Best
Newspaper
Writing
2005

Best Newspaper Writing
2005

American Society of Newspaper Editors
Award Winners and Finalists

Edited by Aly Colón

The Poynter Institute for Media Studies
and

CQ PRESS

A Division of Congressional Quarterly Inc.
Washington, D.C.

The Poynter Institute for Media Studies
801 Third Street South
St. Petersburg, FL 33701
Phone: 888-769-6837
Web: www.poynter.org

CQ Press
1255 22nd Street, NW, Suite 400
Washington, DC 20037
Phone: 202-729-1900; toll-free, 1-866-427-7737 (1-866-4CQ-PRESS)
Web: www.cqpress.com

Cover design, interior design, and typesetting by Auburn Associates, Inc., Baltimore, MD.

Cover photos, clockwise from top right: Stefanie Boyar/*St. Petersburg Times*; Jim MacMillan/Associated Press; Peter DeJong/Associated Press.

Photos in the Community Service Photojournalism section were provided by the photographers. Photos of winners and finalists were provided by their news organizations. Photos of M.J. Wilde are courtesy of Stacia Spragg/*The Albuquerque Tribune*. All other images are accompanied by source information.

Newspaper articles and photos are the exclusive property of the authors and their newspapers and are reprinted with permission.

∞ The paper used in this publication exceeds the requirements of the American National Standard for Information Sciences—Permanence of Paper for Printed Library Materials, ANSI Z39.48-1992.

Printed and bound in the United States of America

09 08 07 06 05   1 2 3 4 5

ISBN 1-933116-51-X
ISSN 0195-895X

*To all journalists who remain
lifelong students of the craft*

Contents

PART 1 Writing on Deadline   1

Part 2 Narrative Writing   83

PART 3 Column Writing   253

PART 4 Obituary Writing   285

PART 6 Community Service Photojournalism 361

Foreword:
Why Newsrooms Matter

BY KAREN BROWN DUNLAP

The first time I heard about an attitude shift among some journalism students, I was intrigued. The second time it came up, I became more interested. Then others mentioned a certain change among students, and now I'm concerned.

I'm concerned that many of the most talented students who want to become journalists don't want to work in newsrooms. I'm also concerned that the atmosphere in some newsrooms could drive away the best and the brightest.

This isn't about all journalism students; maybe it's not about the majority of them. It is about students across the country, in large schools and small, who have drawn the attention of journalism educators.

These student journalists excel in the basics of the craft: they know the meaning of news, and they know how to generate good story ideas. They excel in critical thinking, and thus they are equipped to dig beneath the surface, to ask questions about meaning, context, history and its effects. They are creative and try new writing, editing and producing techniques. They have the skills to work across media platforms and report in print, broadcast and online, regularly using words, sound and visuals.

Most of them understand the purpose of journalism. They know that journalists help people act in their role as citizens. They know the real work of reporters and editors, news directors and producers and designers and photojournalists is to provide information needed for democracy to work.

This group of players oozes with potential, but there's one problem: They don't want to work in newsrooms.

Trevor Brown, retired dean of the Indiana University School of Journalism, explained it this way: "Some students come back from internships in newsrooms and question whether they want a career in daily journalism."

They wonder how much they will grow when they receive little guidance from supervisors or co-workers. They become discouraged by the regular complaints of disgruntled journalists who are worn down by staff reductions and other corporate changes.

Jim Carey, CBS Professor of International Journalism at Columbia University, said he's seen a growing interest in freelance journalism among his graduate students. With technology providing lightweight, affordable tools for newsgathering, students can more easily travel to distant spots, produce reports and sell them to various news outlets. They see themselves working in a newsroom at some point, but they feel no rush to do so.

Susanne Shaw talks with educators around the country in her role as head of the Accrediting Council on Education in Journalism and Mass Communications. She fumed about journalism students who shy away from newsrooms. She said some of the reasons are timeless: students are concerned about low salaries and long hours. Other concerns are more recent. Many students shy away from asking tough questions. They don't want to challenge and risk offending news sources. They like writing but dislike the gritty task of confrontation.

So what's the problem with talented communicators who serve society without working in newsrooms? Frankly, I'd hate for them to miss the valuable training that comes from being in the midst of journalists. And I'd hate for them to miss the fun, even as the industry goes through budget cuts, staff cuts and the bothersome technological, big-picture shift in the role and meaning of news media.

In newsrooms, reporters refine their understanding of news as they explore story ideas. Newsroom conversations should sharpen ethical conduct as leaders and colleagues review what is acceptable behavior. Journalists learn about a community as local characters and history are discussed throughout the day. Craft skills improve as staff members learn the methods of the best journalists and watch the madness of others in a newsroom. In this atmosphere, good journalism emerges, which brings us to "Best Newspaper Writing 2005."

The award-winning writing here comes from journalists who were tied to newsrooms and supported by them, even when they traveled or were based far from them. Read the stories and interviews and feel the newsroom fervor that produces award-winning journalism.

Keep in mind that the future of journalism is bright. News organizations are profitable and will remain so for some time. The public still turns to credible, thorough, well-crafted reports for daily information. Even recent changes in the news environment provide an opportunity to those entering the industry with fresh ideas and new skills, along with a traditional grounding in language, newsgathering and journalistic values.

Richard Prince, in his online column for the Maynard Institute on March 18, 2005, focuses on some students seeking a future in newsrooms.

In "Voices from the Next Generation," he quotes from applications of students who want to work for a college wire service.

Shawnee McFarland of Dillard University said coverage of Sept. 11, 2001, motivated her:

> "I saw some of the best reporting and read some of the most beautifully written stories I have ever experienced," she said. "I was a senior in high school and I knew then that I wanted to be a print journalist."

Alexander Marius Ford, a student at Hampton University, explained why he chose a career in reporting even though, he said, some see it as "an undesirable profession":

> "It takes a truly stubborn person who is not easily rattled to fight for the truth and ask the tough questions that help to strengthen the community," he wrote. "That's why I want to be a journalist. I want to help people find answers."

If you want to help people by engaging and inspiring them with information about the world around them, you ought to be in journalism. If you call yourself a journalist, it helps to experience the passion and pressures of a newsroom.

* * *

This book is possible because a number of smart people became journalists and served the industry as judges for this year's ASNE Distinguished Writing Awards. We are grateful to the following:

Jim Amoss, *The Times-Picayune,* New Orleans
Caesar Andrews, Gannett News Service
Amanda Bennett, *The Philadelphia Inquirer*
Susan Bischoff, *Houston Chronicle*
Neil Brown, *St. Petersburg* (Fla.) *Times*
Jeff Bruce, *Dayton* (Ohio) *Daily News*
Jerry Ceppos, Knight Ridder
Mike Connelly, *Sarasota* (Fla.) *Herald-Tribune*
Jim Crutchfield, *Akron* (Ohio) *Beacon Journal*
Dan Habib, *Concord* (N.H.) *Monitor*
Charlotte Hall, *Orlando* (Fla.) *Sentinel*
Karla Garrett Harshaw, *Springfield* (Ohio) *News-Sun*
Deborah Howell, Newhouse News Service
Kenny Irby, The Poynter Institute

Ed Jones, *The Free Lance-Star,* Fredericksburg, Va.
Marty Kaiser, *Milwaukee Journal Sentinel*
Carolyn Lee, retired, *The New York Times*
Diane McFarlin, *Sarasota* (Fla.) *Herald-Tribune*
Tim McGuire, retired, *Star Tribune,* Minneapolis
Robert Miller, *The News & Observer,* Raleigh, N.C.
Greg Moore, *The Denver Post*
Sue Morrow, *St. Petersburg* (Fla.) *Times*
Chris Peck, *The Commercial Appeal,* Memphis, Tenn.
Skip Perez, *The Ledger,* Lakeland, Fla.
Jim Willse, *The Star-Ledger,* Newark, N.J.

Karen Brown Dunlap is president and managing director of The Poynter Institute as well as a trustee at Poynter and a member of the board of directors of the Times Publishing Company. She is co-author of "The Effective Editor" with Foster Davis and co-author of "The Editorial Eye" with Jane Harrigan.

Preface

This annual celebration of the best American newspaper writing began as an idea nearly 30 years ago, when Eugene Patterson, then-president of the American Society of Newspaper Editors (ASNE), decided to acknowledge distinguished writing. In doing so, Patterson sought to highlight, as he once stated, the "lilt and the loveliness" of the language. Such writing, he had concluded, is characterized by "clarity, grace, brevity. But clarity above all."

To honor exemplary work, ASNE created and still sponsors an annual contest that recognizes and rewards the finest daily newspaper and wire service writing and the most outstanding community service photojournalism. To produce "Best Newspaper Writing," ASNE partners with The Poynter Institute for Media Studies, a school for journalists in St. Petersburg, Fla. This 2005 edition features the work of winners and finalists in the following categories: the Jesse Laventhol Prize for Deadline News Reporting by a team and by an individual; the Freedom Forum/ASNE Award for Distinguished Writing on Diversity; ASNE Distinguished Writing Awards for non-deadline writing, commentary/column writing, editorial writing and obituary writing; and the Community Service Photojournalism Award.

This volume marks the beginning of a new publishing arrangement for "Best Newspaper Writing." CQ Press, a division of Congressional Quarterly, is now the book's publisher. Nelson Poynter founded both Congressional Quarterly and The Poynter Institute, which continue their corporate relationship through the Times Publishing Company. This change has improved the book's quality and made it a more useful teaching tool. A new interior design, including numbered selections, helps readers navigate the book and easily locate information. More and larger photos further enhance the visual presentation.

How to Use This Book

"Best Newspaper Writing 2005" offers readers examples of excellent writing and photojournalism. A number of features complement the outstanding work produced by the winners and finalists:

- **Interviews:** discussions with the winners about their craft, focusing on news judgment, reporting strategies, developing sources, collaborating, working with editors, writing with context and more
- **Lessons Learned:** essays by the finalists revealing the trials and tribulations of producing their honored work

- **Writers' Workshop:** discussion questions and assignments providing an opportunity to analyze and emulate winning work
- **X-Ray Readings:** Roy Peter Clark's deconstruction of the language and rhetoric in three stories offering a toolbox of techniques for reporting and writing
- **Topical Guide:** a useful, at-a-glance selective index pointing readers to places in the interviews and essays that address the craft of writing, such as generating story ideas, conducting interviews, drafting stories, writing leads, finding a focus, addressing ethical issues, writing about difference and selecting and organizing information
- **Narrative Writing:** Pulitzer Prize–winning journalist Thomas French's examination of the narrative techniques used by three reporters, explaining how the narrative style captures color and action and advances each story and highlighting portions of the writing that show the narrative tool at work

"Best Newspaper Writing 2005" is divided into six parts to better follow the structure of classroom teaching and to assist professional writers and others in locating topics of greatest interest. Representing different types of newspaper writing, the parts are Writing on Deadline, Narrative Writing, Column Writing, Obituary Writing, Editorial Writing and Community Service Photojournalism. This structure makes it easier to learn more about a particular form of writing and to compare different styles of reporting and writing. The foreword, written by Karen Brown Dunlap, president of The Poynter Institute, and the introduction, written by Aly Colón, editor of "Best Newspaper Writing 2005," set the stage for understanding how the winners and finalists fit into journalism as practiced today.

About the Interviews and Other Materials

Poynter faculty and fellows interviewed ASNE winners by e-mail and in some cases by phone. The interviews were then edited for clarity, flow and brevity. Faculty and fellows also wrote biographies of winners based on information provided by the journalists and their news organizations.

ASNE provided Poynter with electronic versions of the winners' and finalists' stories. These selections may differ slightly from their original print versions, because "Best Newspaper Writing" editors made minor changes to spelling and grammar. The newspapers' original styles, however, were retained, while other parts of the volume were edited to conform to AP style or to Poynter's style. For example, *The New York Times* uses the spelling "Falluja" in its stories, but Poynter uses "Fallujah." Many newspapers do not italicize the names of newspapers in their stories, but newspaper names are italicized here in the interviews and the elements written to accompany the selections.

There are two datelines for some stories. For example, in *The Washington Post*'s "Sea Surges from Massive Quake Kill Over 13,000 Across South Asia," the story carries a date of Dec. 27, which reflects the date of publication, and a dateline of Dec. 26, which indicates when the article was filed.

All photographs are reproduced as they originally appeared, but with captions edited for length, spelling and grammar. The photos that accompany M.J. Wilde's columns have been cropped for better presentation in a book format.

The goal of "Best Newspaper Writing" is to help students of the craft become better journalists. Reporting and writing can be messy. Journalists, based on their experience and comfort with newspapers and language, may make choices in their writing that some teachers and editors might not allow, such as using incomplete sentences or the passive voice. Students who read "Best Newspaper Writing" can learn from those who know when and how to break the rules.

Some readers may object to the language in "About Face, Part One," where author Josh Peter quotes someone who used a racial epithet. Poynter editors discussed how to handle the text and decided to publish it as it originally appeared because it reflects an element of the story that would not otherwise be told. Students can discuss what they might have done as a reporter or editor in that situation.

Unfortunately, it was not possible to reproduce within these pages all the work honored by ASNE. In some instances, however, all parts of a series are presented. For example, Julia Keller's work, because it also won a Pulitzer Prize, is featured in its entirety. (This volume contains stories and/or images from four 2005 Pulitzer Prize-winning packages.) The entries not published in this volume are available at http://www.poynter.org/bnw2005.

Community Service Photojournalism at NewsU

For the first time, the work featured in the Community Service Photojournalism section is available in an enhanced and interactive form online. It appears on the Web site of News University, or NewsU, at http://www.newsu.org/bnw2005 and includes comments by the photojournalists and ASNE judges discussing basic skills, connecting with under-covered communities, gaining access as a photojournalist and bringing a fresh perspective to the work. In addition, it explores ways to strengthen critical thinking and improve picture editing. NewsU, a partnership between the John S. and James L. Knight Foundation and The Poynter Institute, also offers interactive e-learning, self-directed and faculty-led online seminars.

Acknowledgments

Many people helped make this book possible, beginning with the journalists whose work is featured in these pages. Without them, we would know less about reporting and writing. Thank you also to ASNE, especially executive director Scott Bosley and assistants Alison Wilcox and Suzanne Martin.

"Best Newspaper Writing 2005" benefited from the extraordinary effort and work of Poynter Online managing editor and publications manager Julie Moos and publications coordinator and copy editor Vicki Krueger. Billie M. Keirstead and Mimi Andelman provided copy editing assistance. Poynter faculty and fellows contributed to this volume, and their work is greatly appreciated, as is the work of other Poynter colleagues, especially Elizabeth Carr, Maria Jaimes, Larry Larsen, Meg Martin, Bill Mitchell, Steve Outing, Ola Seifert, David Shedden, Anne Van Wagener and Cary Pérez Waulk. Thanks to staff at News University who created the online course featuring ASNE Community Service Photojournalism winners and finalists: Howard Finberg, Vicki Krueger, Ben Russell and Paige West.

The following people at CQ Press made this a better book with their creativity, attention to detail and enthusiastic support: Brenda Carter, Bonnie Erickson, Colleen Ganey, Charisse Kiino, Gwenda Larsen, Erin Long, Rita Matyi, Steve Pazdan, Robin Surratt and Margot Ziperman. Ann O'Malley proofread the pages.

—Aly Colón

About The Poynter Institute for Media Studies

The Poynter Institute is a school dedicated to teaching and inspiring journalists and media leaders. Through its seminars, publications and Web site (http://www.poynter.org), the Institute promotes excellence and integrity in the practice of journalism craft and in the practical leadership of successful news businesses. Poynter stands for a journalism that informs citizens, enlightens public discourse and strengthens ties between journalism and democracy.

Each year at its campus in St. Petersburg, Fla., the school offers approximately 50 seminars for professionals, educators and students including programs for high school students and recent college graduates. Poynter also teaches via the online training portal News University (http://www.newsu.org). NewsU, as it is also called, offers interactive e-learning and self-directed and faculty-led online seminars. Poynter faculty and staff also work with journalists at various locations around the nation and the world.

The Poynter Institute was founded in 1975 by Nelson Poynter, chairman of the *St. Petersburg Times* and its Washington affiliate, Congressional Quarterly. Poynter, who died in 1978, willed the controlling stock in his companies to the school. As a financially independent, nonprofit organization, The Poynter Institute is beholden to no interest except its own mission: to help journalists seek and achieve excellence.

About the Editor and Contributors

About the Editor

ALY COLÓN is The Poynter Institute's Reporting, Writing and Editing group leader and director of diversity programs. He presents regularly at the Poynter-sponsored National Writers Workshops and consults with news organizations on diversity, ethics, writing and leadership.

Prior to joining Poynter, Colón worked at *The Seattle Times* as diversity reporter and coach. As a reporter, he focused on the intersections where people of different races, cultures, gender and abilities meet. As a coach, he helped reporters and editors address diversity issues. He also was a *Seattle Times* assistant metro editor for urban affairs, health care, ethics and values, religion and social issues. He worked at *The Herald* in Everett, Wash., as an executive editor responsible for business and features and at *The Oakland Press* in Pontiac, Mich.

Colón is the recipient of a Knight-Bagehot Fellowship in business from Columbia University, a National Endowment for the Humanities fellowship in ethics, Knight Center for Specialized Journalism fellowships in health care and race and a Robert Bosch study fellowship on European unity and German reunification.

Colón received his bachelor's in journalism from Loyola University in New Orleans and his master's in journalism from Stanford University.

About the Contributors

ROY PETER CLARK is vice president and senior scholar at The Poynter Institute, where he has taught writing since 1979. He founded the Writing Center at Poynter, lending support to the writing coach movement. He is the co-editor of "America's Best Newspaper Writing: A Collection of ASNE Prizewinners" (2000) and previous editor of "Best Newspaper Writing." Clark formerly worked at the *St. Petersburg* (Fla.) *Times* as a writing coach and briefly as a reporter, feature writer and critic.

THOMAS FRENCH, The Poynter Institute's first writing fellow, began work as a *St. Petersburg* (Fla.) *Times* reporter soon after his graduation from Indiana University. His first newspaper series, "A Cry in the Night," is an account of a murder investigation and trial that French turned into the book "Unanswered Cries." A year spent reporting in a public high school produced the series and book "South of Heaven." His series

"Angels & Demons," about the murder of three women visiting Florida, earned him a Pulitzer Prize for feature writing.

THOMAS HUANG, an ethics fellow at The Poynter Institute, is features editor of *The Dallas Morning News*, where he has worked since 1993. As a writer, Huang was a two-time finalist for the Livingston Award for Young Journalists and a two-time finalist for the Missouri Lifestyle Journalism Award for feature writing. Before moving to Dallas, Huang worked for five years as a metropolitan reporter for *The Virginian-Pilot* in Norfolk, Va. He contributes monthly to a column on diversity issues for Poynter Online (http://www.poynter.org/difference).

KENNY IRBY, visual journalism group leader at The Poynter Institute, is the founder of Poynter's photojournalism program. Before joining Poynter, Irby worked as a photographer and deputy director of photography at *Newsday* and contributed as a photo editor to three Pulitzer Prize–winning projects there. Irby is the recipient of numerous awards from the National Press Photographers Association, including the 1999 Joseph Costa Award for outstanding initiative, leadership and service in photojournalism and the 2002 Presidents Award.

KELLY McBRIDE is the ethics group leader at The Poynter Institute, where she trains reporters, photographers and editors in the skills of ethical decisionmaking, critical thinking and reporting and writing. She also writes an ethics column for Poynter Online (http://www.poynter.org/ethicsjournal) and is director of the Institute's annual News Reporting and Writing Program for College Graduates. Prior to joining Poynter, McBride was a reporter for 15 years, spending most of her time at *The Spokesman-Review* in Spokane, Wash., where she covered the police beat for six years and the religion and ethics beat for eight years.

SARA QUINN is a member of the visual journalism faculty of The Poynter Institute. She also is co-director of Poynter's annual Visual Journalism Program for College Graduates. She was formerly assistant managing editor for visuals at the *Sarasota* (Fla.) *Herald-Tribune* and spent 11 years at *The Wichita* (Kansas) *Eagle*, where she was presentation director. Quinn has won numerous awards from the Society for News Design.

CHRISTOPHER SCANLAN is senior faculty in the Reporting, Writing and Editing group at The Poynter Institute and director of the Poynter-sponsored National Writers Workshops. Scanlan joined the Poynter faculty in 1994 from Knight Ridder Newspapers' Washington bureau, where he was a national correspondent. From 1994 to 2000, he edited the "Best Newspaper Writing" series. In two decades of reporting, he earned 16 awards, including a Robert F. Kennedy Award for international journalism. Scanlan is the author of "Reporting and Writing: Basics for the 21st Century" (2000) and co-editor of "America's Best Newspaper Writing: A Collection of ASNE Prizewinners" (2000).

AL TOMPKINS is The Poynter Institute's group leader for broadcast and online. He writes the daily column "Al's Morning Meeting" for Poynter Online (http://www.poynter.org/morningmeeting), providing story ideas that journalists can report locally. Tompkins joined Poynter's faculty from WSMV-TV in Nashville, Tenn., where he was news director. He is the author of "Aim for the Heart: A Guide for TV Producers and Reporters," a broadcast writing textbook. In addition, he has co-authored three editions of "Newsroom Ethics" for the Radio-Television News Directors Foundation. During his two and a half decades as a journalist, Tompkins has won a national Emmy, the Peabody Award (group award), the Japan Prize, the American Bar Association's Silver Gavel for Court Reporting, seven National Headliner Awards, two Iris Awards and the Robert F. Kennedy Award for international journalism.

BUTCH WARD is Distinguished Fellow at The Poynter Institute. He joined the staff of *The Philadelphia Inquirer* after working at *The News American* in Baltimore. At the *Inquirer*, he was New Jersey editor, assistant managing editor for the Sunday paper, assistant managing editor in features, metropolitan editor and managing editor. He left the *Inquirer* in 2001 and spent three years as vice president for corporate and public affairs at Independence Blue Cross.

KEITH WOODS is dean of the faculty at The Poynter Institute. In 16 years at *The Times-Picayune* in New Orleans, he worked as a sportswriter, news reporter, city editor, editorial writer and columnist. His professional writing won statewide and national awards, including the 1994 National Headliner Award, which he shared with colleagues for the 1993 series "Together Apart/The Myth of Race." He joined Poynter in 1995 and led the institute's teaching on diversity and coverage of race relations as part of the ethics faculty; he then served as Reporting, Writing and Editing group leader. Woods is a previous editor of the "Best Newspaper Writing" series.

Topical Guide

Below is a topical guide that loosely follows the writing process developed by longtime columnist and author Don Murray. The process includes generating ideas, collecting information, focusing stories, ordering elements and drafting and revising. This guide references the pages in "Best Newspaper Writing 2005" where journalists describe the tools and techniques they used to create and refine their award-winning work.

Background and context in writing	Collecting information	Ethical issues	Focusing the story	Interviewing	News judgment	Personal challenges	Reader response	Reporting and writing on race and ethnicity	Reporting strategies
63	20	128	23	21	18	25	133	129	20
71	21	132	29	28	19	29	167	132	21
81	24	309	52	29	52	51	274	185	51
	162	324	70	76	76	129	324	370	125
	310	367	132	77		130			128
		368	163	128		133			129
			251	134		134			130
			267	165		349			134
			309	250					278
				308					308
									310
									313
									367
									370

Writing devices		Writing for the reader		Writing for the Web		Writing on deadline		Writing scenes/sense of place		Writing the lead		Writing with authority		Writing with detail		Writing with humor	
30	✓	30	✓	21	✓	25	✓	20	✓	31	✓	22	✓	21	✓	134	✓
56		358		24		28		21		32		28		22		268	
163		359		126		52		22		70		134		28		270	
164						55		23		319		251		52			
165								28						56			
166								52						71			
268														77			
274														81			
283																	
324																	
347																	
348																	
350																	

Introduction:
The Power of Stories

BY ALY COLÓN

When I was a child, I loved listening to family stories.

I remember the story about how my grandfather survived a hurricane, left the family farm and became a policeman who shot it out with a fugitive known as Richard the Brave.

I haven't forgotten the World War II story about my aunt, who waited faithfully for an American soldier who promised to return and marry her. Five years passed without a word from him. Then one day, on the plaza of her hometown, she saw him—dressed in his uniform, ready to propose.

Stories shape the way we see the world. They chronicle the journeys of the people around us. They connect us to others. They take us to places far away. They draw us into the mind of the storyteller.

The stories in "Best Newspaper Writing 2005" do all of that and more.

As you read the award-winning deadline and narrative stories selected by the American Society of Newspaper Editors (ASNE), you will discover reporting joined with crisp, clear, compelling writing. You'll also find commentaries, editorials and obituaries filled with distinctive voices and pertinent details. You'll see photojournalism that offers intimate community views, captured by journalists who provide a special lens on life.

This book, which has been produced annually for 27 years by The Poynter Institute, grew out of ASNE's desire to improve newspaper writing by rewarding journalists with cash prizes and by showcasing their work. This year's edition builds upon the fine work done over the years by previous distinguished editors and my Poynter colleagues: Roy Peter Clark, Don Fry, Karen Brown Dunlap, Christopher Scanlan and Keith Woods. Each brought his or her own touch to the book. This year's edition continues that tradition:

- We've structured the first five sections of the book by the type of writing: deadline writing, narrative writing, column writing, obituary writing and editorial writing.
- The community service photojournalism section is accompanied, for the first time, by an extended learning opportunity online at Poynter's News University (http://www.newsu.org/bnw2005).
- The interviews in each section focus on the writing process. Interviewers asked each award winner to comment on the steps he or

she followed when reporting and writing news: generating the idea, collecting information, focusing the story, ordering elements, drafting and revising.

- We've expanded our offering of "X-Ray Reading." Poynter's Roy Peter Clark uses the technique on three stories to examine the writing strategies employed.
- Thomas French, a Pulitzer Prize–winning journalist and Poynter Writing Fellow, shares his thoughts about the narrative approach taken by three of the winners.

The book begins with the foundational experience that all journalists face: the deadline-driven story.

The Washington Post's team deadline stories transport the reader to South Asia, where a tsunami engulfed coastal areas. Foreign correspondents Alan Sipress and Peter S. Goodman framed the magnitude of the disaster this way:

> Walls of water as high as 30 feet littered the shorelines of southern Asian countries with death and debris. The toll was most devastating along the coasts of Indonesia, Sri Lanka and India, where hundreds of bodies washed back ashore and entire villages were demolished.

In India, *Post* correspondents Rama Lakshmi and John Lancaster sought out the personal stories of survivors. They gathered details about the destruction that made their coverage personal and poignant.

> "I was holding my cousin's hand, my two sons were walking behind me, and suddenly . . . we saw a huge wave coming at us," said Brajita Poulose, who lay exhausted in a hospital bed, as her eldest son, Jiyo, sat weeping at her side. "We did not have enough warning."

Post staff writer Michael Dobbs rounded out the team coverage with a personal account. He was on vacation in Sri Lanka, in the midst of his morning swim, when he witnessed a biblical scene: "As the waters rose at an incredible rate, I half expected to catch sight of Noah's Ark," he wrote. Dobbs' account captured a disaster that occurred without warning, and on a picture-perfect day.

ASNE's individual deadline award went to a reporter who ventured into a violent situation. Dexter Filkins, a *New York Times* correspondent, joined U.S. Marines as they battled their way into Fallujah, where insurgents held sway.

Filkins filed 15 stories in eight days, his senses attuned to the unpredictable rhythms of war. With one eye on the enemy and the other on the

Marines, he captured moments that show how life and death are but a bullet away. His writing weaved the extraordinary with the ordinary:

> [T]he snipers tensed when they heard movement in the direction of a smoldering building. A cat sauntered out, unconcerned with anything but making its rounds in the neighborhood. "Can I shoot it, sir?" a sniper asked an officer. "Absolutely not," came the reply.

The narrative writing section features Babita Persaud, a former *St. Petersburg* (Fla.) *Times* writer who won the diversity award, and Helen O'Neill, an Associated Press special correspondent who won the non-deadline award.

Persaud presents the promise and the perils associated with an arranged marriage. She followed Vibha Dhawan, a young woman of Indian heritage raised in the United States, as she experienced the traditions associated with this custom:

> Vibha's parents were taking her to see a Hindu priest. He would use astrology to predict when she might get married.
>
> She never guessed that she would be the kind of woman to even consider an arranged marriage. In her mid 20s, strong-minded, a feminist, she hoped one day to sit at the head of a boardroom table.

O'Neill's riveting story places the reader in the home of 88-year-old Hedwig Braun just before she is kidnapped:

> Braun was in bed reading when the lights went out but she didn't pay much heed. . . . Pulling on her dressing gown and slippers, she lit a candle and padded into the kitchen. . . . The clock was stopped at 12:50 a.m.

For column writing, the judges selected M.J. Wilde, of *The Albuquerque* (N.M.) *Tribune.* Wilde brings a personal style and a unique voice to this collection. In one piece, she attacks the promises made by bathing suit designers:

> It happens every summer. And it's a big, fat lie. There has never been a bathing suit made that can "hide your figure flaws." Unless, of course, your figure flaw is a tiny heart tattoo on your size 2 tushie. And if it is, I hate you.

In addition to the writing awards mentioned above, each year ASNE grants an award in a rotating category. In 2005, that category was obituary writing, and the winner was Alana Baranick, of *The* (Cleveland) *Plain*

Dealer. Baranick skillfully resurrected the lives once led by people in her community. She uncovered intimate details and captured them in a series called "A Life Story." Here's one example:

> Clementine Werfel blessed priests at St. Joseph Catholic Church . . . with heavenly desserts, memorable meals and seemingly miraculous coffee. The retired parish housekeeper . . . routinely walked around the dining table in the rectory, offering coffee to each priest.
>
> "Would Father like regular or decaf?" the 4-foot-something Werfel asked them one by one.
>
> Regardless of the priests' individual preferences, she filled all their cups with coffee from the same pot. The coffee drinkers silently accepted what they got, as though Werfel really could turn regular coffee into decaffeinated, much the way that the biblical Jesus turned water into wine.

The editorial writing section of this book features a repeat winner. David Barham, of the *Arkansas Democrat-Gazette,* who shared this award in 2003, employs a conversational tone that sounds as if he is speaking directly to the reader:

> The strangest thought came to mind as we stood at the intersection of Arkansas Highways 5 and 89 early Monday afternoon:
>
> What were their nicknames?
>
> All daddies give their daughters nicknames, don't they? . . .
>
> It was the strangest thought. Here we were looking at the memorials, and we were thinking about their *nicknames.*
>
> What goes on in the human mind.

The final section of the book focuses on the award for Community Service Photojournalism. Read the interview with award-winner Carol Guzy of *The Washington Post* in this volume and then go to News University's Web site (http://www.newsu.org/bnw2005) to see more of her photos.

Whether you're a student, a professor or a professional, we hope you find this book helpful and stimulating. Use it as a reference and a tool to create compelling stories your readers—and families everywhere—will remember.

Aly Colón is The Poynter Institute's Reporting, Writing and Editing group leader and director of diversity programs.

Best
Newspaper
Writing
2005

Writing on Deadline

Michael Dobbs, Peter S. Goodman, Rama Lakshmi, John Lancaster and Alan Sipress
Team Deadline News Reporting

At 7:58 a.m. local time on the day after Christmas 2004, an earthquake measuring 9 on the Richter scale occurred 18 miles under the Indian Ocean off the west coast of Sumatra. Over the next four hours, the quake—the fourth most powerful since 1900—triggered a tsunami that caused one of the worst natural disasters recorded.

The numbers are staggering:
- more than 300,000 people either missing or killed
- more than 1 million people displaced in 10 countries in South Asia and East Africa

Walls of water up to 55 feet high rushed inland without warning, leveling entire villages and crushing inhabitants under cars, buses and shacks. Entire families were wiped out. Among reporters, the suddenness and epic proportions of the disaster—a violent reminder of the destructive power of nature and the fragility of life—immediately inspired biblical references.

Visiting the devastated areas more than a week later, then-U.S. Secretary of State Colin Powell was overwhelmed. "I've been in war and I've been through a number of hurricanes, tornadoes and other relief operations," Powell said. "But I've never seen anything like this."

For that matter, neither had the reporters from *The Washington Post,* who combined, on that incredible Sunday, to produce three newspaper stories that provided readers with an amazing amount of information, context and drama, even though the disaster's magnitude was only beginning to reveal itself.

Four of the reporters responsible for the *Post*'s first-day coverage were based in Asia. Alan Sipress, stationed in Jakarta, and Peter S. Goodman, the *Post*'s Shanghai reporter, collaborated on the lead story—a sweeping report on the disaster's 5,300-mile rampage across the Indian Ocean. The story, written by Sipress and based on his and Goodman's reporting, was impressive not only for its content but also for the difficult circumstances under which reporters in Asia had to work that day.

Reporters Rama Lakshmi and John Lancaster, based in India, collaborated on a sidebar scene story that used vivid anecdotes to illustrate the devastation and human suffering wreaked by the tsunami. Lancaster, just beginning a family vacation in the Indian state of Kerala when the disaster occurred, worked the phones and wrote the sidebar in a Meridien hotel. Lakshmi flew to the Indian state of Tamil Nadu. There she made several key reporting decisions that quickly led to poignant interviews with families and friends of people lost in the great wave. Her resourcefulness was crucial to the unique nature of the *Post*'s first-day report.

But if key decision-making played an important role in the *Post*'s reporting, so did fate. *Post* reporter Michael Dobbs was on vacation thousands of miles from his office in Washington. He was midway through his

The Washington Post's First-Day Tsunami Coverage

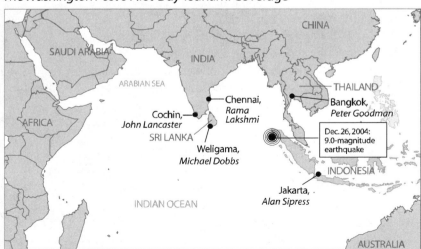

ASSOCIATED PRESS/POYNTER

morning swim off the Sri Lankan coast when the seas rose at least 15 feet in less than a minute. In the moments that followed, Dobbs used one stray catamaran, then another, to safely reach the shore; there, eventually, he found his wife—also alive. Hours later, with all family members together and safe, Dobbs sat in the candlelight and composed a first-person account of what he called a "life-changing experience." The next morning, thousands of *Post* readers shared his vivid narrative.

Together, the three stories pay tribute to the fundamentals of journalism: aggressive fact-gathering, effective interviewing, careful observation and spare, concise storytelling. According to David Hoffman, the *Post*'s assistant managing editor for foreign news who coordinated the tsunami coverage, these stories showed foreign correspondence at its best.

"The greatest single attribute of a foreign correspondent," Hoffman said, "is someone who is obsessed with their subject. You see it in their files: immersed, forever curious, acute observation, vivid description—always original and authentic. When you have people like this, the best thing to do is let them do what they do best. You can't do much more anyway—because of the great distances and difficulties in communications.

"And when they do it well, it seems like a small miracle."

About *The Washington Post* Team

Michael Dobbs is *The Washington Post*'s national education reporter. He has been on the *Post* staff for 23 years, mainly as a foreign correspondent, covering the collapse of Communism in Russia, Poland, Yugoslavia and elsewhere. He returned to the United States 10 years ago and, before assuming the education beat, covered the State Department and worked as a foreign investigative reporter.

Peter S. Goodman has been the *Post*'s Asian economic correspondent in Shanghai since 2002. Raised in New York City, Goodman graduated from Reed College in Portland, Ore., and received a master of arts in Asian studies from the University of California, Berkeley. He began his journalism career in Asia in 1989, just after college, first writing features from Kyoto for the English-language *Japan Times*, then freelancing for several American newspapers from Southeast Asia. He wrote about the war in Cambodia, economic reforms in Vietnam and repression in East Timor.

Goodman returned to the United States in 1993, taking a job in Alaska as a metro reporter on the *Anchorage Daily News*. He joined *The Washington Post* in 1997, working first as a political reporter on the Maryland desk and later covering telecommunications for the financial desk.

Rama Lakshmi is a special correspondent in *The Washington Post*'s New Delhi bureau. She joined the bureau as a news researcher in 1990 and gradually began writing under her own byline. She has written on a range of topics, including politics, women's empowerment, the caste system, India-Pakistan ties, and Kashmir and Hindu nationalist politics.

A native of the southern state of Tamil Nadu, Lakshmi graduated with a degree in English literature from Delhi University in 1988. She also has a diploma in art history from India's National Museum and in refugee studies from York University, Toronto. She was awarded a fellowship on women's representation in politics by Carleton University, Ottawa.

John Lancaster is the *Post*'s South Asia bureau chief, based in New Delhi, India. He joined the paper in 1986 and has worked as a reporter and editor. He covered transportation and the Maryland State House for the metropolitan staff and the environment, the Pentagon, the State Department and Capitol Hill for the national desk. He also served as the Cairo bureau chief and deputy foreign editor. Lancaster previously worked for *The Des Moines Register* and *The Atlanta Journal-Constitution*.

Alan Sipress is a Southeast Asia correspondent for the *Post*, based in Jakarta, Indonesia. Before taking the position in 2002, he worked as a diplomatic correspondent, covering the State Department and National Security Council, and as metropolitan transportation writer. From 1987 to 1998, Sipress wrote for *The Philadelphia Inquirer*, where he covered New Jersey politics and government and regional transportation. He also served as the *Inquirer*'s Middle East correspondent. He previously worked for *The Virginian-Pilot/The Ledger-Star* in Norfolk, Va., and *The Daily Register* in Red Bank, N.J.

A native of New Jersey, Sipress graduated from Princeton University in 1983 with a degree in public and international affairs. He studied for a year in the master's program at the Delhi School of Economics. He is married to Ellen Nakashima, the other half of the *Post*'s Southeast Asia bureau, and has a young daughter, Natalie.

—Butch Ward

The Jesse Laventhol Prize for Deadline News Reporting by a team is funded by a gift from David Laventhol, a former Times Mirror executive, in honor of his father.

1. Sea Surges from Massive Quake Kill Over 13,000 Across South Asia

DEC. 27, 2004

By Alan Sipress and Peter S. Goodman

JAKARTA, Indonesia, Dec. 26—A gargantuan earthquake centered off the western end of the Indonesian archipelago unleashed a series of tsunamis Sunday that crashed into coastal towns, fishing villages and tourist resorts from Sri Lanka to India, Thailand and Malaysia, killing more than 13,000 people in at least nine countries and leaving thousands missing.

The 9.0 magnitude quake was the strongest in 40 years and the fourth most powerful since 1900, according to the U.S. Geological Survey.

The resulting convulsion in the vast Indian Ocean was felt as far away as East Africa, more than 3,000 miles from the epicenter, where fishermen were stranded and resorts were closed by the surging tides.

Walls of water as high as 30 feet littered the shorelines of southern Asian countries with death and debris. The toll was most devastating along the coasts of Indonesia, Sri Lanka and India, where hundreds of bodies washed back ashore and entire villages were demolished.

The initial quake struck the western end of Indonesia's Sumatra island at 6:58 a.m. local time, flattening buildings and sending a wall of water higher than the tops of coconut palms into the towns and villages in the province of Aceh, witnesses said. The epicenter was located 155 miles southeast of the provincial capital of Banda Aceh and 200 miles west of Medan, Sumatra.

Indonesian Health Ministry officials put the toll in Aceh and the neighboring province of North Sumatra at nearly 4,500 and predicted more victims would be discovered after rescue teams reached remote hamlets cut off by the disaster. In Indonesia, as elsewhere throughout the region, it was impossible to determine the exact toll, which will likely not be known for some time.

In Sri Lanka, about 1,000 miles west of the epicenter, a massive surf struck nearly the entire coast of the island nation. National police reported that at least 6,090 people were killed, many of them on the eastern shore near the port of Trincomalee, as well as in the south. About 170 children were feared lost in an orphanage, the Associated Press reported.

The death toll elsewhere was estimated at 3,000 in India, as many as 1,000 in Thailand, 48 in Malaysia, 10 in Burma, and 32 in the Maldives. In Somalia, on the eastern coast of Africa, at least nine people were reported killed by floodwaters, according to news services. At least two children were killed in Bangladesh.

At least three Americans were among the dead—two in Sri Lanka and one in Thailand, according to Noel Clay, a State Department spokesman. He said a number of other Americans were injured, but he had no details.

In Aceh, the tsunami "destroyed buildings, homes, markets and streets in almost all coastal areas," said Mauludi, an Indonesian Red Cross worker north of the affected area. He recounted hearing what sounded like repeated explosions coming from the coast. When he left his home to investigate, he spotted a wave towering above the tree line about a mile inland. Military authorities said they expected to retrieve many more corpses from the trees, where they remained after the waters receded.

[More than 1 million people were left homeless in Indonesia, and rescuers on Monday combed seaside villages for survivors, the Associated Press reported.]

More than half the deaths in Indonesia were reported in Banda Aceh, where Tia Andarita, a telephone operator, said she watched from her third-floor office as two buildings collapsed and then seawater surged through the streets. "Many people were panicked and ran away to rescue themselves," she said.

Over the following hours, tsunamis triggered by the sudden, traumatic shift in the seafloor raced across the Andaman Sea and Bay of Bengal toward coastal communities.

In Sri Lanka, witnesses reported seeing the sea retreat as swiftly as it had struck, leaving corpses floating in the lingering floodwaters and the remains of homes, cars and fishing boats littering the beach. Roads, electricity and telephone lines were severed. Reports that more than 1,000 had died in the rebel-controlled northeast of Sri Lanka were impossible to confirm.

Thousands of people were unaccounted for in Sri Lanka. One million others, about 5 percent of the population, were displaced as many fled for higher ground, hauling their radios, televisions and other valuable possessions on bicycles and seeking refuge in schools and temples.

"I think this is the worst-ever natural disaster in Sri Lanka," N. D. Hettiarachchi, director of the National Disaster Management Center, told Reuters.

President Chandrika Kumaratunga declared a national disaster, deploying Sri Lanka's 20,000-member armed forces to help evacuate people from stricken areas, and appealed for international relief. Rescue efforts were proceeding slowly because police and military bases had been flooded.

"Our naval base in Trincomalee is under water, and right now we are trying to manage the situation there while rescuing people," Jayantha Perera, a spokesman for the Sri Lankan navy, told Reuters.

Officials said that the waves had dislodged land mines and unexploded ordnance left over from the country's two-decade civil war, posing hazards not only for rescue teams but villagers who remained in the area.

In India, a tsunami inundated a broad swath of the country's southeastern coast and flooded offshore islands. Hundreds of bodies washed up on the long, popular oceanfront near Madras, the capital of the state of Tamil Nadu, and officials said they expected more to come ashore in coming days. Officials reported that about 1,700 people had died in Tamil Nadu.

The Indian interior minister, Shivraj Patil, told local television that at least 200 others had died in the neighboring state of Andhra Pradesh. But local residents said that at least 400 fishermen were missing, and 200 Hindu worshipers who had gone to the beach in the early morning hours to take a sacred dip were unaccounted for. About 100 fatalities were also reported in both Pondicherry and Kerala.

The official Press Trust of India news agency, quoting a local police commander, said another 1,000 people had perished on India's Andaman and Nicobar islands, located off the western tip of Sumatra. "The situation is very grim," said Inspector General S. B. Deol of the Indian police.

In Thailand, tsunamis also crashed into the country's west coast. Authorities said at least 392 bodies had been retrieved and that they expected the toll to approach 1,000. The dead included foreign tourists who had packed into the country's beach resorts for the Christmas and New Year holidays.

"Nothing like this has ever happened in our country before," Prime Minister Thaksin Shinawatra said.

On the Thai island of Phuket, one of Southeast Asia's most popular destinations for backpackers and surfers, a 30-foot wave surged over the sand and into the crowded tourist strip, destroying hotels lining the seafront, tossing vehicles around like driftwood and sowing panic during one of the busiest times of the year.

"People were coming up the roads, running and screaming that the beach was disappearing," said Borge Carlsson, a Swede who owns a guesthouse about 200 yards back from the beach. "Cars were upside down, floating around. It's amazing to see anything like this."

At the southern tip of Phuket, on Nai Harn Beach, the waves dismantled a crowded strip of restaurants, tailor shops and motorbike rental outlets. At nearby hotels, amid shattered glass and broken concrete, a pickup truck was deposited in a swimming pool and a car came to rest in a lobby.

"There were thousands of people on the beach then," said Richard Motein, a Canadian who runs a dive shop on Phuket. "I looked up and saw a wall of water coming at me full of lawn chairs, boats, umbrellas. It just totally wasted the beach."

Moments later, many of the people who had been lying on the sand had vanished.

"We're looking at 500 to 1,000 dead, easy," he said, taking issue with the official fatality figures.

The Thai government ordered tourists to evacuate Phuket and other flooded beach resorts. Hundreds of Western and Asian visitors, as well as local residents, were evacuated by sea and air from other small islands off the coast, including 200 people plucked from the tiny island of Ko Phi Phi, featured in the Hollywood film "The Beach."

Helicopters surveyed the islands of the Andaman Sea for stranded divers and snorkelers while rescue workers pulled more than 100 people from the water, officials said.

Besides the deaths on Phuket, officials reported fatalities in Phang Nga, Ranong, Krabi, Satun and Trang.

In Malaysia, authorities also ordered the evacuation of communities along the country's northwest coast after 42 people were killed on the seafront in the states of Penang and Kedah. Several of the dead were jet skiers and picnickers swept out to sea, while many of the missing were fishermen who had set out in the morning and had yet to return by nightfall.

"Our country has never experienced such a disaster before," Malaysia's deputy prime minister, Najib Razak, told reporters. But he acknowledged, "Among the tsunami-hit nations, we are the least affected." He added that about 200 houses had been swept away by the flood.

In Indonesia, authorities said they had dispatched senior officials to Aceh to oversee rescue operations. That effort will be hampered by an ongoing war between government forces and separatist rebels.

The province has been largely off-limits to foreign aid organizations and journalists since the government launched a new military offensive last year. Sutedjo Yuwono, secretary to Indonesia's welfare minister, said international aid groups and journalists would now be allowed to enter Aceh but that access would be tightly regulated.

The small Indian Ocean nation of the Maldives, which consists of 1,200 coral islands resting barely a yard above sea level, declared a state of emergency and closed the international airport after two-thirds of the capital, Male, was inundated. In addition to the 32 dead, 51 people were missing, authorities said.

A Maldivian government spokesman told Reuters by cell phone that none of the dead were believed to be tourists, who are drawn to the Maldives by its idyllic palm-fringed islands and famed scuba diving.

Severe flooding also struck the Seychelles, a string of islands off the east coast of Africa. A six-foot ocean surge disrupted power to hundreds of homes and abnormally high tides repeatedly littered the airport runway with fish, forcing firefighters to hose down the airfield between flights.

2. It Seemed Like a Scene from the Bible

DEC. 27, 2004

By Michael Dobbs

WELIGAMA, Sri Lanka, Dec. 26—Disaster struck with no warning out of a faultlessly clear blue sky.

I was taking my morning swim around the island that my brother Geoffrey, a businessman, had bought on a whim a decade ago and turned into a tropical paradise 200 yards from one of the world's most beautiful beaches.

I was a quarter way around the island when I heard my brother shouting at me, "Come back! Come back! There's something strange happening with the sea." He was swimming behind me, but closer to the shore.

I couldn't understand what the fuss was about. All seemed peaceful. There was barely a ripple in the sea. My brother's house rests on a rock 60 feet above the level of the sea.

Then I noticed that the water around me was rising, climbing up the rock walls of the island with astonishing speed. The vast circle of golden sand around Weligama Bay was disappearing rapidly, and the water had reached the level of the coastal road, fringed with palm trees.

As I swam to shore, my mind was momentarily befuddled by two conflicting impressions—the idyllic blue sky and the rapidly rising waters.

In less than a minute, the water level had risen at least 15 feet, but the sea remained calm, with barely a wave in sight.

Within minutes, the beach and the area behind it had become an inland sea that rushed over the road and poured into the flimsy houses on the other side. The speed with which it all happened seemed like a scene from the Bible, a natural phenomenon unlike anything I had experienced.

As the waters rose at an incredible rate, I half expected to catch sight of Noah's Ark.

Instead of the ark, I grabbed a wooden catamaran that the local people used as a fishing boat. My brother jumped on the boat next to me. We bobbed up and down on the catamaran as the water rushed past us into the village beyond the road.

After a few minutes, the water stopped rising, and I felt it was safe to swim to the shore. What I did not realize was that the floodwaters would recede as quickly and dramatically as they had risen.

All of a sudden, I found myself being swept out to sea with startling speed. Although I am a fairly strong swimmer, I was unable to withstand the current. The fishing boats around me had been torn from their moorings, and were bobbing up and down furiously.

For the first time, I felt afraid, powerless to prevent myself from being washed out to sea.

I swam in the direction of a loose catamaran, grabbed the hull and pulled myself to safety. My weight must have slowed the boat down, and soon I was stranded on the sand.

As the water rushed out of the bay, I scrambled onto the main road. Screams were coming from the houses beyond the road, many of which were still half full of water that had trapped the inhabitants inside. Villagers were walking, stunned, along the road, unable to comprehend what had taken place.

I was worried about my wife, who was on the beach when I went for my swim. I eventually found her walking along the road, dazed but happy to be alive. She had been trying to wade back to our island when the water carried her across the road and into someone's back yard. At one point she was underwater, struggling for breath. She finally grabbed onto a rope and climbed into a tree, escaping the waters that raged beneath her.

Our children were still asleep when the tsunami struck at 9:15. They woke up to find the bay practically drained of water and their parents walking back across the narrow channel to safety.

The waves raged around the island for the rest of the day, alternately rising and receding.

It took us many hours to realize the scale of the disaster, because we could see only the tiny part in front of us. The road from Weligama to Galle was cut in many places. The coastal road was littered with carcasses of boats, dogs and even a few dead sharks. Helicopters flew overhead and loudspeaker vans warned residents to leave low-lying areas for fear of more tsunamis.

My brother's little island, called Tapbrobane after the ancient name of Sri Lanka, was largely intact, although a piece of our gate ended up on the seashore half a mile away. The water rose about 20 feet toward the house.

We have no water and no electricity and are cut off from the rest of Sri Lanka. It is impossible to buy food. We are existing on cold ham and turkey sandwiches, leftovers from Christmas dinner.

The holiday that we planned and dreamed about for many months is in ruins. We feel fortunate—fortunate to be alive.

3. In India, Death Roars in from the Ocean

DEC. 27, 2004

By Rama Lakshmi and John Lancaster

MADRAS, India, Dec. 26—On a balmy Sunday morning at Marina Beach, Brajita Poulose, 45, her husband, two sons and four other relatives strolled along the shore in the sunshine, enjoying the ocean breeze. Young men were playing cricket, joggers trotted past food vendors, fishermen hauled in their nets. Then, without warning, the placid ocean turned violent.

"I was holding my cousin's hand, my two sons were walking behind me, and suddenly . . . we saw a huge wave coming at us," said Poulose, who lay exhausted in a hospital bed, as her eldest son, Jiyo, sat weeping at her side. "We did not have enough warning."

The water quickly rose to Poulose's shoulders, she recalled, and a torrent caused by a tsunami in the Indian Ocean swept her inland, across the main road along Marina Beach, a broad ribbon of golden sand at the edge of this bustling commercial city in the state of Tamil Nadu.

Jiyo, 29, tried to keep his mother in sight, but the surging current pushed them apart. "In no time I was alone, and I couldn't see anyone," he said. "It was one continuous wave."

He caught up with her hours later at a government hospital. The bodies of his father and younger brother Sebastian were in a nearby morgue. The rest of the family was missing.

Indian authorities said Sunday night that more than 3,000 people had died in the tsunami, generated by a massive underwater earthquake early Sunday off the coast of the Indonesian island of Sumatra.

The tsunami swept across the Indian Ocean along a 1,100-mile stretch of India's southeastern and southern coast, with a heavy toll in Tamil Nadu, on the Bay of Bengal. Among the dead were fishermen and other residents of coastal villages, as well as city-dwellers and visitors out for morning walks on the oceanfront of Madras, the capital of Tamil Nadu. Hundreds of fishermen and others were missing Sunday night.

Authorities in Tamil Nadu put the death toll in the state at 1,705. India's private NDTV television channel reported that 1,000 people had died in the remote Andaman and Nicobar Islands, an Indian territory between Sumatra and Burma.

In the state of Andhra Pradesh, more than 200 were killed, according to Indian Interior Minister Shivraj Patil, and local officials said 280 had died in Pondicherry, a former French colonial outpost on the southeastern coast. In the state of Kerala, a popular winter destination for foreign tourists on India's southern tip, more than 120 people were reported to have died. Seawater flooded villages more than a mile inland in the state, the Press Trust of India news agency reported.

Waves also caused devastation in Sri Lanka, surging across roads and railroad tracks and pouring through coastal villages, markets and beach resorts. Authorities said late Sunday that at least 6,090 people had died. Elsewhere, the dead included more than 4,000 people in Indonesia and more than 300 in Thailand, where more than 5,000 people were reported injured.

Indian television channels carried video footage of helicopters hoisting people to safety in Madras. They also showed turbid waters swirling around stranded buses, beaches strewn with wreckage and women wailing over the bodies of children laid out in makeshift morgues.

Dev Anand, 22, said he had been playing cricket with four friends at Marina Beach when the waves swept them inland. Three of his friends survived. But one, whom Anand called "Sheik," could not be found. "He was too thin," Anand recalled after making the rounds of hospitals and morgues with the three other friends to look for the missing man. "We kept yelling out to him to hold on to the lamppost, but he could not."

Ravichandran, a fisherman from Elliot's Beach in Madras, said he noticed something was amiss as he pulled his morning catch from his net. "I saw the waves climbing alarmingly," Ravichandran, 32, told the Reuters news agency. "I rushed back and pulled my wife and two children out of our home. Water had rushed into our hut by then."

'Wailing and Crying'

Rajani Unni, also from Elliot's Beach, said the tremors felt like being on a train. "I turned around, and I saw that a small glass table with a flower vase was shaking," she said. "We saw people rushing away from fishermen's colonies lining the beach. Women were wailing and crying."

Ekambal Nayakar, 50, who lives with her 75-year-old mother in Pattinappakan, a shantytown on the seafront in Madras, said she waded and swam to safety while others rescued her mother. "The water entered the house this deep," Nayakar, 50, said, pointing to her neck. "Then I heard voices outside—'Sea water! Sea water!'—and people were running helter-skelter toward the tallest building they could see."

Pazhani, a fisherman, told Reuters he was taking a bath when sea water entered his bathroom. "I got so scared that I ran out," he said.

His wife, Lakshmi, said she was having breakfast with her three children at the time. "We had to leave everything and run to safety," she said. "We don't know what has happened to our TV, radio, utensils."

Muthalakshmi, a fisherman's wife, told the news agency that her mother had gone to the oceanfront to buy fish and was swept away by the waves. "It took us an hour to recover her body," she said. "Thank God my husband had not gone to sea, as he was unwell."

Some small boats were swept far inland by the ocean surge, while others were washed out to sea. P. Pamanamurthy, a resident of Kakinada in Andhra Pradesh, said he saw fishermen holding on to overturned boats as the receding waters pulled them seaward. "I was shocked to see innumerable fishing boats flying on the shoulder of the waves, going back and forth into the sea, as if made of paper," he told the Associated Press.

In New Delhi, Prime Minister Manmohan Singh ordered senior cabinet ministers to stricken coastal areas to survey damage and directed army and naval units to help with search and rescue operations. Reports from isolated coastal villages indicated that the death toll was likely to rise, Indian officials said. They expressed particular concern about the fate of thousands of people in the Andaman and Nicobar archipelago.

"About 10 to 20 villages have been reportedly washed away, and it has become difficult to get information from there," Home Secretary Dhirendra Singh told reporters in New Delhi. "We're keeping our fingers crossed."

In Sri Lanka, President Chandrika Kumaratunga declared a national emergency, and the military scrambled to mount search-and-rescue operations, although troops were hampered by wave damage to naval installations, officials said.

The port in Colombo, the capital, was closed. Resort areas and villages south of Colombo were heavily damaged, as were isolated communities on the island's less developed eastern side, authorities said.

Sri Lanka, a teardrop-shaped island off the southern tip of India, is known for its lush tropical forests, tea plantations and idyllic, crescent-shaped beaches. It has experienced a tourist boom since government forces and rebels from the country's ethnic Tamil minority declared a cease-fire in 2002.

Coastal areas in the northeastern districts of Mutur and Trincomalee were smashed by waves as high as 18 feet, D. Rodrigo, a Mutur district official, told the AP. "The police station in Mutur is under water," Rodrigo said.

The Associated Press quoted one of its photographers, Gemunu Amarasinghe, as saying after a tour of the area south of Colombo: "I counted 24 bodies in a stretch of only six kilometers. . . . I saw bodies of children entangled in wire mesh. . . . There were rows and rows of women and men standing on the road and asking if anyone has seen their family members. . . . I also saw people bringing in bodies from the sea beaches and placing them on roads and covering them with sarongs."

'The Sea Stood Up'

Amarasinghe said he had been told that some people were killed when they ran out to retrieve stranded fish after the first waves hit, then were caught by a second onslaught.

Roland Buerk, a BBC correspondent vacationing in Sri Lanka, was in bed in his hotel room in Unawatuna, a resort town on the southwestern coast, when the waves struck. "We suddenly heard some shouts from outside," he wrote on the BBC News Web site. "Then the water started coming under the door. Within a few seconds it was touching the window."

He and a companion pushed through the rushing water to a tree and climbed into its branches, but it collapsed under the force of the current. "We were swept along for a few hundred meters, trying to dodge the motorcycles, refrigerators, cars and other debris that were coming with us. Finally, about 300 meters inshore, we managed to get hold of a pillar, which we held on to, and the waters just gradually began to subside."

Buerk described shattered buildings and cars in trees. He said he had counted four bodies, including two Sri Lankans—an elderly woman and a young woman—and a Western boy "who looked to be about five years old."

Another witness in Unawatuna, Swati Thiyagarajan, described the wave to an NDTV reporter: "It was literally like the sea stood up and walked to your door."

Lancaster reported from Cochin, India.

Conversations with
Alan Sipress and Peter S. Goodman;
John Lancaster and Rama Lakshmi;
Michael Dobbs; and David Hoffman

The Lead Story

Edited e-mail interviews conducted by Poynter Institute Distinguished Fellow Butch Ward with Alan Sipress and Peter Goodman, members of The Washington Post *team that won the ASNE deadline news reporting award. Sipress and Goodman collaborated on the lead story, "Sea Surges from Massive Quake Kill Over 13,000 Across South Asia."*

BUTCH WARD: Where were you when the tsunami hit, and where did your assignment come from?

ALAN SIPRESS: When the tsunami hit, I was at my Jakarta home on a Sunday morning, working on an unrelated article based on reporting I had recently completed in Thailand. As I do most days, I frequently checked the wires to see if there was any significant breaking news in Southeast Asia, which is my area of responsibility. The wire services reported there had been an earthquake on Indonesia's Sumatra island, but initial accounts said fewer than several dozen people had been killed.

So, at first, I did not pursue the story.

But the death toll began to increase quickly. By lunchtime it became clear this was a major story, and I decided on my own to begin the reporting process. I asked my Indonesian assistant, Noor Huda Ismail, to come into the office on his vacation and called *The Washington Post*'s office in New Delhi to ask that it get involved. I also called Peter Eisner, an editor on the foreign desk in Washington, at home, waking him up in the middle of the night, to let him know about the tsunami. Peter is the deputy foreign editor in charge of Asia bureaus. He told me that Peter Goodman, usually based in China, happened to be in Thailand and was available to begin reporting the story there.

PETER GOODMAN: I was on an airplane from Shanghai, where I am based, to Bangkok. I was headed to Indonesia to do a China-related story, and I had to overnight in Bangkok to catch a flight to Jakarta the next day. I had just finished an assignment in Africa and, before that, another one in Europe, all of this in a three-week stretch. I'd had to rush back to China before the end of the year to get a visa for the following year, before the deadline, then get down to Indonesia. So, I was feeling a little traveled out and ready to catch my breath. It was a Sunday, and I didn't mind the daylong layover. I was looking forward to a little session by the pool with some Indonesia prep reading, followed by a nap, an early dinner and bed.

When I got to the hotel in Bangkok, the woman who checked me in said there had been an earthquake that morning. They had felt it during breakfast and some people were scared, but most people were amused. I didn't think much of it, but when I plugged in my computer and got online to send a customary note with my contact information to our foreign desk in Washington, my browser took me to the newspaper's home page, and there was an AP story showing an earthquake of over 9.0. The story didn't say anything about a tsunami at that point, and the concern level seemed less than intense because the quake was out in the middle of the ocean.

I knew the desk could reach me now that my contacts were in place, but I have to admit—and maybe this is lousy news judgment on my part—I didn't really see this as something that would involve me. The wires made it sound like not such a big deal. But then the phone rang. It was my editor, Peter Eisner. He was calling to see if I could help Alan Sipress, who is in our Jakarta bureau and was already working the story. Just make a few phone calls within Thailand, I was told. I called Alan and he asked me to make a few calls to Phuket, Thailand's primary resort island. That was the plan.

At this point, the wires were showing that the tsunami had hit through much of the region, though the loss of life was not at all clear. Indonesia was reporting very few deaths, owing to the fact that the wave hit Aceh, which had been shuttered to the world for years. Early reports made it seem like it was really a South Asia story, with our people in India and Sri Lanka likely to be doing most of the work. But Phuket had clearly gotten hit, too, and this little piece of the puzzle was now mine to focus on.

Talk about how you collected the information.

ALAN SIPRESS: Most of the information was collected by telephone. My assistant, Huda, and I spent several hours calling all the telephone numbers in Aceh we could think of, including local officials, academics, activists and even hotels where I had stayed during previous visits, and the man I had used there as my driver. Repeatedly, the calls failed to go through. If we had known then how badly the tsunami had disrupted communications, we might not have spent so much time trying to reach people by telephone. Our smartest decision, born in part of this ignorance, was to keep dialing for hours. But in the end, we were fortunate because we were able to get through to several people.

In Thailand, Peter Goodman likewise worked the telephones from his hotel in Bangkok. Peter and I remained in contact primarily through the *Post*'s in-house e-mail system.

It would not have been practical to head immediately to Aceh for several reasons. First, there is only one flight a day from Jakarta to Aceh and that flight had already left. Second, about two years ago, the Indonesian government placed tight restrictions on the entry of foreign journalists into Aceh province because of a separatist revolt there. I doubted I would be able to enter Aceh without spending several days or more trying to obtain government permission. It made more sense to anchor the story from Jakarta for the first day and then think about trying to get to Aceh after that.

PETER GOODMAN: I am a regular visitor to Thailand. I took my first trip there in 1987 as a backpacker tourist and have been in and out of there ever since, both on vacation and for reporting trips. (I had been a Southeast Asia–based freelancer right after I graduated from college in 1989, and I often passed through Thailand en route to Vietnam and Cambodia.) I had been to Phuket several times. In fact, two years earlier, I had spent Christmas and New Year's right there on a fairly major Phuket beach with my kids. So I knew immediately what the scene must have been like. The thought of a wave taller than the coconut palms sweeping over major resorts on the Sunday morning after Christmas on an island that is a mecca for Asia-based expats and tourists from all over the world: It was chilling.

Obviously, for any story, your reporting is improved immeasurably by being there on the ground, seeing what there is to see and wandering around for yourself. But there was no chance to do that on that first day. Getting to the airport and onto a plane would have taken several hours and the airport was shut anyway, according to the wires. The drive from Bangkok to Phuket would have been at least 10 hours. So, on a story defined by images and narrative, I was going to have to make do with the telephone.

The wires were reporting that phone lines were down and electricity was cut in places. I knew that people on the island would be frantically trying to reach relatives all over the world, jamming up the phone lines. Alan was properly keen to file something to our Web edition as soon as possible to replace the wire copy that was running there. So I needed to reach a few people as quickly as possible to simply find out what was going on down there, what had happened, what it looked like. . . .

Being in a modern hotel with good broadband and phone lines was hugely helpful. I could quickly gather as much information as was then available on the wires and figure out which parts of the island I should call. I had access to as many phone numbers as I needed.

How did you find the people—especially the tsunami survivors—whom you interviewed?

ALAN SIPRESS: Huda and I spent hours dialing telephone numbers, trying to get a call through. In one case, we were able to reach a telephone operator in Aceh's main telephone office who had stayed on the job despite the tsunami, watching the wall of water from an upper-floor window. In another case, we reached an Indonesian Red Cross worker whose cell phone still worked, apparently because he was close to a neighboring province where there was less destruction.

PETER GOODMAN: I knew that the biggest, most developed stretch of beach in Phuket is called Patong, which is an unbroken strip of resorts. The wires had reports of particularly intense damage there. So, I went to Google and typed in something like "Patong Phuket resort" in the search window and started clicking on links to hotels. I was inclined to call smaller guest houses away from the beach, figuring that they would be more likely to have chatty people answering the line, unhindered by the corporate codes of media engagement that I was likely to confront at the Meridiens and Hiltons of the world. . . .

Sure enough, on my first try, I got hold of a Swedish guy who owns a little guesthouse in Patong. He had just come back from as close to the beach as one could get. He had seen the second wave and gave me a detailed account of what he had encountered—cars floating upside down, the sea 100 yards inland from its normal confines. I made a few more calls and reached another small guesthouse where a clerk handed the phone to a Malaysian tourist who had seen the first wave from high up on a bluff and described the sense of terror to me.

That was really enough for the first go, enough to put in a feed for Alan. We had confirmed what the wires were reporting, and we had our own color, our own voice, a little narrative to work with to give the story a sense of reality for readers so easily dulled by the "newspaperese" that can make even a biblical-scale tragedy sound like just another dispatch from that other planet on which news happens. So, I typed it up and sent it to Alan through our internal messaging system. . . .

After that, I got back on the phone and called some hotels in different parts of the island to get an idea of how widespread the damage was, how it varied. There was a BBC report of a bunch of scuba divers missing, so I started to call dive shops all over the place, trying to confirm it. Again and again, I was told that all the boats had made it back safely and no one was missing. It seemed that people on boats were relatively shielded from the impacts.

I used these calls as a way to get more color, more voice, more description. Of particularly high value was an interview with a Canadian guy who owns a dive shop and had seen a beach covered with sunbathers and children playing in the water in the instant before the wave hit. He took issue with the official death toll and said—in what now is way low—that there had to be at least 500 to 1,000 people dead. I typed up a second feed for Alan for use in the print edition.

How did your familiarity with the area affect your work?

ALAN SIPRESS: My familiarity with Aceh was helpful because I could evaluate the information we were receiving from witnesses, wire services and local television about the impact of the tsunami. I knew the geography of the province and the layout of the provincial capital, so I could better judge the severity of the floods. I also had many contacts inside the province that I tried to reach. As I mentioned, however, these calls failed to go through.

PETER GOODMAN: It was huge, the key. Thailand is a place I have spent a lot of time over the last 18 years, Phuket in particular. I didn't have to waste time making futile attempts to get down there from Bangkok that day, and I didn't have to pull out any maps to locate the best places to call. I knew Patong was the spot right away. I was also able to process immediately what was being told to me by the people on the end of the phone. They could speak quickly and casually, as if telling their story to a buddy at the bar in their guesthouse, without having to stop to handle too many questions about the place that would have halted the flow. We could get right to the meat of what I needed and what they were most eager to talk about—the wave and its aftermath.

Most critically, I had been right there on the beach at the same time of year. I knew instantly what the scene had looked like before the wave hit, who was there, what they were doing. Most times on disasters, reporters have to reconstruct for themselves both the before and after. A plane crashes and you have to figure out who was on the plane, where were they going, whether it was crowded. In this case, I knew the "before" intimately from my own experience. That allowed me to very quickly conjure up an image of what had happened down there and it gave me an obvious set of questions to work with. I already had the before; all I needed was the after.

How did you decide what the focus would be?

ALAN SIPRESS: The story did not have a specific focus but rather was an overview of the breadth of the disaster. Within the story, I decided to highlight witness accounts from Indonesia and Thailand because most of the material from India and Sri Lanka was to be used in separate articles.

PETER GOODMAN: This did not require a lot of thinking. Meat and potatoes: What did it look, sound and feel like when a surge of water taller than the coconut palms swept over a jam-packed stretch of tourist resorts on the morning after Christmas? What happened? What did the place look like afterward? We spend so much time these days thinking about new ways to lead readers into stories and keep them there, something we have to do in an age of media saturation, in which people can easily become inured to the content. In this case, we had a biblical-scale disaster in which the simple facts alone, the images, were more than enough to command attention.

How did you work together? Did one of you serve as principal writer? How did the two of you share information?

PETER GOODMAN: Generally at the *Post*, there is one lead writer and it was clearly Alan in this case. He is based in Southeast Asia. I was merely passing through and helping out. So, my job was to get as much as I could from Phuket as quickly as possible and ship it down to him and let him put it together. I glanced at the story in the system and then I saw it on the Web. We talked a couple of times on the phone, mostly just about what he was hearing from elsewhere—Indonesia, India, Sri Lanka. I left it to him to decide what of my material should go in and how, since he had to handle multiple threads of the story and he was the one tasked with fitting it all together.

ALAN SIPRESS: Peter sent me his notes by internal e-mail in the form of storified memos. I took his material along with what we had from our reporting in Indonesia and wrote the article.

You utilized a lot of feeds from various wire services and other reports. How did you keep track of all the information and how did you decide what to include and what to attribute?

ALAN SIPRESS: Over the course of the day, I received feeds from Peter and Huda as well as our reporters in South Asia. As these feeds and wire accounts came over the computer, I printed them out and then underlined important or telling details in each one. I tried to use as much of our own material as possible. In several cases, the wire services had details or quotes that we could not obtain or confirm ourselves, so I attributed these. For instance, I was taken by the quote from the Sri Lankan naval spokesman saying his base was under water, so I decided to use this with attribution.

How did you organize your story? What thread did you decide to use to tie this incredibly large story together?

ALAN SIPRESS: The story opens with several paragraphs of broad sweep, trying to convey the almost biblical proportions of the tsunami, by quickly describing its geographic and geological magnitude along with a smattering of dramatic detail. Then there are a few paragraphs about the two worst-hit countries: Indonesia and Sri Lanka. After that, the story goes back into greater detail about these two countries before moving on to India and Thailand.

Though Thailand was not as badly struck as the first two countries, the story provides ample room for Peter's strong material from Thailand, which included some of our best eyewitness accounts.

How many drafts did you do? Were you aware of deadlines? Editions?

ALAN SIPRESS: I essentially wrote two drafts. The first was filed to *The Washington Post* Web site around early evening, Jakarta time. This meant we had a staff story about the tsunami on the site by the time most American readers woke up Sunday morning. Most of the reporting by

Peter, Huda and me was finished in time to be incorporated in the Web version. The Web site article served as the basis of the second draft, which I later filed for use in the Monday morning newspaper. That draft was edited and added to by the editors in Washington.

As I recall, I hit the send button for the second version and went to bed.

PETER GOODMAN: I just wrote my feeds straight through and sent them down to Jakarta. When time is of the essence, you try to write clean and fast. I was relieved of the responsibility to craft perfect transitions since I knew I was handing building blocks off to the mason, so to speak, who would then decide how best to fit them together.

What role did your editor play?

PETER GOODMAN: After he called me to put me on the story, Peter Eisner let me do my thing without any intrusion. He then kept an eye on the wires from Washington just to be sure we weren't missing anything important.

ALAN SIPRESS: Editors in Washington had the responsibility of ensuring that the article was comprehensive but did not step too heavily on the separate site-specific pieces filed by the other *Post* reporters. Also, since Jakarta is 12 hours ahead of Washington, the editors monitored developments over the course of my nighttime and updated the article before it was sent on for publication.

How did you deal with the effect the event was having on you personally? How did it help or impede your efforts?

PETER GOODMAN: When a huge story hits, there simply isn't time to focus on what it means for you personally. It really wasn't until later—particularly when I got down to Phuket the next day—that I could think about what it would have been like if I'd have been there with my own children on that beach, to reflect on how this could have been anyone I know. You have a job to do and that's pretty much all you're thinking about.

ALAN SIPRESS: The tsunami did not have an emotional impact on me immediately. During the first day, I was still far away from the actual event and, like others, did not fully appreciate the staggering extent of the disaster. The impact only began to hit me after I arrived in Aceh two days later and saw for myself hundreds of bodies in the streets. When that sight became upsetting, I focused my mind on where I was walking, watching my steps in the rubble.

Setting the Scene

Edited e-mail interviews conducted by Poynter Institute Distinguished Fellow Butch Ward with John Lancaster and Rama Lakshmi, members of The Washington Post *team that won the ASNE deadline news reporting award. Lancaster and Lakshmi collaborated on "In India, Death Roars in from the Ocean."*

BUTCH WARD: Where were you when the tsunami hit and where did your assignment come from?

JOHN LANCASTER: I had just arrived in Cochin, in the Indian state of Kerala, to begin a vacation with my family, including my parents and my sister, who had traveled to India from the United States. The tsunami hit while our flight from Delhi was in the air. I learned of it while we were waiting to collect our luggage when I received a text message on my cell phone from Rama Lakshmi, my Indian colleague. Although the extent of the damage was far from clear, I realized that I needed to find out more.

It was the middle of the night in Washington, so I made the decision without talking to an editor. I apologized to my family and expressed the hope that I would be able to join them later in the day (little did I know— I was gone for nearly a month). Then I borrowed $500 from my dad and headed to the Meridien hotel in Cochin, while my family headed off to a rented houseboat.

RAMA LAKSHMI: The managing editor of the *Post*, Steve Coll, was in India with his family for the Christmas holidays. I met them late Sunday morning to show them a 12th-century monument; we had planned a leisurely lunch after that.

Before I left my home, I checked the news and learned about an undersea earthquake and how some coasts in India had been flooded. As I left my home, the numbers of dead in Tamil Nadu were fairly low. Just a dozen or so. I dismissed it as a small story, but, because it had hit several states, I also didn't want to take any chances. I was the only one in New Delhi. John

Lancaster had just boarded the plane for his family holiday in the south. So I sent him a text message on his mobile with the bare details. He was flying, so the message took time, and he read it only when he landed, a few hours later.

When I was at lunch with Steve and his family, I got a call from Alan Sipress in Indonesia. He said he wanted me to send him a brief on what had happened in India. He said, "Although the epicenter was here, it looks like most deaths have taken place in India. But because I am in Indonesia, the site of the earthquake, I will anchor the story from here."

So I hurried through lunch and headed toward my office. By then, John had landed, and he called me. He wanted me to file a brief to him, after reading the wires in the office and talking to New Delhi officials. When I reached the office, I realized it was a story bigger than I had imagined (but I still had no idea how big). I called John. We debated whether he should go to Tamil Nadu, or I should, or both. We concluded that he would go to Sri Lanka the next day, and I would go to Tamil Nadu.

Talk about how you collected the information.

JOHN LANCASTER: I went to a hotel so I could log on to the Internet and start reading wires. Communication was not an issue, at least for me, as Kerala was relatively unscathed by the tsunami. Rama had a much more challenging time in Chennai [also called Madras]; the smartest decision I made was to send her there, before the extent of the damage was clear. I figured it was better to be safe than sorry.

RAMA LAKSHMI: I went home to pack my bag and asked the travel agent to meet me on the road to the airport with my ticket. It was an evening flight, two and a half hours long. So I knew I had very little time and I was debating whether I should report in Chennai or drive out to the worse-affected areas of Cuddalore (three hours from Chennai) or the Nagapattinam districts (six to seven hours from Chennai). I knew if I went to those places, I would get the story but not have enough time to file. I didn't have a satellite phone either. The bureau has one, and John had taken it with him.

The flight arrived in Tamil Nadu about 40 minutes late. By then I knew I should not attempt to leave Chennai. It was already around 9:30 p.m. when we landed.

There were some Indian media reporters on the flight who were heading out to Cuddalore and Nagapattinam. But I chose to stay in Chennai that night. I had to get voices of people as quickly as possible. John was writing the story from Cochin based on wire reports, TV images. But I knew I had to get him the lead and the characters for the story.

How did you find the people—especially the tsunami survivors—whom you interviewed?

RAMA LAKSHMI: From the airport, I rushed straight to the government hospital. By now it was 10:30 p.m. or so. The wards were closed for visitors; the doctors and the nurses on the night duty didn't let me in. They kept saying I should first get "written permission" from the chief medical officer (because it was late, beyond visitors' hours). I knew this was impossible. So I kept walking into the ward, inch by inch, talking to them all the while, assuring them. They said the patients were asleep and that I should not disturb them, that the patients were traumatized and would need to rest. So I assured them that I just wanted to see the scene inside and that I would only talk to the ones who were awake and wished to speak. I assured them I would not wake anybody up, that I would take just a few minutes.

Once I was inside, I saw some relatives who were crying by the bedside of injured patients. I could not shoot off questions right away, even though I was on deadline. So I just went and sat with them quietly for a couple of minutes, writing down their muffled words. Then one woman began talking to me. Then another came up to me and wanted to speak, too. I got three people who had either lost family members or got injured. Before I could go on, the doctors came and asked me to leave.

I wanted to send the quotes and remarks to John immediately by phoning him, but my cell phone signal was very low inside the hospital. So I had to run all the way out of the building to call him. The signal was clearer outside.

I told him as much as I could about the scene: what the survivors had seen, what they looked like, what they had experienced.

Then I went to the morgue; I knew I would find some relatives of dead people there. But when I went there, I found a group of five young men looking for a lost friend. They had been playing cricket on the beach when their friend had disappeared with the water. I decided to follow them from one hospital to another, from one morgue to the next, as they looked for their friend by removing the sheets from the faces of the row of corpses in the morgue or going through the hospital register.

How did your familiarity with the area help you?

RAMA LAKSHMI: I belong to Tamil Nadu, and I understand the Tamil language well. This helped me enormously, because I could afford to not shoot off questions right away—to either the people in the hospital or the men who were searching for their friend. At the hospital, I just wrote down whatever the family members were saying as they wept. It took them a few minutes to open up to me and then I began my questions. The young men also were talking amongst themselves as they went through the bodies in the morgue. The understanding of the language helped me there. The smartest decision was to hit the hospital and the morgue first instead of the beach areas. That way I got the story quicker—all the characters I wanted were in one place.

How did you work together?

JOHN LANCASTER: Rama was the reporter, I was the writer. As soon as she hit the ground in Chennai, well after dark, she made straight for the disaster zone and began calling me on her cell phone with notes and anecdotes from survivors. She must have called me half a dozen times with various bits and pieces, which I then wove into a scene story with other information gleaned from the wires, various Web sites (including the BBC) and television.

How did you decide what the focus would be?

JOHN LANCASTER: We didn't really have much time to reflect. Rama's brief was basically to scoop up as much scene and anecdotal material as she could. I had initially thought that we would be writing an India-specific story; at some point during the evening, David Hoffman, the foreign editor, told me that our story would wrap in scene material from other places, including Sri Lanka. So I had to recast it a bit. Basically, we just tried to capture the human drama with a series of small-focus anecdotes. Bear in mind that the story was a sidebar to the main news story, so we really didn't have to dwell too much on context. That made it fairly easy to write.

How did you deal with the effect the event was having on you personally? How did it help or impede your efforts?

RAMA LAKSHMI: I was too tense and too rushed to think about these things at that time. I saw dead bodies, grief, loss and immense human tragedy that night. But all I could think of was how soon I could get the information to John. I knew he was waiting on the other end. When I reached the hotel, I was too tired to think. I had to leave for Cuddalore the next morning at 4 a.m. It was only when I reached Cuddalore the next day and saw mass burials, children's corpses in clear daylight, that the tragedy really hit me.

The First-Person Account

An edited e-mail and phone interview conducted by Poynter Institute Distinguished Fellow Butch Ward with Michael Dobbs, a member of The Washington Post *team that won the ASNE deadline news reporting award. Dobbs wrote "It Seemed Like a Scene from the Bible."*

BUTCH WARD: Writing in the first person is not always successful. Editors spike attempts at writing in the first person every day. Why do you think your story worked so effectively?

MICHAEL DOBBS: This was such a dramatic event that it really wasn't all that difficult to write. I would like to make it sound like it was extremely difficult to do—but I just tried to write truthfully about the extraordinary thing that happened to me.

After all, it's very rare to get caught in a tsunami—and I wasn't there as a reporter. I just happened to be on holiday with my family in Sri Lanka. The night before, I had had Christmas dinner with my family. We were very relaxed; I wasn't thinking about anything to do with journalism. Then I got caught in this extraordinary event. So I just tried to very simply put my thoughts in order and tell the story in a straightforward, chronological fashion.

I have taught writing to non-journalists. When they are having trouble, I advise them to forget that they are writers and to pretend they are talking to their best friends or writing a letter home. When I was teaching at Princeton a couple of years ago, I had a student who was struggling with her writing and using very academic, bureaucratic words. I asked her whether that was the way she talked to her college roommate. Of course it wasn't. When she told a story to her friends, she talked in very simple, straightforward terms. That's not bad advice for a writer.

I actually did not even think about writing the story until several hours later. I thought I had been caught in some kind of weird, freak tide. I knew a lot of people had died in the area where I was. But it wasn't until later that day, after I had heard BBC reports on a friend's radio, that I began to realize the scale of the disaster.

Once you decided to write, how did you gather your thoughts? Had you already told the story several times to family members and others?

Yes, I had told the story several times. I didn't have a computer, just a few scraps of paper from a legal pad, and I worked by candlelight.

I paid attention to the lead ("Disaster struck with no warning out of a faultlessly clear blue sky") because I wanted to capture the contradiction of it all. On the one hand, I was caught in a terrible catastrophe. But, at the same time, there was a peacefulness about it all—the most perfect day you can imagine. That contradiction summed up my experience that day. So once I had the lead, I just told the rest of the story in a very chronological way.

If you're in a situation like that, your faculties become much more acute. I was describing a period of about 15 minutes, but it's not like 15 minutes sitting in an office. Being there, your whole experience is heightened. I've been in combat situations, wars, had people shoot at me. At such times, your impressions are just much more vivid.

I could have written the story much more elaborately—but I think the story would have suffered from overwriting. Simplicity is probably a virtue.

The Editor's Role

An edited e-mail interview conducted by Poynter Institute Distinguished Fellow Butch Ward with David Hoffman, The Washington Post*'s assistant managing editor for foreign news. Hoffman coordinated coverage of the tsunami with reporters who were thousands of miles away.*

BUTCH WARD: The *Post* produced three stories: mainbar, scene and the first-person account. Was that your lineup from the start or did it evolve? Clearly, the magnitude of the disaster was growing throughout that day. As it grew, how did your thinking change—especially as it concerned the management of your people in Asia? How much of your thinking on that first day was already jumping ahead to how you would dispatch reporters on succeeding days?

DAVID HOFFMAN: I first heard of the disaster in a call from Michael Dobbs before dawn. Michael called on a Hong Kong cell phone that was rapidly losing battery power. I had the presence of mind to get that phone number. I then headed to the office; the wires were still sketchy, and I didn't make any real decisions until about 8 or 9 a.m. Eastern time, when I got downtown. The first thing I tried to do was get Michael back on the phone. This took several hours (he was recharging the phone, I later learned, off a generator). When I reached him, I took his dictation.

We were fortunate that Peter Goodman was in Thailand, and he and Alan Sipress in Jakarta both weighed in pretty early. My concern with Alan was getting him moving toward the epicenter, but frankly I do not recall knowing precisely where that was until later, and I recall he was on his way quickly. I also recall that I needed to get John Lancaster moving to Sri Lanka and Rama Lakshmi toward the Indian coast.

In addition to providing the overview and the most recent developments, what role does the main story play in establishing the tone for the coverage? How quickly did you know this was a story of such proportions that biblical references would be appropriate?

In a big story like this, the "ledeall" is critical. A ledeall needs to tell the reader in a fast-paced, fluid and powerful way what happened. It is the anchor and beacon of the coverage. A story like this cannot wander; it must deliver. And I think the key here was signaling to readers that this was a really large-scale event. We didn't have a clue the toll would go so high, but I think the reporters did understand the scope of the event—just from their own day-one fact-gathering—and wrote the ledeall with that in mind. The first biblical reference I heard was from Dobbs, as he dictated, and it was telling. Normally, as an editor you want to say, "Whoa! Are you sure?" But in this case, the story was extraordinary, and I didn't even pause to ask the question.

First-person narratives often fail to work as well as the one Michael Dobbs wrote. Was this event such a "can't miss," or did Michael do something important with his observation or writing that made it work? Did you coach him at all through the writing? I was fascinated by his recall of the details of his ordeal, especially since he says he didn't think about writing until several hours afterward.

Frankly, this one was less thought-out than that. I think three hours—or maybe four—elapsed from his first call to me at home and the time he dictated. I did not coach him. I immediately approved the first-person narrative. My only role was to ask questions for clarity. For example, I had to ask him to clarify the proximity of the house to the beach. I remember asking him about clinging to a catamaran and why that was important in saving him. I also remember his very clear impression of the peacefulness—the clear blue sky—as the tsunami hit. So there wasn't a lot of drum roll. As he dictated, I did feel that he was moved—deeply moved—at having survived.

What makes a good scene story work? It seemed clear to me that Rama's resourcefulness and familiarity with the local language really made a difference.

I agree that Rama's hustle and drive made a big difference. We had no idea so much damage had happened so far away, and her reporting contributed again to the larger understanding. I wasn't even sure she'd make it out there in time for the first edition but she did, and we were incredibly grateful. We realized if a wave that big had hit so far from the epicenter that this was one mighty tsunami.

What makes a good scene work? Observation taken at first hand, voices of the victims, description.

Finally, can you share any thoughts about how you approach editing stories such as these—filed on deadline, from far away, by people you rarely see? Is it a different process from editing the local education reporter?

Yes, hugely different. I would say the strongest assets an editor can have in such a situation are the eyes and ears of the correspondents. There's all kinds of tweaking you can do at the margins of the written story, but the truly great strength of a paper is in the talent you have in the field.

I believe the greatest single attribute of a foreign correspondent is someone who is obsessed with their subject. You see it in their files: immersed, forever curious, acute observation, vivid description—always original and authentic. When you have people like this, the best thing to do is let them do what they do best. You can't do much more anyway—because of the great distances and difficulties in communications.

And when they do it well, it seems like a small miracle.

So the strongest approach is to find such people and train those who want to learn. Editing is just polishing the vase; the molding and shaping and creative work is all in the hands of the journalists.

Writers' Workshop

Talking Points

1. As soon as *Washington Post* reporter Rama Lakshmi arrived in Tamil Nadu, she decided to go immediately to the hospital and the morgue, because she could "get the story quicker," she said. "All the characters I wanted were in one place." Considering the time constraints she faced, where else might Lakshmi have gone to find "all the characters"?

2. Alan Sipress said that if he had known so many telephone lines were down, he probably would not have spent so many hours trying to gather information by telephone. What other options did he have? Make a list of the resources available to a reporter who does not have time to get to the scene and has been cut off from telephone access.

3. Peter Goodman, describing his role in reporting for the lead story, said he wrote his "feeds straight through and sent them down to [Sipress in] Jakarta. . . . I was relieved of the responsibility to craft perfect transitions since I knew I was handing building blocks off to the mason, so to speak." Identify the transitions in the lead and scene stories, and discuss their roles. Which transitions work best? Which are unnecessary? What would you do differently?

Assignment Desk

1. The compelling details in Michael Dobbs' first-person account of surviving the tsunami are all the more impressive because he did not think about writing a story until hours after the event. His ability to reconstruct the ordeal—images, thoughts, feelings—was crucial to the story's effectiveness. Recall a recent incident in which you were involved and reconstruct it from memory, recording in as much detail as possible the images, thoughts and feelings you experienced at the time.

2. Members of *The Washington Post* team said their familiarity with the region and the language was a major factor in their ability to quickly and accurately gather information for these stories. What are the

areas in your region with which you are most familiar, and how could you exploit that knowledge in the event of a deadline crisis? In what subjects do you have a particular expertise? Are you fluent in any languages other than English? Do your editors know about your areas of expertise and those of other members of the staff? If not, how could you implement a system to collect that information?

3. In addition to gathering information about the earthquake and tsunami, the *Post* reporters needed to explain with authority the science involved in this natural disaster. What sources of information could you turn to on deadline? If the disaster had involved a chemical explosion in your town, where would you turn for quick—and credible—information on the science involved in the event?

Dexter Filkins

Individual Deadline News Reporting

In a story he filed for *The New York Times* on Oct. 10, 2004, Dexter Filkins described how hard it had become to cover Iraq. Reporters found themselves hemmed in because of the escalating violence: "On some days, it seems, we are all crowded into a single room together, clutching our notebooks and watching the walls."

A month later, Filkins began filing stories outside those walls. He placed himself in the midst of one of the most violent confrontations in Iraq at that time: the assault on Fallujah. In a nominating letter to the ASNE judges, the *Times* noted that Filkins joined "the Marines of Bravo Company [as they] embarked on the most grueling street-by-street combat mission American forces have carried out since Vietnam."

Filkins' dispatches from Fallujah covered eight days of ferocious fighting. His stories transported readers to battles so intensely intimate that "soldiers [were] often close enough to look their enemies in the eyes," he wrote.

Filing stories from chaotic places was not new to Filkins. He worked for *The Miami Herald* in the early 1990s, playing a major role in the coverage of Hurricane Andrew's aftermath for which the *Herald* received the 1993 Pulitzer Prize for public service. He later moved to the *Los Angeles Times,* where he was responsible for coverage in seven countries, including Afghanistan, India and Pakistan.

Filkins joined *The New York Times* in October 2000. Before being based in Iraq, he covered the war in Afghanistan and was the Istanbul bureau chief. He became the *Times'* Baghdad correspondent in October 2003.

Filkins grew up in Cape Canaveral, Fla., and earned a bachelor's degree in government from the University of Florida. He later received a master's of philosophy in international relations from Oxford University. He also has worked as a deckhand on a commercial fishing boat in the Atlantic Ocean and as a welder's assistant on a pipe-laying barge in the Gulf of Mexico.

His reporting experience, his practical knowledge and his educational background made him an excellent reporter in Iraq. Filkins was literally on the run during this coverage and used all the skills he had acquired over the years to capture stories that could only be told from firsthand experience.

—Al Tompkins

The Jesse Laventhol Prize for Deadline News Reporting by an individual is funded by a gift from David Laventhol, a former Times Mirror executive, in honor of his father.

4. Urban Warfare Deals Harsh Challenge to Troops

NOV. 9, 2004

FALLUJA, Iraq, Nov. 8—The two marines were pinned down on a roof on Monday, pressing themselves against a low, crumbling wall as insurgents fired rocket-propelled grenades at them from a building near the middle of town.

Hours before, they had clambered over a railroad embankment—a berm, to the engineering-minded—and started their advance into this rebel-held city.

Commanders called in artillery fire on the building where the grenades were emerging, their tails spitting and glowing like sparklers across the sky. But the artillery only flattened the building next door to the one occupied by the insurgents.

"This is crazy," one of the marines said. "Yeah," his buddy said, "and we've only taken one house."

This is urban warfare, where the technological advantages of the American military can be nullified, at least for a few terrifying hours, by a few determined fighters in a warehouse or an abandoned home.

During the night, the insurgents fired off brilliant red and blue flares, blinding the Americans' sensitive night-vision equipment, and slipped quickly from house to house in hopes of confusing the artillery spotters.

For hours, they succeeded, pinning down perhaps 150 marines led by Capt. Read Omohundro, a strapping graduate of Texas A&M who has a habit of walking around upright during bursts of mortar and grenade fire while everyone else is hugging an outcropping of concrete.

Even the captain concedes that this is nothing like a fight in the open desert, where the Americans are always fated to win, quickly. "The challenge is that the battlefield is three-dimensional," he said. "Not only do you have to look in front of you and behind you, but also above you and below you, even subterranean."

This night would become a textbook illustration of those complexities. Captain Omohundro's unit started rolling toward the berm in armored personnel carriers from an encampment about a mile north about 7 p.m. He was supposed to meet up there with another outfit, but it had gotten lost.

Finally he found it, and his men started their part of the invasion by firing a 200-yard cord containing 1,800 pounds of explosive southward from the berm, toward downtown Falluja. The marines worried that their way into the city had been mined. But when the charge exploded, it also set off any mines in a narrow path around it.

That tactic worked, but when the marines climbed the berm in pitch blackness and went over, they discovered rocky ground with rusty junk littering the way—a typical railroad district on the edge of town. They worked their way toward their first objectives, a small traffic circle, and beyond that, the first buildings of the city.

But the marines were getting shelled even before they went over the berm. The area exploded with sporadic gunfire, rocket-propelled grenade rounds and mortars. The advance bogged down as spotters tried to locate pockets of insurgents and wipe them out with the big guns.

For a time, this frightening urban battlefield became a pulsing cacophony of strange and deadly sounds. The mosques in the city broadcast calls to jihad through their speakers. F-18's fired 3,000 rounds a minute in bursts that sounded oddly like burps. AC-130 gunships droned overhead, their big cannons going thunk, thunk as they found targets.

Perhaps strangest of all, the American troops brought in their own "psyops" trucks—for psychological operations—and blared sounds that created a nightmarish duet with the mosques: old AC/DC songs, something that sounded like a sonar ping, the cavalry charge.

Captain Omohundro did not like sitting still in this theater of doom, and for good reason. "My biggest fear is staying in the same place for too long," he said. "Then they'll pinpoint us and start firing."

Eventually the artillery found the house that had been spitting the grenades and flattened that one, too. An AC-130 passed overhead but decided that the threat had been annihilated along with the building.

Then the shooting started again, from some other window among the cracked streets and twisted alleyways of Falluja.

5. Hard Lesson: 150 Marines Face 1 Sniper

NOV. 11, 2004

FALLUJA, Iraq, Nov. 10—American marines called in two airstrikes on the pair of dingy three-story buildings squatting along Highway 10 on Wednesday, dropping 500-pound bombs each time. They fired 35 or so 155-millimeter artillery shells, 10 shots from the muzzles of Abrams tanks and perhaps 30,000 rounds from their automatic rifles. The building was a smoking ruin.

But the sniper kept shooting.

He—or they, because no one can count the flitting shadows in this place—kept 150 marines pinned down for the better part of a day. It was a lesson on the nature of the enemy in this hellish warren of rubble-strewn streets. Not all of the insurgents are holy warriors looking for martyrdom. At least a few are highly trained killers who do their job with cold precision and know how to survive.

"The idea is, he just sits up there and eats a sandwich," said Lt. Andy Eckert, "and we go crazy trying to find him."

The contest is a deadly one, and two marines in Company B, First Battalion, Eighth Regiment of the First Marine Expeditionary Force have been killed by snipers in the past two days as the unit advanced just half a mile southward to Highway 10 from a mosque they had taken on Tuesday.

Despite the world-shaking blasts of weaponry as the Americans try to root out the snipers, this is also a contest of wills in which the tension rises to a level that seems unbearable, and then rises again. Marine snipers sit, as motionless as blue herons, for 30 minutes and stare with crazed intensity into the oversized scopes on their guns. If so much as a penumbra brushes across a windowsill, they open up.

With the troops' senses tuned to a high pitch, mundane events become extraordinary. During one bombing, a blue-and-yellow parakeet flew up to a roof of a captured building and fluttered about in tight circles before perching on a slumping power line, to the amazement of the marines assembled there.

On another occasion, the snipers tensed when they heard movement in the direction of a smoldering building. A cat sauntered out, unconcerned with anything but making its rounds in the neighborhood.

"Can I shoot it, sir?" a sniper asked an officer.

"Absolutely not," came the reply.

This day started at about 8 a.m., when the marines left the building where they had been sleeping and headed south toward Highway 10, which runs from east to west and roughly bisects the town. At the corner of Highway 10 and Thurthar, the street they were moving along, was a headquarters building for the Iraqi National Guard that had been taken over by insurgents.

Almost immediately, they came under fire from a sniper in the minaret of a mosque just south of them. Someone in a three-story residential building farther down the street also opened up. The marines made 50-yard dashes and dived for cover, but one of them was cut down, killed on the spot. It was unclear what direction the fatal bullet had come from.

"I don't know who it was," Lt. Steven Berch, leader of the fallen marine's platoon, said of the attacker, "but he was very well trained."

After two hours of bombardment, the sniper at that mosque ceased firing. But just around the corner at the famous blue-domed Khulafah Al Rashid mosque, another sniper was pinning down marines, and airstrikes were called in on it, too. The issue of striking at mosques is so sensitive in the Arab world that the American military later issued a statement saying that the strike on the Khulafah mosque was unavoidable and that precision munitions merely knocked down a minaret.

By noon, the marines had worked their way down to the national guard building, still taking fire from the sniper, or snipers, on the other side of Main Street. Inside was a sign in Arabic that said: "Long live the mujahedeen." Soon the marines had spray-painted another sign over it: "Long live the muj killers."

But for the next five hours, they could not kill whoever was running from window to window and firing at them from the other side of Main Street, despite the expenditure of enormous amounts of ammunition.

"We're not able to see the muzzle flashes," said Capt. Read Omohundro, the company commander. "As a result," he said, "we end up expending a lot of ammunition trying to get the snipers."

At one point, they thought that they had a bead on someone running back and forth between the two buildings. Then Capt. Christopher Spears exclaimed: "He's on a bike!"

And somehow, through a volley of gunfire, whoever it was got away.

At 5 p.m., the marines finally crossed Highway 10 and searched the smoking remains of the two buildings. At 5:30 p.m., a sniper opened up on them.

6. Black Flags Are Deadly Signals As Cornered Rebels Fight Back

NOV. 12, 2004

FALLUJA, Iraq, Nov. 11—The stars began to glimmer through a wan yellow-gray sunset over Falluja on Thursday evening. The floury dust in the air and a skyline of broken minarets and smashed buildings combined for the only genuine postcard image this country has to offer for now.

Sitting on a third-story roof, Staff Sgt. Eric Brown, his lip bleeding, peered through the scope of his rifle into the haze. Moments before, a lone bullet had whizzed past his face and smashed a window behind him. "God, I hate this place, the way the sun sets," Sergeant Brown said.

Sgt. Sam Williams said, "I wish I could see down the street."

But these marines did see a black flag pop up all at once above a water tower about 100 yards away, then a second flag somewhere in the gloaming above a rooftop. And the shots began, in a wave this time, as men bobbed and weaved through alleyways and sprinted across the street. "He's in the road, he's in the road, shoot him!" Sergeant Brown shouted. "Black shirt!" someone else yelled. "Due south!"

The flags are the insurgents' answer to two-way radios, their way of massing the troops and—in a tactic that goes back at least as far as Napoleon—concentrating fire on an enemy. Set against radio waves, the flags have one distinct advantage: they are terrifying.

The insurgents are coordinating their attacks at a time when they have nowhere left to run. American forces have pushed south of Highway 10, the boulevard that runs east to west and approximately bisects Falluja. American intelligence officers believe that many of the insurgents have retreated as far as the Shuhada, a relatively modern residential area that is the southernmost neighborhood in Falluja.

But beyond Shuhada is only the open desert, patrolled by the United States Army. So the insurgents are turning and fighting. And at night, they are setting up deadly ambushes in the moonless pitch blackness of Falluja's labyrinthine streets.

Going straight up the gut in the center of the American advance on Thursday was Bravo Company, First Battalion, Eighth Regiment of the First Marine Expeditionary Force. Those marines, including Sergeants

Brown and Williams, started their day by getting mortared in a building they had captured at Highway 10 and Thurthar Street.

The building's windows were blown out. Parts of the ceiling had collapsed. The mortars drew closer and closer and then stopped, as if the insurgents were temporarily short of ammo. "I thought, 'This is it,' " said Senior Corpsman Kevin Markley.

At about 2 p.m., the company walked 100 yards east along the highway, then turned south into the Sinai neighborhood, with its car garages and fix-it shops as well as concealed weapons caches and bomb-making factories.

Immediately, shooting broke out, pinning down the marines for an hour. Finally they moved south to a mosque with the stub of a blasted minaret. An armored vehicle drove up from the rear and dropped its hatch. Out walked a group of blinking, disoriented Iraqi national guardsmen. They had been brought in only to search mosques.

Meantime, the marines went to the rooftop, saw the flags and got into a firefight. It was silenced when they called in a 500-pound bomb from above onto a house where some of the insurgents had concentrated. The strike was so close that the marines had to leave the roof or risk being killed by shrapnel.

The Iraqi guardsmen left the mosque and trooped back into the vehicle, which drove off. Soon the marines were headed south again, through a narrow alley between deserted houses.

"Enemy personnel approaching your position in white vehicle with RPG's," someone said over a radio, referring to rocket-propelled grenades. A few seconds later, the same voice said: "More enemy personnel approaching your position from the south."

The alley exploded with gunfire and RPG rounds. Somehow the company commander, Capt. Read Omohundro, got two tanks in place to fire down the alley. They let loose with a volley and a building crumbled.

Captain Omohundro turned to a lieutenant and said, "Are they dead?"

"They must be, sir," came the reply.

But the insurgents had gotten off an RPG round and disabled one tank; the other tank mysteriously stopped working as well.

The company had moved 500 yards south. They regrouped in the pitch blackness and pushed on at about 11:30 p.m. without the tanks, trying to keep up with the rest of the front, but after moving 25 feet they were attacked again in what appeared to be a well-organized ambush.

Two more tanks came in, but one had a problem with its global-positioning system unit. There was an hour's delay. The 50 or so men of the First Platoon, which had taken casualties, started bickering. Then they moved forward, behind the tanks.

At 1:30 a.m., now roughly 700 yards south of Highway 10, they stopped and entered a house, intending to find a place to sleep. There was a huge boom inside. "Oh no! Oh no!" someone shouted. "My leg!" someone else screamed. "My leg!"

They looked further around the house and found tunnels underneath. They retreated and a tank fired rounds into the house, which caught fire.

They looked for another place to sleep.

Black Flags Are Deadly Signals As Cornered Rebels Fight Back

FALLUJA, Iraq, Nov. 11—The stars began to glimmer through a wan yellow-gray sunset over Falluja on Thursday evening. The floury dust in the air and a skyline of broken minarets and smashed buildings combined for the only genuine postcard image this country has to offer for now.

Sitting on a third-story roof, Staff Sgt. Eric Brown, his lip bleeding, peered through the scope of his rifle into the haze. Moments before, a lone bullet had whizzed past his face and smashed a window behind him. "God, I hate this place, the way the sun sets," Sergeant Brown said.

Sgt. Sam Williams said, "I wish I could see down the street."

But these marines did see a black flag pop up all at once above a water tower about 100 yards away, then a second flag somewhere in the gloaming above a rooftop. And the shots began, in a wave this time,

Marginal annotations:

vivid adjectives create sense of place

words in tension describe the surreal: skyline/postcard clashes with broken/smashed

active verbs build action

object of danger and mystery

first character introduced, he has something at stake

quotes inside action = dialogue

odd, antique poetic phrase

exclamation points add fuel to fire

another odd phrase, recalls Ali boxing

subject-verb at beginning introduces long sentence

movement from narrative to background

short, emphatic phrase at end of paragraph

"gold coins"— using imagery as a "gold coin" to reward the reader for staying with the story

nice tension between elegant word and earthy word.

as men bobbed and weaved through alleyways and sprinted across the street. "He's in the road, he's in the road, shoot him!" Sergeant Brown shouted. "Black shirt!" someone else yelled. "Due south!"

The flags are the insurgents' answer to two-way radios, their way of massing the troops and—in a tactic that goes back at least as far as Napoleon—concentrating fire on an enemy. Set against radio waves, the flags have one distinct advantage: they are terrifying.

The insurgents are coordinating their attacks at a time when they have nowhere left to run. American forces have pushed south of Highway 10, the boulevard that runs east to west and approximately bisects Falluja. American intelligence officers believe that many of the insurgents have retreated as far as the Shuhada, a relatively modern residential area that is the southernmost neighborhood in Falluja.

But beyond Shuhada is only the open desert, patrolled by the United States Army. So the insurgents are turning and fighting. And at night, they are setting up deadly ambushes in the moonless pitch blackness of Falluja's labyrinthine streets.

Going straight up the gut in the center of the American

advance on Thursday was Bravo Company, First Battalion, Eighth Regiment of the First Marine Expeditionary Force. Those marines, including Sergeants Brown and Williams, started their day by getting mortared in a building they had captured at Highway 10 and Thurthar Street.

flashback, restarts narrative elements

The building's windows were blown out. Parts of the ceiling had collapsed. The mortars drew closer and closer and then stopped, as if the insurgents were temporarily short of ammo. "I thought, 'This is it,'" said Senior Corpsman Kevin Markley.

variation of sentence length and structure

straight quote

At about 2 p.m., the company walked 100 yards east along the highway, then turned south into the Sinai neighborhood, with its car garages and fix-it shops as well as concealed weapons caches and bomb-making factories.

what filmmakers would call an "establishing shot," place and action viewed from a distance

Immediately, shooting broke out, pinning down the marines for an hour. Finally they moved south to a mosque with the stub of a blasted minaret. An armored vehicle drove up from the rear and dropped its hatch. Out walked a group of blinking, disoriented Iraqi national guardsmen. They had been brought in only to search mosques.

Meantime, the marines went to the rooftop, saw the flags and got into a firefight. It was silenced when they called in a 500-pound bomb from above onto a house where some of the insurgents had concentrated. The strike was so close that the marines had to leave the roof or risk being killed by shrapnel.

The Iraqi guardsmen left the mosque and trooped back into the vehicle, which drove off. Soon the marines were headed south again, through a narrow alley between deserted houses.

"Enemy personnel approaching your position in white vehicle with RPG's," someone said over a radio, referring to rocket-propelled grenades. A few seconds later, the same voice said: "More enemy personnel approaching your position from the south."

The alley exploded with gunfire and RPG rounds. Somehow the company commander, Capt. Read Omohundro, got two tanks in place to fire down the alley. They let loose with a volley and a building crumbled.

Captain Omohundro turned to a lieutenant and said, "Are they dead?"

"They must be, sir," came the reply.

But the insurgents had gotten off an RPG round and disabled one tank; the other tank mysteriously stopped working as well.

The company had moved 500 yards south. They regrouped in

the pitch blackness and pushed on at about 11:30 p.m. without the tanks, trying to keep up with the rest of the front, but after moving 25 feet they were attacked again in what appeared to be a well-organized ambush.

Two more tanks came in, but one had a problem with its global-positioning system unit. There was an hour's delay. The 50 or so men of the First Platoon, which had taken casualties, started bickering. Then they moved forward, behind the tanks.

At 1:30 a.m., now roughly 700 yards south of Highway 10, they stopped and entered a house, intending to find a place to sleep. There was a huge boom inside. "Oh no! Oh no!" someone shouted. "My leg!" someone else screamed. "My leg!"

chaos and violence

They looked further around the house and found tunnels underneath. They retreated and a tank fired rounds into the house, which caught fire. They looked for another place to sleep.

no closure, just the sense of more danger to come

Roy Peter Clark is senior scholar and vice president of The Poynter Institute.

A conversation with
Dexter Filkins

An edited e-mail interview conducted by Poynter Institute faculty member Al Tompkins with Dexter Filkins, winner of the ASNE individual deadline news reporting award.

AL TOMPKINS: Where did the idea for this story come from, traveling eight days with the Marines' Bravo Company as they did street-by-street fighting?

DEXTER FILKINS: The idea of going into Fallujah with the Marines was pretty obvious at the time. The city had become a safe haven for insurgents, and the American military was determined to take the city back. It was shaping up to be the biggest battle of the entire war.

Why did you take on this assignment at such great risk to your own life?

It wasn't possible to cover the fighting any other way, as it was in other conflicts, because the insurgents were killing journalists. So it was go with the Marines or not at all.

Where were you exactly during these stories?

I traveled with Bravo Company on foot into the heart of the city.

Paint a picture of what you were carrying, what you were wearing, where and how much you slept, what you ate.

The conditions were very difficult, the most difficult part of the assignment . . . We were under fire, sometimes very heavy fire, almost continuously for eight days. With a helmet and flak jacket and pack, I carried about 70 pounds of gear. I carried most of my food and water with me for the first few days. Running and walking with that much stuff, while being shot at, was not easy.

How did you collect information?

I collected information as any reporter would, by watching and listening and asking questions. That part was actually pretty easy; the story was hard to miss. The drawback—being in a war zone and embedded with Marines—was that I could talk to Iraqis only rarely. The city was almost empty of civilians.

The other difficulty was finding the time to talk to the Marines; they were usually fighting or sleeping. A moment would come and then it would pass.

How did you decide what the focus of these stories would be?

This wasn't very difficult, as far as stories go. It wasn't like I was going to a zoning hearing and couldn't find anything to write about. The events were so dramatic and so intense that that part was a snap. I filed 15 stories in eight days.

Usually, there were two pieces per day. First, there was the news—how far did the Marines advance into the city, what were the main obstacles to their advance, the biggest events of the day, that sort of thing. Then I usually tried to file some sort of color piece, which focused on what I thought was most interesting or a dramatic scene, which would convey some of the feeling and intensity and human drama that was unfolding there. So, I typically focused on a scene and went from there.

One day our company of 150 guys was pinned down for several hours by a single sniper. The Marines fired thousands of rounds at the guy, dropped bombs and artillery on him, and still he kept firing. That was pretty bizarre and quite indicative of what was going on. Fallujah during the fighting was like another universe. I was just trying to convey that.

Another time, I filed a piece based on a battle for a mosque, which was extraordinarily up close and intense and bloody.

One time, we built an entire story around a flock of geese that flew over the city in a large V-formation, which disintegrated when it passed over the fighting.

How did you organize the stories? What was your process?

I don't have much of a process. Ordinarily, I just sit and write, let things occur as they may, and I check the quotes and small details later. In this case, the writing process was especially hard, given that we were under fire and moving most of the time.

There was no electricity. There were no phone lines. On most days, I would try to gather my thoughts and notes on a rooftop, usually at night, when it was pitch-black and when the Marines insisted on having no visible lights on whatsoever.

So, I usually worked from my sleeping bag, which I would zip up to keep the light of my computer or flashlight from escaping. (Ashley Gilbertson, the photographer I was with, filed twice from inside an outhouse. Fortunately, I didn't have to do that.) It was stifling inside that bag.

I could not have accomplished anything without the help of Jim Glanz, a colleague of mine who was in Baghdad at the time. On most nights I would call him on a satellite phone and dictate what I had as best I could. He did a lot of the work and a lot of the writing. He's amazing.

What revisions did you make from draft to draft?

There was no time for revisions.

What role did your editor play in the story?

I rarely spoke with editors.

Given where you were, and the conditions under which you worked, what was the mechanical process of filing these stories?

The mechanics for filing were very, very difficult. I had a laptop with me and a satellite phone and several batteries. But the batteries ran out after about the first day.

I've traveled in the Third World for some time, and I'm used to scrounging around for electricity and phone lines. This was something else. The most useful piece of equipment I brought with me was an AC converter with battery clips. That allowed me to charge my phone and computer batteries off of car batteries. There weren't many cars on the streets during the battle. So whenever I spotted one, even during the fighting, I would run out to the car and try to pry its hood open so I could hook my converter up to it to charge the battery.

After a few days of really intense fighting, troop carriers started showing up to bring supplies and take out the wounded, and they would sometimes stay for a while, or even overnight. I was able to run off their batteries, which really saved me. I'm not sure what I would have done without that converter.

At one point during the battle when I was almost out of electricity, my colleagues in Baghdad wrapped a bunch of charged phone batteries into a box and had them flown out by Marine helicopter to Fallujah. But given the logistical problems and the fighting, I didn't get them until the day before I left.

When you wrote these stories, what did you hope the result of your work would be?

I wasn't really thinking about that. I was trying to stay alive. We were in mortal danger almost continuously; I almost died at least a half-dozen times. The journalism was secondary.

Writers' Workshop

Talking Points

1. Dexter Filkins' work is distinguished by his careful attention to "telling details"—details that capture the character or scene. For example: "Staff Sgt. Eric Brown, his lip bleeding, peered through the scope of his rifle into the haze. Moments before, a lone bullet had whizzed past his face and smashed a window behind him. 'God, I hate this place, the way the sun sets,' Sergeant Brown said." Analyze one of Filkins' stories, counting the number of details he includes.

2. Filkins describes scenes so vividly that he makes the reader feel like a firsthand observer of the action. Identify specific portions of his stories that capture such scenes. Discuss how he used the five senses to take the reader to the scene.

3. Objective adjectives are specific, factual, measurable, quantitative. They enhance a reader's understanding more than subjective adjectives, which convey an opinion or feeling. Underline the adjectives Filkins uses and note which are objective and which are subjective.

Assignment Desk

1. Look at one of your most recent stories. What details did you include? What details did you omit? As you write your next story, look for at least three details you can include to take the reader to the scene.

2. Compare the number of active verbs with the number of passive forms of "to be" in one of your recent stories. What active verbs can you substitute? As you select verbs, ask yourself who or what is taking action.

3. Filkins said he was in mortal danger almost continuously. You may not face such physical danger, but every journalist must face fears. Legendary journalism professor Melvin Mencher encourages reporters to be counterphobic—that is, to tackle what they fear. Identify one of your fears and map out how you can confront it in your reporting and writing.

Narrative on Deadline

BY THOMAS FRENCH

Any journalist who whines about deadlines—and who among us has not joined that chorus—can only feel humbled when reading Dexter Filkins' astonishing combat dispatches from the streets of Fallujah.

It's hard to imagine a reporter working under more nightmarish conditions. Last November, as he followed a company of Marines fighting their way through the Iraqi city block by block, Filkins witnessed his subjects suffering injuries and even dying. Chronicling this reality put his own life at considerable risk.

Filkins reported while trapped by sniper fire. He reported under the threat of mines and rocket-propelled grenades. When the power cells on his satellite phone were depleted, he snuck back out onto the streets and stole a charge from the batteries of parked cars. At night, when it was time to write, he'd cocoon himself inside his sleeping bag so the insurgents would not see the telltale glare of his laptop. All of this under a daily deadline.

With the assistance of James Glanz, a colleague in the *Times'* Baghdad bureau who compiled and wrote up many of Filkins' observations, the ASNE winner turned out one masterfully reported story after another. His accounts of the battle for Fallujah are riveting, haunting, deeply human. Some passages shimmer with a stark, surrealistic beauty:

> With the troops' senses tuned to a high pitch, mundane events become extraordinary. During one bombing, a blue-and-yellow parakeet flew up to a roof of a captured building and fluttered about in tight circles before perching on a slumping power line, to the amazement of the marines assembled there.
>
> On another occasion, the snipers tensed when they heard movement in the direction of a smoldering building. A cat sauntered out, unconcerned with anything but making its rounds in the neighborhood.
>
> "Can I shoot it, sir?" a sniper asked an officer.
>
> "Absolutely not," came the reply.

Think about the grace it took for Filkins to notice these quiet moments, amid the smoke and the explosions and the screaming, and then to make room for them in his story. Consider how effortlessly he allows time to slow, and almost stop, as the parakeet lands on the power line, and then as the cat makes its entrance from out of the ruins. Consider his choice of "saun-tered." The way he lets us hear the exchange between the sniper and the officer. The way he makes no judgment about the sniper's request.

Again and again, Filkins puts us there. Through a handful of simple narrative strategies, he transports us onto the streets of Fallujah. He brings scenes alive with snippets of dialogue, concrete details, even a well-chosen simile:

> Marine snipers sit, as motionless as blue herons, for 30 minutes and stare with crazed intensity into the oversized scopes on their guns. If so much as a penumbra brushes across a windowsill, they open up.

Filkins leads us from one extreme to the next. His accounts shift between moments of terrible stillness and moments of frantic, lethal movement. A sergeant with a bleeding lip peers through his riflescope and talks about how he hates the approach of darkness. The sky fills with "a pulsing cacophony" of sounds:

> The mosques in the city broadcast calls to jihad through their speak-ers. F-18's fired 3,000 rounds a minute in bursts that sounded oddly like burps. AC-130 gunships droned overhead, their big cannons going thunk, thunk as they found targets.
>
> Perhaps strangest of all, the American troops brought in their own "psyops" trucks—for psychological operations—and blared sounds that created a nightmarish duet with the mosques: old AC/DC songs, something that sounded like a sonar ping, the cavalry charge.

In a handful of relatively short pieces, Filkins manages to catalog the battle for his readers. He describes the black flags of the insurgents, the red and blue flares they launch to stymie the Americans' night-vision equipment. He captures the cries of a wounded soldier, the overwhelming sense of confusion and randomness. He invites us to understand all the ways a human being can die in this place.

Nothing escapes his attention. He shows us the bleeding lip on the ser-geant, enabling us to visualize the man at his post. He allows us to hear not just the "thunk, thunk" of the gunship cannons, but the soldiers play-ing AC/DC and the calls to jihad issuing from the mosques. Many jour-nalists, reporting from this scene, would have included one sound or the other. But how many of us would have thought to describe the way the two formed a duet?

Reading these stories again, for the third and fourth time, what's most striking is that Filkins never seems to be showing off. The action is described clearly and straightforwardly, without ornamentation. Almost without exception, his word choices are simple, clean, strong. And although his eye and his sensibility shape every paragraph, he keeps himself out of the frame. From the first word to the last, he remains focused on the soldiers around him, on the enemy in the distance, the streets in which both are dying.

These pieces remind us of what one reporter can accomplish in a day, under even the most awful pressures. They're a testament to the possibilities of daily journalism.

Thomas French is the first Writing Fellow at The Poynter Institute and a Pulitzer Prize–winning reporter at the St. Petersburg *(Fla.)* Times.

THE WALL STREET JOURNAL

Finalist

Amy Merrick and Dennis K. Berman
Team Deadline News Reporting

7. Kmart to Buy Sears For $11.5 Billion

NOV. 18, 2004

After slipping from their perch as America's top two retailers, the much-diminished Kmart and Sears chains are merging in an $11.5 billion deal that will propel them back into the No. 3 position.

The announcement of Kmart Holding Corp.'s proposed acquisition of Sears, Roebuck & Co. gave a dramatic lift to their stocks, suggesting that investors regard marriage as a promising solution for two chains long hampered by outdated stores, inefficient operations and weak management.

Behind the historic merger of two iconic names in American retailing is Connecticut investor Edward Lampert, whose hedge fund controls Kmart and is the largest shareholder of Sears, with a stake of about 15%. Now the 42-year-old financial whiz is taking on a high-profile role as an operating executive in a punishing industry.

Wal-Mart Stores Inc. and Home Depot Inc., the nation's two largest retail chains, are battering department stores like Sears and discounters like Kmart by delivering a wider selection of products at lower prices in better locations. In orchestrating the second-largest retail merger ever, Mr. Lampert is gambling that he can wring out efficiencies, allow Sears and Kmart to sell each other's exclusive products and move to address a flaw in the Sears business model: a reliance on mall locations in a retailing landscape that has shifted to stand-alone big box stores.

Far from seeking to catch up with Wal-Mart, Mr. Lampert described plans to improve the profitability of existing stores—and sell off those whose earnings don't meet his goals. Many Kmart stores located in prime spots outside malls will now be converted to Sears stores.

Sears shares surged $7.79, or 17%, to $52.99, in 4 p.m. composite trading on the New York Stock Exchange. Kmart shares rose $7.78, or 7.7%, to $109, as of 4 p.m. on the Nasdaq Stock Market.

The stock-market reaction reflected Mr. Lampert's track record as founder of ESL Investments Inc. Since 1988, returns on his funds have averaged about 30% annually. Yesterday's gains in shares of Kmart and Sears meant that ESL's holdings in the two retailers rose nearly $600 million in a day.

In the proposed deal, Sears shareholders will choose either $50 in cash or one-half share of Sears Holdings Corp.—the name of the new company—for each current Sears share. Kmart shareholders will get one new share for each share they hold. ESL, Mr. Lampert said yesterday, will convert all of its Sears shares into Sears Holdings shares. In an interview, Mr. Lampert said ESL will own a percentage of the combined company "in the high-30s to mid-40s," depending on whether Sears shareholders choose cash or stock.

Some of Kmart's biggest shareholders are taking a cautious view. "This deal materially enhances their prospects, but the verdict is not in yet," said Marty Whitman, the chief investment officer of Third Avenue Management, which with 5.5% of the Kmart shares outstanding, is the second-largest holder. "Why don't we talk again in three years."

The deal arose from a development that seemed innocuous when Sears and Kmart announced it in June: Sears was buying about 50 Kmart stores. Kmart had been downsizing ever since its early 2002 descent into bankruptcy court, from which it had emerged in May of 2003 with fewer debts and with a new majority owner: Mr. Lampert. He had been scooping up the retailer's debt, and invested more during bankruptcy proceedings until he had gained control.

After the sale of stores, Mr. Lampert and Sears Chief Executive Alan Lacy talked throughout the summer about a larger deal. Originally talk centered on a Sears acquisition of Kmart. But then Kmart stock soared, largely because Mr. Lampert had boosted profits by cutting back on inventory, slashing costs and stopping rampant discounting. The higher stock price forced Sears into the target role.

Early this month, another hitch developed: Vornado Realty Trust, a New York real-estate fund, disclosed that it had amassed a 4.3% Sears stake. Observers speculated that Vornado saw value in Sears real estate that wasn't reflected in the stock price. The Vornado news boosted Sears stock, raising the possibility that Sears would become too expensive to acquire. Messrs. Lampert and Lacy pushed hard to quickly strike an agreement. One board member said the prospects of a deal weren't even discussed at an October board meeting. "We still didn't have a final deal on price until Tuesday at midday," says one person familiar with the matter. "We were concerned the Sears price might get away from us."

Both Mr. Lampert and Mr. Lacy saw a merger as a possible solution to the Sears chain's old affinity for traditional malls. Sears stores followed the population growth into the suburbs over the decades, but by the late 1990s malls had lost much of their retailing prowess. More than 80% of consumer shopping dollars, excluding purchases of food and drugs, are now spent in locations outside malls, according to research by Customer Growth Partners LLC, a consulting company in New Canaan, Conn. That compares with about 60% in 1995. And six of the nation's largest retailers aren't part of malls—double the number in the late 1990s.

"The problem is they are not where the customers are, and that's the big opportunity," said Mr. Lampert of Sears yesterday. "It is not that the retailer per se is weak, but if you have the greatest store and it's not where the customers are, that's a problem."

The son of a lawyer and a homemaker in the New York suburb of Roslyn, N.Y., Mr. Lampert started focusing on his financial future after his father died of a heart attack when Mr. Lampert was 14. He aggressively courted well-connected classmates and professors as an undergraduate student at Yale University. Mr. Lampert joined Goldman Sachs after college, finding a mentor in Robert Rubin, who was at the time head of risk arbitrage at the firm and eventually U.S. Treasury secretary. Mr. Lampert left to start ESL in 1988, at the age of 25, with just about $25 million to invest.

Mr. Lampert's investors amount to a who's who of the wealthy and smart set, including representatives of the Ziff and Tisch families, as well as David Geffen and Michael Dell.

ESL also owns large stakes in AutoZone Inc., an auto-parts retailer, and car dealer AutoNation Inc.

Last year, Mr. Lampert's desire for secrecy was reinforced, say people close to him, when he was kidnapped from the garage of his office building in Greenwich, Conn. He eventually persuaded the kidnappers to let him go in exchange for $40,000, according to published reports.

During the four-year reign of Mr. Lacy, a former chief financial officer, Sears has cut costs but failed to update its image as yesteryear's retailer. Even after it bought the relatively high-end Land's End brand, sales continued to sputter.

Mr. Lacy, 51, will be chief executive of Sears Holdings. Under him, as chief executive of Kmart and Sears Retail, will be Aylwin B. Lewis, 48, who joined Kmart one month ago as CEO. Before that he was a top executive of YUM Brands Inc., owner of the KFC and Taco Bell chains.

Speculation has been rampant that Sears might recruit Vanessa Castagna, the number two executive at J.C. Penney Co. who recently resigned after failing to get the top job. In an interview, Ms. Castagna said she has been flooded with offers, and that she has been contacted by Sears but is not currently involved in any negotiations. She said she would not be making any decisions until after Jan. 1.

Ms. Castagna said she was surprised by the merger. "I think this will make Sears more competitive with Lowe's and Home Depot," she said. But "I think it is going to take a lot of capital to execute their vision."

Lehman Bros. was Kmart's financial adviser and Simpson Thacher & Bartlett LLP its legal counsel. Morgan Stanley was Sears's financial adviser and Wachtell, Lipton, Rosen & Katz its legal counsel.

Calling Sears the stronger brand, Mr. Lampert yesterday spoke about the chance to expand that chain's products and presence into Kmart country. Mr. Lacy said that "several hundred" Kmart stores could be converted to Sears stores. Some would be part of a new chain called Sears Grand, which adds products such as food and CDs to the typical Sears store.

Both stores have popular exclusive brands that could cross from one store to the other. Investors clearly expect Martha Stewart Everyday products—a big seller for Kmart—to gain access to Sears stores, because shares of Martha Stewart Living Omnimedia Inc. rose yesterday on news of the acquisition. Martha Stewart products already sell in Sears stores in Canada.

Among the brands for which Sears long has been famous, Craftsman tools will likely be introduced to the shelves of Kmart, perhaps bolstering its ability to compete against Home Depot. A bigger question is whether Sears will move its home-appliance products into Kmart stores. Through its Kenmore brand as well as through the sale of Whirlpool, General Electric and Maytag models, Sears is the nation's largest purveyor of refrigerators, washers and dryers, although it has been losing market share in recent years to Home Depot and Lowe's Cos.

The two retailers in yesterday's deal went wrong in different ways.

Beginning with its first large mail-order catalog in 1896, Sears pioneered retailing in the U.S., dotting the land with department stores from coast to coast. In the 1980s, it expanded into a brokerage business and real estate, but it later decided those businesses were distractions and disposed of them.

The rise of discounters and popularity of high fashion squeezed middle-brow department stores such as Sears. Customers wanting low price started going to Wal-Mart and Target Corp. Customers wanting quality would step up to Nordstrom or specialty retailers such as Gap. Meanwhile, so-called category killers such as Home Depot came along and weakened Sears.

During Mr. Lacy's four-year tenure, Sears has repeatedly overhauled its stores and cut costs in an effort to compete with a host of fast-growing rivals, from Wal-Mart and Target to Home Depot and Lowe's. In 2002, Sears purchased the Lands' End apparel brand for $1.86 billion. In July of 2003, it sold its credit-card business for about $3 billion to Citigroup Inc. While better known for its department stores and selling Craftsman tools and Kenmore appliances, credit cards had been a big part of the company for 91 years.

Kmart is a tale of bad management, going back decades. Kmart, with roots that stretch back to 1899 under the Kresge chain, opened its first Kmart store in 1962. It quickly flooded the country with discount stores. In the late 1970s, Wal-Mart's sales were 5% of Kmart's; it had 150 stores to Kmart's 1,000 or so, mostly in urban locations. Wal-Mart, meanwhile, invaded rural America, where it quietly perfected a format of using technology to reduce inventory, keep shelves stocked and offer the lowest prices. By the time it began meeting Kmart head on, Wal-Mart enjoyed a significant price advantage that a series of Kmart executives failed to overcome.

Following a disastrous management scheme to load up on inventory and slash prices to compete with Wal-Mart head-on, Kmart filed for Chapter 11 bankruptcy-court protection in January 2002. Mr. Lampert then made his move. Through ESL, he acquired enough debt to emerge from the company's reorganization with about half of Kmart shares. The company emerged from court protection in May 2003, with Mr. Lampert as its chairman.

The combined company will be based in Hoffman Estates, Ill., where Sears has its headquarters. Kmart will continue to have offices in Troy, Mich. Of the combined company's 10 directors, seven will come from Kmart's board, the other three from the Sears board.

The deal is likely to be investigated by the Federal Trade Commission, which reviews most retail mergers, but seems unlikely to face significant antitrust opposition given the changing marketplace and the power of industry leader Wal-Mart.

Ann Zimmerman and Joann S. Lublin contributed to this article.

To read additional stories by The Wall Street Journal *team, go to* *http://www.poynter.org/bnw2005.*

Lessons Learned

BY AMY MERRICK AND DENNIS K. BERMAN

We first heard about Kmart's plans to buy Sears the night before the announcement was made. We just didn't know it at the time. About 10 p.m., Dennis got word that "something big was happening in retail, perhaps involving Sears." Late into the night, we made rounds of calls to tight-lipped sources who eventually stopped calling back. Sleeping was impossible. There was a huge announcement coming—we could just feel it—and we didn't have the story.

At 6 a.m. in New York, the announcement crossed the wire. Our first reaction was disappointment, to come so close to the scoop and miss it, rather than amazement that these two giants were uniting.

Every media outlet would have the same news, at the same time. When they picked up the next day's paper, most readers already would know the basics. To stand out, we knew we would have to say something insightful and detailed about the history of these two iconic companies, where they went wrong, how a secretive investor brought them together and what the deal meant to consumers and investors, all while meeting deadlines that began in the morning for the Asian editions and continued throughout the day. Other than the caffeine, here's what got us through:

You have to write the little stories to write the big stories. Our story, the centerpiece of a larger package, had to cover an expansive swath of territory. To pull readers along, we tried to include both wide-angle views and close-ups—at times pulling back for a broader view of the roles of Kmart and Sears in American culture, at other times zooming in for the behind-the-scenes details on how the deal came together.

Some of the information obviously came from interviews the day of the announcement, but we couldn't have retraced all that reporting in a day; we'd been laying the groundwork with previous stories for months and years. In fact, those pesky little stories—the quarterly earnings reports, executive changes and other retail merger pieces—gave us the fluency we needed on deadline.

Divide and conquer. As a team, we pulled together six stories that first day, and our wire reporters contributed several more for the paper. It was critical that reporters and editors updated one another about what areas of the news they were attacking and what they still needed to learn.

Someone also had to act as a clearing-house, to save time and effort by verifying small facts and making sure different parts of the package didn't duplicate themes. As the retail beat reporter, while working on the main piece, Amy answered questions for other stories and vetted portions of the copy. From 8 a.m. to 9:30 p.m., she sent more than 150 e-mails.

Likewise, for the lead story, instead of hunting down every last fact ourselves, we reached out to other reporters with specific knowledge that we could tap quickly, in areas from appliance sales to the recent history of shopping malls to the Federal Trade Commission. There are numerous reporters who answered a single timely question or contributed one sentence. Their names don't appear on the final story, but their help was invaluable.

Dennis K. Berman is The Wall Street Journal's *mergers and acquisitions reporter. He joined the paper in 2001 as a telecom reporter and technology columnist and was one of the* Journal *reporters awarded the 2003 Pulitzer Prize in explanatory journalism for a series on corporate scandals. Amy Merrick is a staff reporter for the* Journal, *covering retail from the Chicago bureau. She joined the paper in 2000 as a reporting assistant and subsequently covered banking.*

San Jose Mercury News

▌ Finalist

Julia Prodis Sulek
Team Deadline News Reporting

8. Next For Killer: Life or Death?

NOV. 13, 2004

Before the verdict Friday, Scott Peterson walked into the courtroom as he always does: confident, grinning. He leaned over to a member of his defense team and shared a few laughs.

Then the jury came in. And confidence turned to calm. His face turned pale. He gulped, deeply.

The man who had told his mistress he had "lost" his wife before she disappeared, whose alibi put him within a mile of where the bodies of his pregnant wife and unborn son washed up, was found guilty of first- and second-degree murder Friday. Within a few weeks, the same six-man, six-woman jury will decide whether the former fertilizer salesman from Modesto should be put to death or spend the rest of his natural life in prison.

The case of the 27-year-old dimpled substitute teacher with the bright smile, who threw dinner parties and painted her nursery nautical blue, became a media sensation from the start. It created fodder for nightly cable talk shows. Web sites and blogs devoted to the case sprung up. Al-Jazeera TV broadcast part of the story.

It was a verdict Laci Peterson's family had waited nearly two years to get, and one that was anything but certain during the course of the five months of testimony in Redwood City that pitted a well-heeled Los Angeles defense lawyer against a Central Valley prosecutor.

When the guilty verdict was read, Laci Peterson's mother, Sharon Rocha, broke down sobbing. She threw her arms around her son, Brent Rocha, whose son was born shortly before his sister's baby—a boy she planned to name Conner—was due.

Scott Peterson's mother, Jackie Peterson, who has never wavered in her support for her son, stared straight ahead during the verdict reading. Like her son, she didn't cry. During the penalty phase beginning Nov. 22, when witnesses will testify on Peterson's behalf, she will surely plead for his life.

Dad, Lawyer Missing

Absent from the courtroom were Peterson's father, Lee Peterson, whose whereabouts were not disclosed, as well as Peterson's main lawyer, Mark Geragos, who had promised jurors in June he would prove his client "stone cold innocent." Geragos was at his Los Angeles office Friday afternoon working on another case. His co-counsel, Pat Harris, sat with Peterson instead.

Because the penalty has yet to be decided, Judge Alfred Delucchi maintained the gag order on all parties to the case: jurors, witnesses, lawyers and family members. But in front of the courthouse, emotions were unleashed among as many as 1,000 people who had a 90-minute notice the verdict was at hand. They let out cheers when the guilty verdict spread through the crowd.

"I followed this case from day one," said Anne Morrison, 31, of Foster City, who said she traveled to Modesto to leave flowers at the Petersons' home as well as the edge of the San Francisco Bay near Richmond where the bodies were discovered. "I wanted to see justice brought and I'm so happy. A baby was involved and seeing Laci's sweet face on TV—it really touched my heart."

Finding someone outside the courthouse who had hoped for acquittal wasn't easy. One man, 23-year-old Xavier Taylor, of Oakland, said the conviction stunned him. Taylor knows Geragos and became a friend of the Peterson family during the trial, which he attended almost daily.

"There were many doubts in this case. I don't understand why the jury said guilty," Taylor said. "The defense had an explanation for everything the prosecution tried to put forth. Justice will be served, hopefully in a higher court."

Over the seven days of deliberations, drama and chaos seemed to overtake the jury, leaving many to speculate that a hung jury and mistrial were imminent. Two jurors were dismissed this week, including the foreman, a man educated in law and medicine who the defense had hoped would lead the jury to an acquittal.

But Friday, hours after the verdict, the first juror kicked off this week said that when she was removed Tuesday, the jury, including herself, leaning toward guilt. She broke a court order when she conducted her own research on the case.

"I think they had a good idea of where they were going before deliberations," said Frances Gorman outside her Foster City home. Without disclosing specifics, she said she understood why she was dismissed from the jury. "I checked something and had a knee-jerk reaction." It didn't affect her position on the case, she said.

Early Defense Victories

Over the course of the trial, a conviction seemed far from a sure thing. For the first couple of months, the defense dominated the trial as Geragos seemed to turn each prosecution witness into his own.

Because the case was circumstantial, Geragos tried to convince jurors that there was an innocent explanation for each suspicious circumstance. Peterson was just a cad using a pitiful line on his mistress when he said he had lost his wife. He took several trips to the Berkeley Marina after his wife disappeared, not to look for evidence he left behind, but to check up on the search operation. He bleached his hair and grew a goatee not to disguise himself from police, but from the relentless media.

But the prosecution seemed to come on strong when Peterson's mistress, Amber Frey, took the stand and played hours of taped calls for the jury. At one point, minutes before attending a vigil for his wife at a Modesto park, Peterson told Frey he was partying under the Eiffel Tower with his friends Francois and Pasqual.

Prosecutors Rick Distaso, Dave Harris and Birgit Fladager maintained their momentum when detective Craig Grogan outlined some of the "41 reasons" police believed they would find Laci Peterson's body in the bay. They all pointed to Scott Peterson.

Geragos, who was expected to come back strong when presenting his own witnesses, faltered when he put fertility specialist Charles March on the stand. March was supposed to convince the jury the fetus was so big, it obviously lived past the day of Laci Peterson's disappearance. But he became so flustered during cross examination by Harris that he ended up begging the prosecutor to cut him "some slack."

During closing arguments, Distaso told jurors it was a "common sense" case. The defense's contention that Peterson was framed and someone else put the bodies in the bay, he said, was ridiculous.

Laci Peterson was a mother-to-be who disappeared on Christmas Eve, and in the estimation of her family and friends had the perfect marriage and perfect, handsome husband. Some people suspected him early: He refused to appear on the TV news early on and showed little emotion the night of her disappearance. He told police he had spent the day fishing in the bay in his new boat, but hesitated when asked what he was fishing for and what bait he used.

Even so, Peterson opened the volunteer center each morning and put up fliers. What Laci Peterson's family didn't know for weeks was that Peterson was having an affair with Frey, a Fresno massage therapist who didn't know Peterson was married. As soon as she found out, a week after the disappearance, she called police and began secretly taping his calls.

They talked as many as 16 times a day, with Peterson telling her that he was "longing to hold onto" her.

When the affair hit the front page of the National Enquirer, Laci Peterson's family immediately turned against him. In mid-April 2003, the bodies washed up separately along the edge of the bay, within a mile of where Peterson told police he motored from the Berkeley Marina to go fishing.

A pathologist testified for the prosecution that although Laci Peterson's head, arms and legs had broken away from her body over the course of $4\frac{1}{2}$ months underwater, her womb held the baby inside until nearly the end. A storm churned up the bay, the top of her uterus gave way, and mother and child floated apart, he said. They were discovered a mile apart, the baby in remarkably good condition.

Peterson's lawyers had argued that strangers abducted Laci Peterson while she walked the dog. The abductors held her alive for days or weeks, Geragos said, then threw her in the bay to frame Peterson, whose alibi was widely reported. Geragos tried to convince the jury that knotted twine found around the baby's neck was not bay debris as the prosecution asserted, but part of a plastic bag the killers used to dispose of the baby.

Still Under Gag Order

Jurors obviously didn't buy it. They are still under the gag order, so it is uncertain what evidence pushed them beyond reasonable doubt.

Was it the location of the bodies, or the fact that Peterson returned to the Berkeley Marina five times in rented or borrowed cars in the days after her disappearance? Maybe it was the conversation he had with Frey weeks before his wife's disappearance, when he said he had "lost" his wife and would be spending his first holidays without her.

When he was arrested in San Diego, his newly purchased used Mercedes was filled with survival and camping gear—and $15,000 cash.

In the courtroom Friday, each juror was polled by the judge to make sure the verdicts were unanimous. He was found guilty of first-degree murder for the death of his wife, and second-degree murder for the death of his son. From the time the second alternate replaced the jury foreman Wednesday, it took 7 hours and 14 minutes to reach the verdicts.

As the jury filed out of the jury box, one of the jurors, an accountant who rarely hid her emotions during the trial, looked Laci Peterson's mother squarely in the face and gave her a firm nod.

Flanked by deputies, Scott Peterson was escorted back to jail.

To read additional stories by the San Jose *(Calif.)* Mercury News *team, go to http://www.poynter.org/bnw2005.*

Lessons Learned

BY JULIA PRODIS SULEK

Remember that scene from "Caddyshack" in which the priest gets caught in a storm while playing his best round of golf ever? He is a man possessed, refusing to stop playing despite lightning strikes and gale-force winds nearly blowing him off the course. When writing this story on the Scott Peterson trial, I felt a little like that.

I was in the midst of a media storm. The small courthouse pressroom was jammed with stressed reporters and photographers on deadline. But with a key observation, a little luck and confidence in my knowledge of the story, I was focused and on a roll. When my editor told me he had put together background "a-matter" that I could tack onto the end of the story if I pressed up against deadline, I said, "No! I'm in the zone!"

It didn't start that way. Two hours earlier, I was nervous. Not about the fate of Scott Peterson, but about whether I could deliver a compelling main story on deadline. My colleague Jessie Seyfer and I had covered the murder trial for the past eight months. Expectations were high.

A couple of things were on my mind: With all the media reporting the same story, how could I distinguish our coverage? How could I write an engaging story when we already knew that none of the key players would talk afterward—no lawyers, no family members and no jurors?

I decided to play up the inherent drama of the case and take advantage of a court ruling: cameras were forbidden in the courtroom. This meant that describing the reactions of Peterson and family members was key to giving readers something extra. I lined up early and jockeyed for the courtroom seat with the best view. When Peterson walked in, I was struck by his arrogance. When the jury pronounced him guilty, and his reaction was so subtle, I realized the power was more in the before-and-after contrast than the reaction itself. I had my lead. Because it was on the softer side of a hard-news story, I ran it by my editor, Alvie Lindsay, who had guided Peterson trial coverage. A persuasive advocate, he got buy-in early from upper editors. The most difficult part of the story—the lead—was done. I was on my way. And the tone was set for storytelling.

I wasn't distracted by numerous feeds from other reporters: David Early and Kim Vo were writing a sidebar about crowd reaction, and Patrick May captured the sentiment in Peterson's hometown of Modesto. Seyfer and Howard Mintz wrote a forward-looking legal analysis.

With a gag order on the main players, I relied on what made this story a national obsession and drew 1,000 people to the courthouse steps. The murder had all the elements of great drama—fascinating and sympathetic characters, sex, betrayal, mystery. And the trial itself didn't disappoint either—a legal battle between lawyers with opposite styles and a daily courtroom horse race that left trial watchers uncertain about the outcome until the end. I put that context high and used it as a guide for the rest of the story. I added two quotes I got from people in the crowd out front and an important quote from a dismissed juror tracked down by my colleague Julie Patel.

Then I set about helping readers understand how this legal tug of war came down to a guilty verdict, by giving them enough detail to figure it out for themselves. It was also important for readers to get a picture of Laci Peterson, who painted her nursery nautical blue and whose womb held her baby tightly even after her head and limbs were gone. That image had stuck with me throughout the trial.

I ended the story where I started, in the courtroom, with the one detail I got from a juror—a firm nod to Laci Peterson's mother—followed by a not-so-arrogant Peterson being taken back to jail.

I finished the story, whew, before deadline.

Julia Prodis Sulek is a general assignment/enterprise reporter for the San Jose *(Calif.)* Mercury News. *She joined the* Mercury News, *her hometown paper, in 1998 after 10 years with The Associated Press across the country, most recently as the AP's Southwest regional writer in Dallas.*

Los Angeles Times

Finalist

Kim Murphy

Individual Deadline News Reporting

9. Killers Set Terms, a Mother Chooses

SEPT. 3, 2004

BESLAN, Russia—Zalina Dzandarova cradles her son Alan as he sleeps with his small face buried against her stomach. He is the child Dzandarova was able to save. The child she chose to save, really.

It is the other one, little Alana, her 6-year-old daughter, whose image torments her: Alana clutching her hand, Alana crying and calling after her. Alana's sobs disappearing into the distance as Dzandarova walked out of Middle School No. 1 here Thursday, clutching 2-year-old Alan in her arms.

Guerrillas armed with automatic rifles and explosive belts who are holding hundreds of hostages at the small provincial school in southern Russia allowed 26 women and children to leave. About a dozen mothers, like Dzandarova, were allowed to take only one child, forced to leave another behind.

"I didn't want to make this choice," a stunned-looking Dzandarova, 27, said in the reception room of her father-in-law's house a few miles from the school. "People say they are happy that my son and I are saved. But how can I be happy if my daughter's still inside there?"

Violence often selects its victims randomly, but seldom is a mother asked to make a Sophie's choice: Save one child and leave behind another, possibly to face death. The standoff in North Ossetia republic involving about 20 guerrillas—most likely linked to the neighboring separatist republic of Chechnya or adjacent Ingushetia—has stunned a nation accustomed to war and its horrors after the many ethnic and territorial conflicts that accompanied the breakup of the Soviet Union.

Even with the downing of two Russian jetliners and two street bombings coming in just one week, the thought of schoolchildren surrounded by veiled female suicide bombers and masked guerrillas has traumatized the country. "They Have Taken Hundreds of Our Children," read a banner headline in the daily newspaper Izvestia.

And they took Alana.

"They said they would let us go only after the [Russian] troops are withdrawn from Chechnya," said Dzandarova. She said the attackers had identified themselves as Chechens. "I said we have nothing to do with that, but they wouldn't listen."

Her description provided one of the first accounts of what was happening inside the school, where Dzandarova said as many as 1,000 children and parents were being held in a gymnasium planted with explosives. Authorities officially listed the number of hostages at 354, a figure Dzandarova disputed.

"The director of the school was taken to a TV where they were saying there were 354 of us in here, and the director came back and she was in a state of shock, because there were in fact many more people there," she said.

"There were definitely 1,000 people in that one room," she said, referring to the gym. "I saw it with my own eyes."

On Wednesday, Dzandarova took her daughter to the first day of first grade. As students and parents began lining up, they saw the attackers sweeping into the school. Dzandarova ran with her children to hide in a classroom, but they were rounded up with the others and taken to the gym.

"Everyone was ordered to sit down, and they began to set up booby-traps around the perimeter, right in front of our eyes. They had lots of guns and explosives with them."

At first, she said, everyone was allowed to drink water from the tap. But the hostage-takers soon stopped that, she said, because they were angry that officials, including the presidents of North Ossetia and Ingushetia, had not come to meet with them.

Without water, the powdered milk the guerrillas supplied for the children had to be spooned into their mouths.

The gym was sweltering, even after the window panes were broken out.

"They were telling us, 'Your government is not allowing enough water for your kids.'"

In just two days, she said, the problem became acute. "You see, the kids won't survive these negotiations," she said. "They're not getting enough water. What we have to hope is that they'll survive this night without water."

At the beginning, 20 men in the gym were led to a different room. On Thursday, Dzandarova said, 10 of the men returned. The hostages presumed that the others were dead.

"They told us that it was 'your own side' that had executed them, who had shot them dead," Dzandarova said.

Two women who had been wearing suicide belts apparently detonated them Wednesday in an adjoining room, she said.

"They left the gym, and all of a sudden we heard two loud explosions. We thought the storming [by Russian police] had begun. But then they told us, 'Our sisters have won a victory, and there's no other cause they want to pursue.' "

The male guerrillas, she said, "took it calmly."

Much of the time, she said, the guerrillas appeared tense: running around the room, waving their guns in the hostages' faces, shouting at them to sit still and stop talking.

When Alan began to cry from hunger, Dzandarova was allowed to join several other mothers in an adjacent room, which had its own water and was several degrees cooler.

After a former local political leader visited the school Thursday, the women in the adjacent room were told there was "good news": They would be released.

"They said, 'Pack your things quickly, and take your babies with you,'" Dzandarova said.

Shortly after, she learned that she would have to choose between taking her son or her daughter.

Dzandarova had both Alan and Alana with her and made a snap decision to pass Alana to her 16-year-old sister-in-law. But the guerrillas saw through the ruse and refused to allow her to take the older child.

"Alana was clinging to me and holding my hand firmly. But they separated us, and said: 'You go with the boy. Your sister can stay here with her.' I cried. I begged them. Alana cried. The women around us wept. One of the Chechens said: 'If you don't go now, you don't go at all. You stay here with your children . . . and we will shoot all of you.'"

She couldn't save both of them. She could only die with both of them—or save one of them and herself.

"I didn't have time to think what I was doing," she said. "I pressed Alan even stronger to myself, and I went out, and I heard all the time how my daughter was crying and calling for me behind my back. I thought my heart would break into pieces there and then."

Dzandarova cried as she talked. Her tears fell on Alan, who was sleeping. Even when his mother shook quietly with sobs as she cradled him, he didn't awaken.

Times staff writer Sergei L. Loiko in Moscow contributed to this report.

To read additional stories by Kim Murphy, go to
http://www.poynter.org/bnw2005.

Lessons Learned

BY KIM MURPHY

As reporters, all of us are storytellers. Of course, we are responsible for gathering the facts—the "what happened," the "who it happened to," the "how many"—that one day will become history. But it is through stories, not data, that history transcends. Some stories have the power to leap across generations, nations and time itself. Ask Homer.

None of us would be journalists if we didn't already know this. We spend our lives foraging through facts, sifting like oyster fishermen through people's celebrations and fury and loss for the story that will not only help readers find out what has happened, but force them to take it home, take it to bed, wake up in the morning having learned a little bit about their own humanity, often without even realizing it.

Because we are reporters, we recognize these stories immediately.

If there were lessons to be learned from Zalina Dzandarova's story, they were, first, making the time to let her tell her story. And second, using the vehicle of the story to carry the weight of crucial factual information.

Running on fumes on day two of the hostage crisis at Beslan, where hundreds of schoolchildren, teachers and parents were taken hostage by Chechen and Ingush insurgents, I heard at around 6 p.m. that Zalina had left the school with only one of her two children. *Immediate gut-level story alert.* This story speaks to the most basic of instincts—a mother's love for her children. Just think of the mother cat who keeps going back into a burning building until each one of her kittens is safely removed.

Did I have time to hassle with this? No. I had a big "ledeall" daily to write on all the various developments in the hostage crisis. Zalina's father-in-law, after I knocked on the door, said she was too upset to talk to anyone and told me to go away. Out of aggravation, fatigue and the urgent need to file the other story, I almost did. Instead, I sat down on his front porch with him and started asking about the vodka factory where he worked. Half an hour later, we were ruminating on the ethnic rivalries of the North Caucasus, discussing the various shortcomings of the Russian government—*please hurry!*—and 15 minutes later, I was showing him pictures of my 7-year-old daughter. Well, he allowed, Zalina might want to see you.

I was in. But the story wasn't going to come out the way it needed to come out, I knew, unless Zalina could take her time telling it. It would need the details. I didn't have time for details. I wanted to rush in, grab her by the collar and shout "Why did you leave your daughter behind?" Instead, I fixed on the 2-year-old son she was cradling in her arms. "Look at that darling little boy. What a great shirt, where did you get that?" She smiled softly. (*Shopping: the transnational, transgenerational obsession that will bond women everywhere for as long as there are markets.*)

I spent three hours with Zalina. We talked about every moment she spent in the school gymnasium: what the captors looked like, how the hostages were surviving, how she escaped, how her daughter did not. As a result, I was able to go back and write the story—a mere sidebar to the daily—that ended up being far more memorable than the main news story. The details of what Zalina told me also provided crucial facts, including the first news that the hostages numbered not about 350 but more than 1,000 and that many of them were nearly dying of thirst. All of this could be woven unobtrusively into the framework of Zalina's tale, providing a window into a hellish world that was just across the schoolyard fence in that anxious little town and into every mother's furious love for her children.

Part of the time I was talking to Zalina, we were both crying. When I left, we hugged each other for a long time. It was as though she had transferred part of her pain to me. I went back and wrote the story and transferred part of that pain to all those who read her story. I like to think it lightened Zalina's burden a little.

Kim Murphy won the 2005 Pulitzer Prize for the international reporting that appears in this volume. She is Moscow bureau chief for the Los Angeles Times, *where she has been a reporter since 1983. She has worked as a foreign and national correspondent for the past 15 years covering assignments in the Middle East, the Balkans, Afghanistan and the Pacific Northwest.*

San Francisco Chronicle

10. Spirit Begins Hunt For Water Signs

JAN. 16, 2004

PASADENA, Calif.—The roving Martian voyager called Spirit finally planted its six wheels firmly onto the sands of Mars early Thursday to begin one of the most significant ventures in the history of human exploration—a search for evidence that water, and perhaps life, ever existed on another planet in the solar system.

After a looping seven-month flight through space and a precarious arrival by parachute and rocket only two weeks ago, the spacecraft rolled on command about 10 feet, leaving its landing pad and halting atop a flat clutter of sand and pebbles less than 3 feet away. It took all of 78 seconds and was over at precisely 12:41 a.m.

At the consoles of Mission Control, engineers and technicians leaped from their seats and cheered as word of Spirit's safe arrival on the Martian surface came down through the giant radio antennas of NASA's Deep Space Network in the Mojave Desert and Australia.

It was "a night that's extraordinarily rich and significant for discoveries to come," Steve Squyres, the Cornell astronomer and chief scientist of the mission, told the cheering crowd.

The celebrations continued. At a 3 a.m. briefing for reporters, Jennifer Trosper, Spirit's mission manager for surface operations, popped a champagne bottle and poured for all the hands she could reach. "Now, we're really on the mission that we all envisioned $3\frac{1}{2}$ years ago," she said. "Your efforts are historical."

Despite the triumph of a successful descent onto the surface, mission scientists wasted no time in planning for Spirit's next tasks.

A detailed image of the space between the rover's back end and the rumply Nomex fiber off-ramp from the landing pad shows impressions of the cleated tracks left by Spirit's black anodized aluminum wheels, with sand grains and what seems to be sticky soil clinging to its wheels and tracks.

On either side of the rover lie more sand and clusters of tiny pebbles barely a half-inch in diameter. Some of the soil appears to be sticking together as if it were moist, which, of course, it can't be in the deep cold and arid climate of the Martian surface.

One of Spirit's early tasks, Squyres said, will be to examine that material with the spacecraft's Microscopic Imager, which is capable of examining and taking close-up images of sand grains less than 2 millimeters across, or barely thicker than the Martian grains themselves.

"There's a lot of fascinating soil mechanics to study on Mars," Squyres said, "and it's hard to wait until we check out every instrument."

Squyres and his science team have tempting targets ahead of them. Only 2 or 3 meters to the northwest, there is a sharply pointed, 2-inch rock that scientists have named Adirondack and whose vertical face has apparently been scoured clean by the Martian winds. It is a natural object for the spacecraft's Rock Abrasian Tool that the scientists liken to a geologist's field hammer.

The abrading tool, named the RAT, will grind away half-inch-wide circles of the rock surface to expose as much as two-tenths of an inch beneath the surface for the Microscopic Imager to examine and the spectrometers to analyze for evidence of minerals that might have formed in water billions of years ago.

"Adirondack has a hell of a lot going for it; it's fascinating," Squyres told his colleagues at Mission Control in an irrepressible burst of enthusiasm at 2 a.m.

Then there's what Squyres' colleagues call the Wasabi Range, two rough-surfaced pillow-shaped inch-high rocks named Sushi and Sashimi, which appear made of totally different minerals than Adirondack. These also are near-term targets to be studied over the next day or two.

To the entire scientific team, the first priority is to identify sand and rocks that are typically Martian, and only then to seek out material that is atypical or unusual in order to "characterize the geological diversity" of Earth's nearest planetary neighbor.

Right now, the days on Mars are actually nights at the mission headquarters at the Jet Propulsion Laboratory. Each Martian day, called a "sol," is exactly 24 hours, 39 minutes and 35 seconds in Earth time because the planet rotates more slowly on its axis than Earth on its axis.

Many on the Mars teams carry two watches—one set on Earth time, and the other a special watch that keeps only Mars time. As a result, the crews here often find their Earth days all bollixed up. The rules require them to take three Earth days off every four sols, a rule many scientists and engineers are constantly breaking.

One of them is Squyres, who at 4:30 a.m. was still joyfully explaining to reporters the jobs his science team hopes to accomplish in the next few sols. Today, for example, under the guidance of the mission's chief engineer, Pete Thiesinger, the entire engineering team will test Spirit's mobile arm that carries the various spectrometers, the Microscopic Imager and the RAT. On the next sol, Spirit will be driven a few tentative meters, with all its instruments in operation.

In coming sols, the highest priority for Spirit's science team is to look for evidence of ancient water on the sandy slopes and low-lying terrace that the scientists have named Sleepy Hollow.

Another priority is the small nearby crater with its 15-foot-high rim that intrigues the scientists because it may be a "secondary crater" created when debris from a far larger impact crater gouged out a hole in the Martian surface and threw out a blanket of ejected rocks that fell back in layers, much like layers of sedimentary rocks on lakeshores and ocean cliffs.

The scientists are eager for Spirit to extend itself. At minimum, the rover's mission is expected to last for 90 days, but Thiesinger said he wouldn't be surprised if Spirit and its sister rover, Opportunity, held up for twice that long. But before it gets to work, the engineers insist on testing every instrument and every motor drive.

"Testing in a real Martian environment has just begun," Thiesinger said.

"Our job is to put this marvelous vehicle with its marvelous payload in a place and in a condition that the scientists can do their marvelous science. It's their vehicle now, and we'll be ready to go where they want."

Next week, the engineers' job will become more difficult. Spirit's twin, the rover called Opportunity, is due to land Jan. 24 at about 9 p.m. Pacific time. Its landing site, called Meridiani Planum, is halfway around the equator from Gustav Crater. Although it is flat, unlike Gusev Crater, it lies at a higher altitude with different weather, more dust storms, and fewer craters.

For three sols at that time, Spirit will stand down and perform its geological and chemical research in place so the engineers can focus exclusively on Opportunity's perilous high-speed descent, as filled with tension as Spirit's was 13 sols ago.

To read additional stories by David Perlman, go to
http://www.poynter.org/bnw2005.

Lessons Learned

BY DAVID PERLMAN

Spending a lifetime as a reporter helps, of course, with deadlines hammering at you all the time. But even a short-timer can write fast and get it right with enough background stashed in a scribbled notebook, in a file stored in your laptop that's keyworded for accessibility or in a list of links to favorite Web sites we all keep just in case.

It also helps—at least some of the time, and even if only on clear nights—that your eyes look at the stars and planets, so you have cultivated an unabashedly naive sense of wonder and believe exploring other worlds is something we humans are meant to do, a kind of destiny.

I don't mean swallowing everything that NASA—or any government agency—tells you. But I do mean that a reporter can and should recognize a solid achievement, particularly a spectacular one, and write about it without any ifs, ands or buts.

Digging into the politics, the bickering among scientists and engineers, the battles between robot lovers and only-humans-can-do-it partisans— that's all part of the job of any reporter covering space, whether full time or part time.

But in this news of Spirit's climactic first success, the joy of those who made the bang-on landing possible was well worth communicating wholeheartedly, without cynicism and quickly disregarding sleep when the news breaks at 3 a.m. (Coffee helps.)

This story required advance preparation, which meant demanding time from editors well ahead of time to become aware of the extraordinary difficulties involved. It also required—on that climactic night when Spirit landed, for example—being at Mission Control's pressroom armed with an understanding of what was at stake, what the odds of failure were and who the people were on whose skills and savvy success depended.

Some background we needed to follow up: time on Mars passes differently than on Earth, and a Martian "sol" is different from a day on Earth. (It's 24 hours and 39 minutes). So a calculator is handy, even essential. I have a few conversion factors scribbled inside mine: kilometers convert to miles if you multiply by .6214, Celsius turns to Fahrenheit easily (multiply by 1.8, add 32). That's just preparation. And you can juggle numbers fast if you have the proper tool in your pocket or bookmark the best converter going, www.onlineconversion.com, and have time to use it.

Preparation is the key to every story, I think, and it certainly doesn't apply only to fast-breaking space news. Elections, battles, baseball games, zoning conflicts at City Hall—they all call for reporters who have gathered the background ahead of time and have studied it well. Across the country, parents, teachers and school boards are trying to cope with the requirements of No Child Left Behind, and controversy grows over teaching evolution as proponents of "intelligent design" or "creation science" increase their pressure. These are difficult stories for any reporter to cover without sensitivity as well as solid background.

Then the challenge of covering any story—on Earth or in the cosmos— really begins.

David Perlman is science editor at the San Francisco Chronicle, *where he has worked since 1951, starting as a reporter and city editor before moving to the science beat in 1960. Before joining the* Chronicle, *he served as a European correspondent at* Collier's *magazine and the* New York Post *as well as a reporter for the* New York Herald Tribune *in Paris and at the United Nations.*

Part 2

Narrative Writing

Babita Persaud

Diversity Writing

Babita Persaud grew up wondering: Who am I?

As a child raised in an immigrant family, Persaud sometimes rebelled against her parents' culture, including the
Indian custom of arranged marriage. Ultimately, however,
the central question of identity drove the reporter to examine the age-old custom—and the pressures it placed on
another young, Indian-American woman and her family—
in a three-part series, "A Husband For Vibha."

Persaud was born in Guyana, a former British colony in
South America with a large Indian population. She was 4
years old when her parents immigrated to New York City in
1971. She grew up in the suburbs of Long Island, Atlanta
and Orlando. Her father was a cab driver and her mother
worked at Woolworth's before they became small-business
owners.

Persaud never intended to become a journalist. She studied music history and specialized in playing the flute at
Rollins College in Winter Park, Fla. For a creative writing
class during her senior year, she wrote an essay on her difficulties finding a job. The *Orlando Sentinel* published the
piece on its op-ed page and then hired her to answer
phones.

In 1994, she received a master's degree in journalism
from the University of North Carolina at Chapel Hill and

St. Petersburg Times

worked part time for *The News & Observer* in Raleigh for two years. The *St. Petersburg Times* hired her in 1996 to work in a suburban Tampa bureau.

Later, as a metro reporter in Tampa, Persaud wrote features about the community, as well as arts and pop culture stories. Persaud said she cringed whenever an editor handed her a story idea related to the Indian community. She did not want to be pigeonholed into writing about "her" people.

But then she began to think about the custom of arranged marriage. She had argued with her father when she dated the British man whom she would later marry. She became curious about what it was like for daughters who allowed their parents to pick their husbands. It took Persaud a year to find Vibha Dhawan, a student at the University of South Florida. Persaud spent the next three years following Vibha's and her parents' efforts to find a husband.

Persaud, who left the *Times* in January 2005 to write short stories, said she wanted to understand the mind-set of immigrant parents, as well as the cultural divide between these parents and their children. She said the series was the most fulfilling set of stories she has ever written.

"I have come to understand my own upbringing," she said. "Immigrant parents really have a task on their hands. American culture can gobble up their ancient customs in one generation, and that is a loss."

—Thomas Huang

The award for Distinguished Writing on Diversity is funded by the Freedom Forum, which has partnered with ASNE on many diversity efforts.

11. An American Girl

DEC. 19, 2004

Vibha Dhawan fidgeted in the back seat of the family car, her body wrapped in a beaded Indian tunic. Up front, her father drove. Her mother sat beside him, complaining about a book someone had borrowed.

Vibha tuned them out. Her mind was filled with images, photo after photo of the eligible bachelors her parents had shown her—the kind of young men they thought their daughter should marry, if only she would let them arrange it.

"When is Vibha getting married?" her mother chimed almost daily.

In the white Monte Carlo, they were headed down Interstate 4 toward Orlando, 30 miles from their Deltona home. Vibha looked out the window and watched the traffic flowing past: families bound for Disney World, truckers barreling toward Tampa, teenagers looking for something to do on a Saturday.

Vibha's parents were taking her to see a Hindu priest. He would use astrology to predict when she might get married.

She never guessed that she would be the kind of woman to even consider an arranged marriage. In her mid 20s, strong-minded, a feminist, she hoped one day to sit at the head of a boardroom table.

Born in India, Vibha came to the United States with her parents at age 2. She grew up in Florida, an American girl who was Indian too.

Now she was at the University of South Florida, savvy enough to organize a charity basketball game, poised enough to stand before her peers with a microphone and talk about the importance of community involvement.

Vibha looked at her mother and father in the front seat. The couple, who treated driving as a collaborative venture, were debating a lane change. Thirty years ago, they were like her, alone, until their families put them together. Was an arranged marriage to be her destiny too?

Vibha adjusted the long shawl draped over her shoulders and stared out the window.

* * *

Her world was a swirl of sociology term papers, Dr. Kaplan's Racism in America class, midnight movies at University Mall, dinners with friends at Sawatdee Thai's all-you-can-eat buffet.

An unidentified person holds a photograph of Vibha Dhawan. (Photograph courtesy of Stefanie Boyar/ *St. Petersburg Times*)

This was the fall of 2000. Vibha was just months from completing her bachelor's degree and would soon enter graduate school. She worked for USF parking services, dispatching jumps to cars with dead batteries, while juggling midterms and juvenile delinquency projects. Bulletin boards advertised keg parties. But even 110 miles from her Volusia County home, Vibha could hear her mother's high-pitched voice.

"College doesn't mean party. College doesn't mean fun."

"Parents didn't send you to college to go find a boy and sleep with him."

"Don't give boys a chance to cross the line."

Boys and dating had been off-limits to Vibha, the only child of Devindra and Promila Dhawan, who came from the Punjab region of India. In high school, when her American girlfriends lengthened their lashes for evenings out, Vibha stayed home.

Rules were firm in the Dhawan house. No parties. No racy movies. No HBO.

She had grown up in Daytona Beach, a few streets from U.S. 1, but caught only fleeting glimpses of spring break. Vibha worked at a Baskin-Robbins her senior year, scooping ice cream for college students in swimsuits. When her family visited friends who owned motels near the beach, she saw the crowds gathered for MTV concerts.

Vibha's mother kept her away from all that. MTV wasn't high on Promila's list. It taught that there was nothing wrong with nudity, nothing wrong with drinking, nothing wrong with sex before marriage.

Vibha was permitted male friends, but no boyfriends. She went to her high school prom with four other girls. She wore a powder-blue sleeveless dress with matching high heels. Her mother told her to put on a jacket to cover her arms. Vibha didn't.

At the Adam's Mark hotel under a stars-and-moonlight theme, Vibha danced to fast songs in a group and sat out the slow songs.

After Vibha moved to Tampa and into a USF dormitory, her mother would call late at night to make sure she was in her room.

Vibha did not always adhere to her parents' wishes. They wanted a medical career for her. Her father was a pharmacist; her mother, a hospital lab technician. But in her sophomore year, Vibha made social sciences her major. She was interested in people and society.

Vibha plunged into campus life. During India week, she passed out bumper stickers that beckoned, "Kiss Me I'm Indian," but kissed no one. She started the Organization of Hindu Minds: OHM. The group drew mostly from the vegetarian, toe-ring set, many non-Indians.

Vibha caravaned to Clearwater Beach with friends. She saw Jon Bon Jovi at the USF Sun Dome, her first concert. With her friend Monica Bassi, a fellow Punjabi, she went to the Hindi movies brought to campus each week by the Students of India Association.

Growing up, Vibha had spent many a lazy Saturday afternoon with her mother watching Indian movies rented from the local east-west grocery. The movies almost always had an arranged marriage.

A sari-clad mother would announce to her daughter, "Beta, I found a boy for you." The young woman would throw herself on the bed weeping.

A long-haired beauty learned to love the stranger she married.

A hero secretly pined for the love he could never have and sang about his heart breaking like glass.

The Hindi movies of Vibha's childhood were made in the 1960s. There was no kissing, no couples disappearing behind closed doors.

Marriage remained a leading theme in the Indian movies shown at USF. But now the female actors showed their navels and danced provocatively. Still, Vibha noticed: no kissing.

She went to few college parties. On weekends, she drove her Hyundai Elantra home to Deltona, near Daytona Beach.

It was during those visits that Vibha, who was about to graduate, noticed talk of arranged marriage seeping into her life. Her father would see a young man sitting cross-legged on the floor at the Hindu temple and nudge Vibha: "There's our future son-in-law."

Her mother would slip the topic into conversation at the dinner table. "When you graduate from college, we'll get you married," she would say.

Vibha let the comments evaporate.

* * *

Arranged marriage was born of the caste system. Around 1500 B.C., a tribe of Aryan herdsmen from central Asia crossed the lower slopes of the Himalayas into northern India and settled alongside the darker-skinned natives.

A caste system evolved. In the top tier were the priests or Brahmans, mostly Aryans; in the bottom, laborers or Shudra, mostly natives. At first, marriage was permitted among the top tiers, but in time a more rigid social structure emerged. The community you were born into became your marriage pool, your support system during hardship, your identity in a nation of villages.

To keep the community intact, parents arranged the marriages of their children. It ensured harmony in houses shared by extended families. Parents ruled. Children obeyed.

The practice of arranged marriage survived thousands of years, virtually unaltered. Through the Gupta dynasty and the invasion of the Huns. Through the Turko-Afghan chieftains, the Moghul empire and centuries of Muslim rule. Through European trade and the arrival of the British.

In the past century, Indians have fanned out around the globe seeking a better life. More than 1-million Indians now live in the United States. For customs to survive, the arranged marriage had to evolve.

"Bengali father invites alliance for his 33/5'9" handsome son," reads the ad under the Wanted Brides column of the Indian newspaper *Desi Match*, based in New York. "Father owns a jewelry showroom in Texas. Seeks only U.S. citizen, educated, beautiful girls below 30 years from respected family. Contact with photo."

Hundreds of dating sites dot the Internet: marryindian.com, indiasoulmate.com, suitablematch.com. On shaadi.com, a New York accountant posts her profile: "Fun loving and happy, from a family who are an impressive blend of traditional and modern ideologies."

Each year, Gujarati parents—originally from western India—gather their children for the three-day Charotar Patidar Samaj, commonly called the

At a late-night event during the 2002 Patel Convention, Brijesh Amin of Riverview dances with a young woman he has just met. (Photograph courtesy of Stefanie Boyar/*St. Petersburg Times*)

Patel Convention. North Carolina hotelier Ravi C. Patel and his brothers started the convention in 1989. They had noticed that in suburban Charlotte, marriageable Patels weren't meeting other Patels, a proud family name.

Today, the convention attracts thousands from across America and has fierce competition from a half-dozen similar gatherings.

The conventions are typical of singles socials, with lots of mingling and ice-breaking games.

"Name five things you would need if you were stranded on a desert island," said the host at the Patel Convention in Orlando two years ago.

At table 54, the discussion was lively:

"Unlimited booze."

"A genie and a magic lamp."

"Matches," suggested a young man.

"You going to start a fire?" teased a smiling young woman.

While the 20-somethings joked—*If you were a dessert, what kind would you be?*—parents sat in an adjacent ballroom, arms folded.

One father was near tears as he spoke of culture lost: "My son doesn't even know how to pronounce my hometown."

"They have not accepted as their culture the arranged marriage," said another father.

Parents discussed proms and dating, and talked about what to do if a daughter-in-law, a meat eater, used their vegetarian pots and pans to make chicken curry.

One mother worried aloud: What if the children didn't know how to cook Indian food at all?

* * *

Back in Deltona, Vibha's parents worried, too. Was their daughter Indian or American? Would she accept an arranged marriage?

At USF, Vibha thought she was doing fine on the relationship front without any help from home. She was dating young Indian men she met at school. Not all the guys were Punjabi or Hindu, as her parents had wished.

Vibha went to college networking conferences where young Indians discussed world affairs and exchanged phone numbers. But she disliked the meat-market atmosphere of those gatherings. The dates were always disappointing. The young men "wouldn't look at me seriously the way I was looking at them seriously," she said.

Vibha was in her senior year at USF the next time her parents brought up arranged marriage. The tone was more serious. Her mother showed her a photo of a young man, a doctor who lived in Punjab. He was in his late 20s, a friend of Promila's family in India.

Vibha looked at the photo and wrinkled her nose. The doctor had a mustache, which Vibha didn't like, and his hair was thick, what she liked to call "Indian-guy-hair-from-India."

"Don't go just on looks," her mother said. "Write to him."

Vibha stalled for weeks.

She knew exactly what she wanted in a husband. Someone who wouldn't hold her back from her goals. Someone secure. The sort of man who wouldn't mind if she kept her male friends. A man who wouldn't expect her to be home cooking every night. An understanding guy.

"I wouldn't have to feel like I had to hide things from him," she said.

She wanted a modern man. Not someone from an ancient system.

* * *

An arranged marriage had been the fate of females in Vibha's family for generations.

Vibha's grandmother, Kamlavati Khanna, was wedded at 10, before puberty. Her parents gave her up as a young virgin to please the gods and to end years of misfortune.

Kamlavati was shrouded from head to toe in a red sari for her wedding. No man saw her face, not even her betrothed, who was 10 years older. The child bride paraded around the sacred matrimonial flame behind him, the two connected by a small cord tied to her sari.

After the ceremony, Kamlavati returned to her family's house. When her first period came, at 14, she was sent to live with her husband and his family.

Kamlavati raised 10 children in Amritsar, an industrial city in Punjab state. The youngest of her four daughters was Promila.

Promila's sisters quickly married after high school. Promila didn't; she wanted to go to college. Her brothers objected, telling her it was no place for girls. Finally, one brother yielded and Promila became the first woman in her family to attend college. She earned a bachelor's degree in psychology and a master's in Sanskrit, the ancient language of India.

Promila was a caring daughter, caring for her mother after her father's death, cooking for her and keeping her company between college classes.

At 26, Promila was still unmarried. She wanted to be independent. She wanted her own job, "my own everything," she said, "because then you don't have to bear the stupid behavior of a man."

One day in 1972, when Promila's mother was in the hospital diagnosed with liver cancer, a cousin came to visit. He saw how Promila cared for her mother. He saw her prettiness.

When Promila left, the cousin told Kamlavati about a man he knew. His name was Devindra Dhawan and he had just come back from college in the United States. Do you want me to arrange a meeting, the cousin asked.

Kamlavati relayed the offer to her daughter. She wasn't interested.

One night soon after, while Promila was massaging her mother's head, Kamlavati gave her a talk she would never forget:

"I know you don't want to get married, and I wish I could fulfill that wish for you, but now God has a new plan and I am dying. In two or three days, I will not be alive. I am not forcing you to get married, but I don't want you to live alone. Nor do I want you to live with your sisters or your brothers. They are going to use you like a servant. You are so giving. You are going to lose your dignity and your self-respect, which I don't like. So better you get married and have your own life."

Days later, Kamlavati died.

Promila's sisters pushed her to meet Devindra. He had a doctorate in pharmacy from the University of Florida and was working as a drug inspector for the Indian customs department. His family's background

was not Punjabi, but Devindra grew up in northern India and was familiar with Punjabi customs.

Promila agreed to meet Devindra. The meeting, at a friend's house,
was brief, and Promila never once looked up at him. Devindra spoke first,
expressing sympathy for Kamlavati's death. Then, he became blunt.

"I have to tell you, I am a smoker," he said. "I am a chain smoker. I
drink and I go out, and I am not going to live in India. I am going to move
back to America."

Promila's head stayed down.

"After marriage, you can't say, 'Why you are smoking? You didn't tell
me. Why you are drinking? You didn't tell me.' Well, I'm telling you now."

Promila could see Devindra's profile in a mirror on the wall. He had on
a tie, maroon jacket and blue shirt. She wore a sari, with two petticoats
underneath to add volume to her bony body.

"Do you have any questions?" Devindra asked.

Promila shook her head.

"You are going to answer me? You want a few days?"

She didn't respond.

Her sisters came into the room. "I want to go now," Promila said.

Two weeks later, she still had no answer for Devindra.

Then, the doorbell rang. Promila opened the door to find herself face-
to-face with Devindra for the first time. He was a large man, visibly older.
They were alone, which was inappropriate.

"I'm sorry," he said. "I'm passing through. I thought I would see you.
Have you decided on marriage?"

Promila was shivering. She asked him to come in and offered him a soda.

"Looks like you are under pressure," Devindra said. "I don't want to
force you. Whatever your heart says, you have to go with that."

"I will let you know," Promila said, expecting him to leave.

Instead, he asked her to go for a ride. He was on his way to a work
luncheon and had a driver waiting. Promila telephoned her older sister for
permission. "Be careful," her sister said.

The trip lasted four hours. Devindra was very polite. He didn't pepper
her with stupid questions. Promila enjoyed his company.

That night, she lit a candle by a small altar in her home and prayed.
"God show me who is the one," she said, closing her eyes.

When she opened them, she saw an image of the Hindu god Shiva, the
destroyer, and by his side, the goddess Parvati. They were exchanging garlands, a ritual in marriage.

Promila didn't have a picture of either god on her altar. She usually prayed to Mata, a North Indian god. Yet, there before her were Parvati and Shiva, a younger woman and an older man, just like she and Devindra. It had to be a sign.

The next morning, Promila told her sisters, "Go ahead with marriage. God has a plan."

* * *

When Vibha was born to Promila and Devindra in a Madras hospital on Sept. 24, 1977, her hands were wide open, her arms stretched out. The doctor remarked to Promila that the child would not stay in India. "She is reaching," the doctor said. "She will take you far."

The night Vibha came home from the hospital, a letter from U.S. immigration authorities was waiting. Devindra's papers had come through. The family had a passage to America.

* * *

Promila looked at her college student daughter—hair long like a Hindi film star, nose pierced on the left, but so American on the inside. Promila knew Vibha dated at USF, and that not all the men were Punjabi or Hindu. What if Vibha married a non-Indian? What would become of customs, of all that was important to her parents?

Promila had always strived to make her daughter as Indian as possible. She toted Vibha to *poojas,* Hindu prayer services, held in the homes of local Indians. She enrolled Vibha in Hindi classes and cooked lavish Indian dinners.

She stressed Punjabi culture, which has roots that date back 3,000 years. Punjabi people sacrificed much for India, Promila told her child. During Partition in 1947, it was this northern region that fell divided between a Muslim Pakistan and a Hindu India. Thousands of families were uprooted amid riots and bloodshed, Devindra's family among them.

Promila told Vibha stories about Lord Ganesha, the remover of obstacles, summoned before all ceremonies, including marriage. At bedtime, Devindra would play cassette tapes from the Hindi film singer Lata Mangeshkar.

But Vibha was not always receptive. She found Indian food too spicy. She wanted pizza, hot dogs and hamburgers, a taste she developed in the cafeteria of Holly Hill Elementary School near Daytona Beach. She spoke limited Hindi, with an American accent.

Promila Dhawan kisses Vibha Dhawan in the living room of their Deltona home. (Photograph courtesy of Stefanie Boyar/*St. Petersburg Times*)

When Vibha turned 13, Devindra and Promila decided to send her to India for a year to learn more about her homeland's culture. Even before she walked into the boarding school in Jaipur, 165 miles from New Delhi, classmates were gossiping about "the American."

Vibha felt like a foreigner. She fell behind on school work, especially in her study of Hindi. In class one day, the students had to recite a prayer. Vibha said the prayer as best she could. The headmistress stopped at her desk.

"Vibha, say that again," she demanded.

Vibha's pronunciation was mangled. Her classmates burst out laughing.

But she returned to the United States with newfound interest in her heritage. She started to like being Indian, being Punjabi. When American friends asked her, "Why so many gods?" she knew the answer: Hindus believe in one god, but a god who takes different forms. A figure like Ganesha was symbolic.

She grew to love Indian food, dal and pepper-laden curries. She bought mounds of eye-catching Indian clothes and dazzling jewelry. She wore metal bangles up to her elbows and rhinestone-studded bindi dots between her eyebrows.

With Vibha in her 20s, Promila felt she was standing at a crossroads. She felt a burden. Family traditions, thousands of years old, were threatening to dissolve in just one generation in America.

A Punjabi husband could help Vibha carry traditions to future generations.

Years ago, Promila herself had resisted arranged marriage. Now, she knew better. It was a necessity.

* * *

Promila had one agenda. Vibha's girlfriends at USF had another.

Monica Bassi, a Punjabi born in Toronto, was adamant. "I don't want you to have an arranged marriage!" she said. "You will meet someone at the right time, whenever it happens. You can't force these things."

"You need to find someone that fits the lifestyle you want," said Sheetal Dharia, a member of the Organization of Hindu Minds.

Vibha had tried the American way of dating. She went to parties and met boys and realized that it was hard.

"I get attached very easily," Vibha said. "I don't know how to disconnect."

Would the Indian way—having her parents as a go-between—be better?

The arranged marriage had evolved, changed even from her parents' time. Her parents were dutiful, holding hands to help each other up the stairs or out of the car. Could it hurt to have their help in the search? To have a shepherd? A protector?

Vibha had great respect for her parents. Her father lived with a handicap, the shortness of his left leg. Her mother was strong, not at all submissive. Promila's motto: "Always put your hand in your own pocket; never put your hand in someone else's pocket."

Vibha doesn't remember exactly how she arrived at her decision. Only that she did.

"Okay," she said somewhat out of the blue during a weekend trip back to Deltona. "I will give the boys you find a chance."

Vibha had one condition: She wanted veto power. Her parents, seated in a living room filled with framed family vacation photos, agreed.

Months passed before Vibha heard anything more about marriage. She became caught up in preparations for her December graduation. She knew her mother was planning a trip to India and assumed it was to see family. Then Vibha noticed a stack of photos of herself and a list of her clubs and activities at USF.

Vibha realized: Her mother wasn't going to India just to visit. She was crossing the globe to find her daughter a husband.

ABOUT THIS STORY

St. Petersburg Times reporter Babita Persaud met Vibha Dhawan in January 2002. For three years, Persaud followed Vibha as she and her parents confronted the issue of arranged marriage and how it is evolving for Indians in the United States.

The reporting in this story is based on events Persaud observed and interviews she had with Vibha, her parents and friends in Florida and India. By necessity, some events—Vibha's childhood and her family's years in India, for example—have been reconstructed from interviews. The conversations between Promila and Devindra Dhawan were based on Promila's recollections.

Background information on India and the caste system was obtained from *The Penguin History of Early India* by Romila Thapar, and *India, an Introduction* by Khushwant Singh. Anjula Bedi's *Gods & Goddesses of India* was used as a reference. Explanations of Hinduism were provided by Sudarsan Padmanabhan, who teaches the subject at the University of South Florida.

12. The Match Game

The television flickered with the faces of blonds and brunets, their hair flat-ironed, their evening dresses stretched over pushup bras.

"Who will go home broken-hearted?" the voiceover said.

Vibha Dhawan was watching *The Bachelor* on a 13-inch Magnavox in her dorm room, feeling anything but elegant. Her room was a wreck, clothes strewn everywhere. She studied and ate at the same cramped desk, her textbooks piled on the floor.

On TV, the bachelor, a Harvard graduate with a fondness for snow skiing and Italian food, stood before his harem of beautiful women. Arranged marriage, American style. A tray of long-stemmed red roses awaited the bachelor's whims.

"The first rose goes to . . ." He paused hard before giving up a name.

Lipstick smiles froze in anticipation until one rose was left.

"The final rose goes to . . ."

The camera flashed to those without flowers. The discarded. The disappointed. Love was never easy, not even on television.

* * *

Promila Dhawan telephoned friends and relatives in India who might know a suitable young man. Once Vibha's mother had a name, she called the man's parents, or, sometimes, an aunt, and listened to how they spoke. Were they educated? Overly boastful? Did they seem interested in Vibha?

She phoned neighbors and friends in India who might know the family. "How do they treat people?" Promila asked. "What kind of business do they have? How are their children growing up?"

Vibha was at the University of South Florida, trying to stay calm. She had picked up her cap and gown for winter graduation. She had agreed in principle to her parents' wishes.

"The arranged marriage is all about duty," she explained to her girlfriends.

But at the same time, she told her mother, "There is no way a boy from India would understand me." What did an Indian man know of American ways? Would he let her be a feminist? Have a career?

Her mother was adamant. She wanted a Punjabi boy from India. Indian boys in America were too Westernized, hardly spoke Hindi, knew little about Indian culture and Hinduism.

"What will you teach your children?" she asked Vibha.

In late December 2000, just after Vibha's graduation, Promila boarded a plane for India. She had five interviews lined up. Vibha stayed at home in Deltona with her father.

After flying 8,700 miles to Bombay, her mother traveled 1,500 bone-rattling miles by train to Delhi, then Jaipur and her hometown of Amritsar in Punjab.

Back home, Vibha baked brownies from a box for her dad. In India, Promila sipped hot chai tea in living rooms and quizzed prospects: What do you do for a living? What do your parents do? What are your plans?

Every few days, Vibha got a phone call from her mother. Bachelor No. 1 was off the list, Promila reported. He kept making excuses and didn't want to spend time with Promila.

Another call: Bachelor No. 2 had a girlfriend. "You can't drink milk with a fly in it," her mother told her.

Bachelor No. 3, who had told Promila he was 6 feet 6, turned out to be 5 feet 9. "He was lying, one after the other," she said.

No. 4 was looking for an easy passage to the United States: a green card. Vibha was not about to be used as a one-way ticket to America.

Then came the doctor with the mustache, the one whose photograph Vibha had seen. Promila asked about his plans. He would stay in the United States for five or six years, the young doctor said, but then he would return to India.

"My daughter doesn't want to leave the States," Promila told Bachelor No. 5. "She is an American."

Ten days after leaving, Promila flew back to Florida. Vibha was waiting at Orlando International Airport. Her mother was finished with India. The entire nation of 1-billion had been stricken from her list. She told Vibha, "None of those boys were good enough!"

Vibha felt relief.

But other countries dotted the map. And her mother still had steam.

* * *

Maybe an Indian from the United States really was better-suited for her daughter, Promila decided. She had tried tradition. It was time for modern magic: the Internet. Promila assembled a report known in Indian matrimonial circles as a bio data. On a computer, Promila typed:

VIBHA DHAWAN
DOB: September 24, 1977
Height: 5'5"
Social: President of the Organization of Hindu Minds

Promila listed sports—softball, volleyball and bowling, among them—but, deliberately, did not list Vibha's weight. In Promila's mind, her plus-sized daughter needed to slim down.

With the resume came a cover letter.

Vibha was born on September 24, 1977, at 10:30 p.m. in Madras, India, to Dr. Devindra Dhawan and Mrs. Promila K. Dhawan. She is an only child that comes from a big family located in Punjab, Delhi, Mumbai, Surat, London, Canada, California, New York and Illinois.

Her relatives' professions range from doctors, scientists, lawyers, engineers, to the P.A. of the prime minister of India. Even though she has lived in the United States most of her life she hasn't forgotten her traditional values and religious practices.

Vibha graduated from the University of South Florida in December of 2000 with a B.A. in Sociology and Communication Sciences/Disorders. She is currently working and studying toward her M.A. degree in Political Science and Communications. Her future goals are to live a successful life with her family and to become a politician or news broadcaster.

One could say that she is a sincere, social and open-minded person with a warm heart. She is looking for an independent individual with similar futuristic goals for a prosperous life.

Sincerely,

Promila Dhawan

Vibha flipped through albums looking for a photo to accompany the bio. She chose one of herself smiling from a cream-colored sofa. She was wearing an earth-toned salwar kameez, tunic and draw-string pants, with a Bindi dot between her eyebrows.

Vibha, instructed by her mom, posted the bio data package on punjabimatrimony.com, whose home page offers "eternal bonds" and "everlasting relationships."

Responses poured into Promila's Yahoo account. "The computer is magic," Promila marveled.

Vibha, now in graduate school, checked the account from USF's computer lab between classes. She poked fun at the guys' names, creating

Promila Dhawan pours freshly brewed chai tea in her Deltona kitchen. (Photograph courtesy of Stefanie Boyar/*St. Petersburg Times*)

unflattering rhymes. If a guy couldn't spell, if he wasn't careful in the way he wrote, she didn't take him seriously.

"We would like to have the latest photograph of dear Anita," stated the note from Beavercreek, Ohio.

"Who's Anita?" Vibha said to her mother, and they both burst out laughing.

Promila evaluated the responses. She noted height; she wanted a tall man for Vibha. She noted age. Six years older was out.

She did not make an issue of caste, which could be confining given the smaller pool of single Indian men in the United States.

If the e-mail stated, "I am looking for a girl who knows how to cook and clean"—and some did—Promila zapped it into the trash. She knew Vibha was not domestic.

Promila responded to likely prospects by e-mail, asking for the young man's horoscope—date, time and place of birth—so that she might compare it with Vibha's. Ancient Hindus used astrology to launch battles and unite kingdoms. Promila believed the stars held the messages of God.

Despite the deluge of responses, the first Web posting netted only one prospect: Anil, 24, a chiropractor from California.

He telephoned once. Vibha discovered she didn't know exactly what to say to a man. At least not this man.

"What's up?" she tried.

Anil filled the dead air, raving about California's sunny weather.

The two did not click.

* * *

Her mother was impatient. It was June 2001. Six months had passed since the trip to India. Promila decided to take Vibha to see a Hindu priest—a pandit—near Orlando. Pandits advised on the physical—marriage, death and birth—and the metaphysical, the will of God. Maybe he could tell them something.

In a community center used as a temple, Vibha sat cross-legged on the bare floor, next to the pandit. He seemed young and bony to her. A piece of cloth the golden color of turmeric draped his chest. In front of him was a chart of the stars and the moons.

"When is she going to get married?" Vibha's father asked eagerly.

The pandit looked at his chart. "The guy will come into her life after September," he said. "He will be someone she already knows."

Vibha searched her mind. Who could that be? Faces popped up. She pushed them aside.

"The boy will live in the United States," the pandit said.

Her mother seemed pleased.

"He will be into computers, well-off," continued the priest. "You will have nothing to worry about."

He turned to Vibha. "You're going to get married 18 months from your birthday coming up."

Vibha did the calculation in her head. She would turn 24 in September. Eighteen months from that would be March 2003.

That was awfully close, she thought. She sat silently. While her parents obsessed over *when,* Vibha worried about *who.*

* * *

"I'm not that desperate!" Vibha fumed.

She was at home in Deltona one weekend in January 2002 when she noticed a pile of envelopes in the living room. Responses to the bio data usually came by e-mail. What was going on?

Promila confessed. She had placed an ad for Vibha in *India Abroad,* a weekly newspaper offered at U.S. markets frequented by Indians. Vibha had been revealed to the world as a Punjabi girl, 24, with a wheatish complexion, well-educated and from a good family, who was seeking a Punjabi boy.

"Embarrassing!" Vibha said. She had agreed to the India trip, the bio data, the Web posting. But a classified ad? What was she, a car?

Promila was not only fielding the responses, she was scanning the other ads in *India Abroad*'s matrimonial columns. One day the words "tall" and "attorney" caught her eye.

Without telling Vibha, Promila answered the ad. A few days later, an e-mail arrived from California.

> *Thank you for your response to the ad I had placed in* India Abroad *for my son, Sandeep. I am attaching Sandeep's photo and bio data to this e-mail. If you could kindly respond with a photograph and bio data of your daughter, it would be much appreciated.*

Sandeep was north Indian, 29, 5 feet 10 and 195 pounds. He had been in the United States since he was a baby and was a lawyer in Los Angeles.

Vibha was on the verge of scolding her mother for again snatching the reins when she examined Sandeep's photo and bio data. He was tall and smiling, with thick hair. She liked that he listed both Indian and American hobbies.

She gave her mother the go-ahead, and Promila sent off Vibha's bio data. Within days, Vibha got an e-mail.

> *Hi Vibha,*
>
> *This is Sandeep. I got your e-mail address from my parents who got it from your parents. Where in Florida do you currently live? Besides going to school, are you also working, or are you a full time student?*
>
> *I live at home with my parents, and we live in a suburb of Los Angeles called Porter Ranch. I have a younger brother and a younger sister.*
>
> *Your parents also gave my parents your cell phone number. Would you mind if I called you?*
>
> *Take care, Sandeep*

Vibha was impressed. He was casual and nice. Plus, no spelling mistakes.

> *Hey Sandeep,*
>
> *How are you? I go to school full time and I work full time on campus. I have no problem with you calling my cell phone.*

What type of attorney are you? Personal injury? Corporate? What do you do for fun? Do you travel? Have you been to Florida?

Take care, Vibha

That weekend in February 2002, Vibha hooked her cell phone to her purse and toted it everywhere. She was having lunch with a girlfriend at Perkins Restaurant & Bakery on Fowler Avenue when a strange number flashed on her caller ID. She kept getting calls meant for a real estate office. Expecting yet another, she answered rudely: "What?"

"Hi, is this Vibha?" a deep voice said. "This is Sandeep."

Vibha sat up. "Oh, hi."

The moment wasn't private. "I'm having lunch with my friend," Vibha said. "Can I call you back?"

Forty-five minutes later, she did, catching him in line for a ride at Disneyland.

"So how have you been?" he asked casually, as if Vibha was a lifelong friend.

"Fine," she said.

"How was your week?"

"Fine," she said.

Pauses filled the air and Vibha could tell the timing was not right.

"Can I call you tomorrow?" he asked.

The next day, Vibha waited for his call at an indoor racquetball court at USF. She rarely played racquetball, but thought it would make good background noise. Perhaps Sandeep would think she was athletic and slim.

For 10 minutes, they talked about the weather, before moving to geography.

"Is Tampa east or west of Orlando?" he asked.

He told her he had traveled to Hawaii and Las Vegas. He liked to gamble.

Oh, Vibha said.

Sandeep named some fast-food restaurants he liked.

"I stopped eating beef in 1996," Vibha said. "I eat seafood."

"I can't stand seafood," Sandeep said.

"Oh, that's another thing we have in common," she said, and they both chuckled.

* * *

The next call, Vibha initiated.

Should she tell him the truth? That her bio data photo was dated. That she had gained 30 pounds.

"I'm not, like, a size 5," she said.

He didn't get the hint and went on gabbing about movies and dating.

"Do you think we should meet?" he said.

It was only their second conversation. Maybe he did get the hint.

The Indian celebration of spring, called Holi, passed. Vibha's midterm exams passed. The conversations with Sandeep continued, lasting an hour, then two.

She asked him the husband questions she had been rehearsing in her mind.

"If a girl cooks, will you do the dishes?"

"Yes," he said.

"When you were 14 and your baby sister was born, did you change her diapers?"

"Your questions are weird."

She remained silent until he gave in.

"Yes, I changed her diapers."

"Did you help your mom? Did you cook for her?"

"Are you one of those girls who believe in 50-50 all the way?"

"No, I believe in 51-49," Vibha said. "You for the 49."

They laughed.

He asked her, "Do you get lonely, being an only child?"

"All the time," she said. "I always feel lonely."

She liked the question. It showed sensitivity.

Promila was cautious about Sandeep. She noticed his ad was still running in *India Abroad.* But Sandeep's mother sent Promila a list of the family's summer travel plans. They wanted to meet Vibha.

Vibha told her mother to stall, hoping to buy some time to lose weight.

"Eat more broccoli," Promila nagged. "Lay off the bread."

* * *

The musical chime on her cell phone went off while Vibha was in her dorm. Sandeep wanted to fix a date to meet—urgently.

It was May 2002. Almost four months had passed since their first e-mail.

She asked him to pick two numbers. Twice, he chose seven.

"Okay, I'll meet you on July 7," Vibha said. "I'll come with my mom and dad."

"Will they let us be alone?" Sandeep asked.

* * *

She had already gone to bed when he called one night not long afterward. Somehow the conversation turned to sex. Sandeep asked Vibha how she felt about sleeping with her fiance if she got engaged.

She was stunned. Her upbringing taught her such subjects were private.

"If I get to a point where I feel comfortable, then I will have this conversation with you," she answered, "but you shouldn't expect it."

For weeks, Sandeep didn't call. Vibha sent him an e-mail birthday card in June, when he turned 30. His response was brief and completely ignored their last phone conversation.

For the first time, Vibha felt she couldn't talk to Sandeep. She didn't answer his e-mail. He didn't call.

July 7, 2002, came and went, and Vibha was still like a girl on *The Bachelor,* waiting for her red rose.

* * *

Vibha's mom threw more bio data packages her way, including two men from Houston, both named Manish. Manish One and Manish Two, Vibha dubbed them.

Her bio data was now posted on another popular site, shaadi.com. Promila updated the photo: Vibha in the sleeveless, powder-blue dress she wore to her high school prom.

In Russia, a young Punjabi named Ashu noticed. He e-mailed her on Feb. 25, 2003.

I am ambitious, caring, friendly, possess good sense of humor, family values, professionally sound, dedicated hard worker. I have lust for life, don't let people be sad around me and don't want to hurt them with wrong deeds and action.

Vibha, under Promila's tutelage, had become more demanding.

Dear Ashu,

Your description of yourself sounds vague, could you tell me some of your flaws?

* * *

March 2003 arrived. Vibha was still single. The pandit had been off in his prediction.

The search was in its third year. It reached all the way to New Zealand. A friend of Promila's knew a Punjabi woman whose nephew was

At an Indian potluck, Vibha seasons curried baby eggplant alongside Shantanu Shevade. (Photograph courtesy of Stefanie Boyar/*St. Petersburg Times*)

studying there. "Very tall and handsome," the woman said. His name was Rahul.

Rahul e-mailed Vibha. His first note was short and sweet, which Vibha liked. He ended it with "Be good!"

They set a date to meet—on the Internet—where they would trade instant messages. Online, Vibha waited for an hour. It was as if she had been stood up at a bar. Finally, a message popped on the screen: *Sorry. I had something to do.*

She didn't ask. He didn't volunteer.

* * *

Vibha moved out of the USF dorms and into the nearby Excellence Apartments. Anand Warude, a fellow graduate student, lived at Excellence with five roommates who took turns cooking, and Vibha often went to his apartment for dinner. While *Fear Factor* played on the TV and the friends squirmed at the outlandish stunts, they joked, talked about their day, their professors, USF politics, India.

Vibha particularly enjoyed the stories about India that one of Anand's roommates, Shantanu Shevade, told. Like Anand, Shantanu had grown up in Bombay, and, like Anand, he had come to Tampa to study engineering at USF. Shantanu entertained Vibha and his roommates with tales of the stricter climate at Indian colleges. You couldn't bring food into classrooms, he said, or even a soft drink. Yawning in class was out, too.

Shantanu was nice, Vibha thought. She had thought he was a bit scruffy when they first met, in need of a shave, but she noticed right away that his eyes were hazel—shimmering like pennies—not pitch black like most Indian eyes.

Then, in an instant one evening, he became just another male disappointment.

It had been a long day at school and work. After dinner, Vibha dozed off for a few minutes on Anand's couch. When she opened her eyes, her friends were huddled around the computer, looking at something that made a loud, gasping noise.

"What is that?" Vibha asked.

"That's you snoring!" one of them announced.

The villain was Shantanu. He had recorded Vibha while she slept, much to the amusement of the others.

She left the apartment embarrassed and with Shantanu crossed off her list.

* * *

The online relationship with Rahul had improved after the awkward start. Toward the end of summer last year, Rahul's aunt in Pittsburgh phoned Promila. The aunt wanted to meet Vibha.

With Rahul in New Zealand and his parents in India, the aunt had become the point of contact, typical of Indian matchmaking.

Promila was pleased. She liked Rahul's family. Vibha felt some excitement, too. After three years, she was finally going to meet prospective parents. Vibha wore a fancy Punjabi outfit for the meeting in Pittsburgh, which was held in an Indian restaurant that Rahul's family owned.

The aunt greeted Vibha warmly. "How's school?" she asked.

She raved about Rahul, his good looks, his hobbies. "He might be coming to America soon for a visit," she said. "Maybe you two can meet."

As Vibha and her mother boarded the plane for the flight back to Tampa, Promila took up Rahul's cause.

"You should talk to Rahul more," Promila told Vibha.

In her mind, Vibha was running through the gallery of faces the long search had produced.

The candidates from India were out, or were they? She knew her mother still kept in touch with Bachelor No. 5, the doctor. Promila liked his family.

The Manishes from Houston also came from good families. Manish One was always complimenting Vibha, but was he sincere? Manish Two was worldly and liked to describe at great length the places he had visited, but his monologues sometimes turned Vibha off.

Ashu the Russian wore his heart on his sleeve and was convinced that he and Vibha were destined for each other.

Rahul was kind and liked to cook, but he didn't always share Vibha's sense of humor.

Yet, as Vibha fastened her seat belt, her mind was far from muddled. She didn't let on to her mother, but the picture was becoming clearer. One man was starting to stand out.

ABOUT THIS STORY

For three years, *St. Petersburg Times* reporter Babita Persaud followed Vibha Dhawan as she and her parents confronted the issue of arranged marriage and how it is evolving for Indians in America.

The private nature of some events meant they had to be reconstructed later from interviews. For example, the phone conversations with Sandeep, the suitor from California, were recounted to Persaud by Vibha soon after they occurred.

E-mails and biographic data from suitors were provided by the Dhawan family to illustrate the intricacies of arranged marriage.

13. The Boy Next Door

DEC. 26, 2004

Vibha's cell phone went off. It was Shantanu.

"You want to get something to eat?" he asked.

For weeks after Shantanu recorded her snoring, Vibha vowed not to talk to him. Then, her girlfriend Athy Fitos persuaded her to give him a second chance. Actually, Athy confided, he likes you.

Vibha offered to drive, and slipped on nice jeans, a frilly red blouse and strappy heels.

"You're all dressed up," Shantanu said when she knocked on his door.

"Oh, I just threw this on," Vibha said.

He was in shorts. It was June 21, 2003, a sunny day in Tampa. Shantanu wanted to dine outdoors.

Vibha knew a place in Hyde Park. In her Hyundai, they drove down Kennedy Boulevard. Vibha became lost. Where was the turn for Old Hyde Park Village? On Howard Avenue, she spotted TC Choy's Asian Bistro. Not exactly alfresco, but Shantanu said okay.

A waiter dressed in black took their order for California rolls and fruity drinks. A laughing Buddha statue stood in the corner while a sushi chef rolled rice onto seaweed at the bar. This would be a great date place, Vibha was thinking.

After dinner, she had an idea. "Want to see my favorite house?"

They drove to Tampa's grandest street, Bayshore Boulevard. Vibha slowed in front of the Mediterranean mansion of RV tycoon Don Wallace.

"It's my dream house," she said.

"Wow," said Shantanu, imagining the price tag.

He looked beyond the balustrade of Bayshore Boulevard to Hillsborough Bay. His hometown of Bombay is near the Arabian Sea.

"I want to go near the water," he said.

Vibha knew just the spot. They drove through downtown and across the bridge to Harbour Island. She felt like a tour guide, introducing Shantanu to a Tampa he had never seen.

It was almost 9 p.m. when they sat down behind Jackson's Bistro, on the brick steps along Seddon Channel. Shantanu was an arm's length from Vibha, two steps above her. For the longest time, they just sat there, looking at the skyline across the channel and at each other.

"You're so good," he said, breaking the silence.

He was teasing her, just like he often did at Anand's.

"You don't know me that well," Vibha said. She wanted to prove she wasn't goody-goody. "I dare you to kiss me," she joked.

"Oh, I dare you to kiss me," Shantanu said.

Vibha wasn't sure if he was joking. Or was he challenging her? She was not one to back down.

"All right," she said. But she did not move.

Minutes went by. Should she do it?

She scooted closer to him and kissed him on the cheek.

"See," she said, smugly.

She was feeling playful.

"I dare you to kiss me, too," she said.

And he did.

* * *

She could hardly pronounce his name at first and had to think it through phonetically: Shan-TAN-oo. She asked what it meant, and he explained: One who heals.

Like a doctor, Vibha thought.

He had seeped into her life. She had met him the year before. He was a friend of Anand's and a graduate student. Vibha would go to Anand's for dinner and Shantanu would be there, along with Anand's girlfriend and many other people. Then, when Vibha moved into Excellence Apartments, Shantanu was there with Anand to help.

He would tease her about being ABCD, American Born Confused Desi, a term for Indians confused about their identity after years in America. She joked he was FOB: Fresh Off the Boat.

She began to notice little things about him. He never raised his voice. He helped with the dishes after meals and told her he did things 50-50. In his eyes, men and women were on equal footing.

Perhaps if she had seen his bio data, she would have dismissed him for some superficial reason.

Perhaps, he might have dismissed her, too. At first sight, Shantanu thought Vibha was plump, but soon he was noticing the shine of her hair and the delicacy of her nose. When his car broke down, it was Vibha who canceled her movie plans to pick him up.

Before coming to America, Shantanu Shevade had never left India. He lived in a suburb of Bombay, the country's financial capital, which was renamed Mumbai in 1995 as politicians sought to break away from India's colonial heritage. His mother, Maitreyee Shevade, taught Sanskrit in a high school. His father, Sudhir Shevade, was a retired computer manager for the State Bank of India.

Shantanu chose mechanical engineering as his career. It fit with his fondness for airplanes and engines. He went to Mumbai University and got a job at a software company, but he was not happy. Why not try graduate study at USF, his childhood friend Anand suggested.

Two hours after arriving in Tampa in August 2002, Shantanu was wading in the swimming pool at Campus Walk apartments. Five hours later, he was at the Greenery, the campus hangout.

The next year, he moved into Excellence Apartments with Anand. His building was just 100 yards from Vibha's.

Her mother had searched the Earth for a husband for Vibha.

Vibha found Shantanu next door.

* * *

The e-mails from Rahul, the student in New Zealand, ceased not too long after the trip to Pittsburgh. He and Vibha fell out over a joke Vibha made that he did not get.

Ashu the Russian didn't have a college degree, Vibha discovered. Her mother gave her permission to stop responding to his e-mails. Calls from Manish One and Manish Two of Houston faded with "I'll call you later." Vibha did not follow up. Neither did they. The others faded. But not Shantanu. He and Vibha became inseparable in the summer and fall of 2003. It was Vibha who brought up the subject of marriage. Shantanu didn't shy away from the suggestion.

Vibha's mom knew nothing.

Would Promila approve? Vibha realized Shantanu didn't meet several of the standards her mother had set. He didn't have a steady job. He didn't even have a green card. He was younger than Vibha, by a year.

And there was another problem.

* * *

"Ma." Vibha was talking to her mother on the cell phone, on her way to pick up Shantanu. They were going to Ybor City.

"Remember that guy who helped me move into the apartment?" Vibha asked.

"No."

"The one who assembled the bed?" Vibha said.

"No."

Vibha pushed ahead. "Well, I think he likes me," she said quickly. "I think he's the one."

Vibha filled in the silence. He's from Bombay, she said. He's a graduate student at USF, getting his master's and eventually his doctorate.

What was her mother thinking, Vibha wondered. She didn't know. But she plowed on. There was one more thing she needed to say. She knew her mother wanted to keep Punjabi customs alive in America, to pass them on to future generations.

"Ma," she said, "he's not Punjabi."

* * *

Shantanu came from the western state of Maharashtra. At home, he spoke Marathi, a regional language. He ate different foods than Punjabis. He worshiped a different god, Lord Ganesha, rather than Mata, the North Indian god Promila worshiped.

There were different wedding customs, too. Maharashtra weddings take place in the day and the bride wears green bangles and a 9-yard sari. In Punjabi weddings, typically held at night, the bride traditionally wears red.

Promila wondered whether infatuation was clouding Vibha's judgment.

She summoned her sister, Poonam, who lives in Mumbai, to investigate. Poonam met Shantanu's parents and reported: The mother was friendly with Punjabis. She and her husband were highly educated.

Promila spoke to Shantanu's parents on the telephone. They were polite, she quickly discovered, but would they demand a dowry?

Some Indian families still followed the ancient custom, which was outlawed in 1961 in an effort to stop the suicides of young women seeking to spare their parents the financial burden. Promila believed her daughter was gift enough.

The Shevades did not ask for one.

Promila spent weekends with Vibha and Shantanu. They went to *poojas*—prayer services—at the Hindu temple near Orlando. They watched Indian movies on satellite Zee TV in the living room.

Promila noticed at dinner that Shantanu fixed his own plate of food.

"If he was a Punjabi boy, maybe he would sit there and say, 'Get me a glass of water,'" she said later.

But Promila was still cautious. And so, one evening after dinner, while Vibha was in another room, she launched a cross-examination of Shantanu.

"My daughter, she wants a 50-50 relationship," she said, "but it might more be like 60-40. Is that okay with you?"

Shantanu said yes. He was willing to do more than his share.

"My daughter, she is not Marathi. She is not from India. Doesn't your mother want a Marathi girl for you?"

He said his parents would accept his choice.

Promila asked about Shantanu's degrees. He was applying to the Ph.D. program in mechanical engineering at USF.

"What about a job?" Promila asked. She did not want them to depend on Vibha's paycheck alone.

Shantanu felt his education would land him a good job in the United States.

The questions went on and on. Finally, Promila asked: "Why do you want my daughter? She doesn't cook. She doesn't do housework. What do you see in her?"

Shantanu did not freeze.

"She has a good heart," he said.

And that was when Promila knew Shantanu was the husband for Vibha.

* * *

Vibha knew exactly the kind of wedding she wanted: a full five-day Punjabi wedding, with an opening ceremony, two days of bridal preparation, an all-night wedding, a reception the next day. And she wanted it in India.

Promila was ecstatic. Her daughter was sticking to tradition. An auspicious wedding date—deemed special by the gods—was set by the family pandit in Mumbai. The priest weighed the moons and stars and determined the lucky number for Vibha and Shantanu: nine.

They would become engaged on Jan. 18, because one and eight added up to nine.

The wedding in India would be June 27.

* * *

Shantanu was a modern man from a modern India. His friends dated. He liked Western music and he had seen Bryan Adams in concert in Bangalore.

He told Vibha he didn't want to wait for the wedding in India to live together. They should move in together, he said, after the civil ceremony they planned at the Volusia County Courthouse Annex in Daytona Beach. A civil wedding would streamline immigration for Shantanu; it was a step many Indians took.

Vibha's apartment lease was almost up. She wanted to live with Shantanu, but she didn't want to upset her mother. You ask Promila, she told Shantanu.

He waited until he was alone with Promila one day in the den of the Dhawans' Deltona home. Shantanu started his preamble.

"Do you think a court marriage is a marriage?" he said. "I think it is."

Promila opened her mouth, as if to say something, but Shantanu kept on talking.

"I want to move in with Vibha," he said.

Promila couldn't believe her ears. There was marriage in the eyes of the law. Then there was marriage in the eyes of God. To live together without Hindu sanction conflicted with tradition.

But moving to the United States had taught Promila this: Adaptation was part of life. She had cut her hair when she first arrived. She had let her American friends call her "Pam," and now she was allowing her daughter to marry a non-Punjabi.

Promila listened to Shantanu. His plea wasn't coming from an American. It was coming from an Indian.

"Okay," she said.

Vibha was stunned at her mother's approval. But not Shantanu.

"She is very open-minded," he said.

* * *

On Jan. 18, 2004, Vibha and Shantanu exchanged rings in Deltona in front of relatives. Two days later, they were married in the hallway of the Volusia courthouse. Only nine people attended, plus a small crowd of bystanders who were at the courthouse to pay traffic tickets: a woman in an embroidered lighthouse sweater, a man holding a motorcycle helmet, a woman with long acrylic fingernails who admired Vibha's lavender sari.

From a red folder, the deputy clerk read words born of another culture's traditions: "For better and worse, for richer and poorer, in sickness and health . . . I now pronounce you husband and wife. You may kiss the bride."

But there was no kissing in front of relatives.

Rose petals fell upon the two.

"You happy now?" Vibha's father whispered to her.

"Yes."

On Valentine's Day 2004, Shantanu and Vibha moved into a two-bedroom apartment off Fletcher Avenue in Tampa. The newlyweds had a roommate, Promila's sister Poonam, 63, who was visiting from Mumbai.

In the evenings, Vibha and Shantanu held hands and hugged in front of Poonam. When bedtime came, Shantanu headed north down a narrow hallway to a room with a twin bed and a huge Shelby Mustang poster.

Family and friends toss flower petals on the newly married couple after a short ceremony in the hallway of the Volusia County Courthouse in Daytona Beach. (Photograph courtesy of Stefanie Boyar/*St. Petersburg Times*)

Vibha headed south to a room with clothes everywhere. Poonam followed. In a queen-sized bed, Vibha slept with her aunt.

* * *

Vibha stepped off the Delta flight with her father, exhausted from nearly 24 hours of traveling. She knew immediately she was in India. Frail women wrapped in saris swept the floor of Chhatrapati Shivaji International Airport in Mumbai with short straw brooms.

Vibha's formal wedding was 16 days away. Her mother and Shantanu were already in Mumbai.

Would his family like her, the Indian girl from America? She had worked out for weeks before the flight and was wearing cream pants and a black top.

"You look good," Shantanu said, greeting her.

Vibha searched the airport crowd for Shantanu's mother and spotted a woman smiling. Maitreyee Shevade looked exactly like her photo.

"Namaste, mammi-ji," Vibha said, "Hello, my dear mother."

She gave Maitreyee an American greeting, a hug.

Shantanu's family surrounded Vibha: his brother, cousins, aunts and nieces. Vibha glanced over at her own mother, who stood alone, and wondered if she felt left out.

Outside the terminal, as Maitreyee was about to step into the car, Vibha gave the Indian greeting. She knelt to touch Maitreyee's feet.

"Why don't you come over to our place?" Vibha asked her new family.

The U.S. dollar stretches far in India and Promila had been able to rent a three-bedroom apartment for the family's monthlong stay. She had also hired a car and a driver.

Vibha hardly knew what to say to her in-laws in the car. She showed them her engagement ring. She told them things about her mother and father that she knew they already knew. She sat silently for the longest time.

At the apartment, Vibha put the fan on high and served her guests tea and water. She made small talk and hugged them when they left.

Later, Vibha called Shantanu.

"What did they say about me? What did they think," she asked.

There was nothing about her weight or clothes, Shantanu said, none of the things she had worried about. His relatives were impressed that Vibha still had enough energy after a long flight to serve them tea.

* * *

Vibha slept that night on a floor mattress. She awoke to noise, the clattering of dishes and Hindi. Aunties and uncles hugged her. A 12-year-old cousin with a short bob and dangling earrings wouldn't let go of her hand.

At the Gandhi Market, three-wheeled scooters—autorickshaws— whizzed by, their horns buzzing like swarms of bees. Vibha climbed over boards and litter, maneuvered around chickens and dogs and a beggar with one leg. The smell of diesel fumes and dung burned her throat. Her clothes stuck to her skin in the 100-degree heat.

One of Vibha's first stops was Friendship Sarees, to pick out her wedding attire. A sign hung above the door: *No bargaining, fixed rate.* Mats covered the floor, as if the store were a gymnastics studio. About a dozen salesmen sat on cushioned benches. All were barefoot. None smiled as Vibha entered.

At the manager's instruction, vibrant fabrics were draped over the salesmen's arms and across their chests, as if they were bullfighters. Vibha sat on the floor. Color after color appeared in front of her: azure, then garnet, then saffron lined with mossy green and champagne, then wine. Vibha ran her fingers over the beadwork, flecks of mirror and sequins.

"I like this one," she said. "I don't like this one."

Her final choice was not red, as is Punjabi tradition, but fashionable fuchsia and plum.

In one shopping spree, Vibha and her family spent 100,000 rupees, about $2,200, the sum an Indian might earn in a year.

* * *

She was an American in India, hiding behind sunglasses. Her fancy Indian outfits—bought at the best stores in America—seemed out of place.

Vibha complained endlessly about the heat. She retreated for hours to the only room in the apartment with air-conditioning.

Language shut her out. Shantanu's family spoke Marathi. Vibha would turn to him for help: "Translation?" She barely understood the formal Hindi the TV news anchors spoke.

Even her name sounded different. In America, friends called her "Veebs." With a heavy Indian accent her name came out "Veeb-HA."

She couldn't go out after 10 p.m. She wanted to go to a nightclub with Shantanu, but her relatives did not approve. Dating rules are strict in India, even for engaged couples. It was easy to forget that, back home, the two were already married.

From India had come the *Kamasutra,* but displays of public affection would draw glares.

She and Shantanu settled for outings to coffee shops, like many young Indians. No alcohol. No dark corners. Yet, still intimate.

Shantanu didn't take Vibha to his old hangouts, worried she might find them too dumpy. He didn't want her to make a face, as she did that day in the rickshaw. The monsoon rains had begun, and the sweltering air was giving Vibha a headache. Shantanu flagged down a rickshaw and Vibha hopped onto the seat, only to find it was wet and torn.

"Gosh," she said to Shantanu, "if you are going to stick me in a rickshaw, at least stick me in a nice rickshaw."

"A rickshaw is a rickshaw," Shantanu said.

In India, Vibha acted very American. Shantanu was right at home.

* * *

There was one place they could hold hands without fear.

Vibha had never been to the Taj Mahal, the symbol of everlasting love built near New Delhi in the 1600s by emperor Shah Jahan for his favorite queen.

On June 21, the one-year anniversary of their first kiss, Shantanu and Vibha made the pilgrimage. They posed on a bench made famous by Princess Diana and felt the coolness of the stone under their bare feet.

The sun was starting to set. With the marble dome blushing pink, Vibha and Shantanu strolled along the reflecting pool of the Taj, hand-in-hand, as lovers had done for centuries.

* * *

A string of marigolds was tacked to the door of the Dhawans' apartment in Mumbai. The wedding's five days of ceremonies were about to begin that day, Thursday, June 24, with a *pooja*—prayer service—to Lord Ganesha, the remover of obstacles.

If a wedding was to take place without hurdles, Lord Ganesha had to be consulted and appeased.

"Pray to God. Listen to God's stories," said the pandit in Hindi.

Vibha and Shantanu sat inches from the priest on the apartment's bare floor. Agni, the fire god, flared from a stone pot. He was the most destructive force known to ancient Hindus. To bring him on the couple's side meant nothing could stand in their way.

Marigold petals and leaves were tossed into Agni's mouth. Twigs and branches, too.

Two hours later, the pandit stood—wearing the loose pajama pants, *dhoti,* popularized by Gandhi during his fasting days—and rang a small brass bell. Everyone sang the hymn that Vibha grew up hearing in Daytona Beach.

"Om Jaya Jagadeesha harey Swaami Jaya Jagadeesha harey" It began, "Salutation to Thee, O Lord of the universe . . ."

Their voices escaped through the open window, past the bird-filled neem trees and into the warm evening air.

The next day, the scent of menthol filled the apartment.

Vibha was having mehendi applied to her hands and feet by two female artists. They hovered over her, creating intricate tattoos that would last a week. It is said that the goddess Parvati would crush the leaves of the henna plant and make such intricate designs on her body that her consort, Lord Shiva, could not look away.

Vibha sat for four hours while the mehendi artists squeezed the brown paste from cone-shaped tubes. Vibha's hands looked as if she were wearing lace gloves. Among the swirls, the artists drew a drum, a peacock, a groom with a turban and a bride with a nose ring. Shantanu's name was written among the designs.

"He has to find it!" said the aunts gathered around Vibha.

"Then, he gets a gift," they giggled.

"What?" Vibha asked.

"A kiss!"

* * *

Wedding day dawned. Vibha bounced out of a hotel bed, still reeling from a party there the night before. In two hours, her body would be purified for marriage.

Then she heard her mother's voice. Promila sounded alarmed.

"Vibha," Promila said, "come in the car."

Vibha's father, Devindra, had collapsed at the apartment. An ambulance had taken him away.

At the hospital, in a room separated by curtains, Vibha saw her father lying on white sheets.

"I had a mild stroke," he said softly.

Vibha could see he was weak. "When are you coming home?" she asked.

The doctors said they needed to run more tests. Vibha's wedding was at 7 that night. Would he not be there, she wondered.

Promila spoke. She told Devindra he had better give his blessing to Vibha now.

Vibha knelt beside her father's bed and felt his hand on her head. Her sobs filled the room.

* * *

When her aunties dabbed turmeric onto her forehead, she thought of her father. When they slipped the red wedding bangles onto her mehendi hands, she thought of him.

Her body purified after being rubbed with turmeric and her hands adorned, Vibha was ready for marriage in the eyes of God, prepared to walk in front of Agni and pledge to be true to Shantanu. But she didn't want to get married without her father.

Maybe the hospital would allow him to come for an hour, Promila said. She would talk to some of Devindra's relatives who were doctors.

Her aunties and cousins didn't agree. Why risk it, they said. Let him stay in the hospital. Best to have him healthy and alive.

Vibha felt selfish and called Shantanu for advice.

"I want him there," Vibha said. "Is this bad?"

Shantanu, whose body was also being purified with turmeric, didn't side with the aunties. Nor was he wishy-washy.

"I think your dad should be there," he said. "If you think he can be there, I think you should fight for him to be there."

Vibha thought about Shantanu at that moment, the husband she had picked on her own.

"I knew I made the right choice," she said later.

* * *

Under a half-moon, the wedding of Shantanu and Vibha began with the beating of steel drums and a procession. Shantanu, a turban on his head, rode a white mare decorated in sequins. A veil of pearls covered his face. His relatives skipped and danced around him. Firecrackers popped.

The parade left the Dhawans' apartment and headed down a busy road to the Delicacy Restaurant. In a back room of the restaurant, Vibha was having a last-minute press-on nail crisis. So many aunties and cousins were helping assemble her beaded veil and shawl that she resembled a Hindu goddess with many hands.

When the procession reached the restaurant, Shantanu's cousins—in turbans and double-breasted suits—shouted "Jai Maharashtra!" which meant "Maharashtra warrior!"

Rickshaw drivers tooted their horns. Passers-by cheered. Even in India, the Indian wedding fascinates.

"Treat Shantanu like a king!" the cousins shouted.

The restaurant's glass doors opened and Promila appeared in a sari the color of Florida oranges, her arms wide open. She separated Shantanu's veil of beads and allowed his face to show. She hugged him. He had been welcomed, symbolically, into her family.

On the red-carpeted stage, Shantanu took his spot on a gold and red velvet throne.

Minutes later, Vibha emerged. Her fuchsia and plum *lengha*—floor-length skirt and blouse—glittered under the chandeliers. A medallion necklace, the *rani haar,* shimmered from her bodice. Golden charms hung like wind chimes from both wrists, to make music over the heads of those who would be next to marry.

When Vibha's grandmother, Kamlavati, married, her face was completely shrouded. On Promila's wedding day, a sari's edge obscured her eyes and nose. Vibha showed her entire face, with a row of bindi dots on her forehead for glamor.

Vibha and Shantanu exchanged long Indian jasmine and rose garlands.

"How are you feeling?" the groom's side shouted in Hindi.

"Great!" replied the bride's side. "We're getting married!"

And with that, everyone headed for the food line, where vegetarian curries steamed in chafing dishes.

It was nearly 11:30 p.m. when the matrimonial ceremony began.

Shantanu took his seat by the pandit, beneath pillars and marigold vines, for the blessing. Vibha sat quietly in the audience, her eyes forever checking the restaurant door. Would her father make it?

Then, at three minutes before midnight, a feeling came over her. She felt as if her father had already entered the room. She glanced at the doors again. One started to open, then the other.

Devindra Dhawan gives his only child, Vibha, his blessing after her wedding. (Photograph courtesy of Stefanie Boyar/*St. Petersburg Times*)

She ran toward the doors. If it was him, she wanted to be the first person he saw.

Devindra had a bandage and an intravenous tube on his left arm. Abu, the family's driver, helped him through the doorway.

"Look Pa, what do you think?" said Vibha, crying and showing off her wedding sari.

He looked at her and smiled weakly. It was all Vibha needed. As a child, she used to cling to her father by his fingers. Tonight, she held his hand firmly until he was safely seated. She hugged her mother in appreciation.

Vibha joined Shantanu under the canopy of marigolds, in front of the potted flame. The pandit dotted their foreheads with red powder, the tikka, a symbolic dot representing the mind's eye.

He knotted a red string—holy thread—twice around their wrists for good luck, long life and happiness. He called out to Lord Brahma, the creator, so that the couple would enjoy good health, and to Lord Vishnu, the preserver, so the couple might avoid calamities.

The wedding was running late. The restaurant staff started to clean up, stacking chairs, but the pandit kept chanting.

Vibha and Shantanu, clinging to a single pink sash, stood and circled the sacred fire. First Vibha led. Then Shantanu. Then both, side-by-side.

The wedding's finale was the ancient ritual of *sindoor.* Shantanu sprinkled a red powder onto the parting in Vibha's hair. She lifted her head to reveal a marked forehead, the stamp of a new wife.

* * *

Weeks later, after a honeymoon at a resort outside Mumbai, Vibha and Shantanu were back in Tampa. Shantanu returned to his classes at USF, working on his doctorate in mechanical engineering. Vibha started her new job as a speech pathologist's assistant at Foster Academy in Seminole Heights.

They were building a life together, piecing together a household: a ladybug welcome mat, a vacuum cleaner, a 32-inch TV. On weekends, they drove to Deltona to see Promila and Devindra, who was recovering well. They honored the Indian custom. Forty days after her wedding, Vibha slipped off the red bangles and wrapped them for safe-keeping, as is Punjabi custom.

One afternoon, Vibha popped open her Dell laptop to clean out her mother's little-used Yahoo account. Amid all the spam, Vibha found a response to one of her postings on the matrimonial Web sites.

The e-mail was from a young man. He wrote that he was looking for a woman from a good family, and he included a link to his bio data Web page. If Vibha was interested, she should contact his brother.

Vibha did not click on the link, but she did reply. Her note was not long. She thanked the young man for writing and then gave him her news. *I recently married in India.*

There was something more she needed to say. She typed one last line before hitting send:

Good luck in your search.

ABOUT THIS STORY

St. Petersburg Times reporter Babita Persaud followed Vibha Dhawan's search for a husband for three years. The private nature of some of the events recounted—for example, the night Vibha and Shantanu sat on the steps outside Jackson's Bistro—meant they had to be reconstructed later from interviews.

Persaud and photographer Stefanie Boyar went to India for Vibha's wedding. Explanations of Hinduism were provided by Sudarsan Padmanabhan, who teaches the subject at the University of South Florida.

The *Times* wishes to express its thanks to Vibha and her parents for agreeing to be the subjects of such a personal story.

A conversation with
Babita Persaud

An edited e-mail interview conducted by Poynter Ethics Fellow Thomas Huang with Babita Persaud, winner of the ASNE Award for Distinguished Writing on Diversity.

THOMAS HUANG: Where did the idea for your story, "A Husband For Vibha," come from?

BABITA PERSAUD: I like to say this story was not off a beat, or off the news, but off life—my life. I always knew the topic would make a good story. I knew about the arguments, the slamming doors and the tears. My father was very upset when I dated Steve, who is not Indian. For a year, my dad did not speak to me. I walked behind him and yelled, and he ignored me. My father finally came around when he saw Steve and I were determined to marry. But I did not want to write about someone rebellious like me. I was curious about the daughter who allowed her parents to pick her husband.

Where and how did you collect the information?

It took a year to find Vibha. I contacted local Hindu temples and the Students of India Association at the University of South Florida. Tampa has a sizable South Indian and Gujarati population, so I met with leaders and explained my story idea. Nothing was working until I was cruising a list of clubs at USF looking for story ideas and realized there was a smaller Indian group on campus: Organization of Hindu Minds. Vibha Dhawan was listed as its president.

I met her in January 2002 at an on-campus function. I told her I was writing a story on arranged marriages and she said, "What do you want to know?"

Over the next three years, I met with her periodically. I hung out with Vibha in her dorm, her home in Deltona, even by the pool at her apartment complex. I trailed her social activities, such as India Fest, and met her dinner companions and close girlfriends. I became immersed in Vibha's world.

How did you decide what the focus would be?

In November of 2002, I attended the annual matrimonial Charotar Patidar Samaj—commonly called the Patel Convention—and met another local

Indian on a search. His name: Brij Amin. The story now had a new title: "A Husband For Vibha, a Bride For Brij." Four parts.

I spent two years trailing Brij. An entire section was devoted to the convention. Three months from deadline, Neville Green told me to drop Brij and boil the convention down to a few paragraphs. I could have pitched a fit, but Neville phrased it just right: "You have a Romeo and Juliet who don't meet." I could only nod in agreement.

How did you organize your story?

Part One is background. Part Two shows the process of the arranged marriage, including its modernization. This section is fashioned like a whodunit, intended to leave the reader guessing the chosen suitor. Part Three is the wedding.

I wanted to start the story with the trip to the *pandit* [a Hindu priest] because of my experience. I also wanted to start with Vibha's name and not with "They were in the car." A pet peeve of mine is when stories about minorities start with "they," a term that can be demeaning when referring to an ethnic group.

How many drafts did you do?

Writing is rewriting, isn't that the saying? I wrote eight versions and many drafts, some composed before editors came on board.

What revisions did you make to the story before publishing?

The story was cut dramatically. Part One dropped from 1,000 lines to 750 to finally 430 lines. Lots of great stuff was cut. Neville wielded the knife. I did not scream. I wanted the reader to finish the story. Also, before publishing, we moved much of the Hinduism explanations of the wedding ceremony to the multimedia package (http://www.sptimes.com/2004/webspecials04/indianwoman). On the Web site, I narrate customs shown in Stefanie Boyar's photographs.

What role did your editor play?

Patty Ryan, a gifted wordsmith, was the line editor. Her words of wisdom: Tell the story from the inside out. Blend historical sections into the personal story. Patty felt we had the opportunity to tell this story from an insider's perspective. She wanted the reader to look up in the sari shop and see what Vibha (and I) saw, to feel what Vibha felt.

Neville Green was the architect, shaping structure. He encouraged me to use pop culture as a common ground. He also pushed for the story in ways that I am eternally grateful. He and Patty did not balk when they found out the wedding would be held in India. I think this shows the lengths the *St. Petersburg Times* will go to pursue a good story.

It took three years of reporting to produce the series. What challenges came up because of that long period?

The first time I was supposed to formally interview Vibha, she did not show up. I knew then the story would be full of obstacles. Would she wiggle out at the end? Would her husband disapprove of a reporter? For the longest time, we did not know if Vibha would marry. Our story needed some kind of satisfying conclusion. Editors were anxious to wrap it up, almost as much as Vibha's mom.

What techniques did you use to manage and organize your reporting over the years?

I taped most interviews. I did not transcribe word for word; I merely listened to the conversation again—and sometimes again—to make sure I had quotes and details right.

I catalogued my notes into files: Vibha's parents, Sandeep, New Zealand suitor. I wrote long stretches of scenes and pieced the vignettes together chronologically. Then, I worked on sequence.

How did you approach writing the stories during the three years?

I wrote as I went along. It helped me track my notes and the story, which was evolving before my eyes. If I wrote only at the end, I think I would have freaked out.

I spent much of 2004 writing. After Vibha's engagement in January 2004, my general assignment duties were lessened until I went to India in June. When I returned, I had solid work time on the story, about five months.

What tips would you have for reporters who are about to embark on a long-term project like this?

Be patient. I could tell Vibha would ultimately marry by the determination in Promila's eyes. Of course, you cannot tell a daily metro editor, "Uh, I have to work on my project because I see a twinkle of hope." You do what you have to do. But I always returned to Vibha. The topic deserved my attention.

You were a metro reporter at the time. How did you juggle reporting this series with other assignments?

I met Vibha mostly after work because that was when she was available. Our meetings sometimes lasted hours, occurring weekly or monthly depending on what was going on in her life. I blocked off the days that I had to travel to Deltona to see Promila, Vibha's mother. I came in early and wrote for a good two hours before my day became busy. I also listened to my tapes and researched subjects such as dowries and the caste system while waiting for phone calls. I wrote sometimes on Sunday because it was quiet. I did not think of it as work. I really loved reporting this story.

There are several scenes in the stories that were reconstructed because they occurred in the past or in a private setting. What is your philosophy about reconstructing scenes in narratives?

Are we ever there for the murder? The best we can do is interview the witness as a detective would. I felt Vibha was a reliable primary source. I spent lots of time with her.

To reconstruct scenes, I asked her step-by-step questions. "What happened next? And next?" She knew my technique—that I would ask about clothing, her thoughts, what she ate. I am a very direct writer and tend not to stray far from my subject's account.

What techniques did you use to reconstruct the scenes and ensure their accuracy?

For Vibha and Shantanu's first date, for example, I interviewed both of them. I retraced their steps that night and had Vibha show me the outfit she wore.

I asked her questions repeatedly to make sure she did not mix up facts. Of course, lapses in memory occurred. For example, Vibha did not remember the exact moment she decided to accept the arranged marriage. We simply stated she could not remember in the text.

Some scenes are verbatim, such as Promila's account of meeting her husband, Devindra. I was merely a conduit.

In the newspaper, we ran a box alongside the story noting the sources of our story.

You include some e-mails and snatches of dialogue between Vibha and her would-be suitors. Did you have to navigate any privacy issues on using those communications? Were you able to interview any of the suitors?

Vibha volunteered the e-mails. The telephone conversations were recounted to me sometimes days after they occurred. Perhaps, in hindsight, I could have interviewed the suitors, but the story was from Vibha's perspective and we were honest with the readers, telling them in a box the conversations came from Vibha. I felt she was telling me the truth. She did not try to sugarcoat the dialogue. She told me when Sandeep asked her about sex and her weight, sensitive issues with her.

Why were you passionate about telling Vibha's story?

I felt the story clarified misconceptions about Indians and arranged marriages, that it is not always a forced situation. Choice is a factor. Children and parents can meet halfway.

You're a Guyana native of Indian descent. How did your personal background help you in reporting the series? Could a reporter with a different background have reported this series?

I've been thinking about this. Honestly, I don't know. I never feel that you have to be an immigrant to write a good immigrant story. I write about all kinds of people different from myself—Koreans, Filipinos, African Americans, gays—and I'd like to think I give those stories sensitivity and understanding also.

I can tell you, though, because of my background, I knew what questions to ask for this series. I knew to ask about the pandit, because I remember the swami coming to my house and using astrology to predict my marital future. I knew to ask about the strictness of Indian parents, because I experienced it.

I knew what to expect at the Indian wedding, so I was able to prep Stefanie Boyar, the photographer. I knew we'd have to walk during the procession and that the wedding would run late.

Being Indian did not always guarantee trust, though. At the Patel Convention, I met a young woman named Sapna whom I wanted to follow. I even had a title—"Sapna's Search"—but she was suspicious of motives, claiming I wanted to write about how the caste system was perpetuated in America. She looked at me as if I were betraying my people.

What kinds of stories are you attracted to? How did your immigrant family experience shape your approach as a journalist?

My background has taught me that people live amazing lives. When my parents came to America, my dad drove a taxicab and my mom worked at Woolworth's. They are now small-business owners. I really like personal tales from regular people: the veteran Red Lobster waiter adored by his customers, the elderly couple who disco dance, the housewives who play tennis all day and find friendship.

Did your personal background ever get in the way or hinder your reporting of the series?

Being Indian did not always help. In India, Vibha's relatives would address me in Hindi, which I do not speak. "But you look Indian," one said.

Sticking to one's own is not a concept I embrace. Still, I understand the need for immigrants to preserve their history and identity in a melting pot like America.

The series takes a non-judgmental stance on the custom of arranged marriages. Did you have an opinion about the custom before reporting the series, and did your opinion change at all afterward?

Yes, my opinion changed. I see the benefits now of having parental involvement. It might have saved me from heartache in college. Still, I would have married Steve.

One powerful dimension of the series is its depiction of Indian culture, both in the United States and in India. Even with your background, did you have to learn more about the culture? How did you go about educating yourself?

I became more Indian researching this story. I met often with Sudarsan Padmanabhan, who teaches Hinduism at USF. I talked to pandits in America and India. I read books on India and Indian culture and Hindu gods and goddesses. I recorded television programs (using TiVo) about India just so I could learn everything I could on the subject. I read non-fiction—S. Mitra Kalita's "Suburban Sahibs"—and fiction, simply for inspiration, authors like Chitra Banerjee Divakaruni and Jhumpa Lahiri.

The adage goes: Write about what you know. Here, I also wrote about what I wanted to know.

You do a wonderful job painting this melange of customs and traditions that immigrant kids face as they grow up in the United States—in Vibha's case, the melding of Indian and American cultures. How did you go about looking for examples of that?

I remember as a child being dragged to Indian functions, sitting on hard floors and being bored out of my mind. I asked Vibha about her experience with *poojas* [prayer services]. I asked Promila what Vibha was allowed to wear as a teenager. I remember my father quibbled when he found out I had to wear an off-the-shoulder drape for my senior picture.

You also do a wonderful job in exploring the tensions and contradictions within Vibha, as well as the tensions between Vibha and her parents. Why was it important for you to explore these tensions?

Cultural wars were played out in Vibha and Promila's relationship. I saw the weakness and strength in Vibha (strong-minded and submissive in one body) and the highs and lows of her relationship with her parents. To me, this was reality.

Vibha and Promila placed great trust in you. They both opened up to you and gave you incredible access. How did you earn their trust? Over the three years, did the family ever balk or try to back out of the story?

I was scared to meet Promila. When I finally saw her, I thought she looked very motherly.

It is important to me that my subjects know my motives. If Promila asked me, "Why do you want to know that?" I would explain. I told them in the beginning I wanted a truthful story, the ups and downs. I knew Promila and I were on the same page when I heard her explain my presence to a relative: Babita is writing about East/West clash.

I think Vibha and I connected not because we were Indian. I am West Indian and she is East Indian and there are many differences there. I think we clicked because we were American—in similar situations. I really see the story as an American tale.

And yes, I lived in fear that Vibha would "break up" with me. She did not call for months after Sandeep. I gave her space. Then I sent her an e-mail.

Even though Vibha is the focus of the series, Promila's participation in the story adds such depth and resonance. Immigrant families are often hard to crack. Why do you think Promila agreed to participate?

Promila knew families torn because of marriage disagreements. She could see the story was not just about her family. It was a vehicle to tell a greater story. In our first meeting, she asked me, "Will the story help parents understand? Will it help them to talk to their kids?" I said, "I hope so."

Both Vibha and Promila seem to have changed over the years. Vibha increasingly embraces her parents' culture, while Promila seems to become more and more flexible and adaptable. Did this surprise you? Were Vibha and Promila aware of these changes within themselves?

Promila and Vibha evolved before my eyes, to my surprise. I think Promila perceived these changes more than Vibha. Promila knew she was adapting.

Often, in very personal narratives like this, there are things that the subjects ask you to leave out, perhaps because they're embarrassed or they don't want to look bad. Did that ever come up? How did you handle that?

Vibha asked me to leave out one thing, which I did. It really was not necessary to the story.

I'm not going to ask you to divulge Vibha's secrets, but were you able to talk to your editors about the one thing you left out? Did you and they discuss whether her privacy outweighed any greater glimpse the reader could have into her life?

I mentioned it to them casually at first (a tactic of mine). I was afraid they would force me to include the material, but they did not. The editors were very sensitive to Vibha, and we did talk, for example, about how much of Vibha's dating history—prior to agreeing to the arranged marriage—needed to be in the newspaper. We did not want the story to be a gratuitous look at someone's love life.

You've talked about wanting to understand the mind-set of immigrant parents. Why is that? Did you feel that you accomplished that in the series? What have you come to understand?

I have come to understand my own upbringing. Immigrant parents really have a task on their hands. American culture can gobble up their ancient customs in one generation and that is a loss. This series explores that mind-set, but of course, more can be written. You could go deeper. For example, you could write this story strictly from Promila's stance.

A large portion of Part Three takes the reader through the intricacies and pageantry of an Indian wedding. Why was including that important to you, and what do you hope the reader learns from that?

"Colorful" is a word often used to describe Indian weddings—and stories. I aimed beyond the visual. I wanted the reader to understand the *pandit*'s chants, to know the significance of the *tikka* and *sindoor*. [*Tikka* is a symbolic dot of red powder worn on the forehead to represent the mind's eye. *Sindoor* is an ancient ritual that is the finale of the wedding ceremony.] I wanted the reader to experience the wedding—religious and fun parts. I wanted to make the foreign more familiar.

The series, to me, is about a search—or a set of searches. Not only the search for love, but also for identity, for a way to adapt traditions, for a way to make a life within two cultures. Was that your focus as you started reporting the stories, or did that theme emerge later on?

The original slug for the story was "search." (This later changed to "Vibha.") Identity emerged as a theme during my interviews with Promila. She told me she used to fret when Vibha was young: Is this child Indian or American? I could relate. When our family first came to America, my sister Nivedita changed her name briefly to Penny in grade school (after the daughter in the television series "Lost in Space"). I used to wonder myself: Who am I? I was born in Guyana, a former British colony in South America. My heritage is Indian, tinged with Caribbean customs. I was raised in New York and Georgia. "American" seems to be the simplest label.

Narratives often get a tremendous response from readers. What kind of response did you get? What kind of response did Vibha and Promila get?

I received about 100 responses, more online guest book entries and e-mails than calls, although a caller inquired if Vibha was available after Part One was published. I told him to read on. The responses were thoughtful, readers philosophizing about culture, marriage and values. One e-mail writer said American families should adopt the arranged marriage.

My harshest critics were Indian. One said the story was a typical "Desi" (a term for Indian person) story.

Promila received responses from friends and relatives in India, who read the story online.

News about the ASNE diversity award made the *Times of India* and the Marathi-language paper in Mumbai. Vibha was a celebrity for a while, although one friend chided her, "I would not have told a reporter so much."

What do you hope the reader comes away with after reading the series?

Readers from various backgrounds connected with this story, which I liked. Many told me the story altered their perceptions of arranged marriages. I felt I did my job.

Editor's Note: We also asked Persaud, "What lesson or lessons did you learn or re-learn during the writing of this story that might be of help to others interested in the pursuit of excellence?" This is her response.

For the longest time I cringed when an editor handed me a story about Indians. I remember once an editor slipped a *New York Times* article in my mailbox. It was about second-generation Indians who ran high-end hotels, unlike their parents who ran roadside inns. I pushed the article aside and thought, "Gosh, is that all they think I can write?" I wanted to cover cops and write dramatic tales of life and death. I did not want to be pegged.

Many minority reporters reach this dilemma at some point in their careers, whether they are Indian, Korean or African American. Do I write about my people? How much do I write about my people?

I can honestly say that "A Husband For Vibha" was the most fulfilling story I have ever written. It put me in touch with my heritage and gave me a chance to visit my ancestral homeland, India, for the first time.

My lesson learned is this, and here goes my sports analogy: If you played soccer as a teen and want—emphasis on want—to write about the subject, you already have a head start. You know the rules and the spirit of the game. You can write with authority and depth.

So spread your wings. Write the cops and schools stories, but know that you also have a huge reservoir of ideas right in your back yard, and such stories can only make the newspaper a richer and more interesting product, which is the goal.

Other Lessons

Like your subject. I know we are supposed to be objective journalists, but I really liked Vibha Dhawan, and I wanted others to like her also.

Use humor. There is something amusing about an overbearing mother. Promila, Vibha's mother, reminded me of the mom in "Bend It Like Beckham" who scolds her daughter for not making round *chapatis*. Life is humor and sadness. Stories should be also.

Listen for a good subject. Both Vibha and Promila spoke with passion and in great detail. They did not censor themselves. I knew they could be personal.

Have chats, not interviews. I told Vibha about my husband, my father, my beagle. She knew where I was coming from. In a long-term relationship such interaction is necessary.

Go beyond the surface. If you notice, Vibha's story does not have long descriptions of her appearance. I never mention her shade of lipstick. What I wanted from her was her heart and her soul and her mind.

The power of one. Sometimes it is best to tell a story through one set of eyes. But that someone has to be pretty special. Vibha embodied the modern Indian-American woman.

Give them you. I'd like to think that we are hired not only because we perform a skill—i.e., writing, checking public records—but also because we bring personality to the table. We reach into your life, your background, your interests. We pull out something that can only come from you.

Writers' Workshop

1. In Part One, what details and anecdotes does Babita Persaud use to reveal the personalities of Vibha Dhawan and her parents? How does Persaud set up the tension that exists between Dhawan and her parents? How does she set up the contradictions that exist within Dhawan?

2. Discuss how Persaud reveals, layer by layer, the age-old custom of arranged marriage. How does she use historical background, Indian movies, personal ads and the Patel Convention to provide different glimpses of the tradition?

3. The series takes a non-judgmental stance on arranged marriages. What are the upsides and downsides portrayed in the series? Debate the topic.

4. Persaud devotes an entire section to the young lives of Promila and Devindra Dhawan, Vibha's parents. Why do you think she does this? What important things do we learn about Promila and Devindra? What do we learn about Promila's attitudes toward marriage?

5. Baskin-Robbins. "The Bachelor." "Fear Factor." Persaud includes many American pop culture references in the series. What is her purpose in doing so? What effect do these pop culture references have on how you perceive Vibha Dhawan and her friends? Examine, in particular, the use of "The Bachelor" in Part Two. What similarities and differences does "The Bachelor" have with the custom of arranged marriage?

6. Rather than tell us, Persaud shows us what Dhawan and Shantanu Shevade's relationship is like. For example, study the first section of Part Three. Discuss how Persaud uses action and dialogue to reveal what Dhawan and Shevade's dreams are and how they interact as a couple.

7. "A Husband For Vibha" is not just Vibha's story, but Promila's as well. How did Vibha change over the three years that the series covers? How did Promila evolve? Persaud talked about wanting to

"understand the mind-set of immigrant parents." Through Promila's evolution, what do we learn about that mind-set?

8. The series involves a set of searches that an immigrant family undertakes. Identify some of these searches. How does Persaud develop them in the series?

Assignment Desk

1. There are several reconstructed scenes in "A Husband For Vibha." To work on your skills at reconstruction, interview someone about a dramatic event that occurred in that person's life. Ask enough detailed questions that you can reconstruct the event. After you have written a first draft, go back to the person you've interviewed. Check your facts and ask follow-up questions.

2. Persaud uses dialogue between characters to advance her story. Practice using dialogue in your stories. Go to a public place, listen in on a conversation and, in a notebook, record what you hear.

3. In stories about other cultures, it's important to explain unfamiliar customs in a clear and concise way. As an exercise, select another culture's custom that interests you. Do some research on it to get more background. Write three or four paragraphs explaining the custom.

4. As a follow-up, find someone who observes the custom you researched. Interview him. Conduct an interview asking what that person remembers about the custom, how he observes it and how it has shaped his life. Write a story about this person's experience, and weave in your three or four paragraphs of explanatory text.

5. In reporting stories about other cultures and countries, sometimes you have to interview people who don't speak your language. To practice doing this, find a family in which one person speaks English and another person speaks a second language. Interview the second person by getting the first person's help as a translator.

Helen O'Neill
Non-Deadline Writing

Associated Press

In its 152-year history, The Associated Press has granted the title "special correspondent" to only 22 people. Helen O'Neill earned the distinction in 2001. Her specialty: tales of high adventure and human drama.

Before reconstructing "Kidnapping Grandma Braun," O'Neill was one of the first journalists to dive to the Titanic, spending 11 and a half hours at the bottom of the ocean in a three-person Russian submersible. She also flew over a remote Alaskan glacier in a tiny Super Cub for a story about a lost plane rumored to be loaded with Chiang Kai-shek's gold.

A native of Dublin, Ireland, O'Neill graduated from University College Dublin with bachelor's and master's degrees and spent a decade as a reporter for newspapers in Connecticut, including *The Hartford Courant*. She joined the AP as a writer based in New York in 1996 and became a national writer the following year. In 2005, she took "a yearlong break from full-time journalism," she said, "in order to build a house on a little island in Connecticut." She plans to rejoin the AP in 2006.

Among her many writing awards are the Ernie Pyle Award, the James K. Batten Award, four National Headliner Awards, two Associated Press Managing Editor awards, three Front Page Awards from the Newswomen's

Club of New York for stories related to Sept. 11, 2001, and a 2003 Front Page Award for a story about a dying father finding a new family for his children.

Looking for story ideas one day in 2003, O'Neill came upon news of 88-year-old Heddie Braun's kidnapping in rural Wisconsin. But she had to wait nearly a year before she was able to persuade Braun's family to co-operate.

"Kidnapping Grandma Braun" is based on exhaustive reporting and classic serial narrative form, the suspenseful combination of fact and chronology that has been bringing newspaper readers back for more since a young reporter for London's *Morning Chronicle* named Charles Dickens published the first one in 1836.

—Christopher Scanlan

14. Kidnapping Grandma Braun I

LITTLE PRAIRIE, Wis.—It was cold the night Grandma Braun was taken, that bitter dead-of-winter cold when the countryside is sheathed in ice and the stillness is broken only by great gusts of snow that swirl across the fields and back roads, erasing footprints and car tracks and all traces of life.

Eighty-eight-year-old Hedwig Braun was in bed reading when the lights went out but she didn't pay much heed. In her tiny farmhouse on Bluff Road, miles from the nearest town, power outages are not uncommon. Pulling on her dressing gown and slippers, she lit a candle and padded into the kitchen. She poured a glass of milk, settled at the table and continued her book about angels.

The clock was stopped at 12:50 a.m.

A sudden blast of wind. A shadowy figure in the doorway.

"Eddie!" she screamed as the intruder lurched toward her, throwing something over her head. "Eddie come quick."

But her 88-year-old husband, asleep in the other room, didn't stir.

At 5-foot-2, weighing 80 pounds, Braun is a slip of a woman whose toughness is all inside. She had no strength to fight off her abductor. She didn't even try. She just prayed as she was flung into the trunk of her 1992 white Cadillac, kept praying as they tore down the country road, screeching to a halt beside a ditch, prayed even harder as she was tossed into the trunk of another car and they sped away again.

In the darkness, wedged against the spare tire, she wondered, "Why me? I'm just a nobody. What does he want with me?"

* * *

Nothing about the phone call made sense.

Robert Mann's grandmother never called. She was almost completely deaf, so phone conversations were difficult for her. Besides, she wouldn't have dreamed of interrupting her 33-year-old grandson's workday at 12:36 p.m.

It was Tuesday, Feb. 4, 2003. At his desk at Mann Brothers Inc., in Elkhorn, the road construction company his great-grandfather had founded, Mann didn't know what to think.

"Hi, Grandma," he began. "Sorry I missed your birthday. How are you?"

"I'm OK," she said, though her teeth were chattering as though she

Eddie and Hedwig Braun are shown at their home Dec. 23, 2003, at Little Prairie, Wis. (Photograph courtesy of Joan Wolfram, HO/AP)

were cold. "I'm not worried about dying. At my age I thought I would have died a long time ago."

Mann frowned. Where was this coming from? Aside from having to take heart medicine every day, his grandmother was healthy, her mind sharp. She never rambled like this.

"Grandma, you're not dying. You're going to live a long time," he bellowed into the phone. "Where are you?"

"I'm in a dark place. I'm tied up. There's a man. . . . he's shining a light. . . . He says I'm going to die."

"What man? Put the man on the phone."

But all Mann heard was a muffled sound as the phone went dead.

Mann waited for a few minutes, wondering if she would call back.

Still puzzled, he phoned his aunt, Joan Wolfram, who lives a mile down the road from her parents.

"Something is wrong with Grandma Braun," he said.

Wolfram hopped in her truck and drove to her parents' small green home on Bluff Road. Her mother's car was gone. Her father, who is blind, was sitting at the kitchen table.

He hadn't heard his wife since they had gone to bed the night before, though at one point he thought she had cried out. He assumed it was her leg cramps. When he didn't hear her in the morning, he thought she must have gone to visit one of their two sons, Richard or Tom, who both live close by. But when Wolfram raced over to their houses, neither was home.

Back at her parents' house, Wolfram felt a growing sense of unease.

The farthest her mother ever drove by herself was to Wolfram's house, and even then she always called first. She never just took off on her own.

In the bedroom Wolfram found her mother's day clothes laid out in a neat pile. Her Sunday clothes, too. Missing were her nightclothes along with the burgundy fleece gown that Wolfram had given her for Christmas.

Wolfram could feel the panic rising in her stomach. Had her mother been in an accident? Was she lying in a hospital, unable to remember who she was? Was she frozen in a ditch, or huddled in a barn?

And what about the phone call?

"I'm calling the police," Mann said when his aunt called him back.

Wolfram hung up. She opened the yellow pages and began dialing emergency rooms.

* * *

In the frigid, winter wilderness of rural Wisconsin, old people go missing all the time. They forget their medicine, get lost or confused, drive off the road.

When Heddie Braun's car was discovered by a ditch about a 1/2 mile from her house, folks assumed the worst. The temperature was in the low 20s. An elderly woman couldn't last long in her nightgown and slippers.

Little Prairie is just a dot on the map, 12 miles from the small city of Elkhorn. It is no more than a crossroads really, a place of wide open fields and scattered farms, a place of comfort and security and trust. Doors are left unlocked in Little Prairie, car keys are left in the ignition. People know their neighbors. And in a crisis, everyone turns out to help.

Word spread fast that Heddie Braun was missing.

Eddie Braun affectionately calls his wife "my tough Norwegian," though she spent only the first six weeks of her life in Norway. Everyone else knows her as Grandma Braun, the tiny woman with the snow-white hair, who loves animals and her garden and adores her ever-expanding brood of great-grandchildren.

And so, when people learned that Grandma Braun was missing, it was as if the world stopped to join the search.

Family members left their jobs in Elkhorn, population about 7,000, and raced to Little Prairie—nieces and nephews and grandchildren and great-grandchildren all flocking to Wolfram's house. Neighbors arrived with snowmobiles and horses and dogs. Volunteer firefighters came from the neighboring towns of East Troy and Troy Center.

They fanned out over the frozen fields. They combed through the woods, knocked on doors and poked through barns.

"Heddie," they cried, their calls echoing over the countryside. "Grandma Braun."

Helicopters from the Civil Air Patrol flew low over the searchers. Her church started a prayer chain.

Wolfram trudged the fields, calling and crying and praying. When she was too hoarse and exhausted to do anything more, she went home and cooked great pots of chili for the searchers.

Robert Mann stayed at his desk late into the night, hoping for another phone call. He printed large fliers with a picture of his grandmother and asked drivers for Mann Brothers to post them all over the state. He e-mailed everyone he knew.

But the thought kept nagging him. What if there really was a man who had tied up his grandmother and was holding her hostage? But who? And for what purpose?

Walworth County Sheriff David Graves was uneasy, too. Police found power and phone lines cut at the Braun house. This was something more than a case of an old lady who had wandered off.

Graves, a 50-year-old veteran cop and former hostage negotiator, was serving his first term as elected sheriff. Like everyone else, he knew the Brauns and the Manns. His wife's best friend is one of Heddie Braun's granddaughters. He had been to Republican Party fund-raisers at the home of Heddie's eldest daughter, Judy, and her husband, Richard Mann. The Manns are among the wealthiest and most politically connected families in the region.

The money part was too troubling to ignore.

Graves oversees a staff of 84 officers and nine detectives, and more than half were already working on the case. On Tuesday, he drove from Elkhorn to Little Prairie and spoke to the Braun family. By Wednesday, on Feb. 5, he was sure.

"No offense," he told Capt. Dana Nigbor, chief of detectives. "It's time to call the FBI."

* * *

Shackled in the darkness, praying for warmth—and for strength—Heddie Braun lost all sense of time.

This Feb. 2003 photograph from the Walworth County (Wis.) Sheriff's Department shows the small trailer where a kidnapper held Hedwig Braun while he sought $3 million in ransom. (Photograph courtesy of Walworth County Sheriff's Dept., HO/AP)

At one point, she thought she heard helicopters and wondered if she was in a flight path or near an airport. Try to remember everything, she told herself, so when they find you, you can be of some help.

Briefly, she had glimpsed her masked abductor that first night as he carried her across a moonlit field and flung her inside a small, white utility trailer—the kind used for snowmobiles. But she had no idea where she was or how long she had been there.

Her legs were pinned to the floor, the chains cutting into her ankles. At first, he had tied her wrists, too, but she had cried in such pain that he eventually released them.

In one corner a sputtering kerosene tank cast an eerie orange glow on the dirty mattress on which she was lying. A few blankets were thrown over her.

She prayed and dozed fitfully and tried not to think of the pain. Every now and then he came with food—orange juice and a hamburger.

Heddie tried to engage him in conversation, remembering her training from the home for mentally disabled where she had worked years ago. No matter what he has done, he is a person, just like me, she thought.

And so she thanked him politely for the food, asked if everything was going according to plan. But her abductor never said a word.

She knew her family would be searching for her. She knew she couldn't last much longer in this cold. She would bite small pieces of hamburger and press them against her stomach, trying to stay warm.

She worried about not taking her heart medicine. She worried about Eddie.

The first day, her kidnapper had shone a flashlight on a note demanding that she read it to her grandson, Robert, over a cell phone. The note said she would die if his instructions were not followed.

But Heddie was too deaf to understand what Robert was saying, and it was clear when the masked man yanked the phone from her that he was unhappy with the way the conversation had gone.

She was still baffled by her kidnapping.

"Why me? What do you want with me?" she asked, over and over.

* * *

The ransom note was typed in black. It was discovered by Robert Mann's cleaning lady in his mailbox early on the morning of Thursday, Feb. 6, more than two days after Heddie Braun disappeared.

"For the last time, no police.
So do exactly what we tell you
Remove all posted missing person flyers
If not, death will be the end result
$3 million (in black sports bag) is the sum of life."

The words pounded through Capt. Nigbor's head like a line from a bad crime novel. Only this was real.

Staring at the ransom note, the chief of detectives could almost hear her own heart thumping.

"Oh my God," she thought, looking around at the other detectives. "We've never worked a kidnapping before."

There were so many questions swimming around her head. Where was the victim? Who was holding her? How would the kidnapper contact them again?

And the most haunting question of all: How long could an 88-year-old woman, dressed only in her nightgown and slippers, survive the trauma—and the bitter February cold?

"Death will be the end result."

Did the writer mean it? Was this the true kidnapper, or someone playing a cruel prank after seeing Heddie Braun's picture pinned up all over town?

Was there just one person involved, or a gang?

Nigbor, a 40-year-old career cop whose briskly efficient manner is softened by a warm smile, had recently been promoted to chief of detectives after 14 years on the force. She had worked homicides, even a few domestic custody fights where children were taken. But she had never been in charge of anything like this.

She knew all eyes were watching her. She knew some wondered if she was up to the task.

Deep down she prayed they all were.

15. Kidnapping Grandma Braun II

MARCH 22, 2004

LITTLE PRAIRIE, Wis.—At his home on Bluff Road, Eddie Braun sat at the kitchen table, refusing to eat or sleep, sobbing about how he had lost the love of his life. The blind, 88-year-old man was so despondent that at first his children were reluctant to tell him that their mother wasn't missing. She had been kidnapped.

"Kidnapped!" cried the Brauns' 53-year-old daughter, Joan Wolfram, when police told her about the ransom note. "Why would anyone want to take my mother?"

But the motive was clear.

Heddie and Eddie Braun live in a modest one-story home about a mile from the crossroads that marks the area known as Little Prairie. Their only wealth lies in the 100 acres they once farmed.

But the Brauns' eldest daughter, Judy, had married Richard Mann of Mann Brothers Inc., one of the largest construction firms in the state. The Manns are considered the wealthiest, most politically connected family in the area. If anyone could raise millions, it was the Manns.

"Daddy, you can't get sick on us now," pleaded Wolfram. "Mother is strong. You have to believe that she is still alive—and that the best people in the state are trying to find her."

But Wolfram knew she was really trying to persuade herself.

Where was Mother?, she kept thinking. And what was the kidnapper doing to her?

"Please, God," Wolfram prayed, "wherever Mother is, send your angels to protect her."

At police headquarters in Elkhorn, Sheriff David Graves and the FBI Special Agent in Charge of Wisconsin, Dave Mitchell, gathered Heddie's grown children and their spouses: Richard and Tom Braun, Judy and Richard Mann (who had flown back from vacation in St. Martin when they got the news), Joan and Donny Wolfram. Also there was Robert Mann, Heddie's 33-year-old grandson, who had received the ransom note earlier that day.

It was Thursday morning, more than two days since the abduction. Temperatures were dropping into single digits. Hope was fading, too.

In grim silence, the family listened as police told them there was a 65 percent chance they knew the kidnapper.

Joan Wolfram and her brother, Richard Braun, sit March 5, 2004, at Wolfram's home near East Troy, Wis., with photos of their mother, Hedwig Braun, who was kidnapped from her home a year earlier. In the foreground is a picture of Hedwig and her husband, Eddie, from their wedding. (Photograph courtesy of Andy Manis/AP)

"He might be a member of your extended family, a co-worker, a friend," Graves said. "We need to know everything about you and your family and your lives. You need to write down everything you did in the three days before Heddie disappeared. We need to know what you had for breakfast, who you talked to on the phone. We need to know the name of anyone you have ever had a disagreement with. There can be no skeletons, no secrets. We need to know EVERYTHING."

Wolfram was unsure whether she felt more angry or scared.

"We are all the people who love Mother the most," she thought, "and we are suspects!"

But the nightmarish reality only got worse.

Police would need fingerprints from every family member, background checks, too. They would need to tap their phones. They would need an ironclad assurance that they would talk to no one, not even their closest friends or other family members about the case.

"You need to move your children to safe houses," Graves said. Police didn't know if they were dealing with a gang, or if this was a vendetta. They had to take every precaution.

The family could tell no one that the FBI had been called, or that the case was being investigated as a kidnapping.

"As far as the public is concerned," Graves said, "this is still a case of a missing person."

The FBI's Mitchell took over. It was time to talk about the ransom.

"The decision to pay or not to pay is yours and we won't question it," he said. "But all decisions about how to handle the drop, how to negotiate it, how to execute it—whether we follow him, whether we take him out. You are not making those decisions. We are.

"Do you understand?"

Around the table, the sons and daughters of Heddie Braun nodded. There was no doubt about the money. They would call their banks. They would raise as much as they could.

They would hand it over willingly in return for their mother's life.

*   *   *

At the command center in the sprawling police complex the atmosphere was electric. Dozens of FBI agents poured in from around the state. At first there was more confusion than cooperation as agencies tried to sort out their roles.

The first logistical problem was simply where to put everyone, though Graves quickly came up with a solution: the newly built but unoccupied wing of the 512-bed county jail next to the sheriff's headquarters. There S.W.A.T. teams suited up and napped on bunks as they waited for action.

Police called off the massive search near Braun's home and began focusing instead on any shred of information that could lead them to her kidnapper. But with just one phone call and one typed note, printed from a computer and delivered two days after the call, there was little to go on.

There were no fingerprints on the note. The local phone company confirmed that the phone used to make the call to Robert Mann was a prepaid disposable cell phone called a TracFone.

"What the heck is a TracFone?" Capt. Dana Nigbor, chief of detectives, wondered, as she assigned officers to write subpoenas for records from the Florida company that makes the phones. But she knew it could be days before they got the information.

In the meantime, the only thing to do was old-fashioned leg work—knocking on doors, interviewing anyone connected to the Braun and Mann families, grilling family members, talking to employees at Kmart in the nearby town of Delavan—the only place locally that sold TracFones.

The sheriff's department and the FBI quickly established a joint system of command: two 12-hour shifts run by a top officer from each agency. Phone banks were set up. Photographs of the white-haired, smiling Braun were pinned to the wall, along with a huge chart detailing both the Braun and Mann family trees.

Blackboards were continually scrawled with potential leads—a former Mann employee, an ex-girlfriend of a Braun relative—only to be crossed out and replaced with others.

"There was a sense the clock was ticking," Nigbor said, "and it was getting louder all the time."

Following the instructions on the ransom note, police placed a cell phone number and an American flag in the windows of Mann Brothers Inc., facing Route 12, the main highway north of Elkhorn. They set up round-the-clock surveillance from the country club across the road.

They worked with the phone company to scour the records of all cell phone calls made in the area on the day the kidnapper had forced Heddie to call her grandson. But there were hundreds, perhaps thousands, of numbers.

"It was a needle-in-the-haystack kind of thing," Nigbor said. "We didn't even know what we were looking for—just anything that might lead us to the kidnapper."

Meanwhile, they waited for his next move.

* * *

Shivering in the cold and the dark, Heddie Braun knew she was failing.

The pain in her feet was excruciating. Her slippers had fallen off and ice encrusted the chains around her ankles. She knew she couldn't last much longer. Yet she didn't feel bitter, or scared.

She felt grateful.

Grateful her abductor hadn't beaten or raped her—her first awful thought when he shackled her legs to the floor. Grateful for the thick fleece nightgown her youngest daughter Joan had given her after fussing for years about her mother not keeping warm. Grateful she had been the one taken, and not a grandchild or great-grandchild.

Most of all, Heddie felt grateful for a life well lived, especially the 68 precious years with Eddie, the dear, charming man she had fallen in love with at a roller rink in Milwaukee all those years ago. They were married two months later, and over the years he had been a factory worker, a ditch digger, a railroad man, a farmer, and they had never stopped loving each other. They raised four fine children, and later, when the children had grown, they had made friends around the country on camping trips in their recreational vehicle.

It had been a simple life, but a good one. And though this wasn't the way she had expected it to end, she could accept it.

She had been to church the previous Sunday. A throng of her grand-children and great-grandchildren had visited on Monday and celebrated her 88th birthday with cupcakes and candles.

She was kidnapped later that night.

She understood now that she was being held for a $3 million ransom. In written notes, the kidnapper had explained everything. She knew there was no hope. Three million dollars! She hadn't even considered a new hearing-aid because it cost $1,000.

Her family couldn't possibly raise that kind of money—and even if they could, she was too old to be worth it. After 88 years, her life was over.

And so, at peace with her life and her Lord, Heddie Braun prepared to die.

Yet, as she drifted into an uneasy sleep, she couldn't help but wonder, "How does he plan to kill me?"

16. Kidnapping Grandma Braun III

ELKHORN, Wis.—The kidnapper was getting nervous. Nothing was going as planned. The old lady was deaf as a plank and she hadn't followed his written instructions about what to say on the phone to her grandson.

He couldn't talk to her—or call the grandson himself—because he was afraid his accent would give him away. He had even tried practicing with a tape recorder, but it was no use. His accent was too strong.

Even the new, disposable cell phone hadn't worked out properly. He had tried to activate it from pay phones so the call couldn't be traced, but it didn't work. After complaining bitterly to customer service representatives, he gave up in frustration and used his home computer line.

The old lady kept moaning about the cold, and though he was feeding her hamburgers every day, he knew she couldn't last much longer in the trailer.

Her picture was plastered all over town. He had to either get the money or get rid of her.

And he had to act soon.

* * *

The e-mail flashed onto Robert Mann's computer screen, terrifying in its directness.

"Are you ready to discuss business so we can send her home healthy?"

"We have contact," an FBI agent yelled, as other agents scrambled for computers and phones at Mann Brothers Inc., a construction company in Elkhorn which, in recent days, had begun to resemble a satellite FBI post.

"Are you ready?" one agent asked Mann.

Mann nodded. He had spent the past few days waiting for this moment, rarely leaving his desk, grabbing just a few hours sleep on an office sofa.

It was 2:11 p.m. on Friday, Feb. 7.

Four days had passed since Mann's grandmother, Heddie Braun, disappeared and, by now, everyone was losing hope. There had been no word from the kidnapper in over 24 hours, since the delivery of a ransom note to Mann demanding $3 million.

Exhausted by lack of sleep and lack of information, frustrated by chasing leads that always seemed to prove false, police were preparing the family for the worst.

This flyer, photographed at the Walworth Sheriff's Department March 6, 2004, in Elkhorn, Wis., was circulated after the disappearance of Hedwig Braun from her home on her birthday in February 2003. (Photograph courtesy of Andy Manis/AP)

"More and more it seemed like we were all hoping for a miracle," said Sheriff David Graves.

Robert Mann didn't believe in miracles. He believed in action. He believed in fighting whoever was terrorizing his family, forcing Mann—at the request of the FBI—to send his fiancee and their children to a relative's home for safekeeping. Other family members had moved to safe houses, too.

At 33, Mann has dark good looks and penetrating blue eyes and the steely intensity of someone who has won tough fights before—from hard-fought construction contracts to recovering from a broken back.

Even some of the most hard-bitten FBI agents marveled at his determination to complete the "mission" as he called it. He would be one tough negotiator.

"Make your grandmother human," the FBI agent assigned to be Mann's "coach" said over his shoulder. There were so many agents swarming around, Mann didn't even know their names.

"Tell him something that makes him relate to her as a person, not just as a victim."

The sender's address was bulletproof_655@hotmail.com

Mann felt pure rage as he stared at it. But he forced himself to stay calm. Taking a deep breath, he started typing, "My grandmother needs her heart medicine," he wrote. "Is there any way I can get it to her?"

Across town at the Walworth County Sheriff's Department, Capt. Dana Nigbor, chief of detectives, combed through the stack of records that had just arrived from the TracFone company. Police had subpoenaed the records when they learned the type of phone the kidnapper had used to make a call to Mann's office earlier in the week.

The records included the serial number of the cell phone and the number from which the phone had been recently activated.

Nigbor paused. It was a local area code.

She typed the number into the computer using a reverse directory service.

An address popped up: N6974 Peck Station Road in the Town of LaFayette, about six miles from Elkhorn.

Nigbor clicked on the computer again. The house belonged to Reinier Ravesteijn.

Another click—this time to run a police background check.

A picture popped up, of a burly looking guy, dark, slightly balding. Ravesteijn had been booked on breaking and entry charges in 1997.

Heart thumping, still uncertain of what exactly she had found, Nigbor printed a copy of the mug shot and showed it to Detective Michael Banaszynski.

"I think we have a suspect," she said.

Banaszynski, universally known as "Bambi" because his name is so difficult to pronounce, had a deep, personal investment in finding Heddie Braun, a neighbor of his in Little Prairie. The families were friends. Banaszynski had been in charge of the massive ground search until it was called off two days earlier.

He stared at the photo intently.

"Oh my God!" Banaszynski cried. "That's Rene."

"You KNOW this guy?"

"I've known him for 20 years."

"What?" Nigbor was incredulous. "Is he capable of kidnapping . . . of killing?"

Slowly Banaszynski nodded.

"I think so," he said. "I mean . . . if he was desperate."

* * *

"When are you ready to do the trade?"

A second e-mail flashed across Mann's screen. Nearly three hours had passed since the last one, and he hadn't moved from his desk. At the urging of the FBI, he had written about a dozen e-mails trying to re-establish contact. But bulletproof_655 had not responded—until now.

It was Friday, Feb. 7 at 5 p.m., nearly four days since the kidnapping.

"Ask for details," urged the FBI agent. "Where you should go? When? Assure him that you have the money and you are ready."

Investigators hadn't traced the e-mail yet but they were working on it, and the longer Mann could keep the connection the better chance they had.

The Mann family had already raised about $180,000 in cash. The banks had promised more. They had bought a black gym bag.

"I'm ready," Mann typed.

He had no idea that police already had a suspect.

At the command center across town, Banaszynski sat at his desk painstakingly writing everything he could about the larger-than-life Dutchman he had met years ago. Ravesteijn, now 45, had immigrated from the Netherlands to marry a local girl, Karen Evenson, after they met on an overseas trip when she was a student. Her sister was once married to Banaszynski's ex-partner.

The Ravesteijns were well known in the area. Karen had worked for years as a waitress at Millie's Restaurant in Delavan. Their three children, ages 10, 12 and 14, attended local schools. Ravesteijn, a carpenter, had a reputation as a good worker, but a difficult one—a hothead who smoked marijuana, used salty language, and didn't much care for authority.

Through the Evensons, the Ravesteijns had become friendly with the Manns. They went to parties at Dick and Judy Mann's house. Once, when Robert Mann was 12, they had all gone on a trip to the Netherlands together.

Though he had never been in serious trouble with the law, Ravesteijn had been in minor scrapes. Banaszynski had no doubt he had a violent streak if pushed.

But premeditated kidnapping? Ransom? Was Rene capable of that?

Banaszynski thought long and hard before ending his report.

"Detective Banaszynski, based on his personal knowledge of Ravesteijn, believes he is capable of committing the kidnapping," he wrote. "Detective Banaszynski also believes Ravesteijn is capable of causing bodily harm to the victim if necessary, to allow his escape or if he is pressured."

Reading it, Nigbor's heart sank.

"Poor Heddie," she thought.

* * *

By Friday evening, Feb. 7, local television stations were reporting the kidnapping despite the best efforts of police to continue to present the case as a "missing person." The family was frantic. Locals were getting uneasy, too. There were so many agents in town that people were calling to report suspicious activity—a van parked near a cell phone tower for an unusually long time (the FBI S.W.A.T. team), strange cars at the country club.

By now, investigators had traced the e-mails to the iColiseum Internet Cafe in West Allis, about 40 miles from Elkhorn. A video surveillance camera had captured a fuzzy picture of Ravesteijn. A manager confirmed it was the man in the police mug shot.

There was no doubt that Ravesteijn was their suspect.

There was no doubt they would arrest him, and soon. The question was when, and where.

Did they take him at his home, risking an emotional scene with his wife and children and the possibility that he would deny everything and never lead them to the victim?

Did they try to stop him on the road, risking a high-speed chase and shootout?

Were they further endangering Heddie's life by leaving her with Ravesteijn one more day?

In the end, they decided, that is what they had to do.

"There was this unanimous feeling that he was going to be in jail by the end of Saturday," Nigbor said. "The question was, would he lead us to Heddie?"

And was she still alive?

17. Kidnapping Grandma Braun IV

MARCH 24, 2004

ELKHORN, Wis.—All night long, S.W.A.T. team members crouched in a snowy embankment, their sniper scopes trained on Reinier Ravesteijn's house, a small, yellow raised ranch on a remote country road about six miles from Elkhorn.

There wasn't even a tree to hide behind, just frozen fields and the roadside ditch. Temperatures dipped into the single digits. The wind was blowing at 20 miles per hour. Agents took two-hour shifts, it was so cold.

Lights flickered on and off, and shadows moved through different rooms, and when finally the house went dark, the S.W.A.T. teams made their move.

In the moonlight, a couple of agents crept up the drive. They placed two infrared beacons near a trailer at the back of the house. They would be used as spotters for aerial surveillance. Then they slipped a transmitter underneath Ravesteijn's white van.

It took just a few minutes before they crept back to the ditch.

It was Friday, Feb. 7.

They would wait through the night and leave before sunrise.

* * *

Saturday morning, around 9 a.m.

"Suspect is mobile."

At the police command center, all eyes latched onto the little red dot as it moved across the computer screen—the transmitter attached to Ravesteijn's van.

Finally, it was time for action.

They were baffled by what happened next.

First Ravesteijn drove to the Ace Hardware store and bought a kerosene tank.

Then he drove to McDonald's and bought a couple of hamburgers.

"What the heck?" Walworth County Sheriff's Department Capt. Dana Nigbor said, voicing the thoughts of everyone else. "Where's Grandma?"

Sheriff David Graves had a bad feeling. The more the clock ticked, the more likely the suspect would panic, dump the body and try to flee.

He's on to us, Graves thought, watching the little red dot as Ravesteijn drove home. He's pretending to be normal, he thought. He's not going to lead us to Heddie.

For the next agonizing hour and a half, police debated what to do. Should they go to his home? Should they wait a few more hours?

Then the cry went up again.

"Suspect is mobile!"

Again the little red dot moved across the screen. Again everyone crowded around to watch. This time Ravesteijn was on the highway, heading north. It looked like he was fleeing town. Another few miles and he would cross county lines.

Graves' head was pounding. He prayed he was making the right call.

"Stop him," Graves cried. "Take him now."

It was 11:15 a.m.

Along I-43, the scene was surreal—a convoy of 30 unmarked police cars trailing the suspect's white Dodge van. Police had blocked the road from other traffic as they waited for word from headquarters.

"Go! Go! Go!"

The two lead cars swept past Ravesteijn's van and another two screeched up behind, barricading him at the side of the road.

Sirens blared. Flashbangs—small popping devices used to disorient suspects—exploded. Officers leaped from their cars, dragged Ravesteijn from his van and shoved him face down onto the road. Guns were pointed at his head. Everyone was yelling.

"WHERE'S GRANDMA?"

An officer grabbed Ravesteijn's shirt and screamed into his face. Another held a gun to his throat.

"Tell us where she's at. Where's Heddie?"

Ravesteijn looked terrified.

"I don't know what you are talking about," he cried. "Let me go. Just treat me like a man."

But the screaming just got louder.

"WHERE'S HEDDIE? WHERE'S GRANDMA?"

Detective Michael Banaszynski watched from a distance. Banaszynski, 43, is short and dark with a round face and friendly eyes and a gentle manner. The nickname Bambi suits him well.

Slowly he got out of the car and walked toward Ravesteijn. His cell phone and radio were turned on, so everyone at the command center could hear what was happening.

From the ground Ravesteijn spotted his old friend.

"Bambi!" he cried. "I'll talk to Bambi."

The screaming stopped. Officers pulled Ravesteijn to his feet.

"Rene," Banaszynski looked him in the eye. "Is she alive?"

"Bambi . . . I was desperate."

"IS SHE ALIVE?"

Ravesteijn nodded furiously. "She's alive."

"How do you know?"

"I saw her this morning."

At the command center, cheers erupted as investigators pulled off headphones and leaped across the room with whoops and hugs.

Only the sheriff held back.

"If he's telling the truth," Graves thought, "what shape is she in?"

* * *

In the police car, Ravesteijn confessed to Banaszynski how he concocted the kidnapping scheme after losing his $32-an-hour job. He hadn't even told his wife about the job, he said. He pretended to drive to work every morning, while secretly driving to a parking place where he could sleep or do cocaine.

Banaszynski listened in silence. He had no sympathy, nor any time for a formal interrogation. That would come later. He just prayed that Heddie Braun was alive.

In the car, Ravesteijn told Banaszynski where Braun was imprisoned. When the police car pulled into the drive, the detective raced to the small white trailer behind Ravesteijn's house.

Banaszynski pushed the door open and peered inside. There was an eerie whooshing sound from the kerosene tank in the corner, and the dank smell of urine. All he could see was a pile of filthy blankets, some McDonald's containers, and some kind of plastic sheet underneath.

"Heddie!" he called. "Heddie?"

Banaszynski heard a muffled moan. He pulled off one blanket.

Heddie's huge blue eyes gazed up at him, startled but calm.

"Who are you?" she said.

"We're the police. We've come to take you home."

Banaszynski put his arms around the old lady, all skin and bones and frozen. She looked close to death. Her feet were bruised and swollen. Ice coated the chains around her ankles. Banaszynski felt sick. How could Rene have done such a thing?

"You're safe now," Banaszynski said.

"What took you so long?" she whispered.

Banaszynski couldn't bring himself to smile. He was crying too hard.

"You are one tough lady," he said, choking on his tears.

Across town, at police headquarters, everyone listening was crying, too.

* * *

At first doctors told Heddie she might lose her left foot, it was so damaged by frostbite. She had blood clots in her legs. Her heartbeat was irregular because she had been off her medicine. Doctors didn't think she could have survived another day.

Heddie just smiles when asked how she remained so strong.

"I'm Norwegian," she says.

Her foot was saved, and she went home from the hospital after two weeks.

The family reunions were joyful. The church dinner to thank the rescuers was special, too. Heddie dressed in a dark blue suit with flowers on her lapel, listened to the speeches and offered a simple thank-you of her own. She showed no anger or bitterness. And she never shed a tear.

She has rarely talked about her ordeal, other than the required interviews with police.

"That's the past," she says. "We can't live in the past."

Once, months later, when her daughter, Joan Wolfram, was driving her to one of her countless doctor's appointments, she said, "I forgive him. You have to, too."

"The forgiving is not the hard part," Wolfram says. "It's forgetting that's hard."

It was especially hard to sit in court at Ravesteijn's December sentencing—the Manns and Brauns on one side, the Ravesteijns on the other—and hear the rambling apology of the man they had once considered a friend.

It was galling to hear his wife, Karen Ravesteijn, plead for leniency. She had, after all, taken part in a botched plan to help him escape by smuggling saw blades in a Bible into the jail. She ended up being placed on two years' probation.

The Ravesteijn children heartbreakingly climbed onto the stand and, one by one, begged the judge to give them back their dad.

And then Heddie's family spoke.

In letters to the judge, in speeches in court, they told of how the kidnapping had robbed them of their sense of safety, peace and trust. They have security systems in their homes now, they said. They worry about someone trying to kidnap their children.

But the worst was the betrayal.

"How do you tell your grandchildren that a 'friend' kidnapped Grandma, and tortured her like she was a prisoner of war?" asked Wolfram. "How can they ever understand?"

At the back of the courtroom Heddie Braun clutched the hand of her wheelchair-bound husband, Eddie, and listened. She didn't feel any joy,

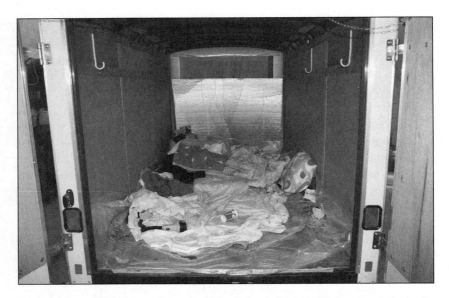

This is a February 2003 photograph from the Walworth County (Wis.) Sheriff's Department showing the interior of a trailer where kidnapper Reinier Ravesteijn held Hedwig Braun, 88, for nearly five days while he sought $3 million in ransom. (Photograph courtesy of Walworth County Sheriff's Department/AP)

she said later. She was curious about what her kidnapper looked like without his black face mask. But mostly she felt sad for his wife and children.

Not Eddie. For Eddie, life in prison was not punishment enough for the monster who had taken his wife.

So he gave a grim smile when the judge sentenced Ravesteijn to 45 years for kidnapping, burglary and false imprisonment. Heddie let out a gasp.

Forty-five years? For kidnapping her?

But I'm just a nobody, she protested.

"No ma'am," Sheriff Graves said.

Her family thinks she may have suffered a mild stroke, brought on by the ordeal. Heddie says the pain in her foot wears her down, and that is why she seems so frail and tired.

She sleeps a lot these days, more than she used to.

She locks the door now. And she always leaves the lights on.

EDITOR'S NOTE

This story is based on interviews with nine members of the Braun and Mann families, including Hedwig and Edward Braun, Joan Wolfram and Robert Mann; with Sheriff David Graves, Capt. Dana Nigbor, Detective Michael Banaszynski and two other members of the Walworth County Sheriff's Department; with Walworth County District Attorney Philip Koss and three members of his staff; with the FBI Special Agent in Charge of Wisconsin, David Mitchell; and with Reinier Ravesteijn's attorney, Larry Steen. It is also based on Walworth County Circuit Court criminal records, sheriff's department police reports, a videotaped sheriff's department interview with Hedwig Braun, and transcripts of Ravesteijn's confession to police.

A conversation with
Helen O'Neill

An edited e-mail interview conducted by Poynter Institute faculty member Christopher Scanlan with Helen O'Neill, winner of the ASNE non-deadline award.

CHRISTOPHER SCANLAN: Where did the idea for "Kidnapping Grandma Braun" come from?

HELEN O'NEILL: As part of my daily routine at The Associated Press, I spent time trolling through newspapers and state wire stories searching for ideas for profiles and serial narratives. I was fascinated by the Grandma Braun story from the start, ever since spotting the first wire stories about the kidnapping in February 2003. My preliminary efforts got nowhere. The family was too traumatized, and the police and prosecutors wouldn't talk until the court case was over.

After the kidnapper was sentenced in December 2003, I approached the family again. They reluctantly agreed to meet with me, still very concerned about the fragile state of Heddie. I flew to Wisconsin and spent days talking to family members, trying to persuade them to let me meet Heddie. Eventually, the family took a vote and unanimously agreed that I should meet her. I knew if I could actually interview Heddie, the rest of the story would fall into place.

Where and how did you collect the information for the story?

I spent about 10 days in Wisconsin interviewing police, prosecutors, FBI agents, attorneys, family members and, of course, Heddie Braun. I drove down country roads, retracing the route the kidnapper had taken, and traipsed across the fields where the searchers had been. I visited the county jail, where the FBI and the SWAT team had stayed, and saw photographs of the massive command center they had set up. I visited Robert Mann in his office, where he had received e-mail messages from the kidnapper, and got a sense of the rising tension and panic as the FBI swarmed all over his company. I spent days in the district attorney's office and the sheriff's office reading huge files on the case, including police records, a videotaped sheriff's department interview with Braun and transcripts of the kidnapper's confession to police. I spent hours with Joan Wolfram, Heddie's daughter, who lives a short distance away from her mother and who was the first to alert authorities that Heddie was missing. Eventually, I spent an afternoon with Heddie and her husband, Eddie, in the kitchen of their farmhouse, where Heddie was kidnapped.

How did you decide what the focus would be?

The focus was always clear: an old lady who considered herself "just nobody," who was, in fact, extraordinary in her resilience and her courage. The focus also extended to the extraordinary effort that went into rescuing her.

How did you organize your story?

This was not a particularly difficult story to organize. By following the chronological narrative—the kidnapping, the panicked search, the ransom notes, the rescue—the story organized itself. The hardest part was figuring out where to begin. I finally decided to start with the unforgiving landscape and the kidnapper bursting through the door and dragging Heddie off into it.

How many drafts did you do?

There were several drafts, but I don't recall any major rewriting.

What revisions did you make to the story before publishing?

The biggest change was length. I originally attempted to write the story as a three-part series, conscious of space and length, which, even with serial narratives, we always have to worry about at AP. But when I handed it over to my editor, Bruce DeSilva, he said he wanted to read more! Writing in four parts rather than three gave me an opportunity to flesh out some of the characters a bit more.

Please describe the editing process. What role did your editor play?

I've written some major serial narratives, so I'm familiar with the form and with the need to end each day with some sort of "cliffhanger" to keep readers interested. In this case, there were so many cliffhangers that much of the editing involved discussions about which one to end with. Again, the biggest role my editor played was really to encourage me to write more, rather than less.

What was the biggest challenge of this story?

The biggest challenge was getting Heddie Braun's family to agree to let me meet her. Understandably, they were very protective and very concerned about anyone "exploiting" her story.

I had to convince them that it might be good for her to talk and that it should be her decision to meet me. I also showed them other stories I had written involving elderly people or sensitive subjects. In the end, I think they felt that the interviewing process and the subsequent story helped their mother. For the first time in her life, she began to view herself (and her life) as special, not "just another nobody."

What surprised you most about this story?

Heddie's toughness. Here is this tiny wisp of a woman, 88 years old, subjected to incredible emotional and physical trauma, and she not only survived but forgave her kidnapper and got back to her life.

Did you have any models in mind—other stories or story types—when you reported and wrote?

No. I simply approached the story the way I always do, by immersing myself in the interviewing and reporting process, reviewing the material and then deciding how to write and structure the story.

What advice would you give someone interested in writing a gripping narrative reconstruction?

You can only write a gripping narrative reconstruction if you have a gripping narrative. The tension has to be inherent in the story. It cannot be contrived. Most of the time, I think the writing should be simple, spare and fast-paced, though there were times in the Grandma Braun story when I felt that more evocative descriptions were called for.

Many of the characters are described in brief, but vivid, fashion. What was your strategy for putting characters, not just sources, on the page?

I think portraying characters, rather than stick figures, always makes a story feel more real, more human. Unfortunately, because of space constrictions, the little human touches sometimes get edited out. Just a phrase here, a word there, can humanize a character—even a minor one—who might otherwise remain just a cardboard cutout.

Throughout the series, sentence lengths vary. The lead in Part One is 49 words long. Paragraph four consists of sentence fragments: "A sudden blast of wind. A shadowy figure in the doorway." What's the reasoning behind the variations?

Actually the long lead is a big departure for me. I can't remember when I've written a single sentence that long. There wasn't really any strategy.

It just felt and sounded right. I was trying to convey the endless icy lone-liness of a particular time and place and how it was brutally shattered in an instant. The longer, descriptive sentence followed by the short, sharp ones just seemed to work.

You sometimes seemed to rely on internal dialogue, as in the questions Joan Wolfram asked herself after she found her mother's clothes laid out in Braun's bedroom. Where and how did you get that material and why did you employ it in that fashion?

When I interview people for any story I am constantly pressing them for descriptions of their emotional state at the time of the ordeal. I want to get inside their heads and their hearts, to understand at some level their deep-est thoughts and feelings and emotions. By digging deeply—but with great care and gentleness and a real investment of time—I find people are willing to open up and tell me the sorts of tiny, intimate details they might not oth-erwise have shared. And those details often lend great richness to a story.

You describe rural Wisconsin in winter, its climate and community spirit, with an authority that helps a stranger understand the region. How did you come to know and understand these things?

I asked lots of questions. I read anything I could get my hands on about the area. I talked to the cops about what kinds of crimes occur in rural Wisconsin in winter. I talked to neighbors and community leaders. And, best of all, I have a sister and nieces and nephews who live in Wisconsin, so I have actually spent time there in winter.

The series alternates between two types of narrative: dramatic and sum-mary. How did you decide when to tell and when to show?

Again, length and word count play a role. I only have so much space, so inevitably some of the narrative has to be summary. But I also tinker around quite a bit, deciding what feels and sounds right. Sometimes my editor will step in and suggest that I change one section from summary to dramatic. I would say this is where most of the rewriting and editing takes place.

How much time did it take to report and write this story?

This is difficult to pin down because I was working on other stories at the same time. I would guess a month or six weeks from start to finish.

You tell the story through vivid scenes and rely on extensive quotes, pre-sumably drawn from interviews and source documents listed in an editor's

note. What conditions had to exist before you used a scene or quote you didn't witness personally?

I wouldn't portray a scene unless several people had described it to me or it was described in documents. The question about quotes is trickier and causes quite a bit of editorial discussion in our department, with some editors feeling that remembered quotes should never be used because they cannot be verified. I tend to think that in some cases when the drama is so intense, people do remember what they said.

For example, I had no problem quoting Heddie crying out for Eddie when she was being kidnapped because it's the most natural thing she could have done and because she remembered it so vividly. The kidnapper also remembered it in his taped confession to police. And he remembered Heddie asking, "Why me?" when she was shackled in the trailer. Most of the other quotes in the story were heard and remembered by several people, which is why I decided, with the blessing of my editor, to use them.

How and why was the decision reached to include all the attribution for the story in a note accompanying the series? Did the editor's note appear with each installment?

This is a decision that my boss, Bruce DeSilva, made some time ago for all major investigative pieces. I believe it is largely to assure newspaper editors, rather than readers, about the depth of research and reporting that went into the story. The note appears with each installment.

Each installment—and often each section of the series—ends with a nail-biting cliffhanger. How did you decide on these devices and why?

To a certain extent these were writing devices, but to a larger extent this was just the narrative flow of the story. These cliffhangers really happened, which made it easy to use them as a way to keep the suspense building.

At the end of Part Three, you quote from Detective Michael Banaszynski's statement. Why did you decide to quote it instead of paraphrasing?

When I sat in the sheriff's department and read Banaszynski's report, this statement leaped out at me. I thought it was more powerful to let readers see the same words, and have that same gulping experience, rather than tone it down by paraphrasing him. Using the detective's own words, I think, added to the sense of dread.

What was the most memorable experience you had while working on this story?

Interviewing Heddie Braun. Despite everything she had been through, she had such spirit and such courage.

Were you surprised by the way readers reacted to the story?

The response was extraordinary. Readers and editors from around the country bombarded me (and their local newspapers) with letters and comments. It was very gratifying.

Can you bring the story and the fate of its subjects up to date for us?

Heddie Braun died of natural causes in December 2004.

Writers' Workshop

Talking Points

1. From the first paragraph, Wisconsin in winter plays a pivotal role in "Kidnapping Grandma Braun," adding suspense and texture to the story. Study how Helen O'Neill repeatedly uses the environment's brutality and menace to add suspense and texture to her story. How well do you know the places you write about, and how effectively do you convey a sense of place in your stories?

2. In his letter nominating the series for an ASNE award, Bruce DeSilva, who edited "Kidnapping Grandma Braun," said that the series was deliberately broken into four parts to draw "readers back day after day." When one newspaper had to delay publication of the final installment, "the switchboard was ringing off the hook with readers desperate to know" how the story ended. Behind the successful strategy is a time-honored narrative device known as the cliffhanger, which leaves a character in a dramatic or precarious situation. Why do you think the endings of Parts One through Three kept readers coming back?

3. "Kidnapping Grandma Braun" is based on extensive reporting, including multiple interviews with family members and law enforcement authorities. Instead of using traditional "he said" or "police said" attribution, the source of the information presented in the series is detailed as an editor's note. Why do you think that approach was taken? What is the effect of such a choice on the reader? How did you react?

Assignment Desk

1. Like any good nail-biting narrative, this series is full of cliffhangers, those dramatic points at which things hang in the balance. Indeed, O'Neill says one of the challenges facing her and her editor was deciding which ones to use. To sharpen your skill at recognizing these critical points in a narrative, see how many moments in the series could be made into cliffhanger endings.

2. Using the reporting and writing that went into O'Neill's descriptions of rural Wisconsin in winter as a model, report and write a one-paragraph description of a place—your beat, your hometown, your campus—that describes what it's like during a particular season.

3. Helen O'Neill, like many good writers, varies the length of her sentences. The lead of Part One is 49 words while the fourth paragraph consists of sentence fragments. Do a word count of the sentences in one of your recent stories to determine how well you use variety in your work.

Using Details, Dialogue and Scenes in Narrative Writing

BY THOMAS FRENCH

Serial narratives brim with subversive power.

More than a decade after they experienced a rebirth of popularity in U.S. newspapers, serials continue to challenge some of the most hallowed traditions of newswriting.

Instead of compressing a story into as few paragraphs as possible, serials are constructed on the belief that, on occasion, readers are willing to read longer pieces—if they are offered something worth reading. Instead of summarizing the action at the top, or giving away the ending, serials allow their stories to deepen gradually, one chapter at a time. Instead of reducing a project's findings into a set of lessons set off by bullets, the insights of a serial are often woven into the fabric of the story itself. Themes are introduced, characters developed. Plot threads twist and turn. Usually the ending is not revealed until, well, the end.

In an age of perpetual acceleration, when it's assumed no one has time to sit down with the newspaper, serial narratives embrace the radical idea of asking readers to actually read.

Two of this year's ASNE recipients—Babita Persaud and Helen O'Neill—won in their respective categories with serial narratives. Their stories unfold in classic serial fashion, through scenes, dialogue and compelling human detail. Both thrive on the pleasures and rewards of unfolding.

Persaud's story, a three-part account published in the *St. Petersburg* (Fla.) *Times*, follows the story of Vibha Dhawan, a young Florida woman searching for love. Dhawan's parents, born and raised in India, are encouraging her to consider the centuries-old tradition of an arranged marriage. She tentatively agrees to consider whatever bachelor her mother finds for her, but reserves the right to find a husband on her own terms.

The narrative, based on three years of Persaud's reporting, is built on the archetypal story pattern of love and courtship, but it explores an intriguing variation on that pattern—a variation that catches the reader off guard because it's set in modern-day America. Will Dhawan find someone for herself, or will she agree to the ancient custom of spending her life with someone her mother chooses for her?

O'Neill, a special correspondent for The Associated Press, wrote a four-part story that appeared in newspapers across the country. The project, a gripping account of an 88-year-old grandmother who was kidnapped and held for ransom, kept readers on edge from Oregon to North Carolina. In one town, people lined up outside a local store early in the morning to buy the next installment.

Based on interviews and police records, the story follows every step of the case: the abduction of Hedwig Braun one winter night from her Wisconsin home, the frantic search to find her, the family's efforts to raise the $3 million demanded by the kidnapper. The most moving scenes take the reader into the tiny trailer where Braun is held in shackles, shivering in the cold and darkness. Here she considers her kidnapper as he brings her a hamburger:

> Heddie tried to engage him in conversation, remembering her training from the home for mentally disabled where she had worked years ago. No matter what he has done, he is a person, just like me, she thought.

Like the rest of the story, the moments inside the trailer are written quietly, simply, without a trace of melodrama. O'Neill's approach is respectful of her subjects and her audience. She does take an interesting chance, sharing Braun's interior monologue from the trailer. Any reader paying attention to these sections can guess that Braun will be rescued and will survive her ordeal; otherwise, how could the writer describe her thoughts and feelings in such detail? Still, whatever tension is sacrificed is more than compensated by the grace and humanity of Braun's insights and the restraint that O'Neill uses in rendering those insights.

Both Persaud and O'Neill gain the reader's trust through such understatement. They each have a strong story to tell, and they know it. They have faith that the reader will stay with them, waiting to find out what happens next.

Thomas French is the first Writing Fellow at The Poynter Institute and a Pulitzer Prize–winning reporter at the St. Petersburg (Fla.) Times.

The Philadelphia Inquirer

Finalist

Adam Fifield
Diversity Writing

18. A Cruel Past Lingers

DEC. 12, 2004

Some call it "Pol Pot sickness." Symptoms include hearing voices, disassociative episodes, depression, nightmares, dizziness, panic attacks, chronic headaches, hallucinations, sleeplessness and flashbacks.

Although Cambodia's barbaric Khmer Rouge leader is dead, the horrors of Pol Pot's 1970s regime, which wiped out nearly a quarter of the population, continue to plague the survivors. Many of them now live in Philadelphia, which has the fourth-largest settlement of these refugees in the country.

The effects of that bloody era have deepened the normal troubles immigrants experience in assimilating. For many, their lives have improved little if at all.

Philadelphia's Cambodians suffer acute mental distress and other health problems, extreme levels of poverty, dependence on public assistance, truancy and difficulties in school, isolation and neglect. And the weight of all these burdens is harming family relationships.

Cambodians "really need a lot of help. More than anybody else, they need help," said Evelyn Marcha-Hidalgo, executive director of Intercultural Family Services, a nonprofit social services agency in West Philadelphia. Yet the city and the state pay them little attention.

And no one has answered for the crimes that forced their resettlement here. But that may soon change. A genocide tribunal is expected to be held outside Phnom Penh next year, which Philadelphia's community awaits with excitement and wariness.

The connection to Cambodia is still profound for these displaced people. Every year dozens journey home, looking for missing relatives.

Without resolution, many who endured that dark period never really escape it. Today, 25 years later, the legacy of the Killing Fields reverberates still—into the neighborhoods of Philadelphia and into the lives of a new generation.

* * *

The Khmer Rouge, Maoist-inspired Communists, undertook one of the most drastic social reorganizations ever attempted in the ruthless pursuit of an agrarian utopia. Anyone in the way was annihilated.

From 1975 until 1979, when the regime was ousted by Vietnam, at least 1.7 million people perished from execution, overwork, starvation and disease.

These zealous radicals employed a particularly vicious, primitive form of oppression. They beat captives with clubs, pulled out fingernails, and cut off fingers. They slashed throats with serrated palm tree branches. They impaled victims on bamboo stakes. They smashed babies against trees. They forced family members to watch as loved ones were raped and murdered and forbade witnesses from showing emotion.

A regime slogan was "to keep you is no benefit; to destroy you is no loss."

Heang Prak was not destroyed, but she was shattered.

In a recurring nightmare, the quiet 54-year-old Olney resident is struck in the head with a club, as she once was in Battambang province. She takes pain medication every six hours for headaches, but they are the least of her concerns. Many afternoons, she hears voices calling her name. Or someone knocking on her door. But when she opens it, no one is there.

Sometimes, though she is awake and in her rowhouse, she is also somehow running through a field. And Khmer Rouge guards are chasing her.

This has been her life for more than 20 years.

Last year, she was buoyed by surprising good news. A friend who had gone back to Cambodia found Prak's son, long presumed dead. He was an infant when she last saw him in 1978. She was fleeing during the Vietnamese invasion and had given him for safety to people with an oxcart. They were to meet up later, but the chaos of battle swallowed their plan. Her son is now 26. She hopes to somehow raise money so she can go meet him.

* * *

City and state officials concede they don't know how big Philadelphia's Cambodian population is. The 2000 U.S. Census estimates 6,570 people; the Cambodian Association of Greater Philadelphia insists the number is three times that many.

Cambodians make up the largest group of Asians in the Philadelphia School District, and Khmer is the second-most predominant foreign language, after Spanish, that district students speak. (Photograph courtesy Akira Suwa/*The Philadelphia Inquirer*)

That numerical limbo—within the city administration, the Philadelphia School District, state and federal agencies, and health and mental health care providers—hampers the ability to get help.

Although no local government agency has studied the problem, case-workers and advocates say that as many as half of the adults are afflicted with profound mental anguish. Alcoholism and gambling are persistent problems. Diabetes and hypertension have become common. At least a third live below the federal poverty level; the per capita annual income, according to the census, is $10,215. Nationally (the only measurement available), nearly one-third of households are "linguistically isolated." In Philadelphia, Cambodians rank fourth among foreign-language populations receiving public assistance. The census places the high school graduation rate at an appalling 47 percent.

But the mental-health problem compounds all others. "It's become a quiet crisis that no one talks about," said An D. Thach, a Cambodian case-worker at Hall Mercer Southeast Asian Mental Health Program at Pennsylvania Hospital. "We have seen parents so traumatized they are emotionally dry and unable to give to their children anymore . . . and the families are falling apart."

Many cannot talk about what happened. "We have had no chance to settle down and mourn our loss," said Bunrath Math, a social worker at Intercultural Family Services. When asked about lost relatives, more than a dozen men and women sobbed and could not finish their stories.

"Cambodians are no better off than they were 25 years ago," said Mary Scully, a psychiatric nurse and executive director of Khmer Health Advocates in West Hartford, Conn., which provides mental-health care and other care for that area's Cambodians. "As a matter of fact, they're worse."

The pain persists, in part, because of the long duration and unusual intensity of the violence they experienced. Scully, who has been treating Cambodians since 1980, said her patients displayed the same level of trauma symptoms they did when they arrived in the United States.

For some survivors, especially those who were forced to spy on their own families, paranoia still thrives. "In the back of their minds, they're always aware of potential danger," said Kim Hort Ou, a revered elder. The fear is not entirely frivolous; it is fed by sightings in Philadelphia of former Khmer Rouge members, who have blended into the population.

These individuals, Hort said, range from low-level operatives to those whose hands are "filled with blood."

* * *

Cambodians didn't choose to come to America. After years in refugee camps, they were placed in Philadelphia by resettlement agencies such as the Nationalities Service Center and Lutheran Children and Family Service. The population grew, as people from other parts of the country migrated to the region for factory and farm jobs.

Because the Khmer Rouge targeted professionals, intellectuals, artists, musicians and monks, those who landed here were mostly uneducated rice farmers. And the task of building a community in an alien, at times hostile, place without the benefit of leaders or traditional structures was gargantuan.

Cambodians clustered in gritty pockets in South Philadelphia near Seventh and Wolf Streets and around Olney and Logan in North Philadelphia. Over the years, they have become the city's second-most concentrated immigrant group, after Russians, according to a study by the Fels Institute of Government at the University of Pennsylvania. While that concentration has provided comfort, it has also isolated them and kept them hidden.

"I think we are unknown to most Philadelphians," said Wutha Chin, president of the Cambodian Association. "Unless you live next to a Cambodian, you're not going to know them."

The picture is not uniformly gloomy. Some Cambodians have made remarkable strides, considering the obstacles they faced. More now attend college and graduate school, become citizens, buy homes, start businesses, and raise healthy families. A new generation of leaders, in their 20s and 30s and educated here, is emerging.

At celebrations in Cambodian neighborhoods, shadows and grief are banished. The camaraderie and hospitality of the old country revive, and these refugees come into their own. Like other immigrants, they add verve and diversity to a great city.

* * *

Trieu Det, 49, walked into a fluorescent-lit waiting room, worry etching her face.

Every Tuesday and Thursday, dozens of people file into the cramped offices of the Cambodian Association on North Fifth Street in Olney. Most are middle-aged and elderly with no formal education. Although they have lived here for years, few speak any English.

They need someone to explain Philadelphia's still unfamiliar world for them. Many feel intimidated by local institutions—the welfare department, the police department, the court system and hospitals—where interpretation is unavailable or inadequate. Some want help scheduling a doctor's appointment, deciphering a gas bill, or navigating paperwork from the Immigration and Naturalization Service. Others want an escort to a parent-teacher conference or a meeting with a caseworker. Without this support, many could not function.

Hands folded in her lap, Trieu listened as a staff member explained a public-assistance form and showed her where to sign. Afterward, through an interpreter, she related the story of her family.

Many parents, concerned that grisly stories of the past could upset their children, don't talk about what happened.

One of her four sons dropped out of school, joined a gang and was killed in a 1997 shoot-out in South Philadelphia. She never learned whether the killer was caught. Last year, her husband died in a local emergency room, but she has never understood the cause of death. She does not like to go out, since a knife-wielding mugger stole a treasured necklace. She did not report the incident to the police.

Trieu is among more than 600 people the Cambodian Association aided in the last year. Others receive services from the Southeast Asian Mutual Assistance Association Coalition and the Cambodian American Seniors Association. But those getting help are a small percentage of the ones with problems. The Cambodian Association, founded in 1979, has only six full-time employees.

"We can't meet all those needs, but we try to," said executive director Cindy Suy. "Because if we don't do it, where are they going to go? Are they going to miss that surgery? Are they going to miss that X-ray? These things are life-and-death."

* * *

The Khmer Palelai Buddhist Monastery, on Greenwich Street in South Philadelphia, was founded in 1987 and has about 1,000 members. It is one of four Cambodian Buddhist temples in the city.

Temples are places of solace, particularly for elderly Cambodians, who seek counsel on spiritual and everyday matters. Some feel so comfortable here, they sleep at night on the floor.

Monk Neang Thol estimated that "almost 100 percent" of congregants regularly suffered "bad feelings."

The monks try to assuage people's grief, Neang said. Live in the present, he advises. "Don't let the bad things invade your head. . . . If you get the bad things, get them out."

* * *

Massachusetts is home to the second-largest U.S. Cambodian population. In 1989, it conducted a survey of refugee mental health; 95 percent of Cambodians reported the loss of relatives in an "unnatural manner," 83 percent felt depressed, and half experienced sleep difficulties or anxiety. Using that information, the state then identified obstacles to mental-health care and expanded services to address the problem.

In Pennsylvania, the depth and breadth of the mental anguish are unmeasured. Language barriers and a stigma about mental illness are formidable obstacles to getting help. In addition, most providers know little of the history and culture of Cambodians and do not reach out to them.

As a result, the majority of those who need mental-health care do not get it, according to advocates and caseworkers.

Cindy Suy is director of the Cambodian Association of Greater Philadelphia, which helps those hampered by a language barrier navigate the bureaucracy and conduct everyday tasks such as making medical appointments. She is holding her year-old son, Aron. (Photograph courtesy of Akira Suwa/*The Philadelphia Inquirer*)

"The city fails to recognize how serious the problem is," said Thach, the caseworker. "There is such a need. . . . It is going to put a lot of stress on the system if they don't tackle this problem."

The city has taken some steps, said Tom O'Hara, an administrator at the city's Office of Behavioral Health: It reimburses Hall Mercer and other agencies that aid Cambodians. In 2000, the city gave two onetime grants, $340,000 to Intercultural Family Services, and $90,000 to Hall Mercer, to provide mental-health care and promote outreach among Southeast Asians—Vietnamese, Laotians, and Hmong as well as Cambodians.

"My sense is that there doesn't seem to be a lack of available outpatient services for people who are Cambodian," O'Hara said.

A major gap is the scarcity of Cambodian therapists, without whom patients will not open up as readily. Pat Palmer, executive director of the

Wedge Medical Center in North Philadelphia, said, "I could use two more Cambodian therapists if I could find them, the need is growing so quickly."

So quickly, in fact, that one of Palmer's two part-time Cambodian therapists, Sivann Douk, juggles the job with college studies. To accelerate his availability, Douk was exempted from some city requirements so he could receive his credentials.

Douk, 29, said some clients were even unaware they were sick. "Some . . . feel this is absolutely normal—flashbacks, depression, panic attacks. They don't even know they've been traumatized until we revisit these events in session."

Compounding the problem, say Douk, Thach and several caseworkers, is an inability or unwillingness among doctors to diagnose symptoms of trauma. Many patients who complain of chronic headaches or chest pain, for instance, are simply prescribed pain medication and sent home. Large stockpiles of aspirin are common in Cambodian households.

"I have clients who literally bring me a brown paper bag of prescriptions that have expired," said Douk. "They don't even know what they are taking."

* * *

In April, David Seng and other members of his fledgling United Cambodian American Youth Association spent more than $3,000 of their own money to host Mayor Street for a seven-course seafood feast.

Enjoying the dinner along with the mayor were Police Commissioner Sylvester Johnson, Managing Director Phil Goldsmith, and Department of Licenses and Inspections Commissioner Robert D. Solvibile. As traditional music wafted from a small stage, community members took the occasion to put their priorities before the city administration.

They asked: Would the mayor support a youth center? Can city departments hire more Cambodian personnel? What is your plan to reach out to and help our people?

The mayor and his cabinet said they would look into the concerns.

Now, eight months later, David Seng wished he had saved his money.

"There's been no follow-through," said Seng, 34. "I was disappointed I wasted all that food on public officials. I was hoping we were constructing a relationship."

Street's appearance before the Cambodian community was rare. Its leaders say the city ignores them.

"I guess the squeaky wheel gets the grease," Seng said. "Our wheel is wobbling and about to fall off, but it doesn't make the squeaking noise."

At the Palelai temple in South Philadelphia, Cambodians hold a ceremony for the dead. The city has the fourth-largest number of Cambodian refugees in the country. "Cambodians are no better off than they were 25 years ago," an advocate says. "As a matter of fact, they're worse." (Photograph courtesy Akira Suwa/*The Philadelphia Inquirer*)

In May 2003, the Cambodian Association got its first significant city grant, renewed in January, at $60,000 a year. And in July, it received $94,846 for a parenting program.

Executive director Suy said Street has never attended any function held by the association, the primary organization representing Cambodians in the city.

"We just want to have our voice heard, like any other community," said Wutha Chin, president of the Cambodian Association. "It seems like you have to work so hard, break down so many walls, to get someone's ear. We've been in existence for 29 years, and we have to remind people, call people and bring every issue to them. It's a one-way thing. If we don't call them, they don't call us."

Barbara Grant, spokeswoman for Street, said the mayor had made "an unprecedented outreach into the Asian community." She expressed regret that Seng was disappointed.

"We want the Cambodian community to feel they are full partners with us in terms of being a part, contributing to the city, getting the services that they have a right to expect from the city."

She added that the mayor's liaison to the city's Asians, Korean businessman Mahn Suh Park, "has taken great pains to make sure that various cultures in the Asian community all have the opportunity to get access to this administration."

Several Cambodian leaders complain that Park neither understands them nor represents their interests. Park disputes that.

"Killing Fields or whatever. Does that mean that they have to have the special treatment? . . . Whether the Killing Fields or not, that's their fault."

He added: "If they say I'm not their leader, if they say I'm not representing their community, it's fine. If they do that, I have less work."

* * *

Though the Killing Fields of Cambodia continue to shape their lives, many teenagers know little about their history.

At the Cambodian Association one evening, adults and teens discussed their heritage, school problems, deportations, and justice for Khmer Rouge members. The conversation turned to the death in 1998 of genocidal dictator Pol Pot, whose regime created the diaspora that had brought these people to this room.

A girl raised her hand.

"Pol Pot was a person?" she asked, surprised.

"I always thought it was just another name for the Khmer Rouge organization."

Many parents, concerned that grisly stories of the past could upset their children, don't talk about what happened.

The closest some young Cambodian Americans come to understanding these events is by watching the 1984 film *The Killing Fields.*

Chamroeun Chow, 17, a senior at South Philadelphia High School who cited Bart Simpson as a role model, said the movie angered him. "My dad had nine brothers and sisters. My mom had eight brothers and sisters. I only have one uncle in Cambodia left."

As Cambodian American children immerse themselves in popular culture, many parents hold all the more tightly to traditional values. The split within families has yawned so wide that some have little opportunity to communicate.

"They don't have the education or the knowledge of how to raise their kids here in America," said Rorng Sorn, program director for the Cambodian Association. "The history doesn't affect the kids directly, but indirectly it's affecting them."

Parents are often uninvolved in their children's education and unaware of their lives outside the house. And some parents avoid contact with teachers, especially if they bear bad news. "The second or third time they hear negative things, they cut their phone lines," said Chiny Ky, a Cambodian who is the Philadelphia School District's liaison to the Asian community.

Some teens, taking advantage of parents' inability to read truancy and other notices, have dropped out of school.

The district says the truancy rate is 14.5 percent, about twice the normal figure. The district could not provide a high school dropout rate. The Cambodian Association estimates that 40 percent to 45 percent of Cambodian students give up high school.

Cambodians make up the largest group of Asians in the school district; 2,032 students identify themselves as living in a Cambodian household. Khmer is the second-most predominant foreign language, after Spanish, that district students speak.

For that population, the district employs 10 Cambodian teachers and 14 Cambodian counselor assistants. Some advocates say that is not enough and that the district overlooks their students.

At Furness High School, which 102 Cambodians attend, there is only one Cambodian counselor assistant assigned two days a week.

Community leaders say that with so little understanding of the culture, mistakes can happen. Thach, the mental-health specialist, recalled working with a family last year whose developmentally disabled daughter was placed in a mainstream ninth-grade class.

Because the girl did not speak much, the teacher assumed she was foreign. The girl's grades sank.

"I saw her report card," said Thach, who went to school on the girl's behalf. "I walked to the special-ed director and said, 'She needs to be in special ed.' "

Through Thach's intervention, the girl at last received appropriate attention.

District officials said they could not comment about the case. In general, said Charles R. Glean, a special services administrator, the policy is to keep students in mainstream classes until a series of assessments can be performed. "We are loath to identify kids as being disabled if disabilities aren't there."

Conversely, Cambodian advocates contend, the school district strands U.S.-born Cambodian students who speak English fluently in the English as a Second Language program.

School district officials said the ESL program was overhauled this fall. Revised testing procedures will better assess who should be in the program, they said. In November, the district hired a firm to provide telephone interpretation services.

In South Philadelphia, Loe Lei (left) and Pros Phen play Cambodian chess. Over the years, Cambodians have clustered in pockets in South Philadelphia near Seventh and Wolf Streets and in North Philadelphia around Olney and Logan. (Photograph courtesy Akira Suwa/*The Philadelphia Inquirer*)

"We are doing our best to hire as many people as we can," district spokesman Fernando Gallard said. "We are a district that is not very wealthy."

Without more people, the children often miss the benefit of valuable mentors. Cambodians, said the district's Ky, have "so many more problems than any other group"—among the biggest concerns are gangs, drugs and fighting.

Gangs, including the Tiny Rascals, were a conspicuous sight in the 1990s, exacerbated by bullying and racial harassment. "If they go to school, they get harassed," said the Cambodian Association's Sorn. "If they go to the library, they get harassed. If they go to the corner, they get harassed. So they organized."

Gang violence has waned as members have been incarcerated and others entered the drug trade, according to Rudy Braxton, a detective with the Philadelphia Police Department's Organized Crime Unit. "They still have quite a few young boys hanging out there."

Nathan Ung, 18, of South Philadelphia, said he started "hanging out with the Bloods" when he was about 8. "I just chilled with them, smoke cigarettes, smoke marijuana." Ung, who admitted he rarely speaks to his parents, said he felt included by the gang. "They keep me company." Now a junior at an alternative disciplinary high school, Ung has been aided by a youth program at Intercultural Family Services.

Advocates say the lack of role models leaves many teens struggling to know who they are. "Some kids don't want to identify themselves as Cambodians," said Sorn. " 'Why do I have to go through this? Other kids don't have to go through this.' . . . They don't have their identity."

Thierry McEldowney, a lawyer who represents many Cambodian clients, said: "The young kids are in serious trouble. They've lost their way. . . . I just don't see where the end of the tunnel, the light, is. . . .

"I just don't see the parents being able to give the guidance they need, not because they don't want to, but when they try, the kids have shut them out."

Max Niedzwiecki, executive director of the Southeast Asia Resource Action Center in Washington, said given the brutality their parents experienced, it's no surprise Cambodian teenagers were so troubled. "All of these psychological disabilities can prevent people from learning new things and from engaging with each other. It's a tragic phenomenon."

To read the rest of this series, go to http://www.poynter.org/bnw2005.

HOW THIS SERIES WAS REPORTED

Staff writer Adam Fifield interviewed more than 170 people, including more than 40 in Cambodia, more than 80 Cambodians in Philadelphia, more than 50 experts, advocates, city and government officials, and national authorities on Cambodians in the United States. His writing on Cambodia also draws extensively on work he has done on the subject since 1996.

The analysis of 2000 U.S. Census data is from the Southeast Asia Resource Action Center in Washington.

Lessons Learned

BY ADAM FIFIELD

As I began reporting this story, I envisioned it as a straightforward, medium-size piece examining how Philadelphia's Cambodians were preparing for a possible tribunal in their native country to try surviving members of the brutal Khmer Rouge regime. During the late 1970s, the Maoist-inspired Communists had transformed Cambodia into a massive labor camp and had claimed at least 1.7 million lives. Thirty-five inches, I thought, maybe 40.

Then I had my first interview.

One evening in February 2004 at a South Philadelphia travel agency that doubled as a nighttime political meeting spot, six Cambodian men gathered to munch on doughnuts and share their opinions and memories. They went around the table, each telling a harrowing story from a quarter-century ago, recounting starvation and torture and the murder of family members. Within a half-hour, four of them had broken down, sobbing, unable to continue.

"We don't talk about it," one man explained to me. "We just joke about it."

I had been writing about Cambodia, on and off, for almost 10 years, and I knew that the evils wrought by Pol Pot had not simply ceased when his regime was toppled by Vietnam in 1979. I knew that some Killing Fields survivors, including my foster brother, Soeuth Saut, still had nightmares and that many yearned for a resolution they might never find.

Sitting in that small, fluorescent-lit room, as these men were gripped by a sudden, shattering sadness, I realized this story was bigger than the one I had set out to tell. This was a story about the continuing legacy of one of the 20th century's most heinous chapters—a legacy even now, 25 years later and halfway around the world, more palpable and devastating than I had imagined. And a legacy influenced, many believe, by the action and inaction of the United States.

The first lesson I learned was to go where the story takes you. Let your reporting dictate the appropriate breadth, depth and life of your story— that is, if your editor allows it. (I was lucky to have one who pushed me to expand this story and helped me see its potential.) Maybe your piece is only 35 inches, a few days of reporting time, but it could be something else, something far more significant and with a lot more layers than you had originally planned.

One challenge I faced was how to dramatize a negative. The Cambodian community in Philadelphia is largely invisible to local government agencies that do not adequately serve it and are even unaware of its actual size. Instead of letting a dearth of information paralyze my reporting, I learned to show that the scant statistics—the absence of an attempt to study this vulnerable population—demonstrated, in and of themselves, a kind of neglect.

I also learned to strike a balance between asking enough questions and giving a subject the emotional and physical space he or she needed. Sometimes you don't need to ask questions. You just have to let the moment play itself out.

Two articles in this series told the story of Bunrath Math, a 38-year-old social worker from North Philadelphia who went back to Cambodia in June 2004 to search for a brother he had not seen in 28 years. Bunrath agreed to let me accompany him on his journey. We traveled together for three weeks, and he shared with me some acutely painful and intimate experiences.

I stood by, for instance, as he closed his eyes and placed his hand on a gnarled tamarind tree in the town of Staung. The tree had been used by Khmer Rouge soldiers to kill children and may have been the site where Bunrath's 4-year-old niece was murdered. After a few seconds of silence, he said, "I can hear them crying."

As I visited remote villages with Bunrath in Cambodia and spent time with Cambodians in Philadelphia neighborhoods, I was at turns outraged and saddened by the hand life had dealt these people. Ultimately, however, I was inspired by their generosity and their determination to improve their lives and their community.

Adam Fifield is a staff writer at The Philadelphia Inquirer. *He is the author of "A Blessing Over Ashes: The Remarkable Odyssey of My Unlikely Brother" (William Morrow, 2000), which tells the story of his relationship with his Cambodian foster brother, Soeuth Saut.*

The Times-Picayune

Finalist

Josh Peter

Diversity Writing

19. About Face, Part One

DEC. 19, 2004

Friday night. Homecoming. An hour before kickoff.

In the darkened locker room, hushed but for the sound of cleats scraping the concrete floor, one voice pierced the quiet.

"Juicy!"

Jarid Caesar called over teammate Anthony "Juicy" Trosclair, captain of the Riverside Academy football team, to hear the song he listens to before each game.

There they sat, side by side on a wooden locker-room bench: Trosclair, the white defensive lineman, and Caesar, the black running back, each pressing a headphone against one ear and nodding to the beat.

It was a moment once unthinkable at this small private school in Reserve.

Opened in 1970, Riverside was founded by white residents in the River Parishes who opposed school desegregation. It was one of hundreds of private schools, known as "segregation academies," that sprouted up across the South in the late 1960s in response to the federal government's call for desegregation of public schools.

More than 30 years later, at Riverside's 2004 season opener, symbols of its all-white tradition were hard to miss.

Old block letters spell out "Welcome to Rebel Land" on the pressbox. The smell of popcorn and jambalaya wafted from the concession stand, next to a stretch of grass where vendors sold team paraphernalia such as temporary tattoos of the Confederate flag.

A smattering of parents carried umbrellas with Confederate designs. Fans filed into the metal grandstands wearing T-shirts emblazoned with the team's nickname, Rebels. And the crowd thundered in applause as 63

Riverside football players, dressed in crisp red and white uniforms, burst onto the field.

Jarid Caesar, 15, was the only African-American among them.

Ticket to a Title?

He is not the first black student to attend Riverside. But unlike the handful of black students who preceded him, Jarid is a rising star on the football team at a school built to exclude people with his skin color. In the football-crazy River Parishes, that alone makes him a controversial figure.

Some in the black community objected to his enrollment at the private academy. They felt the school wanted him not because it was interested in true integration, but because the coaches thought Jarid could push an already-strong football program to the championship level.

"They were founded because parents didn't want the white kids to go to school with the black kids," said Larry Dauterive, the head football coach at public East St. John High School. "All of a sudden they're going to go get the black athletes."

Yet to Jarid's father, Donald Caesar, it was about more than his son helping a white school win football games. It was an opportunity for his son to change a culture—both how Riverside viewed black people and how the black community viewed the school.

A few weeks after Jarid enrolled, his father walked into his son's bedroom and hung on the wall a felt tapestry of Martin Luther King Jr. standing between John F. Kennedy and Bobby Kennedy. "Gaze up there at that," Donald Caesar told Jarid. "Think about it, why you're at Riverside. It's all about the freedom fighters."

That History

Donald Caesar knew all about Riverside's history.

In 1970, the year St. John the Baptist Parish desegregated its schools after steady pressure from the federal government, Donald Caesar was among the first black students to attend Leon Godchaux High School. That same fall, he saw white students leave Godchaux en masse for a new school called Riverside.

White parents had helped clear sugar cane at the site to hastily construct an academy where African-Americans were not allowed.

Clyde Gisclair not only served as Riverside's first principal but was among the white residents who helped build the school. "I put up the first piece of concrete, the first brick, the first mortar, the first piece of wood, the first Sheetrock," Gisclair said. "You name it, I had something to do with it."

"The whole idea was no blacks," added Gisclair, who stayed one year as principal and said he took the position simply because he needed a job. "Everybody that was opposed to integration at the time wanted to attend Riverside."

One of the white students sent to Riverside was Mickey Roussel, now 48 with salt-and-pepper hair, a foghorn voice and a job as the Rebels' head football coach.

After 2003, the Rebels' worst season in 15 years, Roussel came into this fall counting heavily on Jarid, an elusive 5-foot-7-inch, 150-pound back with caramel-colored skin, shy brown eyes and the nickname "Ten Speed."

Jarid had played a few games with the varsity the season before, but this year the freshman was expected to take over as the marquee running back. In the season opener he rushed for 97 yards, returned three kicks for 61 yards and caught two passes for 40 yards. But he fumbled three times, recovering all but one, in a 45-6 loss to Destrehan.

As Donald Caesar headed onto the field to console his son, Jarid was walking off with Roussel. The coach and father shook hands.

But his son wasn't smiling.

"I know I can do better than that," he said, heading home with his parents to their cramped, two-bedroom home, which sits between Rising Star Baptist Church and the Williams Club bar in LaPlace.

With Jarid now starting for Riverside, the Caesars found themselves in a delicate predicament. Their son was well-known in the area, and his emergence as a black athlete at a school founded on racist principles had touched nerves in the black community.

"People looked at each other and said, 'Why? Why would you send your kid to Riverside with that history?' " said Mose Simmons, 39, a black graduate of East St. John High School who lives in Reserve.

Gone were the days when Jarid was just a student at public Glade Elementary, before he started to draw attention on the football field.

Changing Leagues

It was a fall afternoon in 2000, and Riverside's all-white elementary school football team was playing a predominantly black recreation league team called the Heat. Or, more accurately, the little Riverside Rebels were trying to tackle the Heat's running back.

As the boy darted through the Rebels for five touchdowns, Riverside youth coach Thomas Hymel watched and wondered, "Who the heck is this kid?"

They call him "Ten Speed," the opposing coach told Hymel after the game. His real name is Jarid Caesar.

He was a fifth-grader at Glade Elementary and just the type of young star Hymel and the varsity coaches at Riverside were looking for.

At one time, the idea of Riverside courting a black student, or a black student considering Riverside, was unimaginable. For years, Riverside officials maintained they would admit any qualified student, regardless of race. It was an easy thing to say, considering no black student had ever applied, until Michael Townsend showed up in 1987.

Riverside officials were stunned.

Townsend and his mother, who'd spent several years in California before moving to the New Orleans area, initially knew nothing about the school's history. Though they quickly learned the school had no other black students, Townsend's mother, Bettye, thought the benefits of Riverside outweighed the drawbacks.

Her son's application was accepted.

Graduating in 1991, Townsend seemingly blazed a new path, but it was a path no other black students seemed eager to follow. Nearly a decade passed before the school enrolled another black student.

The year Townsend arrived, 1987, was the year Riverside dropped out of the Louisiana Independent Schools Association, a small, all-white private school league where the Rebels had won eight championships from 1970 through 1986. Roussel, a star defensive back on Rebel teams that won LISA titles in 1972 and '73, had grown tired of critics belittling Riverside's accomplishments because the league's teams were not the caliber of those in the larger, integrated Louisiana High School Athletic Association.

Every year, when the Rebels football schedule was posted at Kaiser Aluminum, where Roussel worked for nine years before switching to full-time coaching, co-workers taunted him by crossing out the Rebels' opponents and replacing them with the names of pee-wee football teams such as the "Paulina Packers" and "Gramercy Tigers."

"I wanted to strangle some of them," Roussel, then a Riverside assistant coach, said of his co-workers.

If Riverside was going to prove it could compete against the state's best teams, Roussel felt it had to leave the all-white league. Finally, citing the rising travel expense of playing the shrinking number of LISA teams, enough Riverside stockholders overrode the objections of segregation hard-liners and approved entry into the LHSAA.

Two years after the change, Roussel was promoted to head coach.

Slowly Toward Diversity

Over the next 15 years, he built an all-white powerhouse. The Rebels made the playoffs 14 consecutive seasons. They reached the state championship game in 1993, 1998 and 2000. Riverside lost all three times.

It made Roussel and his staff want a championship ring all the more.

But while the Rebels routinely fielded talented, well-coached teams, Roussel felt the Rebels had little chance of winning the title if they were limited to only white players. Roussel and his assistants had noted that other private schools in the area had teams that were racially mixed. They, too, wanted the chance to attract the best players, white and black.

"If we had just three guys off that team or three guys off that team, we'd probably have four state championship rings," Roussel said he remembers the Riverside coaches saying.

The school administration gave Roussel the green light to diversify his team, but for more than athletic reasons. With the school facing financial hardship, Riverside applied for federal tax-exempt status, which required that the school actively seek black students.

Riverside dispatched its elementary school coaches to recreation departments where Riverside graduates such as Hymel scouted young football players and talked to black parents about how attitudes at the private school had changed. But Roussel decided that, for black people to feel welcome at Riverside, it was going to take more than talk about changed attitudes.

Before the 1998 season, Roussel ordered the Rebel mascot taken off the school's helmets and replaced with the school's initials, RA. He discouraged fans from bringing Confederate flags to games. As word of the coach's wishes spread, the regular sight of dozens of flags dwindled.

Roussel said he regarded the Confederate flag as a symbol of the South's heritage. But he knew many people, black and white, saw the flag as a symbol of slavery and racism. His goal, he said, was to make Riverside's environment more comfortable for potential black students. A year later, the fall of 1999, Riverside enrolled the second black student in the school's history.

Roussel still had no black athletes, but by the fall of 2000, Hymel was working hard to attract Jarid Caesar, the running back he'd watched overrun his team. Hymel met with the boy's parents to tout the advantages of Riverside and stayed in touch with the family. When Jarid struggled in school and Glade Elementary held him back in the fifth grade, his parents grew dissatisfied with the public school and thought more seriously about Riverside.

The boy's mother, Cynthia Caesar, a cook at a nursing home in LaPlace, still had reservations. But his father, employed by the St. John the Baptist water-waste department, liked the idea of his son breaking new ground. He argued that the decision should be left to Jarid, who at the time was 12.

As the enrollment deadline approached, Cynthia asked her son what he intended to do.

"I'm going to Riverside," Jarid told her.

In the fall of 2001, Jarid became a Rebel.

Not Always Easy

One Saturday morning, Donald Caesar was cutting grass in the front yard of his house when one of his old high school football coaches pulled up in his car. "Oh, just the guy I wanted to see," Caesar recalled the coach saying. "They tell me your son's going to Riverside."

"Yes, sir," Caesar said.

"Well, what's the matter?" the coach asked. "You're telling me the black teachers aren't as good as the white teachers? Is that it?"

The coach sped off.

It wasn't long before Cynthia Caesar began to question the decision.

Standing behind the end zone at one Riverside game, she nudged her husband when she saw a white Riverside fan waving a giant Confederate flag and running back and forth in front of the grandstand. Speaking loud enough to be heard by the parents around him, Donald Caesar said, "I hope that motherf—— runs past me."

None of the white fans spoke of the incident with the Caesars. But the couple said they never saw another Confederate flag at a Riverside game.

Another time, the Caesars were in their usual spot behind the end zone, near a group of about 10 other Riverside fans, all of them white. One of the men used the word "nigger."

Donald and Cynthia Caesar raised their hands, a private signal to each other when something offensive occurred.

Again, none of the white parents discussed the incident with them that night. But the next week the man apologized to the couple, who said they never again heard a slur at a Riverside game.

Mostly unaware of the controversy around him, Jarid took the ball and ran.

During the 2003 season, when he was moved up from the junior varsity, Jarid said, some opposing players called him "Uncle Tom" and made other slurs. He understood certain black residents considered him a traitor. Yet the Riverside coaches considered him a trailblazer and hoped Jarid's success would draw other talented black athletes to the school.

In the fall of 2003, Devante White, a promising black 12-year-old football player from LaPlace, enrolled at Riverside. His black friends couldn't understand it.

"Why would you go to an all-white school?" Devante's mother, Shontel, said she remembers other black boys asking her son.

She faced similar questions from her family.

Devante stayed one year and returned to public school.

Entering the 2004 season, Jarid remained the Rebels' only black athlete and one of six black students at a school with an enrollment of 729. Roussel knew the young running back would be pivotal to a turnaround. Despite the team's lopsided loss in the opener, he made sure Jarid continued to get the ball.

Cutting a New Step

By Game 5, the Rebels were 4-1, and Jarid was on a roll. Then came homecoming night.

In the darkened locker room before the game, after sharing his favorite pregame song with "Juicy" Trosclair, Jarid helped his teammate tuck the jersey sleeves inside his shoulder pads. The giant lineman tapped his fists on Jarid's shoulder as if to say, "Ready?"

Jarid scored three touchdowns and led Riverside to a 42-18 victory over Redeemer-Seton and the Rebels' first homecoming victory in three years. After the game, Jarid told his parents that Riverside was holding a dance in the gym for its parents and alumni. Suddenly Hymel showed up to congratulate Jarid on the game.

Hymel turned to Donald Caesar.

"You going to the dance?" he asked.

"Yeah," Donald said.

"You know how to cut a step?"

"You'd be surprised."

It was only this season, prodded by her son, that Cynthia Caesar had started attending the school's weekly pep rallies. Growing up, she'd rarely interacted with white people and still felt uncomfortable in certain settings. Now came the dance.

If not for herself, she would go for her son.

Entering the gym that night, the Caesars found themselves in a familiar situation: The only black parents there.

They watched their son shake hands with the parents of his teammates and mingle with his classmates as Take 5, a local band, played a list of familiar favorites. Donald and Cynthia Caesar stood alone, leaning against a wall in the dimly lit gym, drinking beer.

They talked about their families and how most of their siblings disapproved of Jarid attending Riverside. How only a handful of their brothers and sisters had come to see him play for the Rebels.

"We're in this alone," Donald Caesar said.

Then a couple approached the Caesars and made small talk. Within five minutes several other parents gathered around the Caesars.

One father grabbed Jarid's mother by the hand.

"I'm going to get Cynthia out there on the floor," he told Donald.

"Go on, brother, do it," Donald said.

And onto the floor they went.

Beloved Figure

Weeks later, Cynthia Caesar was wearing a Riverside cap and standing in the checkout line at a convenience store around the corner from her house.

"Oh, Lord, there she goes with that Riverside cap on her head," Cynthia said another black customer blurted out.

"You mean to tell me I can't wear that cap, the school my son goes to?" she replied.

"What you want to wear that cap for?" asked the man, a fan of West St. John High School, a West Bank school where 99 percent of the students are black. "You know what I should do? I should take that cap off your head and stomp on it."

"If you take that cap off my head, you won't be around to tell no one about it," Cynthia snapped.

She paid for her BC headache powder and walked out.

At times, the Caesars still felt caught between two worlds, the one in which they grew up, virtually all black, and the one at Riverside, virtually all white.

Then came the Rebels' regular-season finale. In the game's final minutes, Jarid was knocked out of bounds and into a metal bench. When it appeared the star running back was not moving, someone called an ambulance.

Riverside players, coaches, cheerleaders and parents gathered around Jarid while waiting for the paramedics. Some cried as his spine was stabilized and he was loaded into the ambulance. About 40 Riverside supporters followed the ambulance to River Parishes Hospital.

Relieved upon learning Jarid had suffered only a minor shoulder injury, the group still waited to see him. In pairs, they were allowed to visit.

Early the next morning, the phone rang at the Caesars' house. It was Roussel.

He told Jarid to stay home and rest, to skip the team's 8 a.m. practice, when the Rebels would begin preparation for their first-round playoff game. When Jarid hung up the phone, his father poked his head into the room.

"I'm ready when you're ready," Jarid said.

"Ready?"

"I want to be with my teammates," he said, "even if all I can do is sit and watch."

Donald Caesar drove his son to practice.

After a week off, Jarid returned to the lineup and helped lead the Rebels to a 30-14 victory over Oakdale. The Riverside faithful started dreaming the impossible: a march to the Superdome and the state championship.

That next week, in the second round of the playoffs, Jarid scored two touchdowns and a two-point conversion. But a punt that glanced off him led to a touchdown for Ouachita Christian, which rallied late for a 25-15 victory.

Sobbing after the game, Jarid was devastated. But like the night he was injured and taken to the hospital, a throng of Riverside players, coaches and fans tried to console him.

The season was over. Still, Donald Caesar couldn't help but see all those Riverside supporters and recall the night they filled the emergency room when his son got hurt, and what he thought when he saw them:

"Look at all these people. They must love Ten Speed."

To read the rest of this series, go to http://www.poynter.org/bnw2005.

Lessons Learned

BY JOSH PETER

Riverside Academy is a school where history and traditions die hard. Those who attend a home football game will see Confederate flag tattoos and a sign above the press box that reads, "Welcome to Rebel Land." In 1970, the school opened specifically to avoid desegregation. So it was significant news when Jarid Caesar entered the 2004 football season not only as the first black student from the community to play for the Rebels but also as the team's star running back.

The story initially showed up on the news budget as a "first" story—in this case, Caesar being the "first black kid to start at tailback for Riverside." The story was killed. We saw a better story out there. We decided to go looking for cultural shifts that must be occurring for such an event to be possible.

Lesson number one: Look beyond the obvious. A straightforward story about Caesar being the first black student to star at running back for the Rebels would've been fine, but additional reporting and reframing the idea proved there was a more compelling story to tell.

Academies such as Riverside at one time dominated white communities in the South, and so our initial focus was on the broad story. We gathered the facts and the figures. We crunched the numbers. We talked to the experts. Then we crowbarred it all into one giant story that never ran. Simply put, the story failed. It failed to capture the emotion, nuance and complexity so important to the story, so we turned to narrative.

More than 30 years after the so-called segregation academies opened, we decided to revisit three schools, each at a distinctly different point of evolution in dealing with racial change. Fortunately, during our initial reporting, we found three ideal schools—one in Louisiana, one in Mississippi and one in Alabama.

On Day One and Day Three, we showed that once a comfort level is achieved, things change because people want them to change. On Day Two, we showed continuing resistance from hardliners even when school administrators pushed for change. That day also gave our readers a perspective from a black mother who did not want her son to be the first and only black student in an all-white school. We based each story on a strong narrative.

That's a second lesson. Storytelling proved to be the most effective way to capture the issue's nuances and complexities.

Being a white male and the only reporter on the story presented another challenge: How to ensure we had thoroughly covered the point of view of the white and the black communities? "Too many cooks in the kitchen" has its journalistic equivalent: Too many editors in a room can spoil a good story. In our case, that proved dead wrong. One of the primary editors on the story was a talented, African-American woman. In addition to her expertise, we asked other African-American editors and writers throughout the newsroom to read the story and offer their feedback and criticism.

A third lesson: A single white male reporting a sensitive story involving race is not a recipe for disaster—provided you involve African-American editors and seek feedback from African-American writers to ensure you are covering issues important to the black community thoroughly and with sensitivity.

Josh Peter is a sports journalist at The Times-Picayune *in New Orleans. Peter previously worked at the* Anderson (S.C.) Independent-Mail, The State *in Columbia, S.C., and* The Commercial Appeal *in Memphis.*

Chicago Tribune

Finalist

Julia Keller

Non-Deadline Writing

.

20. A Wicked Wind Takes Aim

DEC. 5, 2004

UTICA, Illinois—Ten seconds. Count it: One. Two. Three. Four. Five. Six. Seven. Eight. Nine. Ten. Ten seconds was roughly how long it lasted. Nobody had a stopwatch, nothing can be proven definitively, but that's the consensus. The tornado that swooped through Utica at 6:09 p.m. April 20 took some 10 seconds to do what it did. Ten seconds is barely a flicker. It's a long, deep breath. It's no time at all. It's an eternity.

If the sky could hold a grudge, it would look the way the sky looked over northern Illinois that day. Low, gray clouds stretched to the edges in a thin veneer of menace. Rain came and went, came and went, came and went.

The technical name for what gathered up there was stratiform cloud cover, but Albert Pietrycha had a better way to describe it: "murk." It was a Gothic-sounding word for a Gothic-looking sky. A sky that, in its own oblique way, was sending a message.

Pietrycha is a meteorologist in the Chicago forecast office of the National Weather Service, a tidy, buttoned-down building in Romeoville, about 25 miles southwest of Chicago. It's a setting that seems a bit too ordinary for its role, too bland for the place where the first act of a tragedy already was being recorded. Where the sky's bad intentions were just becoming visible, simmering in the low-slung clouds.

Where a short distance away, disparate elements—air, water and old sandstone blocks—soon would slam into each other like cars in a freeway pileup, ending eight lives and changing other lives forever.

The survivors would henceforth be haunted by the oldest, most vexing question of all: whether there is a destiny that shapes our fates or whether it is simply a matter of chance, of luck, of the way the wind blows.

* * *

It was a busy day for Pietrycha and his colleagues. The classic ingredients for a tornado—warm air to the south, cooler air north and a hint of wind shear—had seemed imminent most of the morning. Spring and early summer are boom times for tornadoes, the most violent storms on Earth.

What bothered Pietrycha was a warm front that loitered ominously across southern Illinois. If the front's moist, humid air moved north too quickly in the daylight hours, clashing with cooler air, the instability could create thunderstorms liable to split off into tornadoes.

But by early afternoon, it seemed that maybe, just maybe, northern Illinois would escape. If the front waited until after sunset to arrive, its impact would be negligible because the air near the ground—with no sunshine to warm it—would cool off. *Nope,* a relieved Pietrycha said to himself. *Probably not today.*

It was only a hunch. Meteorologists know a lot about tornadoes, but with all they know, they still can't say why some thunderstorms generate tornadoes and some don't. Or why tornadoes, once unleashed, do what they do and go where they go.

That's why forecasting is as much art as science. Too many warnings not followed by actual tornadoes make people skeptical and careless. Too many warnings can be as dangerous as too few. And while meteorologists can spot an approaching hurricane days in advance, the average warning time for a tornado is 11 minutes.

* * *

What she was thinking was, *Gotta beat that rain.*

Frowning up at a sky as flat and gray as a cookie sheet, Shelba Bimm, 65, figured she just might be able to outrun the next downpour. Worth a try, anyway.

Bimm was standing in the driveway of her house at 238 W. Church St. in Utica, population 977, just outside Starved Rock State Park.

It was precisely 5:15 p.m. She had her schedule figured down to the minute. Busy people do that. But this ornery rain—will it or won't it, and if it starts up again, how long will it last?—was irksome.

She was due in Oglesby at 6 p.m. for the weekly class she was taking for her certification as an EMT Intermediate, the next level up from EMT, a rank Bimm had held since 1980, answering the frequent summons from the Utica volunteer fire department. Folks in town were accustomed to the sight of the white-haired Bimm in the driver's seat of her black Honda

CRV, yanking on the wheel with one hand and gripping her dispatch radio with the other.

Shelba Bimm had been a 1st-grade teacher for 42 years. She was retired now—if that's what you want to call it, even though she was at least as busy these days as she'd ever been when running a classroom, what with her EMT work and the dollhouse business she operated out of the front room of her home. And now she and Dave Edgcomb, Utica's fire chief, were taking classes to upgrade their credentials.

Oglesby is a 15-minute drive from Utica, so normally Bimm didn't hit the road until 5:30 p.m. But then again, she thought, just look at that sky.

If she left now, she might be able to get there and dash from the parking lot at Illinois Valley Community College and into class without getting soaked. *It's gonna be,* she thought, *one hell of a storm.*

So she scooted into her car—the one with the can't-miss-it license plate BIMM 2—and took off, backing out of her driveway and heading east on Church Street.

At the four-way stop a few yards from her house she turned south on Mill Street. Near the corner was a bar called Milestone. A block later, at the corner of Mill and Canal Street, she passed Duffy's Tavern.

Bimm turned west on Illinois Highway 71 and then headed on into Oglesby, pulling into the campus parking lot at 5:30 p.m. The western sky was getting blacker and blacker, as if something had been spilled on the other side of it and was seeping through.

All told, it took her less than a minute to cross Utica. Had she happened to lift her pale blue eyes to the rear view mirror as she left the city limits, she would have seen, poised there like a tableau in a snow globe just before it's shaken up, her last intact view of the little town she loved.

* * *

Pietrycha and his colleagues work in a big square room with a central ring of linked desks and a computer monitor perched on just about every flat surface.

Across Pietrycha's work station, six computer screens glowed with radar information that told him, through tiny pixels of perky green and hot red and bold yellow, about hail and rain, about wind rotation and velocity.

To check the screens, Pietrycha, a slender man with short sandy hair and the preoccupied air of someone who's always working out a math problem in his head, quickly rolled his chair back and forth, back and forth, screen to screen to screen, taking frequent swigs from a Coke can.

As 4 p.m. approached, the end of his shift, the warm front was still dawdling in southern Illinois. Looking good. So Pietrycha got ready to go. He lives in Oswego, some 13 miles northwest of Romeoville.

To Mark Ratzer, a fellow meteorologist with a neat blond crew cut who was in charge of the office that day, Pietrycha said, "Hey, if things get out of hand, call me."

* * *

The specials at Duffy's Tavern that night, according to the green felt-tip lettering on the white board above the bar, were: "All You Can Eat Spaghetti w/garlic breadsticks, $4.99" and "Cajun NY Strip w/onions and peppers and potato salad, $16.99" and "2 stuffed walleye, $13.99." The soup was cheesy broccoli.

Lisle Elsbury, 56, had bought Duffy's a year ago. Buying it meant leaving behind the life he knew as a heating and air conditioning repairman in Lyons, and slapping down all his chips right here in Utica.

Elsbury was a compact man with a nervous energy that seemed to oscillate just beneath his skin. His small gray mustache dipped at either end, curling around his upper lip like a parenthesis.

He liked to stand behind the long bar, its rich brown wood so ancient and polished by innumerable elbows that it looked sumptuous, almost liquid. It shimmered in the light.

If he'd glanced out the big front window just then, he might have seen Bimm's black Honda going south on Mill as she headed to class. But Elsbury was too busy to be gazing out windows. When you owned a bar and grill, there was always something to do. Always a ledger to balance, a glass to rinse, a burger to turn.

After a rocky start—Utica is a tough town to break into, with friendships stretching back decades—Elsbury was feeling pretty good. Things were looking up, even though there were four other taverns in town—Skoog's Pub, Joy & Ed's, Canal Port and Milestone—all within a stone's throw.

Duffy's and Milestone were the new kids on the block. Not literally—the buildings were each more than a century old, two-story structures that anchored either end of Utica's roughly one-block business district. The proprietors, not the properties, were new. Elsbury and his wife, Pat, had bought Duffy's; Larry Ventrice and his wife, Marian, were running Milestone.

They were alike in a lot of ways, the Elsburys and the Ventrices. They were two couples trying to make a go of it in a new business in a new town. Money was tight. Hours were long. You worked as hard as you could work, and you still weren't sure sometimes if you were going to survive.

At this time of day, though, with the sun going down and the room filling up, Elsbury was reminded of the reasons he loved running a bar. Toughest work he'd ever done, but Lord, he just loved the feel of the place. The laughter. The talk. The scrape of chair legs on the red-painted plywood floor. A kind of benign, peppy chaos.

Two TV sets were angled on small platforms extending from the wall at both ends of the bar, their screens busy with maps sprouting wavy lines and harsh-looking arrows. Bartender Chris Rochelle, 23, a skinny, good-looking kid with spiky black hair, had changed both sets from ESPN to the Weather Channel.

The sky, he told anybody who asked, just didn't look right to him. Didn't look right at all.

* * *

By the time Pietrycha walked back into the weather service office at about 5:45 p.m., everything had changed. It was as if an orchestra conductor, with a simple flick of the baton, had abruptly altered the room's tempo. What had been casual was suddenly intense. Phones rang, people scurried back and forth, frowning meteorologists hunched over computer screens.

That lackadaisical warm front suddenly had come to life, moving north much faster than any of the forecasters thought it would, initiating the fatal tangle of warm and cold air. Tornadoes darted across the Midwest, making jailbreaks from the thunderstorms.

At 5:32 p.m., Pietrycha's colleague, radar operator Rich Brumer, had issued a tornado warning for north-central Illinois. Typically, a watch—which alerts people to be on their guard—precedes a warning, but the warm front had risen so fast that Brumer went straight to the warning.

Now it was a matter of what meteorologists call interrogating the storm: keeping an eye on the screens as the data pours in, supplied by the Doppler radar tower that rises just behind the Romeoville office. In one sense, Pietrycha and his colleagues are immensely powerful as they compile fact after fact after fact about the atmosphere. They know just about everything there is to know about the air, the clouds, the wind, the rain.

But in another sense, they're utterly helpless. They don't know the "ground truth": the meteorological term for what's actually happening to real people, people who don't just record and measure the weather but must live through it.

That night, the weather service would tally 53 tornadoes in the Midwest. Fourteen whipsawed across north-central and northeastern Illinois.

One of those—born about 2 miles southwest of Granville and cutting a 15½-mile, 200-yard-wide notch from Granville to Utica—seemed to make a beeline for a venerable two-story tavern. It would arrive at 6:09 p.m.

* * *

At 5:55 p.m. the phone rang in Beverly Wood's mobile home in Utica. It was her daughter, Dena Mallie, a vivacious 44-year-old who lives in Peru, just west of Utica.

"We're having really bad hail," Mallie told her mother.

Wood, 67, was in the middle of dinner with Wayne Ball, 63, whom she'd dated for years and who lived in a mobile home right across the road, and Helen Studebaker Mahnke, 81, another friend who lived in the same trailer park just east of the downtown business district.

Wood and Ball were an easy, comfortable couple, with an affection that ran deep and true. When Ball's hands were severely frostbitten during his work with the railroad several years ago, and had to be bandaged and immobile for many months, it was Wood who fed him, who lit and held his cigarettes for him.

Wood had heated up a frozen pizza and mixed a few drinks. Mallie could hear music in the background; the three old friends had settled in for the evening. But Wood deeply feared storms.

"We're going to scoot," she told Mallie. "We're going uptown."

Trailers, as everybody knew, were notoriously vulnerable in bad weather. It made sense for Wood, Mahnke and Ball to hunker down in one of the Utica taverns, one of those big, reliable old buildings that could shrug off a storm like it had been shrugging them off for decades.

Leaving the pizza—minus the three slices they'd just eaten—on the table with the drinks, because they'd be back in a jiffy, Wood, Mahnke and Ball hurried outside and climbed into Wood's car, a taupe Buick Century.

It couldn't have taken Wood more than a minute to drive them to the bar, even pausing for the single stop sign on East Church, even heeding the posted speed limit of 20 m.p.h.

She parked across the street, and they quickly walked in through Milestone's double doors. Wood was in such a hurry she didn't lock the car; for her, an unheard-of lapse. It was just after 6 p.m.

Relief. They were, they thought, safe now.

* * *

For several minutes before the three arrived, Milestone's lights flickered. Larry Ventrice, 49, was getting irritated. On or off, he didn't care. Just wished they'd make up their mind, on or off, on or off. It climbed a person's nerves, real quick.

He was a restless, impatient man, a man with a finger-snap temper but a good heart. He hailed from Bridgeport, a South Side Chicago neighborhood, and was proud of it, and he was proud as well of what he'd done with the tavern: filled it with funky antiques such as a roulette wheel and fake "WANTED" posters that gave the place a toe-tapping, down-home feel. The atmosphere started at the threshold, where a couple of horseshoes served as door pulls, and continued on around to the building's southern exterior, where a big, colorful mural, a rollicking pioneer scene with wagon trains and sod-busters, had been painted on the sandstone blocks.

Larry Ventrice knew about the bad weather heading their way. On the big TV set over the bar he'd heard the stations yakking about tornadoes and seeking shelter and all the rest of it, but he wasn't worried. Why should he be? Milestone, with its thick sandstone walls, flat concrete roof and slate foundation, was as solid as a vault. It was 117 years old, but just as hard times strengthened a person's character, surely rough weather over the years toughened up a building, didn't it? Showed its true mettle. Milestone was a survivor. You'd bet your life on it.

Larry knew just about everybody who was there that night, and they knew him. His cousin Jim Ventrice, 70, was sitting at a table finishing up a bowl of chicken noodle soup while waiting for his second course, a pork chop sandwich he'd ordered from Marian Ventrice, 50, Larry's wife. Everybody called Jim Ventrice "Cousin Junior" or just Junior.

Junior, a slight man who wore his shirt tucked in and his hair combed neatly back from his forehead, had gotten to Milestone at about 5:40 p.m. that night. He stopped in at least once a day because he liked the bar's cozy, nobody's-a-stranger ambience.

He'd taken a seat, spotted Jay Vezain at the bar and called out, "Hey, Jay, how're you?"

Vezain, 47, who worked at the Utica grain elevator just south of Duffy's, was nursing a bottle of beer. "I'm OK, Junior, how're you?"

He had a good sense of humor, Vezain did, and the kind of smile to go with it: quick, mischievous-looking. A lot of folks saved their best jokes for Vezain, just to see that smile.

Over in the corner, Carol Schultheis, 40—Wayne Ball's daughter—was playing the video poker game, shoving in coins and waiting for luck, and taking occasional drags on a Marlboro Light. She'd been diagnosed with multiple sclerosis a few years ago, but so far it hadn't slowed her down; she was a day-shift cook at Joy & Ed's, and everybody in Utica knew her and she knew everybody right back, and if you passed her on the street you'd get a smile and a wave and maybe a naughty joke or two.

Rich Little, 37, a truck driver from nearby Troy Grove, was sitting at the bar, drinking a bottle of Bud Light. He was supposed to meet his girlfriend here at 6:30 p.m.

Back in the kitchen, Debbie Miller, 44, pushed a pork chop around on the grill for Junior's sandwich.

The lights flickered again. The door opened, and Wood, Mahnke and Ball came in.

Just after that, Debbie Miller's family spilled in through the back door, a pinwheeling mass of kids that must have quickly overwhelmed the small hallway and kitchen, a living scribble of elbows and long legs and sneakers and stick-thin arms, talking and pushing.

There was Debbie's husband, Mike, 49, lanky and bushy-haired; sons Mike Jr., 18, Gregg, 14, and Christopher, 8; and daughters Ashley, 16, and Jennifer, 12, along with Gregg's best friend Jarad Stillwell, 13.

Mike Miller's lean, lined, mournful face seemed to carry all the family's woes in its crevices. They'd had a lot of hard luck over the years. Money was tight, and Mike's salary from the Illinois Central Railroad never seemed quite able to stretch from one payday to the next, not with all those skinny tow-headed kids to take care of. Debbie Miller had signed on as a cook at Milestone about a year and a half ago, and Ashley and Mike Jr. sometimes came along, too, to wait tables or sweep up, netting a few bucks from Larry.

So when Mike Miller, back in the family's little blue house a half-mile south on Washington Street, had gotten spooked by those increasingly agitated TV weather reports, he thought of Milestone. Milestone was a second home. And Milestone, he figured, would be safer. It was big and thick-walled and had a stone-floored basement that was reassuring just to think about.

Milestone, anybody would tell you, was as sturdy as a preacher's promise.

Mike had just pulled a frozen pizza out of the oven for the kids' dinner, but to heck with it: They could eat when they got back home in a few minutes, after the storm passed.

So Mike ran down the crumbling steps with his children right behind him, and everybody scrambled into the family's Ford LTD.

By the time he and the kids got to the bar—two minutes later, tops—Debbie Miller was shutting down the grill, just like Larry had told her to.

"Everybody in the basement," Marian Ventrice said. "Kids first. Get the kids." She was a nervous, fretful, excitable woman, and you could hear the anxiety spiking in her voice.

The basement door was toward the front of the bar, under the stairs leading to the second floor. It was an old-fashioned cellar door, flush with the wooden floor, and you pulled up on a metal handle then flipped the door over.

Jarad and Gregg trooped down the wooden stairs, followed by Jennifer, Christopher, Ashley and Mike Jr., and then the adults. They moved quickly, efficiently, but without panic, because they were heading to safety; the basement was a haven, the basement was exactly where you'd want to be at that moment. Thick stone floor, low ceiling. Like a cave.

"Stick together, everybody stick together," Marian said, and she and Larry went to the center of the basement. So did the older people—Wood, Ball and Mahnke—and the Miller family piled up against the north wall, just beyond the bottom of the stairs. Gregg and Jarad headed to the south wall, next to the walk-in cooler.

Everybody was still talking, still speculating about the storm, and Mahnke asked Ashley and Jennifer their names. Marian was agitated, jittery, but everybody else was relaxed and casual, so casual, in fact, that Junior and Little had brought their beers with them. They set them on top of the chest-high freezer against which they stood, waiting for somebody to tell them it was OK to go back upstairs. No big deal.

* * *

At 5:58 p.m., Dena Mallie saw it from her driveway in Peru.

As it blossomed darkly, a huge batwing erasing the sky around it, a Utica contractor named Buck Bierbom saw it from his back yard.

Rona Burrows saw it. She leaned out the front door at Mill Street Market, where she worked as a cashier, and looked up at the sky.

Lisle Elsbury saw it from the alley behind Duffy's.

It was a great black mass, a swirling coil some 200 yards wide at the ground—it was wider in the sky—heading northeast at about 30 m.p.h. They looked up and saw it but they thought: No. Couldn't be. Could it?

There was a wild beauty to it, a fiercely knotted loveliness that was like nothing they'd ever seen. They could see debris swirling in it, pulled in and out and sucked up and around, frenzied sticks of wood, trees, dirt, other things, everything.

The ones who watched it come, watched it fill more and more of the blue-green sky like the canvas of a finicky painter who decides to slather the whole thing in black and start over, felt almost hypnotized at first, rooted to the earth but looking up, up, up. "Awesome" is the word that came instantly to Mallie. And not the way teenagers meant it. Awesome as in something that fills you up with awe.

* * *

Steve Maltas, 23, a Utica volunteer firefighter with a trim goatee and a distinct aversion to small talk, was at the car wash in Utica's south end. He heard the report from the LaSalle Fire Department on his dispatch radio: A tornado was bearing down on them.

Maltas gunned his pickup toward the fire station, just up on Mill across from Milestone. He knew where the switch was to activate the tornado siren, the mechanical wail that would give his friends and neighbors a fighting chance.

He braked in front of the yellow-brick firehouse, cut the engine, raced inside and ran smack into a dilemma: He had no authority. Only the chief was supposed to give the OK to sound the warning. Another firefighter, quiet, blond Shane Burrows, 23—Rona Burrows' son—was there, too. He had tried to reach Edgcomb, but the chief's cell phone was turned off—a requirement for the EMT class.

The two men had seconds to decide and what they decided was:

Screw the rules.

Flip the switch.

A moment later they were joined in the firehouse by Steve Maltas' mother, Gloria, who'd hustled there when she heard about the storm. She, too, worked at the firehouse in her spare time.

But even with the siren, the townspeople weren't paying attention. When Gloria Maltas looked outside, she saw them standing in the street, watching the sky. Maybe they thought the siren was just a precaution, or maybe they were trusting old Utican wisdom: A tornado won't go in a valley. A tornado won't cross water. Both were false.

So Gloria, ordinarily a shy, reticent woman who deeply disliked anything that could be remotely construed as making a spectacle of herself, who usually spoke in a soft, whispery voice that made listeners lean in a little to catch her words, did something wholly uncharacteristic: She directed Steve to one side of Mill Street and she took the other, and they began running and yelling at people who stood in the doorways, telling them to get inside, take cover, *for God's sake, go back in.*

Gloria kept running. She ran faster than she'd ever run before, and she didn't realize how fast she was running. A day or so later, her legs ached and she couldn't figure out why, and then she remembered the running, running up and down Mill Street, screaming at people who must've wondered what on earth had gotten into sweet little Gloria Maltas.

Steve Maltas made it back to the fire station, where his last warning was issued to a few folks who stood in the doorway of the bar across the street. "Get in! Get back in!" he hollered, and he saw that one of them was Jay Vezain, who did as he was told, and then the others who'd been standing behind Vezain went back in, too.

Because the fire station didn't have a basement, Maltas and Burrows and the other firefighters who had gathered there headed for the boiler room. They heaved the door shut behind them, and then they waited, having done all they could do, for whatever the next flurry of seconds would bring.

* * *

Gloria Maltas, whose last warning was to the people standing outside Duffy's, wasn't going to make it back to the fire station. It was only a block away, and she had started back, thinking she could do it, but then she glanced over her shoulder and *Oh, my God* saw the tornado gaining on her, spreading out behind her.

She was running toward the station, running and running, but there wasn't time, there wasn't time. The big black triangle was rising right behind her, capturing more and more of the sky.

At Mill Street Market, the tiny grocery store in the middle of the block, Gloria halted at the glass door—the one with the "We appreciate our customers" sign—and pounded on it. Closed, locked. Nobody stirred inside. Gloria had done her job too well. They were all in the back, she guessed, having fled into the big walk-in freezer.

Still Gloria pounded and hollered, because there was nothing else to do, no other option. She had to get inside somewhere, anywhere, and then she saw Rona Burrows running toward the door, jiggling the key in the lock, twisting it, that lock was always stubborn.

"Hurry up!" cried Burrows, pulling her inside. "If I have to see you flying through the air, I'll kill you!" she added, half-laughing, half-sobbing, and then they got to the back of the store, past the meat display case and into the freezer where the others—Mary Jo and Bruce Conner, the couple who managed the market, and a woman Gloria didn't know—were huddled.

They waited that final minute, not knowing if they were really safe, not knowing if the walls would hold, not knowing if these were the last seconds of their lives, and they embraced, and then—at 6:09 p.m.—there was a sound like hundreds of cars being dumped on the roof, and they knew that it was, unmistakably, upon them.

21. 'Milestone's Gone!'

DEC. 6, 2004

UTICA, Illinois—In the basement of Duffy's Tavern, dirt sifted between the floorboards overhead for 10 seconds. They could hear muffled booms from above, the crashes, the bangs and cracks and rattles. The whole building seemed to shudder, as if bumped rudely in a crowd. Sixty seconds before, they had hurried into the basement, chased there by a tornado flying toward the tiny town of Utica at 6:09 p.m. on April 20.

Down the wooden steps they had come, hurrying, hurrying, but trying not to shove. The lights died. Once at the bottom, they huddled shoulder to shoulder, next to things they couldn't see: shelves with plastic tubs of French dressing and twist-tied bags of the green and white mints that Lisle Elsbury liked to hand out to departing customers.

Elsbury, the owner of Duffy's, was last in line, having gathered everybody—six staff members, six customers—and made sure they were headed down the stairs and then closing the basement door behind him. His foot was still on the bottom step when it hit.

Ten seconds of shaking. Of falling dirt. "Everybody OK?" Elsbury said, once the shaking stopped. A nervous murmur of yeses.

He waited another 45 seconds or so. When he thought it was all over—you couldn't be sure, not really, but you followed your instincts—Elsbury headed up the steps and cautiously opened the door.

He expected chaos. He expected, at the very least, severe damage: splintered bar, overturned tables and chairs, busted windows.

But Elsbury saw little change. Later he would discover a great deal of structural damage to the second floor, but for now, he felt lucky.

Chris Rochelle, 23, the bartender, was right behind his boss. When he saw that Duffy's seemed intact, Rochelle moved straight out the back door to check on the rest of the town. He had good friends up and down this street, but none better than Larry Ventrice over at Milestone, Larry who'd encouraged him to start lifting weights again and take care of himself, Larry who'd lent him a car in which to drive home to Kansas last Christmas. If Duffy's looked OK, then Rochelle wanted to help his friend Larry clean up Milestone.

He ran north through the alley, past the backs of Duffy's and Skoog's Pub and the other buildings, past the blown-down bricks and felled trees and hunks of twisted metal.

When he got to the corner he couldn't believe what he saw. What he didn't see.

Rochelle ran back to Duffy's—he would have no memory of the running, of his knees rising and falling or of the breath tearing in and out of his chest, but he knew he must have done so, because that's where he ended up—and he screamed, "Milestone's gone! Milestone's gone!" Even as he was saying it, even as the words flew out of his mouth, it didn't sound possible. But it was. He had seen it. Or, not seen it.

* * *

Steve Maltas, who had taken refuge in the boiler room of the firehouse along with seven other volunteer firefighters, shoved open the heavy door. Yep, the building was still standing.

Then they all hurried outside, and the first thing they saw was what wasn't there: Milestone.

A knee-high pile of rubble—sandstone blocks, thick wooden beams and a crusty overlay of broken concrete—seethed and steamed in the space where a two-story building had stood since 1887, right across the street from the firehouse.

For a few seconds Maltas and the others were too stunned to move, too numb, their minds utterly rejecting what their eyes were telling them was true: A building had been flattened in 10 seconds, like a sandcastle squashed by a bored kid at the beach.

They broke out of their astonishment and ran across the street to the jagged pile. Where to start? What to do? Good God. The center was absolute mashed chaos—wood and concrete and stone and wire and a thick powdery mist of pulverized mortar—but the edges, the edges looked bizarre: At the edges were huge intact sandstone blocks that had toppled in neat rows, like dominoes.

They started pulling at the rocks, doing what anybody would do: trying to get to whoever was inside, grabbing and lifting and clawing. They could hear screams and calls for help, and it was a healthy sound, God knows, because silence would have been worse.

Seconds later, they were joined by other people, people who had emerged from downtown buildings and looked around to check the damage and then saw—*Good Lord*—Milestone, what was left of Milestone, and so they ran to the site and bent over or dropped to their knees and pulled, scratched, dug and heaved the stones, but there were so many stones and so many layers and it seemed hopeless. They couldn't let themselves think that, though, so they just kept digging and pulling at stones.

So intent were they, so focused, that at first they didn't notice the damage to the rest of Utica. They didn't really see the garage right next to Milestone, where the Fire Department parked its ambulances, wrecked so badly that later it would have to be torn down. They hardly noticed that Starved Rock Bait & Tackle, the century-old building across the alley from Milestone where Jim Collins had sold gas, cigarettes, soda pop and hunting licenses for almost two decades, was a ruined mess.

All anybody could think about was *Milestone, Milestone, Milestone,* because the tavern wasn't just mauled and pummeled, wasn't just grievously damaged. It was gone.

In the top layer of the rubble, two bodies were clearly, excruciatingly visible. And because Utica is a small town, because everybody knows everybody, they knew who they were: Jay Vezain and Carol Schultheis, two local folks who'd been having a drink in Milestone just before the storm.

* * *

By the time Joe Krizel got there about five minutes later, at least two dozen people were tugging at the rubble. Krizel worked at Uniman, a sand plant on a hill just north of Utica. From his vantage point up there, he had watched the tornado move in, watched it churn and whip its way northeast, then saw it pause over Utica—10 seconds, he thought, no more—almost as if it had an appointment there, as if it knew where it wanted to go, right down to the street address. Krizel couldn't tear his eyes away from it.

Then the spinning black cloud moved on, heading up the hill where it broke apart, and Krizel suddenly felt released from whatever spell that awful thing had cast over him.

Krizel, 49, had been a volunteer firefighter for more than two decades. He knew there'd be a lot of damage, so he slid into his pickup to head downtown. Trouble was, the road was blocked by debris—ripped-up trees with their shocked roots still dangling, thrown-down telephone poles, big chunks of roofs, swatches of curled-up sheet metal—and he couldn't get through. He hollered at Blayne Bimm—son of Shelba Bimm, one of Krizel's Fire Department colleagues—who also worked at Uniman, and Blayne hopped into an endloader and cleared the way for the pickup.

Krizel took a look at the mess that had been Milestone. He knew what kind of job this was: technical rescue, which meant equipment and expertise, not just hard work and good intentions. Maltas already had alerted state officials and in the next few hours 52 fire departments would respond. The streets of Utica would be jammed with firetrucks. But right now, it was just Joe Krizel and the Utica firefighters, and they could hear people calling for help from under the rubble.

Krizel dashed into the firehouse, flung open his locker and started yanking on boots and coveralls. He slapped on his hardhat with the light on it.

Back across the street, firefighters had just pulled Rich Little from a corner of the rubble, and Little had pulled out Jim Ventrice. It was the easiest rescue they'd have; from here on out, it would be desperate and difficult work, but the two men who'd been standing next to a couple of freezers in the basement seemed to be fine. It was astonishing, really: Amid the destruction, with an entire two-story building compressed into an appallingly tiny space, two men had climbed out. They were dazed and groggy and dust-covered, but alive.

A woman ran up to Little and embraced him. It was Kristy Kaiser, 35, the girlfriend he was supposed to meet in Milestone that night. But she'd seen the tornado blooming in her rear-view mirror like an assailant who'd been hiding in the back seat, so she pulled her Dodge Ram to the curb, jumped out and ran into a grocery store, where she spent the anxious minutes in a walk-in freezer with strangers.

Now she was here with Little, here amid the confusion and the shouting. It was so chaotic that Ventrice wandered over to a stack of stones and sat down, and minutes later said hello to a friend, and the friend remembers thinking, "Why's he bothering me when we got a crisis here?"—not realizing until much later that Ventrice himself had just been pulled out of the building. It was that kind of scene: wild, surreal, drenched in panic and dread and a kind of crazed disbelief.

Gradually, though, the firefighters took control, moving the townspeople back and back and back, so Krizel could get to work. They were afraid to touch Vezain and Schultheis, afraid they might send the whole fragile mass crashing down on the survivors inside, so they draped the bodies in plastic, and tried to put out of their minds what they would never get out of their memories. They had a job to do; there were more people down there, living people. They could hear them crying and screaming. So there was no time for grief or reflection.

* * *

By 6:20, 11 minutes after the tornado belted Utica, Shelba Bimm and Dave Edgcomb, Utica's fire chief, showed up. They'd been in a class in

Oglesby to upgrade their EMT certifications. When the tornado sirens sounded, their instructor, as protocol required, marched the students into the basement. On the way down, somebody turned on a dispatch radio and everybody got the news: Utica.

"We gotta go," Bimm told the teacher, and she and Edgcomb ran to the parking lot, Edgcomb to his pickup and Bimm to her Honda CRV, and their journey back to Utica was something neither would remember in any detail, because their only thought was get there, *get there,* and it bullied all other thoughts out of the way.

They had to abandon their vehicles at the edge of town, because there was too much stuff clogging the streets: trees and rooftops and hunks of siding, plus toppled power lines that twitched and sizzled. They had to claw their way through branches and shattered glass, around broken pipes and crinkled windowless cars, and they took a crazy, makeshift route under and over and through. It was like moving across a war zone, Bimm thought, like advancing through a dangerous maze during combat.

She made it to Church Street, and she looked at her house for just a second—everything was happening in fragments now, time had been sliced up into smaller and smaller increments—but it didn't make sense. She couldn't figure out at first what she was looking at.

Somebody had made a mistake. A bad, bad mistake. This wasn't her house. This was a place that had been wrenched off its foundation, twisted sideways beneath a battered roof. This looked like one of her dollhouses— the kind she sold in her front room—after somebody had knocked it off a shelf and stepped on it.

She shook her head. Said to herself, *Well, OK, my house is gone. Let's go see what other folks need.*

And the retired 1st-grade teacher with the bright white hair bent over and thrashed her way inside the mess of what had been her house, digging out her fluorescent vest, so people would know she was an EMT. Then she started toward Milestone.

* * *

Please, God. Don't let it be kids.

That was Edgcomb's single thought, the one that kept pace with his racing heart as he ran toward Milestone: *Please, God, no kids. Please. Please.*

He'd been a firefighter for 25 years, he was a powerful, well-built man, a natural leader, and nobody would call Dave Edgcomb weak, no sir. He carried an air of can-do confidence.

But right now he was, in his thoughts, on his knees:

Please, God, just don't let it be kids.

He knew it was bad, real bad, and he knew he could handle anything—but not kids. No dead kids.

In one of his first days as a firefighter, Edgcomb was called to an accident scene on Interstate Highway 80. A drunk driver had crashed her car, the car was burning, the driver had tumbled out and was fine—wasn't that always the way?—but she kept screaming, *my kids, my kids,* and the firefighters did the best they could, but in the end, Edgcomb was asked to retrieve two small charred bodies in the back seat.

Now, as he approached Milestone and saw his fellow Utica firefighters, saw their grim faces, he knew. He just knew. There were kids down there.

Please, God.

* * *

From under the rubble along the southern wall, Krizel heard somebody yell for help. He thought he knew that voice. So he yelled back and, yeah, it was Jarad Stillwell, a pal of Krizel's son Zack.

"How many down there?" Krizel called. "How many, Jarad?"

"A bunch." The raw, choked voice of a 13-year-old, scared out of his mind.

Krizel spotted a dime-sized hole in the jagged debris. "Hey, Jarad," he said, "can you get your finger out there?"

A pale fingernail appeared in the opening, then a pale finger, then a few more fingers managed to spread the hole wider. Krizel touched Jarad's fingers.

The firefighter knew how extraordinarily careful he had to be. If he moved the rocks too much, too fast, he could dislodge a crucial section. He had to consider every gesture he made, every wriggle and bump—but he also had to work quickly, because the people trapped below might be dying.

Krizel probed cautiously at the stones and splintered wood and broken concrete, taking a piece here and then a piece over there, careful, so careful. It required almost two hours just to enlarge the hole.

Finally it was big enough, and Krizel reached down to take Jarad's hand—yeah, yeah, here he comes—and Krizel and four other firefighters pulled the kid up and out. There was a kid next to him down there, Gregg Miller, 14, and they pulled him out, too. Right as the boys emerged there was a moment of panic because they were drenched in something sticky and red—*Is it blood? For God's sake, are they bleeding?*—but it turned out to be syrup for the soda pop served at Milestone, stored in the basement in pressurized containers that had popped open in the collapse. The kids were OK.

Krizel handed off the boys to his colleagues—Shelba Bimm was there, his old friend Shelba, where'd she come from?—and then he got ready for the hardest job of all: reaching the people who were entombed under hundreds of tons of debris.

He knew a technical rescue team from the Sandwich Fire Department was on the way, he knew Edgcomb was coordinating things, but he had to get started. He could hear people screaming.

Krizel looked down in the hole from which he'd pulled the boys. Might work.

He inched himself into the opening, feet first. It was just barely wide enough. A couple of guys held his arms and lowered him on down, on down, until his feet hit something solid and he had to stop. Krizel flipped on a light. He could see a young girl's narrow ankle caught under a beam. He wiggled and turned and twisted so that he was on his stomach, so that he could crawl over to her.

Above him, he could hear the crunchy steps of people walking on the debris, feel the pile shift. One wrong footfall, Krizel knew, might bring everything crashing down. So he climbed back up and stuck his head out of the hole and yelled, "Get offa there! Clear those people off!"

Then he went back down, back on his belly again, and crawled closer to the girl. By this time he could see other bodies, too, some alive and some dead. Krizel was crawling through at least 6 inches of frigid water, through sewage and booze and electrical lines. He used tin snips to clip and bend and poke and push his way forward. *I got $10,000 worth of rescue equipment up there in the truck, and none of it's gonna do me a bit of good,* Krizel thought. *Just these tin snips.*

Water. Wires. Sheet metal. Pipes. Jagged wood. Krizel kept cutting, cutting until his hands were red-raw. Ashley Miller, the girl whose ankle he'd seen under the beam, was crying; she was in pain and wanted out, and he said, "I can't get to you yet. Hang on." She sobbed, "But I can see your light! Come and get me!"

There were other firefighters down in the hole by then, too, coming behind Krizel, cutting and pushing, but gently. They had to be smallish, fit men, like Krizel, because the makeshift tunnel was so narrow, so frail. They didn't know what they were touching or what the touching would do. Before Krizel cut a pipe, he wondered, *Is it gas? Electric? Water?* He couldn't tell. He just kept working, pushing, tunneling, and when he came to a dead body, he kept going, kept going, toward the living.

* * *

For the people buried alive in Milestone, it had sounded like an explosion, like a bomb going off right over their heads, like the end of the world.

Mike Miller was slammed to his knees. His left foot was twisted up under him, and Debbie was jammed against that foot, and they couldn't even flinch, they were pinned in every direction.

Before Jarad and Gregg were rescued, Debbie had called out the children's names, one by one, and after a child responded, she went on to the next one, calling for Christopher, 8; Jennifer, 12; Ashley, 16; and Gregg and Jarad.

When she said, "Mike," there was no answer from 18-year-old Mike Jr., and she knew. She knew.

They started yelling for help, all of them, and the kids cried. In a minute or two they heard answering yells—people on the outside, above them—so they knew somebody was coming.

But when? *When?* Why didn't somebody just unstack these stones and junk and get them the hell out of there? Ashley was crammed up next to her mother; Jennifer was pinned against Ashley; everybody was smushed against somebody else.

They were wet and cold and scared and confused. They could hear pipes bursting and then, because this was the basement of a bar, they could smell alcohol, urine and excrement. Their arms and legs and shoulders and backs were clasped by a vast unfathomable heaviness. They could barely move their chins an inch or shift a knee. They were suspended in a prison of sandstone, concrete and terrible weight.

Mike Miller sensed a presence wedged beside him, and somehow he realized it was Larry Ventrice. Or what had been Larry Ventrice. Mike Miller was as close to Larry as a person standing next to him in a crowded elevator.

He'd had enough. He was done. Sick of fighting. "I'm going to give up," he told his wife.

They could hear the firefighters inching their way toward them, cutting and pushing, and the great heaviness all around them shimmied and creaked and groaned. They could hear Jarad and Gregg being pulled out, and that gave them hope, great hope. Maybe it wasn't that bad. Mike Miller asked the firefighters how bad it was, and they wouldn't give him details. "Bad," one said. That was the only word he would use: "Bad."

After another two-and-a-half hours of work, rescuers had reached Chris, the smallest. They pulled him out, and then it was on to Ashley. Her thin blond hair was caught under a wooden beam, and they told her she'd have to pull out several handfuls before they could free her. Ashley hesitated, but her mother said, "*Do* it, Ashley," and she did, yanking a succession of strands in small painful bundles from the front of her scalp.

Mike and Debbie, though, were bigger, bound tighter, and would require another three hours of delicate work by the rescuers. While firefighters snipped and probed, one managed to lower a flashlight into Debbie's fingers. He also handed her some ice and asked if she wanted anything else.

"Yeah," she said. "A cigarette."

That drew chuckles. And Mike—did he want anything?

"A pain pill," he said. His back, his foot: It was agony, *agony*. It was so excruciating, in fact, that he was finished. He'd had enough. He was done. Sick of fighting. "I'm going to give up," he told his wife. A simple fact: I'm through.

"No," Debbie said. "You're not giving up. You're not giving up."

He hung on not because he wanted to—he didn't want to—but because he had no choice. He couldn't move, he was helpless, he was trapped in life right now, the same way he was trapped under the heavy stones.

Gradually a tunnel widened above them, and they could see hands and lights. Voices were louder. Mike Miller had to push Larry Ventrice's knee to one side to free his own leg. First Debbie, then Mike, were strapped on backboards and hauled out.

* * *

Within the first hour after the tornado, Chief Richard Kell and 30 firefighters from Sandwich had arrived, experts in rescues in collapsed buildings. Kell dispatched two teams—one with two men, the other with three—to crawl under the rubble toward the survivors, and Krizel was told to come up, come back up, they'd take over. Come up. The crew from Sandwich would continue the tedious journey: snipping, bending back metal, scooting gingerly through the water and muck and sharp-edged broken stones.

When Krizel climbed out of the hole he was as tired as he'd ever been in his life. He was angry, too, at having been relieved. He argued, he fought, but he knew they were right. He'd done all he could, but there was so much more to do. Living people were still pinned down there.

The dead were down there, too, people he knew, friends of his, and it was clear the night had really just begun.

He stood there a minute or so, and then Shelba Bimm came forward and hugged him, holding him as his shoulders bobbed up and down with quiet sobs, because now there was a weight on Joe Krizel, too, and it was heavier than any building.

22. After the Storm's Fury

DEC. 7, 2004

UTICA, Illinois—They picked at the pile, inch by inch, stone by stone, just in case. They thought they'd gotten to everyone who was alive, but you had to be sure. You had to. Buckets of debris were passed from hand to hand along chains of firefighters. It began to rain, but nobody noticed.

Earlier that evening—at 6:09 p.m. April 20—a tornado had barreled through the town of Utica in north-central Illinois and, with a tornado's savage whim, had shunned a building here but shredded one over there. Hitting and missing and hitting.

Milestone. That was where the firefighters now were gathered, hundreds of firefighters from 52 units throughout the state. The 117-year-old tavern near the corner of Church and Mill Streets had taken a direct hit and collapsed into a ponderous heap of wood, stone and concrete, trapping 17 people who had sought shelter within its thick walls.

Nine had been rescued earlier that night: Jim Ventrice, Rich Little, Jarad Stillwell, and Mike and Debbie Miller and their children Ashley, Jennifer, Gregg and Chris.

The eight others still down there, firefighters believed, were dead. But they had to be sure.

So they kept working, systematically removing buckets full of rubble, pushing back thoughts of anything except the task at hand: dig, fill the bucket, pass the bucket, dig.

The whole place was lighted like a movie set. The lights cast an eerie glow on the firefighters in their heavy gear and their hardhats, their steel-toed boots and leather gloves. The lights splashed up on their solemn faces, which looked steep and angular in the artificial glare. All of that illumination made it seem as if a strange new sun had been unearthed, a mixed-up one that didn't know night from day.

At about 1:30 a.m., when the listening devices that were dropped down into crevices continued to fetch only silence, they knew the rescue part of their job was over. Now it was a different mission: recovering the bodies.

Buck Bierbom's skid loader was waved forward to handle the larger chunks of debris, but they had to be careful, so careful. When firefighters edged close to a body, the heavy equipment backed off and the painstaking labor by hand recommenced, the tender, awful job of verifying what they already knew.

Bierbom was a local boy, Utica-born and Utica-raised, a slender, wiry man with a creased, weathered, beard-fringed face and the kindest eyes you'd ever hope to see. He and his brothers, Mark and Doug, had run their own construction company for 12 years. Utica Police Chief Joseph Bernardoni had called him at 6:30 p.m., 21 minutes after the tornado leveled Milestone, and asked him to get there with his skid loader and mini-excavator just as quick as he could.

So tonight Bierbom was unearthing the bodies of people he'd known all his life. People he'd grown up with. People he'd waved to on the street maybe twice, maybe three times a day for a whole bunch of years.

Shortly before dawn, when all the bodies had been located, a chain saw cut away sections of Milestone's floor. Bierbom's big machine removed the sections. Then Jody Bernard, the somber, petite LaSalle County coroner, or one of her three deputy coroners, would climb down, examine the body and pronounce the death.

Each body was placed in a blue bag, then the blue bag was lifted out of the hole.

At 6:59 a.m., they lifted out Jay Vezain.

At 7:04 a.m., Carol Schultheis.

At 11:12 a.m., Mike Miller Jr.

At 11:15 a.m., Larry Ventrice.

At 11:17 a.m., Beverly Wood.

At 11:22 a.m., Marian Ventrice.

At 11:25 a.m., Wayne Ball.

At 11:28 a.m., Helen Studebaker Mahnke.

All but Vezain and Schultheis died of traumatic asphyxiation, which means they were crushed to death, probably in the first instant of the collapse, when the walls and floors began to pancake down into the basement. Vezain and Schultheis, who never made it into the basement, died of blunt force trauma.

But those official-sounding causes of death, announced by Bernard at the coroner's inquest May 27 at the LaSalle County Courthouse, hardly hint at what actually happens to human bodies when crushed by a two-story building: the brutality, the blunt and unimaginable violence of hundreds of tons of stone and wood and concrete collapsing upon fragile frames and soft flesh. There were shattered bones and severed arteries and fractured skulls and lacerated organs and one transection of the brain stem—decapitation.

The ones who survived did so because they chanced to be standing in just the right places. The walk-in cooler and the two freezers blocked a portion of the plummeting debris, creating instant, lifesaving lean-tos.

There had been, survivors said, simply no time. No time for final thoughts or last-minute regrets, for so much as a cry of pain or yelp of warning. There was only time, if one is inclined to think that way, for the freeing of eight souls to continue their journeys elsewhere.

* * *

They lived or they died. Among the living, the most serious injuries were the broken ankles suffered by Mike Miller and daughter Ashley, but no one was paralyzed or maimed, which meant there was no middle ground for the people in Milestone. It was life or death.

Whether you ended up on one side of that line or the other depended on whether you went down those basement stairs and what you did when you got there.

Whether you turned left or right. Whether you paused or didn't pause. Whether, when everybody was hustling down the stairs, you waited to let an older person pass or a kid go ahead of you, or whether you didn't wait, or whether you moved to the center of the basement or stayed against the sides. Left, right, forward, backward, life, death.

Schultheis' body was found beneath the video poker machine. Vezain had used his cell phone to call his sisters, making sure they were safe in the storm, and in the last call—suddenly cut off—he talked about trying to close the door, so maybe that's what he was doing, which would have been characteristic of the amiable, thoughtful Vezain, and then there was no more time; time itself was extinguished, and eight histories ended abruptly in a sandstone tavern at dusk.

The funerals began two days later, when Vezain was remembered at a service in LaSalle, and continued for a week after the tornado, in locations that widened out from Utica in concentric rings: Wood, Ball and Schultheis, also in LaSalle; Mahnke in West Brooklyn; Miller in Rock Falls; the Ventrices in Chicago.

* * *

They started on a hill about a half-mile northeast of Utica, where the tornado had worn itself out, and worked their way back, back to where it began, some 15½ miles southwest of that hill.

It was approximately 10 a.m. on April 21, and Albert Pietrycha, Mark Ratzer and Jim Allsopp, meteorologists assigned to the National Weather Service's Chicago forecast office in Romeoville, were doing what they always do after a major storm: surveying the damage, beginning at the end and ending at the beginning. They'd map it on the ground first and then, the next day, by air.

Armed with laptops and GPS tracking software, the men in the Ford Explorer crossed country roads and state highways, cut through farm fields and spongy riverbank, using thrashed trees and flattened vegetation and ripped-off roofs to track the tornado's path. Out in the open ground they found its vivid footprint in the black mud, a herringbone pattern that testified to the violent, switchback winds.

Recording the damage in its wake is how meteorologists rank a tornado's severity. The F scale, named for University of Chicago meteorologist Ted Fujita, is based on the havoc wrought by tornadic winds—not on an actual measurement of those winds. The Utica tornado was deemed an F3, meaning that, based on the destruction the meteorologists observed, it probably had packed winds of between 158 and 206 m.p.h.

Despite all that is known, however, despite all the charts and statistics and technology, tornado forecasting still has a long way to go. Since the 1950s, which saw the first major advance in atmospheric science, little has changed. Tornado forecasting still is filled with ambiguity and uncertainty, with the locked-up secrets of nature's worst tantrums.

It's a mystery why some thunderstorms turn into the supercell variety, whose organized rotating updrafts explode into tornadoes. The questions keep scientists such as Pietrycha, who's worked at the weather service for two years, relentlessly searching a tornado's dark heart.

And there is a point, Pietrycha knows, where the scientific facts abruptly stop, a stark cliff-edge where something else takes over, some inscrutable plan or perhaps just cruel caprice. Destiny—or dumb luck. Who can say which?

That was why, as Pietrycha and his colleagues followed the tornado's crooked trail that morning, they were all struck by a thought they couldn't seem to get out of their heads:

If the 200-yard-wide funnel had moved just a bit to either side during its furious charge, leaning a half-mile left or right, it would have missed Utica altogether. It would have churned up only farmland, and Milestone still would be standing.

And the regulars, people such as Jay Vezain and Carol Schultheis, would have had quite a story to tell, the story about the tornado that nearly hit Utica. Talk about your close calls.

Why the tornado dived straight at Milestone, why it demolished some houses and ignored others, why it turned when it did and didn't turn when it didn't—those were questions the meteorologists couldn't answer.

And neither, come to think of it, could anybody else.

* * *

Mike Miller and his family had been trapped in the Milestone rubble for almost five hours. They were rescued, but sometimes you can be rescued and still be trapped.

Two months after the tornado, Miller sat on the postage-stamp of a front porch of his house in Utica and smoked Marlboros, one after another, through the long summer afternoons. He looked out at the green field across the street. Beyond the field and the tangled mass of trees was the Illinois River. Even if you couldn't see the river you knew it was there; the river's scent rode the breeze, just the faintest tang of moisture and sweet coolness and the tantalizing hint of elsewhere.

His ankle was on the mend. He'd spent a week in the hospital and two weeks in a rehabilitation center. Now he was home, in the small blue rented house on Washington Street.

Miller's skinny legs were propped up on the porch rail. The cast and bulky protective boot on his left foot was the only suggestion of heaviness about him. He was as thin as a matchstick, which tended to make his thick nest of hair—not quite gray but getting there—look even wilder. He had a bountiful mustache and flyaway eyebrows and round spectacles. There was a quietness about Mike Miller, a kind of baffled resignation.

The Miller family had to find someplace else to live. The landlord had evicted them in May—too many complaints about the kids from neighbors, they were told. Granted, Mike and Debbie hadn't been around the house a lot to keep an eye on things; he was an engineer with Illinois Central Railroad, she was a cook at Milestone.

Now both were home all the time, because Mike was on disability leave and there was no more Milestone. But it was too late. Now the Millers wanted to be rid of Utica just as much as Utica seemed to want to be rid of them.

They hoped to find a place in nearby LaSalle, so they could stay in the same area as their three oldest children, Kassi, 24, Brandon, 23, and Michelle, 19, who hadn't been with them in Milestone.

Their next-oldest child, 18-year-old Mike Jr., had died when the tavern collapsed.

It was bewildering sometimes, Mike thought, all that had happened to his family that night. "The Good Lord put us through four-and-a-half hours of hell," was how he phrased it, thinking back on the long rescue and the pain.

And there were times when he wondered, as he sat on the porch with his crutches stacked beside him, if they'd ever really gotten out of that place, ever really broken the surface. There were times when he felt as if things were piled on top of him still, things that made it tough to move forward.

*   *   *

Tear it down. That's what they told him.

And Lisle Elsbury said, *Nope.*

But you could see their point. Duffy's Tavern had long ragged holes on both sides of its second floor, the bricks ripped out as savagely as if someone had been digging for treasure hidden behind them. When the tornado hit, it tore off sections of the grain bins of Utica Elevator just across the canal, turning them into missiles. Two of those sections sliced into Duffy's.

A week after the storm, Elsbury was standing in the middle of Mill Street, peering intently at the building in which he'd stuffed his hopes and his cash. Contractors hired to help him repair it were snapping together the scaffolding to reach the second floor. Elsbury wore sunglasses, a hardhat, black jeans and a bright green T-shirt with "Duffy's Tavern" in yellow letters.

Built in 1892, easily Utica's most distinctive-looking structure, Duffy's sported a tower that flared out over the corner of Mill and Canal Streets with a Disneyesque flourish. That was why Elsbury and his wife, Pat, had bought it the year before. They loved the look of the place.

What it looked like now was a lost cause.

Elsbury had worked in construction in Lyons before buying Duffy's, so he knew the repairs would cost at least $100,000, only part of which would be reimbursed by insurance; already, he was deep in arguments with the agent.

And there was something else.

When you looked at Duffy's, you couldn't help but think about Milestone. They had been a block away from each other. Elsbury and Larry Ventrice, Milestone's brusque manager, had rhyming lives: Both had done other things before deciding, in their middle years, to run a bar in Utica. Both had wives who kept their jobs and lived in other cities so the family could have health insurance.

Marian Ventrice had quit her job just two months before, to join her husband at Milestone.

Pat Elsbury, who worked as a secretary for an oil-recycling company in La Grange, had been contemplating the same kind of bold stroke: Just do it. Forget what everybody says is the smart move. Follow your heart. Lisle was remodeling the second floor, turning it into an apartment—just like

Larry and Marian had done at Milestone—and they'd be living and working together. Just like Milestone.

And then came April 20, when Milestone collapsed and killed the Ventrices and six others. Pat and Lisle Elsbury were haunted by the crazy capriciousness of it all: Two bars. Two couples. One tornado. Two fates.

Why did Milestone fall and Duffy's stand? Pat Elsbury tried to stop thinking about it, but she couldn't. When she drove to Utica, she kept running into the questions as if they were police roadblocks: Why Milestone and not Duffy's? Why had the tornado veered left just before it hit Duffy's, dealing it only a glancing blow, but pounced on Milestone as if on a mission? Why was Lisle Elsbury alive and Larry Ventrice dead?

Pat, a pretty, talkative woman with strawberry blond hair and a quick laugh, soon realized that the only way to outfox her thoughts was to do what Lisle did: stay busy.

So while her husband kept an eye on the crew that was restoring Duffy's, rebuilding the brick sides and shoring up the roof, Pat was there every Saturday and Sunday. When Duffy's reopened after three weeks, Pat would wait tables and grapple with paperwork, unpack supplies and sweep floors. Anything to keep her mind away from that relentless and quietly terrifying, "Why?"

* * *

Jim Ventrice had gone to Milestone every day, for lunch or dinner or both. Now that it was gone, he had to get his meals and his companionship somewhere else.

Through the summer you'd see him at Skoog's Pub, maybe, sipping a Miller Genuine Draft, his favorite, or over at Duffy's, having a burger, or sometimes at Joy & Ed's.

Ventrice and Rich Little were the first two people rescued from Milestone's basement. While the others down there died or were forced to wait hours before being pulled out, Ventrice and Little had escaped right away. Within minutes. The building fell in all around them, but except for a few bruises and cracked ribs, both were fine.

When he'd gone down to the basement that night, Ventrice turned right at the bottom of the stairs. He stood beside Little, a stranger, over by a couple of freezers.

He didn't know why. If Little hadn't been there, Jim Ventrice believed, then he would've gone over next to his cousin Larry Ventrice or Larry's wife, Marian, Milestone's managers, and he would've absorbed the full weight of the falling slabs—the concrete roof, the second floor, the first floor—just as they had.

A week later, Jim Ventrice called Little.

"Were you in the tornado?"

"Yeah."

"I was the guy beside you."

"Well," Little said, "that freezer saved us."

Wasn't much more to it than that. Wasn't much more to say. They didn't talk philosophy or religion or predestination. The freezer had blocked the falling debris, sparing them. It was the freezer, plain and simple. Wasn't it?

Ventrice had plenty of time that summer to sort it all out. He'd walk along Mill Street, hands in his pockets, and think. He'd just about settled things in his mind: You had to live with the fact that for a lot of questions, there aren't any answers. Good people die. And God doesn't have to explain himself. It's his call.

Rich Little had moved in with Kristy Kaiser, the woman he'd been supposed to meet in Milestone. The single parents blended their families, his three kids and her three.

A month after the tornado, he bought a Harley, his longtime dream. On solitary rides he thought about that night, about how he'd been sure it would change him in some fundamental way, but it really hadn't. He was the same guy. Wasn't he?

* * *

Debbie Miller was writing down recipes. It was the best way she could think of to remember Milestone, a job she loved, the first outside job she'd held after 18 years. Fried chicken, burgers, spaghetti, hot wings—garlic was the secret ingredient in the wings—and steaks, all the recipes she and her boss, Larry Ventrice, had concocted together. They'd never put them on paper, because Debbie caught on quickly and repetition did the rest, and even Marian took to calling the back room of Milestone "Debbie's kitchen."

Debbie had lost so much—her son, her job, her best friends, Larry and Marian—and she wanted to hang on to what she could.

While Mike Miller sat on the porch the first two months after the tornado, feet propped on the rail, Debbie often stayed inside the small house, smoking cigarettes until the rooms were hung with a yellow-gray glaze. Blond bangs hung between Debbie's eyes and the world; straight blond hair fell down her back. The big-screen TV that dominated the living room always seemed to be on, and the Miller kids and a few of their friends and Debbie sat on couches and watched. With the curtains closed you couldn't always tell if it was day or night, unless you already knew.

But the Millers had to find a new place to live, so on an afternoon in late June, Mike, Debbie, Gregg and Chris piled into the car—they'd gotten a teal Ford Taurus to replace the LTD damaged in the tornado—and drove to LaSalle. They had called a couple of newspaper ads for rental houses.

The first one was bright blue with a wide front porch. The moment the car stopped at the curb, Chris and Gregg tumbled out and rushed over and mashed their noses against the windows to see inside: "Cool!" "Wow!"

Mike hobbled to the picture window, cupping his palms over his eyes to peer in. "Nice big living room," he said.

But Debbie didn't like it. She looked around, then folded her arms across her chest.

"It needs a lot of cleaning," she said.

A quick, hopeful response from 8-year-old Chris: "I can dust!"

They moved on, though, and reviewed a few more houses that day, a few more the next. On July 1, a week before they had to be out of the Washington Street house, they signed a lease for a good-sized stone house on a corner lot in LaSalle. By July 5, they'd left Utica.

Debbie still drove back there once a week or so for an informal support group of Milestone survivors and families that met evenings at Joy & Ed's. Jim Ventrice sometimes showed up, too.

They didn't talk much about what happened that night. They talked about their lives, about their struggles, about how hard it still was to drive past the corner of Mill and Church Streets, where Milestone had stood, and where the city had put up a makeshift memorial. There were, affixed to white-painted concrete barriers, pictures of the victims and pictures of Utica from long ago.

Rising from the thin layer of gravel spread over the site was a row of white crosses, each inscribed with a name: *Jay Vezain. Helen Mahnke. Bev Wood. Wayne Ball. Carol Schultheis. Marian Ventrice. Michael Miller. Lawrence Ventrice.*

* * *

Shelba Bimm was leaving Utica. She wasn't going far, just to a subdivision on a hill west of town, a pretty little neighborhood of gently curving streets and polished-looking homes with wide driveways.

Bimm had loved living right in the middle of Utica. But she and her neighbors with homes crushed by the tornado faced a tangle of complications. Utica was on a flood plain, and if you rebuilt, you were required to start with an expensively high foundation. Also, state officials long had planned to redo Illinois Highway 178 to divert its noisy truck traffic, and when they did, many of the homes on Church Street would have to go.

At first, Bimm had been determined to rebuild right on the same spot. This was home. Long divorced, this was where she'd raised her two sons, Shayne and Blayne, by herself. But there was just too much up in the air. Bimm wanted to move on, to get going. She didn't like to stand still. So she bought the lot and began planning her new house.

It would be white with cranberry shutters, just like the old one. On June 21, Buck Bierbom dug the foundation, using the same equipment he'd used to help clear tons of rubble from the Milestone site.

* * *

Pat Elsbury had finally had enough. Enough of the dilemmas. Enough of the back-and-forth—both the highway kind and the philosophical kind.

In mid-July she gave her notice in La Grange. Her last day on the job, a job she'd had for 13 years, was July 30. She cleaned out her desk, packed her pickup and drove straight to Duffy's, where by early evening she was drinking a Miller Lite at the bar, and talking and laughing. "This is what I want to do," she said. "This is where I want to be. I don't want to be back there anymore." Simple, declarative statements.

What wasn't so simple, though, was making up for the money Duffy's had lost. It was only closed for three weeks after the tornado, but the tourists who normally thronged into Utica on summer days on their way to Starved Rock were taking other routes. They'd heard about the disaster and, according to what Lisle Elsbury was picking up here and there, they figured Utica was still in disarray. That exasperated him, but what could he do?

One Sunday afternoon in August, he was sitting in the back room of Duffy's, looking grim and discouraged. There were smudges on his forearms; he'd been struggling to fix an exhaust fan in the basement. But what really irritated Lisle was his insurance company, with whom he'd been tangling all week about repairs to the front of the tavern. The threshold was crucial, Lisle believed. The three-sided glass entrance with neat wooden trim was Duffy's signature. You just couldn't do it on the cheap. It had to be done right.

He wasn't going to compromise. He and Pat had sold their house, had sunk every nickel they had into this place, had staked their future on the corner of Mill and Canal Streets. No way would he short-change it all now because some guy in a button-down shirt with a clipboard didn't get it, didn't understand why the entrance had to be special. No way. He was a fighter, Lisle Elsbury was, and he hadn't survived a tornado just to capitulate to some insurance company.

Lisle was bothered, too, by something Pat had mentioned: When she told her boss back in La Grange goodbye for the last time, he'd given her a look. The look, she said, could have meant only one thing: *You're not going to make it.*

Pat had shrugged it off. *Come and see us in a year,* she wanted to shout at him. *Come back and see us then.*

* * *

Mike Miller returned to work part time for the railroad Nov. 9, running a locomotive. He walked with a limp and probably always would, his doctors told him. He didn't mind. "As long as I don't fall flat on my face," Mike told Debbie, "I don't care."

The Miller kids started school in LaSalle, and Mike and Debbie's biggest concern was Chris; at the threat of a storm, the merest hint of one, the quiet little boy was terrified. They alerted his teachers: If a storm came, they'd need to hold him, to tell him things would be OK.

Debbie Miller put in job applications to cook at several restaurants. No luck yet, but she was hopeful. She didn't spend her afternoons in a dark room anymore.

They still had money problems, though, and wondered how they were going to cover Christmas gifts for the kids. And they still hadn't been able to afford a headstone for Mike Jr.'s grave in Sterling, 47 miles northwest of Utica.

On Aug. 16, at about 5:30 a.m., Mike and Debbie's daughter Michelle had given birth to 5-pound, 10-ounce Melodie Marie. Debbie stayed all night at the hospital, and when she returned home mid-morning, exhausted but joyful, there was a lightness in her face that hadn't been there in a while. Her smile was tentative—she still wasn't sure about the world, after what it had taken from her—but the smile came more easily now, lingered longer. The haunted quality in her eyes had receded a bit.

Yet even as she sat on the couch that morning and talked about Melodie Marie, photos spread out on the coffee table, Debbie had to know that just above her head, high on the wall in the Millers' living room, was a picture of Mike Jr.

He was facing the camera, and the tall, skinny young man with the glasses and straight blondish-brown hair wore his mother's smile: shy, cautious, not quite sure he can trust the world, not really certain it has his best interests at heart.

* * *

By the end of November, Bimm's new house was coming along nicely. The walls were up, and so was the crisp white siding, the gray roof.

She loved to stop by and watch her contractor, Tom Trump, and his crew do their work. And she had a little more time on her hands these days; she and Dave Edgcomb had been notified Sept. 17 that they'd passed the test to be certified as EMT Intermediates, so there were no more classes.

The flat crash of hammering, the piney astringent smell of new wood: Bimm liked to walk around the job site and plan what she was going to put where. She hoped to move in by Christmas. She'd been living in a small trailer that her sons bought for her the day after the tornado, setting it up on Blayne's property.

Some afternoons Bimm would drive out to the site of her new house and just stand in the yard, taking it all in, while the wind fingered its way through the trees.

If you glanced up at the sky, the blue seemed to go on forever—up and up, straight through the roof of the world—and to spread seamlessly from horizon to horizon. So blue, so calm, so beautiful. You would almost swear nothing bad could ever come from such a sky.

ABOUT THIS SERIES

To report this story, Tribune reporter Julia Keller interviewed the nine survivors of the Milestone collapse, and their friends, family members, neighbors and colleagues; and the friends, family members, neighbors and colleagues of the victims of the Milestone collapse; over a seven-month period, beginning a week after the tornado.

She also interviewed townspeople of Utica, Ill.; public officials, including employees and elected officials of Utica and the Federal Emergency Management Agency; meteorologists at the National Weather Service's Chicago office; tornado experts such as Howard Bluestein of the University of Oklahoma; public safety officials, including Utica Fire Chief Dave Edgcomb, Utica Police Chief Joseph Bernardoni, LaSalle County Sheriff Tom Templeton and LaSalle County Coroner Jody Bernard.

The reporter also used newspaper and television accounts of the tornado, and consulted historical books about Utica and the surrounding countryside.

Passages describing downtown Utica before and after the tornado were based on first-hand observations by the reporter, and on the observations of townspeople who were interviewed. Descriptions of the interior of Milestone the night of the tornado were based on the recollections of survivors and on the recollections of other townspeople who frequented the bar. Descriptions of the exterior were based on photographs and the accounts of Utica citizens.

Passages describing the rescue at Milestone were based on eyewitness accounts obtained from multiple interviews with firefighters, police officers, EMTs and volunteer citizen rescuers at the scene that night, along with the recollections of survivors and townspeople present shortly after the tavern collapsed.

Scenes of the Miller family's life after being rescued from Milestone—in their Utica home; sitting on the porch with Mike Miller; searching for a new home; the morning their granddaughter was born—were witnessed by the reporter. Scenes of Pat and Lisle Elsbury's life after the tornado were compiled through first-hand observation by the reporter and through interviews; thoughts and emotions attributed to the Elsburys were derived from multiple interviews with the couple.

Passages dealing with Shelba Bimm, Edgcomb, Steve Maltas, Gloria Maltas, Rona Burrows and other townspeople were based on interviews and observations by the reporter.

Scenes that were not witnessed by the reporter were assembled through multiple interviews with people who were present, both named in the story and not named. When thoughts and emotions are presented, those thoughts and emotions come directly from the reporter's interviews. Descriptions of the activities and thoughts of people who died in the collapse were compiled through interviews with those who were present, or those to whom the deceased had confided their thoughts and emotions.

Lessons Learned

BY JULIA KELLER

Allow me to quote that well-known prose stylist Dwight D. Eisenhower, who once opined that plans aren't worth a damn, but planning is essential.

Much of the information gathered for a long series won't ever be used. Many of our most treasured insights will be revised, then revised again and finally abandoned. The majority of our felicitous phrases—the kind that make us pause just after we come up with them and smile secretly to ourselves—will be relegated to the writer's version of the cutting-room floor: the "delete" key.

The finished story would be a different thing, a lesser thing, without all the elements that are dropped or altered along the way. Behind every fact deployed in a story, there are a hundred other facts for which there isn't space or need, but which deepen and sharpen and illuminate the finished product.

It took me awhile to warm up to this truth. After all, I had transcribed dozens of hours of interviews with multiple sources. I had hunted down and verified every last detail about certain moments in the story—eye color, a license plate number, air temperature—and I had composed, scribbling on a yellow legal pad after the day's reporting was done, a covey of long, ornate descriptions of the people to whom I had spoken.

I had charts. I had graphs. I had plans.

Then, when it came time to actually write the damned thing, I had frustration—because, despite the story's length, a great deal of my reporting had to go.

Yet I could not have produced the series without having first produced the pile of material that wasn't ultimately used. My plans may have been shot to hell, but the act of planning was crucial.

Eisenhower's aphorism, then, is terribly apt—or at least it was for me—as I worked for seven months on this three-part series.

There were facts, and then there were the shadows that congregated behind those facts. There were shades and subtleties and nuances that emerged only because I had taken note of the shadow-facts—the scuff marks on the side of a shoe or the way the clouds seemed to stack up in the autumn sky like sweaters in a drawer—and they retained power and influence over the finished story, even though they were not explicitly mentioned.

Quoting Joseph Conrad makes me feel itchy and pretentious—funny, quoting Ike never does that—but Conrad knew his stuff, too. The goal of art, he wrote, is to "render the highest possible justice to the visible universe." Tall order, that, but it's a goal important to journalism as well as to fiction. Perhaps even more important to journalism, as reporters listen and ask questions and look around and dig for fact after fact after fact. And then we select the few facts that bring justice to bear upon this gorgeous heartbreak of a world.

Julia Keller won the 2005 Pulitzer Prize for feature writing for the work that appears in this volume. She is cultural critic and staff reporter at the Chicago Tribune. *Before joining the* Tribune *in 1998, she worked at* The Columbus Dispatch *in Ohio and* The Daily Independent *in Ashland, Ky.*

San Francisco Chronicle

█ Finalist

Meredith May
Non-Deadline Writing

23. Operation Lion Heart, Part One

SEPT. 12, 2004

Dr. Jay Johannigman opened the back door of the Iraqi ambulance. Inside was a boy. His abdomen was ripped open. His left eye was missing. Both hands—blown off.

A veteran of two Gulf wars, the surgeon at Tallil Air Base near Nasiriya had seen casualties this horrific many times. Few had survived. Remarkably, this child was still speaking.

"Mister, I need water," 9-year-old Saleh Khalaf said politely in Arabic.

It was Oct. 18, 2003, seven months after U.S. forces invaded Saleh's country as part of Operation Iraqi Freedom. Johannigman knew that his job was to treat only American soldiers, but Saleh's unwillingness to die moved him.

The Air Force doctor made a split-second decision that would launch a dramatic mercy mission. The rescue operation would involve an airlift from Iraq to the Bay Area, require dozens of life-and-death surgeries and attract worldwide media coverage.

No one could have imagined then that the mission would take so many harrowing turns—or alter so many lives.

The effort to save Saleh would imperil his family. It would force him to endure excruciating physical and emotional pain. It would strand him in a strange land, far from his remote Muslim fishing village.

Yet before it was over, ordinary people would become heroes. And a little boy from a battle-scarred land would show everyone he met that even in the wreckage of war, there could be miracles.

* * *

Saleh's 16-year-old brother, Dia, was up to his usual tricks, switching their conservative uncle's Quran TV station to a channel with dance music.

The younger Saleh was too modest to join the prank, but he giggled anyway. He didn't have all the dance moves like Dia, who wore his hair shaved on the sides and long on the top—just like the American boys.

Their father, Raheem, sometimes couldn't believe his two sons were brothers. Saleh was always reading the Quran, and Raheem could silence him by simply putting a finger to his lips. Dia had a mind of his own. In the family's southern Iraqi village of Bada'a, he spent his time hanging out with friends.

Too reckless, said an aunt, to marry her teenage daughter. That morning, on Oct. 10, the adults in the living room were giving serious thought to a wedding between the youths when Dia interrupted them with his rendition of the Macarena.

Raheem shook his head, but he had to smile. It had been a long time since he had laughed so freely with his relatives.

The family had been much happier in the months since the American bombings sent longtime dictator Saddam Hussein and many of his Sunni Muslim followers into hiding. For the first time in a generation, the oppressed Shiite Muslim peasants in Saleh's village imagined a future without mass graves and whispered fears. Many Shiite men in the run-down village of 300 had lost homes to bulldozers, or their ears to the secret police, for defying the Baghdad regime.

After a seven-month absence from the classroom, Saleh and Dia were to return to school later that morning. Allied forces had recently driven out fugitive Sunni militants holed up in the boys' school. U.S. soldiers had checked the grounds for explosives and assured parents that students could safely go back.

Saleh was looking forward to class. An expert Lego builder who liked to draw, he had the makings of an architect, his parents and teachers thought.

Raheem, a taxi driver, took his sons to school. On the way, he gave them a rare treat and stopped for gyros. Dia ate two.

When Raheem dropped the boys off, Dia yelled back over his shoulder that this had been the happiest day of his life. Raheem cringed.

In Arabic culture, it was bad luck to say that.

* * *

Returning home from school later that day on a barren path, Saleh trotted behind the longer stride of Dia.

They were getting close to an abandoned restaurant, the halfway point on their 2-mile walk to their crumbling mud and concrete house.

Saleh stopped. Something caught his eye in the trench alongside the road. It was a khaki-colored ball, small and smooth—a toy perfect for playing catch with Dia.

Saleh's parents had warned him not to touch strange objects on the ground. But he was still caught up in the giddiness of seeing his school-mates again.

Saleh picked up the object and quickly realized his mistake when a classmate ran away.

He looked down at his hands and began to cry. Dia raced toward him. Just three more steps.

It blew.

* * *

Raheem was washing his taxi in the front yard when he heard some kind of explosion. It was such a common sound: It could have been mor-tar fire, or someone's can of cooking oil. The 35-year-old man with ink-black hair barely looked up.

To celebrate their sons' first day back in class, his wife, Hadia, had splurged for an expensive freshwater fish called *bini,* which she was preparing over a fire in the back yard. She and her husband had always expected great things from their sons in school, and she wanted to rein-force that returning to class was cause for celebration.

Suddenly, a screaming child ran to the house and interrupted their chores: "Dia and Saleh are dead!"

Raheem dropped his cleaning rag. Chickens and ducks scattered out of his way as he ran for a mile down the dirt road. Hadia trailed far behind, stumbling with grief as villagers crowded around her.

Raheem crossed over the lock where ships used to come in from the Diyala River, past the shuttered restaurant and toward his sons' school.

Raheem's slippers fell off. His bare feet began to bleed, but he ignored the pain. He screamed and screamed. He couldn't stop.

Until he saw Saleh.

Lying sprawled on his back, Saleh was motionless, his belly torn open. His right hand was gone, and only a thumb and an inch of his middle fin-ger remained on his left. Blood poured from his eyes. A piece of shrapnel the size of a quarter had torn through his left eye and lodged in his brain behind his right eye.

Raheem thought Saleh was dead.

Dia was trying to get up. Much of his right thigh was missing. A piece of shrapnel had lodged in his neck.

"There's nothing wrong with me," Dia told his father.

Raheem held Dia so tightly that his friends had to fight to get the teenager out of his arms and into a friend's car. As Raheem climbed in the backseat, Dia said: "Dad, really, I'm all right."

Raheem embraced his first son and prayed. Shortly after they arrived at Saddam Hussein Hospital in Nasiriya, Dia bled to death.

* * *

Raheem selected a coffin for Dia at the hospital's morgue. He and a friend immediately set off in a rental car for the 250-mile journey to the holy city of Najaf, where he would bury Dia that same night, as is Muslim custom. They leased a Chevy Suburban so they could fit the wooden box holding Dia in the back.

Raheem would have to attend Dia's funeral without Hadia. In a small Muslim village like theirs, women weren't allowed at funerals. He was desperate for an update from his brothers, who he thought were making burial plans for Saleh. But without phone service, he couldn't contact them or Hadia.

During Dia's service, Raheem helped hold the coffin aloft and circled the tomb of Imam Ali, the holiest leader of the Shiites. A day spent with Imam Ali is said to be worth 700 years of prayer, and Shiites from around the world seek to bury their loved ones in the same cemetery.

"There is no God but Allah," Raheem chanted in Arabic, "and prophet Muhammad is his messenger."

Even though he said the words, Raheem was questioning why Allah had taken his two sons.

Moments before the burial, Raheem and a village elder went to a ceremonial room at the cemetery and bathed Dia with a sponge and soap. They perfumed him and wrapped him in cloth, like a cocoon. Normally, the dead were buried in one shroud. Raheem insisted on eight pieces of fabric because he thought Dia deserved it.

When he arrived back home that night, he went straight to the "sympathy house," where townspeople were chanting Quranic verses to escort Dia's soul to paradise.

Then someone—Raheem can't remember who—told him Saleh was still alive.

Raheem could feel his knees give out. He collapsed.

* * *

Minutes later, an overjoyed Raheem raced in his taxi to Saddam Hussein Hospital in Nasiriya.

When he entered Saleh's room, he found Hadia praying. When he saw his father, Saleh whispered, "Please, please, can I have some water?"

Raheem couldn't believe how pale Saleh's olive skin had turned. His only living son was all bones.

In the hospital hallway, out of Saleh's earshot, Hadia cried as Raheem described Dia's funeral. She then told him what had happened to Saleh earlier that morning.

Just after Raheem had taken a dying Dia to the hospital, Hadia had arrived at the blast scene to find Saleh on the ground. Realizing that her son was alive, she put Saleh's intestines back in his abdomen and held his body together with her skirt.

Hadia could hear the moans of her son and see his intestines shaking during the car ride to the closest hospital, 10 miles away in Al Shatra. But doctors were short on supplies. Without any large bandages, the only thing they could do was to cover Saleh's abdominal wound with plaster, then send him immediately to the larger Saddam Hussein Hospital in Nasiriya, 40 miles away.

Over the next three days, the Nasiriya doctors stitched his organs back together and put simple bandages over Saleh's mangled forearms.

As the week wore on, Raheem grew increasingly worried. There were no medications. The hospital, abandoned during the American bombings, looked dirty and empty to him. The surgeons would leave the orderlies in charge a lot, especially at night.

Nurses privately confirmed Raheem's worst fears: The doctors were waiting to see whether Saleh would die before operating.

Looking for answers, Raheem tracked down Saleh's physician at another clinic.

"Sit down," the doctor said.

Raheem refused. "I already lost my oldest son. I am here to get the truth about this one."

The doctor lowered his head.

"Your son is 100 percent in danger," he said. "Your only shot—and it's a long one—is to go to the Americans."

* * *

The next day, Oct. 18, Raheem drove to the U.S. checkpoint of Tallil Air Base. Armed with the only word he knew in English, he spoke to the jittery guards:

"Mister, mister."

The guards, trained to expect suicide bombers, fanned out in a circle around Raheem, guns at the ready. Shouting in broken Arabic and using hand gestures, they ordered Raheem to stop, raise his hands and spread his legs.

After determining he was free of dynamite and guns, the guards looked at him blankly.

"Mister, mister," Raheem tried again.

Raheem panicked. Shouting in Arabic, he asked to see the general, but no one understood him. The only chance to save his son was about to vanish.

Then Allah delivered Raheem a gift.

One of the interpreters called to the checkpoint was an Iraqi friend who had frequented Raheem's favorite cafe to drink coffee and smoke fruit tobacco through hookah pipes. Raheem couldn't believe his luck.

His friend, Abdel Hassan, asked what was going on.

The story came out in chokes and sobs. Once the Americans got the translation, one of the guards stepped forward and put his hand on Raheem's shoulder.

Now, they understood. The guards told the translator to tell Raheem that they would call an ambulance for Saleh.

* * *

When Johannigman first saw Saleh in the back of the ambulance, Raheem was waving flies off of his son's wounds.

That Saleh was awake and talking contradicted every textbook the physician had ever read.

The bone on the boy's right arm was exposed where his hand had been blown off. Johannigman pulled the blanket back from Saleh and saw the clumsy plaster battle dressing covering his belly.

Johannigman immediately thought, "land mine." Allied forces were unearthing mines every week from schools, villages and even their own base.

The Iraqi doctors had concluded that Saleh's injuries came from an American-made cluster bomb that failed to detonate during the March invasion. Each one scattered 1,000 bomblets that Iraqi children had frequently mistaken for toys.

For Raheem, the origin of the blast did not matter—his son was dying. He handed Johannigman the boy's medical record. It consisted of a small scrap of gray paper with a few notes in Arabic from Saddam Hussein Hospital.

Johannigman looked at the document. Useless.

It was now or never. Johannigman didn't have high hopes, but he hugged Raheem and headed for the trauma tent.

* * *

In a makeshift emergency room, Johannigman scrubbed his hands and prepared for surgery.

For several weeks, he had been working in a canvas-covered tent shaped like an airplane hangar. It was triage, all the time.

Johannigman, the trauma director at University Hospital in Cincinnati, was on his third tour of duty in the Persian Gulf as a reservist. The lieutenant colonel thrived under the intense conditions that the Air Force referred to as "austere but adequate," where creativity and quick thinking could mean the difference between a patient living and dying.

It was the type of work he dreamed of when he entered medical school—no HMOs, no insurance forms.

The boyish 47-year-old had always believed that his mission was to save patients one at a time, whether it was a 23-year-old American staff sergeant who had rolled his humvee or a 9-year-old Iraqi boy who had picked up an explosive on his way home from school.

On the operating table, Saleh's pulse was fading.

Air Force doctors hooked him up to an IV and assessed the boy. Saleh screamed as they pried off his plaster bandage. His dressing hadn't been changed and had stuck to his wounds.

When Johannigman got the bandages off, he didn't think he could save Saleh. The stitches holding the boy's colon, stomach, liver and small intestine had burst apart with the swelling of his organs, and gangrene was spreading inside his abdomen.

In the next eight hours, doctors conducted 10 operations, during which they untangled Saleh's organs and put them back in their correct places, closed holes in his bowel and cleaned the infections. They pulled piece after piece of shrapnel out of his body. Doctors used a plastic IV bag to close Saleh's abdomen because he didn't have enough skin.

Saleh hung on. After every surgery, Johannigman would remove the breathing tube from Saleh's mouth, and the little boy would wake up, asking for something to eat. His resilience was like nothing the doctor had ever seen.

* * *

It was sunrise when Johannigman finally peeled off his scrubs and fell asleep in his cot. Within a few hours, nurses paged him. Saleh was throwing up blood.

In the trauma tent, Raheem called for help. Saleh heard the worry in his father's voice. "Don't cry, there's nothing wrong with me," he said. Raheem had heard that before.

"Don't let him die! Don't let him die!" Raheem shouted at the Air Force doctors through an interpreter. "Please, please, give him water!"

Johannigman thought one of the stitched holes in Saleh's stomach had broken loose. But that didn't account for his rapid pulse. He was slipping away.

The doctors couldn't give him water, because it could have entered his lungs and made him choke. "Get the chaplain, we may lose him this time," Johannigman called out.

Saleh went into shock. Six nurses, Johannigman and a second surgeon gathered with the Air Force chaplain around Saleh's bed.

"Our father, who art in heaven, hallowed be thy name . . ."

Raheem didn't understand their prayer, but he saw the doctors with their heads bent down. He knew they thought his son was going to die.

Raheem did the only thing he could think to do. He joined the Americans, turning his palms toward the skies and praying to Allah.

But in the middle of the night, the bleeding somehow clotted and stopped. It strengthened Johannigman's belief that surgeons worked with God's hands.

Saleh had survived again, and Johannigman gave him a nickname.

Lion Heart.

* * *

From that night on, Johannigman slept in a cot next to Saleh.

Soldiers, medics and cooks all came by to visit the boy whose iron will and easy charm made him the talk of the dusty base. Saleh taught the nurses a few Arabic phrases: "Scratch my nose," and "Cover me."

An orthopedic surgeon was called in to saw off the bone that was sticking out of Saleh's right forearm, and pull good skin over the break so it could one day fit a prosthetic.

But by Oct. 25, a week after Saleh had arrived, Johannigman had a new problem that he hadn't anticipated.

His trauma tent wasn't equipped to rehabilitate Saleh. Normally, the Air Force hospital would stabilize wounded soldiers so they could be transported to the United States for long-term medical care. Now doctors had an Iraqi child who needed the same thing, but there was nowhere to send him.

Johannigman knew that his young patient had a realistic chance of surviving—but not in the plundered clinics of Iraq, let alone a bare-bones base in the middle of the desert.

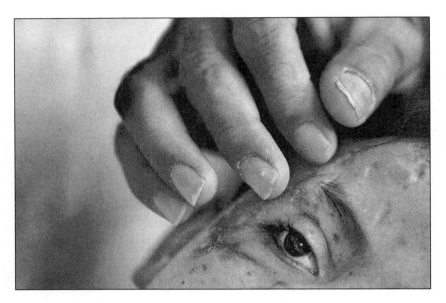

Saleh Khalaf, a 9-year-old Iraqi boy, was severely maimed by an explosion. His indomitable spirit—which earned Saleh the nickname Lion Heart—moved Air Force surgeons in Iraq to launch an international mercy mission to save him. Throughout the ordeal, Saleh's father, Raheem, stayed at the boy's side, ready with a comforting touch like this. (Photograph courtesy of Deanne Fitzmaurice/*San Francisco Chronicle*)

The Air Force surgeon turned to the Internet to consult with pediatric specialists in the United States.

Children's Hospital Oakland, the largest pediatric hospital in Northern California, heard about Saleh's plight on the Web, and administrators agreed to take Saleh as a patient—for free. Of the thousands of injured children in Iraq, Saleh would become one of the lucky few singled out by American military doctors to be treated in the United States. The battle plan was straightforward: Airlift Saleh to Oakland. Restore his organs, give him a new right hand, and build an acrylic left eye. Then send him back home.

To help Saleh survive the airlift, a doctor from San Francisco General Hospital—Peggy Knudson, whom Johannigman had consulted online—shipped a biological dressing called wound vacuum-assisted closure, or "wound-vac." A thin, black spongy material used in cutting-edge trauma rooms, wound-vac sits on top of wounds and absorbs fluid while pulling the skin together slowly.

It arrived four days later in a DHL delivery van. The driver asked Johannigman: "Are you the doctor treating a boy named Saleh?"

In that moment, Johannigman felt proud to be from a country that had the resources and the will to help a boy from a faraway country.

In Saleh, Johannigman had found a piece of war-torn Iraq that he could save.

* * *

On Nov. 8—three weeks after they had frisked Raheem at gunpoint— soldiers escorted Saleh and his father toward a C-130 military plane at Tallil Air Base. Neither Raheem nor Saleh had ever been in an airplane. Neither had ever heard of their destination: California.

The medical evacuation had been cleared by U.S. immigration officials and then approved by everyone from the base commander to the Iraqi Ministry of Health to U.S. Defense Secretary Donald Rumsfeld.

In the dark of night, Air Force doctors gingerly lifted Saleh's cot into the camouflaged military plane. He was unconscious, on his side with his stick legs tucked under him. Barely 40 pounds, he looked like a bird that had fallen out of its nest.

On the tarmac, Johannigman prayed with Raheem again. This time, the doctor lifted his hands to the sky and prayed the way Raheem did.

* * *

Inside the plane, it was pitch black. Doctors showed Raheem where to sit, out of the way of injured American soldiers lying on stretchers.

Raheem was terrified by the thought of flying, and it was agonizing to leave behind Hadia and their two small daughters, Marwa, 2, and Zahara, 4. But he knew this was the only chance to save Saleh.

The pilot started the engine. Raheem bolted upright. The drone of the engine's propellers drowned out all sound, including Saleh's medical monitoring equipment.

During the flight, Saleh suffered chills, and his temperature shot up to 104. His lungs weren't functioning normally.

At stops to change planes in Kuwait, Germany, and Andrews Air Force Base in Maryland, doctors on board ran into the terminals to e-mail Johannigman about Saleh's worsening condition.

After a 35-hour journey, the plane touched down at Travis Air Force Base in Fairfield at about 1 a.m. Nov. 10. Saleh, still unconscious, was placed in a helicopter for the ride to Children's Hospital Oakland.

A hospital staff worker fetched Raheem in a company car. On the way, he was transfixed by the rolling landscape. The freeways. The office buildings. The SUVs. Everything seemed so big.

* * *

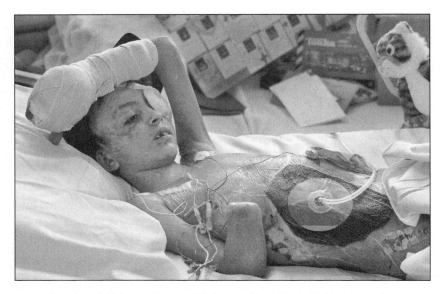

The mission to save Saleh brought him and his father to Children's Hospital Oakland, leaving his pregnant mother and two younger sisters behind in Iraq. The explosion had ripped open Saleh's abdomen, torn off his right hand and most fingers on his left, blown out his left eye and killed his older brother. (Photograph courtesy of Deanne Fitzmaurice/*San Francisco Chronicle*)

As the helicopter landed on the roof of Children's Hospital, chief pediatric surgeon James Betts was waiting with a 6,000-calorie-a-day IV filled with fat, protein and glucose. He knew from Internet chats with Johannigman that Saleh was starving and would need more strength before any more surgeries.

When Betts first saw Saleh, the boy was so emaciated that he looked more like a kindergartner than a 9-year-old. Betts inserted the IV in Saleh's arm and pulled a red blanket decorated with dalmatians over him.

The 56-year-old Betts would lead a team of doctors, plastic surgeons, physical therapists and counselors that would try to restore Saleh to health.

The moment Raheem arrived in Saleh's room, Betts could see the pain in his face. The doctor shook his hand, and through an interpreter, assured Raheem that he would do everything he could to get Saleh home.

It humbled Betts that a father would come so far, under such emotional duress, to seek his help. The tall, lanky surgeon was considered a Bay Area hero for climbing the rubble of the Cypress Freeway in Oakland hours after the 1989 Loma Prieta earthquake and amputating a boy's leg to pull him out. In another high-profile case, he treated a 10-year-old Richmond boy whose face and ears had been torn off by three pit bulls.

In the first few days, all Betts and his team could do was feed the unconscious Saleh intravenously and monitor his weight. Saleh was taken to the operating room multiple times so physicians could change his surgical dressings. They needed to wait until the dressings pulled his abdominal skin closer together, so that eventually they could use grafts from his thighs to close the wound. Saleh also would need skin grafts around the remaining thumb and partial finger on his left hand. An eye specialist cleaned out Saleh's damaged eye socket.

Betts' strategy worked. Saleh regained consciousness, and his temperature stabilized.

Saleh had cheated death one more time.

* * *

"I want to see Mom and my sisters. I want to see them before I die," Saleh moaned in Arabic.

On his fourth day in the intensive care unit, Saleh felt acute pain in his arms and abdomen and realized he was far from home. He was entering what pediatric surgeons call the depression phase. Betts, after 20 years of treating young gunshot victims, recognized it immediately.

"You're not going to die," Raheem told Saleh, sidestepping his son's request to go home. Raheem wasn't sure when they would see Hadia and the girls again.

Saleh had a white patch over his left eye socket. "I want to die!" "I want to die!"

"Shhhh, Shhhh," soothed Raheem. He put on rubber gloves and scratched around the edges of his son's abdominal wound.

Saleh was ready for his first meal. He asked the nurses whether they had a lamb's heart.

Armed with pictures of food on index cards, they suggested he pick something else.

He settled on french fries.

* * *

By mid-November, Saleh was in the news around the world. CNN, local TV stations and dozens of newspapers had reported the boy's airlift to the Bay Area.

Well-wishers sent Saleh piles of stuffed animals and toy cars. A Yemeni couple in Oakland, owners of a Middle Eastern market near the hospital, made daily treks with yogurt and rice. Muslim groups in Oakland and Marin collected nearly $4,000 in community donations for Raheem and Saleh. Arabic professors from UC Berkeley came by to console Raheem.

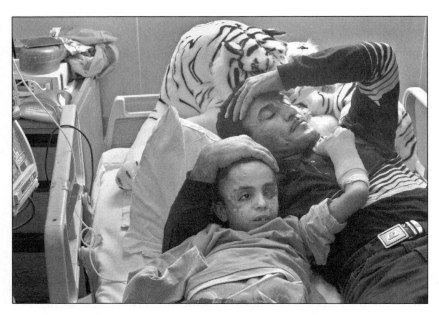

Raheem started most nights in bed with Saleh and then slipped off to a chair when Saleh fell asleep. He was still grieving the death of his oldest son, Dia, killed when Saleh was maimed. Two months after the incident, Raheem had not told Saleh his brother was dead. (Photograph courtesy of Deanne Fitzmaurice/*San Francisco Chronicle*)

Schoolchildren made Saleh quilts and cards. Nurses brought balloons. Firefighters dropped by with a red hat and miniature fire truck.

Saleh was too weak to play with any of his gifts, and instead watched an Arabic cartoon videotape that the hospital provided.

Raheem sat in a chair next to his son during the day, always in the same brown, button-down shirt and knit vest that he had worn on the plane. At night, he crawled into bed with Saleh, forgoing the hospital apartment provided to him in the Family House two blocks away. He prayed five times a day facing east, unless there wasn't space in the emergency room for his prayer rug. Otherwise, Raheem recited his prayers in his head.

As Saleh had done at the Tallil Air Base, he charmed his nurses at Children's. A doctor's wife brought him the Quran on CD. A secretary brought him balloons shaped like dolphins.

His favorite American was 40-year-old Leslie Troutner, a ward clerk in the intensive care unit for more than a decade. Though she had seen many children at the hospital, she had managed not to get too attached to any one patient. But there was something about Saleh that defied words.

She began trying to communicate with gestures and an Arabic dictionary. Her broken Arabic was the only thing that could make Raheem laugh. She brought fast food to Saleh's bedside and taught him one of his first English expressions: "Burger King."

She had the same long, dark hair and chocolate eyes as Saleh's mother.

* * *

One evening in the last week of November, Raheem bent down to pray alongside nearly 100 other Muslims at the Islamic Cultural Center of Northern California on Madison Street in Oakland. It was his first time in public since arriving in California two weeks earlier.

He thanked the crowd for including him in their regular service and said he felt the force of their special prayer for Saleh. Even though Raheem had momentarily doubted his God at Dia's funeral, Saleh's recovery and the support in America were restoring his faith.

Afterward, as Raheem dined on rice and curried chicken in the mosque basement, dozens came by to meet their special guest and take his picture. Everyone wanted to know about Saleh.

Raheem said Betts and his team had just taken sheaths of skin from Saleh's inner thighs and covered his abdomen with them. For the first time since the blast, Saleh's organs were protected by skin.

Raheem told his hosts that his son was going to make it. When they heard the good news, they all had the same reply: "Allahu akbar" (God is great).

Since the Oct. 10 blast, Saleh had endured 20 operations in four different hospitals. Even though months of rehabilitation remained, the prognosis was good.

Raheem felt that he and his son were finally heading toward better days. But he was careful not to talk about his happiness.

In Arabic culture, it was bad luck to do that.

To read the rest of this series, go to http://www.poynter.org/bnw2005.

Chronicle reporter Meredith May and photographer Deanne Fitzmaurice began documenting Operation Lion Heart on Nov. 11, 2003, when Saleh Khalaf first arrived in Oakland with his father.

Over a 10-month period, May and Fitzmaurice worked with Arabic translators to extensively interview Raheem and Saleh inside the hospital, in their new apartment, at McDonald's, at the mosque, at their respective schools and at Middle Eastern cafes and markets. The *Chronicle* was granted access to operating rooms and to doctors and officials inside Children's Hospital Oakland, and spent many hours every week with Raheem and Saleh in the intensive care unit.

Chronicle reporter Matthew Stannard traveled to Saleh's hometown of Bada'a in southern Iraq to interview his mother, Hadia, through an interpreter. He also interviewed Saleh's grandfather and other relatives. Neighbors took Stannard to the site of the blast and to Saleh's school. He interviewed doctors at the Al Shatra hospital, where both Saleh and his older brother, Dia, were taken immediately after the blast.

The scenes in Oakland were witnessed by May and Fitzmaurice.

In most cases, direct quotations used in this story were heard by the reporter, and when necessary, translated for her. In some instances, when a scene was reconstructed based on interviews, direct quotations were provided by interview subjects.

Here are details about how specific scenes in Part One were reported:

- The scene in which Saleh picked up the explosive was recounted by Saleh to his father, Raheem, who recounted the story to May through an interpreter. The interviews were translated by Rima Rhodes, an Arabic speaker hired by Children's Hospital to translate for patients. Houida Alhaimi, owner of the Middle Eastern grocery Pyramids Market in Oakland, also helped translate Raheem's account on a separate occasion.

- The scenes detailing Raheem's involvement at the chaotic blast site and at Dia's funeral were based on five extensive interviews that May conducted with Raheem. Rhodes and Alhaimi translated. Hadia's involvement at the blast scene was based on Stannard's interviews in Iraq.

- The remaining scenes from Iraq were reconstructed through May's translated interviews with Raheem, as well as conversations over the phone and in person with surgeon Jay Johannigman, who treated Saleh at the U.S. air base.

- Raheem recounted Saleh's treatment in Iraqi hospitals, and explained to *Chronicle* reporters how he sought help for his son at the U.S. Air Force base in Iraq. His interviews were translated by Rhodes. His story was confirmed by Johannigman. Both Johannigman and San Francisco General abdominal surgeon Peggy Knudson (who was consulting via e-mail with Johannigman during that time) were interviewed about Saleh's three-week stay on the base. An Air Force photographer on the Iraqi base provided descriptions and photos to the *Chronicle*. Johannigman shared photos as well.

- Scenes of Saleh's first week at Children's Hospital Oakland were reported by *Chronicle* reporter May from his bedside. Details of his first medical procedures were confirmed through interviews with Saleh's pediatric surgeon, Dr. James Betts. Arabic conversations between Saleh and his father, and Raheem's comments during this time, were translated by Rhodes and market owner Alhaimi.

- Raheem's visit to the Islamic Cultural Center of Northern California in Oakland was attended by *Chronicle* reporter May and photographer Fitzmaurice. Muslim members at the prayer service provided Arabic translation.

Lessons Learned

BY MEREDITH MAY

I was in a foul mood. My editor had interrupted my lunch to send me to the hospital for a story. Something about an injured Iraqi kid.

The news conference had already ended. I didn't even have a reporter's pad. I scrambled for a napkin and a pen.

When I walked into the hospital room, Raheem Khalaf, who had just traveled 35 hours from a remote fishing village in southern Iraq, locked eyes with me and pulled the blanket off his son so I could see what an explosive does to a child.

I gasped. I knew war was awful—I'd seen it on TV. But there it was, forcing me to really look for the first time. Saleh was so emaciated he reminded me of a bird that had fallen out of its nest. His hands were missing. His left eye gone. His abdomen was held together with surgical skin and tubing. Doctors were pretty sure he was a goner.

Lesson number one: Never lose your soul. Here I was so mad about a missed burrito that I had forgotten where I was going and what I was doing. I wasn't prepared, and I had to step into the hallway to hide my tears. When I stepped back into the room, Khalaf and I didn't need to speak the same language—one look told us we would be there for each other. I would be his son's storyteller.

Reporting "Operation Lion Heart" brought daily challenges working with language and cultural barriers. Because my main characters spoke Arabic, I often had to watch events unfold and get the translation days later when I had an interpreter available.

The story taught me a second lesson: Be flexible. The Arabic sense of timeliness is hours away from American punctuality. Many of my interviews were missed but made up at night while Khalaf smoked hookahs at a Middle Eastern cafe.

The story took me to the Jordanian-Iraqi border to meet Saleh's mother and three siblings after the U.S. government granted the family asylum. Meeting someone at the border during wartime is like finding a stranger at the World Series.

I learned an important third lesson about international journalism: It can only happen through the graciousness of others. Photographer Deanne Fitzmaurice and I spent most of our trip to the Middle East negotiating with the U.S. Embassy, Jordanian government officials, underground "fixers" who get important documents signed and countless military guards, drivers and airline officials who were willing to help once they heard Saleh's story. Our Arabic interpreter, Rima Rhodes, helped us meet Saleh's family at the border and fly with them to San Francisco for the critical reunion. Our trip would have been a failure had we not been respectful and patient with the officials and insiders who didn't have to go out of their way to help us.

My editor David Lewis taught me an all-important lesson in writing "Operation Lion Heart": scene work. The story's theme—that hope could be salvaged from the wreckage of war—needed to be reflected in each chapter or else the scene hit the floor. Once we figured out what the story was about, it was easy to see which quotes, details and moments would best illuminate Saleh's story.

Saleh taught me the most important lesson of all: Immerse yourself in the story. Many times I worried I was getting too wrapped up in his family to remain objective. I was losing sleep worrying whether I would be able to meet his mother in the Middle East and fly back with her. In hindsight, I learned that you have to put yourself on the line if you want to elevate a story beyond mere fact-telling. You have to get close to be able to tell the story with intimate authority.

When I saw Saleh run into his mother's arms in San Francisco, I knew I had a great story with a happy ending. But more important, one brave Iraqi boy had survived the horrors of war and was happy once again.

Meredith May started as a reporter for the San Francisco Chronicle *in 1999. Prior to joining the* Chronicle, *May worked as a social welfare reporter for the* Contra Costa Times *in northern California. She also has written for* The Boston Globe, The Examiner *in San Francisco,* The Daily Review *in Hayward, Calif., and KGO-TV in San Francisco.* Chronicle *photojournalist Deanne Fitzmaurice won the 2005 Pulitzer Prize for feature photography for her "Operation Lion Heart" images. Fitzmaurice has worked at the* Chronicle *for 16 years.*

Column Writing

M.J. Wilde
Commentary/Column Writing

If humor columnist M.J. Wilde is playing it straight, which is, at the least, suspect, then many of her columns in *The Albuquerque Tribune* are drawn from a life best viewed through a funhouse mirror.

Even her name is a story with a punch line. She was born Melissa Jeanelle Jaramillo and grew up answering to M.J. But "I never really felt like a 'Melissa,' " she said. The name had a discordant ring in the ears of one with a resume that includes writer, actor and recorded jazz singer. So after years of hearing people fumble around—"I've been called everything from Michelle Armijo to Martha Marillo"—she legally changed her name to M.J. and borrowed a surname from her favorite humorist, Oscar Wilde.

Wilde, the columnist, joined the *Tribune* in 1982 as an editorial assistant. Little by little, her writing started to appear in the paper in the form of movie synopses, photo captions and TV copy. Then she took over putting together the newspaper's TV book and became the "TV Queen," a title she adopted for the critic's column that gave readers an often-irreverent glimpse of the day's television offerings.

In 1990, she became a feature writer for *The Post-Star* in Glens Falls, N.Y., but missed her family. So a year later she returned to Albuquerque. In fall 2002, the New Mexico native began writing her humor column, meant, she said, to poke fun at life and then "turn tail and run away. Fast and far."

The description holds up in her winning columns, and it is clear that Wilde plays no favorites, poking away with equal mirth at homophobic folks in Tennessee or the body she sees when she looks in the mirror. For Wilde, the joke begins before the first word and doesn't end until the last paragraph. Each of her columns is accompanied by a mug shot tailored for the day's emotion. Shock. Dismay. Sarcasm. There are lots of sarcasm mugs.

"When we were getting ready to launch the column, the editors wanted to do something fun but weren't sure what that would be," she said. "But I knew. Being ... quite animated and wanting this column to have a unique life of its own, I just couldn't see how one mug shot could capture all that. And since the column was going to cover a wide range of topics, including all the voices in my head, I thought, 'Why not put a face on all those voices?'

"I also thought it would be fun to be able to pick a mug shot that would express the emotion behind the topic of each column—cynical, childlike, overwhelmed, angry, frightened, etc. We took about 140 shots—not one the same. It was a gas. Then we whittled that down to a more manageable 40 shots, and each week I choose a mug that fits the column. And the mugs have become as much a part of the column as the writing."

The writing can be a wild trip full of free association and a vocabulary stretched beyond the dictionary by Wilde's imagination. Writing is the thread that connects all her pursuits, the common denominator of a most uncommon life.

"I'll never give it up," Wilde said. "It feeds me. I'm drunk on it. I'm writing a novel, a killer thriller and a one-woman show.

"But every day is a column. Every day is a new idea or a thought that blooms in my head at odd angles until I have to put it into words. God, I love words. You may have noticed that."

—Keith Woods

24. Anti-Gay County Inherits the Windstorm

MARCH 26, 2004

In the last several days, there has been a lot of voting going on in Rhea County down in Tennessee.

First, the Rhea County commissioners unanimously voted to ask state lawmakers to introduce legislation amending Tennessee's criminal code so the county can charge homosexuals with "crimes against nature."

Of course, that's ridiculous. Homosexuals love nature. Especially pool parties.

The most outspoken commissioner, J. C. Fugate (a name for the ages), put it this way: "We need to keep them out of here."

In fact, County Attorney Gary Fritts was asked by Fugate to "find the best way to enact a local law banning homosexuals from living in Rhea County."

Was it a surprise? Well, no. All this is coming from the same county that still has an annual festival commemorating the 1925 trial that convicted John T. Scopes on charges of teaching evolution, even though the verdict was thrown out by the Tennessee Supreme Court.

But this recent gay ban did not sit well, as you can imagine, with the rest of the civilized and, yes, evolved world and brought a poop storm down on Tennessee's most conservative county. So, in a lily-livered backpedal, the county's commissioners got together and reversed their 2-day-old decision.

That's right. Two days, and they caved.

Come on! If you're gonna be ignorant, go all the way.

I say, let them ban gays and lesbians from their county. I say take it beyond that. I say ban everything that even suggests gayness. And there's only one way to be sure, and that's to strip Rhea County of all things fabulous and/or sparkly.

The only colors that should be allowed in Rhea County should be beige, navy blue and brown. All comfortable shoes for women and all high heels over a size 10 should be burned. Toy poodles, Chihuahuas, Shih Tzus and Pomeranians should be bused to the nearest Gay Accessory Shelter. Feather boas should be plucked naked, and all cosmetics—especially hair gel and glitter lip gloss—should be destroyed.

Of course, certain subversive CDs and/or albums that make you feel like dancing, thinking, connecting emotionally or being happy, i.e. gay, in any way—Cher, Judy Garland, John Lennon, Johnny Mathis, Melissa Etheridge, U2, Prince, Bruce Springsteen, Donny Osmond—gotta go. (Marie Osmond is OK, 'cause she's a little bit country. But Donny, well, he's a little bit rock 'n' roll.)

Now, any restaurant that serves expensive food in small, attractive portions should be shut down immediately, and the owners run out of town. I mean, it's not like they can be rehabilitated to overcook food and put gravy on everything.

School drama departments, swim teams, wrestling teams, community theater and musical groups of all kinds should be immediately disbanded. All participants should be required to sit and watch a re-edited, redubbed version of "Footloose" in which the kids realize that banning rock music is a *good* thing. The added anti-gay message at the end will, of course, be re-enacted by puppets.

Cable TV? I don't think so, mister.

Finally, Rhea County residents might wanna think about building a really big wall around their county. You can't be too careful. But they should keep in mind gays and lesbians have been known to get around just about any barrier put in front of them.

Oh, and just FYI, I believe the Bush administration's chemists are developing a substance called Gay-B-Gone. It smells like a combination of feet, canned green beans, motor oil and Fritos. But it's just in the testing stages.

Seriously, I do think gays in Rhea County could do a couple of things to draw attention to their cause. First, they could drop planeloads of glitter and confetti all over the county. I mean, who wouldn't love that? Or they could release as many monkeys as they can find into the next County Commission meeting.

Who knows? Maybe the monkeys can take over and make more enlightened decisions. They've evolved a lot since 1925, you know. The monkeys, I mean.

25. Life's Scary. Ask My Bosom Buddies.

You know, it's not death I fear so much. It's everything leading up to it.

When you get to a certain age and the people you love have bad, bad things like cancer and emphysema and diabetes, it tends to shrivel your view of life to pinpoints.

My aunt has emphysema. My sister has breast cancer. My cousin has uterine cancer. My mother, father and brother-in-law have diabetes. My brother has heart problems and a knee that needs an operation. Another cousin has to have some serious back surgery. And a good friend has terminal cancer.

So when it was time for me to go in and get a physical, I was a little, um, freaked out. OK, I was really freaked out.

The physical wasn't such a bad experience. Except you're naked, draped in a thin paper gown and sitting for 20 minutes on butcher paper. I felt like a club sandwich without the toasted bread. All that was missing was a pickle and a side of cole slaw.

Every time my doctor said, "This is going to feel a little uncomfortable," she was being completely honest with me.

It turned out I had a questionable little bump on my left breast. The doc said it was probably just a little swollen node. OK, I bought that. It was nothing. Then she said it would be a good idea to have a mammogram, just to be sure. I hadn't had one yet, and so it sounded like a sensible idea.

Aaaaaaaaahhhhhhhh!

My sister had just had a mastectomy, and my cousin a partial hysterectomy. Both were undergoing chemotherapy, and both were doing well. This news did not calm me.

In the three days before my mammogram I kept having the same dream. I was in some 1930s Hitchcock movie. Everything was black and white and slightly tilted. I was in a ritzy hotel lounge having a drink with friends. I was so happy, so carefree.

Then a bellboy who looked like a young Harrison Ford appeared at the door to the lounge and yelled out: "Mammogram! Mammogram for Ms. Wilde! Mammogram!"

Everyone turned and looked at me and froze. I'd wake up in a sweat.

So the day finally came, and I soldiered on over to the radiology place, filled out some papers and sat among the brave. Women of all ages sat, acting casual and reading golf magazines as though the secret to life were hidden in the pages. We all had that same look. The look that said: "This is nothing. No big deal. It'll be fine, and then I'll go get ice cream. Maybe buy a sexy new bra. Or a bottle of bourbon."

They called my name.

"M.J. Weeeldee?"

"Um, that's *Wilde*," I corrected. Geez, I thought in a panic, I hope they're better at reading mammograms.

During the mammogram, the technician made small talk as she cavalierly squashed my perky girls into Play-Doh pancakes between panes of glass. By the time she was done, we each knew the other's life story, and my mammos were now hanging to my knees. In fact I almost asked if they had one of those canned ham keys so I could roll 'em back to their original positions.

After a week of waiting for the results, my doctor called me at work.

That's gotta be bad news, right? They never call you at work. Heck, they never call you.

But she was calling to give me good news. I was fine. All the tests were normal, including the mammogram.

I should've been happy. But all I could think of was why was I the lucky one?

There's no answer really. We wake up every morning, hold on to hope with both hands and laugh as much as we can.

It's not much to go on, but it's all we've got. Besides, hope and laughter beat fear any day of the week. And if we're lucky, maybe even cancer.

26. Bathing Suit (My! Oh!) Can't Skim Flaws

JULY 16, 2004

It happens every summer. And it's a big, fat lie.

There has never been a bathing suit made that can "hide your figure flaws." Unless, of course, your figure flaw is a tiny heart tattoo on your size 2 tushie. And if it is, I hate you.

And there has never been a bathing suit made that can "draw attention away from your figure flaws." I imagine, in my case, this miracle suit would have to come with a juggling monkey I would wear as a hat as I approached the pool area.

Every time I log on to the Internet these days I see the happy little feature stories on how to go about buying the bathing suit that would flatter, fix and forgive even the worst of my fatty and/or genetic flaws.

The idea, you see, is to camouflage the problem. Blend in. Make your 2-foot moons glow less brightly in the light of day. This works about as well as when guys wear those camouflage outfits to the grocery store so the "enemy" can't see them in the cereal aisle.

And magazines glare out at us every year with advice on how to fix big butts, small butts, small chests, big chests, short legs, long legs, big tummies, short torsos, long torsos and everything else they know we consider just plain ugly. The reason they know we consider ourselves just plain ugly is they helped put the idea in our heads in the first place.

You can ask any normal woman—from a chick-on-a-stick to a-roast-on-a-platter—and each will tell you, point by point, what is wrong with their bodies. And, unless they're on the cover of Sports Illustrated, they'll also tell you how much they hate wearing a bathing suit.

Some of the suggestions of the bathing suit gurus are such lies that it's silly even to point them out. So I will.

I like the one where they suggest wearing one of those shiny metallic suits to create an optical illusion about just what the heck is wrong with you.

Yeah, this way the sun can point you out to those who might have thought that slap-slap-slapping sound was coming from the pool's water instead of your thighs. Happily, just before they register your face, you will reflect said sun so intensely they will be blinded for life.

Win-win sitch.

Then there's always the skirted bathing suits decorated with dizzying geometric patterns. These make people feel nauseous and fall down, giving them no time to notice your poochy stomach/floatation device.

I have one word for you: Lycra.

This is the magic word used in many catalogs for women larger than a size 8. It is usually found in the bathing suit section, which is one page squashed between the 20-page "why don't you just stay home and wear a caftan?" section and the 12-page "thank-you-God-extra-wide shoes" section.

Lycra, my friends, is not found in nature. It was not discovered on a hippo who was using it to quell the gibes of hyenas as she approached the watering hole.

Lycra is the trademark for a substance called Spandex, a man-made elastic fiber used in all types of clothing, especially leotards, unitards and Halle Berry's cat suit. And yards and yards and yards of it is used in bathing suits. It will flatten your tummy and hold in your tush. But I must caution you. On some of us, it can smoosh those flaws out the leg and arm holes and leave you looking like the Michelin Man.

I say flaws be danged. I say embrace your figure flaws and show the world it's those very figure flaws that make you the gorgeous, saucy, unique individual you are.

Personally, I'm gonna do my bit by stripping and going nekked to the next office swimdig.

Of course, I'll wear the juggling monkey as a hat. I mean, I'm not crazy.

27. I'd Like to Teach Sodas to Live in Perfect Harmony

JULY 23, 2004

A Pepsi drinker once asked me why I'd never joined Pepsi's "Next Generation."

Honey, I replied, Pepsi is a cult. But Coke is a religion.

You see, there are two kinds of people in this world. There are Coke people and there are Pepsi people.

Coke people are smart and very awake. Pepsi people think they're smart and very awake. But both are good people. Except for Pepsi people.

Not that I'm a soda bigot. We all have a right to drink whatever we like without having it held against us. And if someone out there decides that drinking a weak, sorry-excuse-for-a-soda like Pepsi makes them happy, well, good for them.

Now, this is just the kind of open-mindedness that has made me proud to work here at The Tribune.

You see, we here at The Trib are all about diversity. We're all about choice. We're all about thirst-quenching freedom.

And nowhere could you find better proof of those ideals than in our soda machine.

That's right. Stressed out, cotton-mouthed employees could choose from Coke, Diet Coke, Pepsi, Dr Pepper, Slice, Mountain Dew and even some kind of atrocious grape soda.

All you had to do was pay 55 cents, and you were instantly rewarded with a cold can of the heaven of your choice.

It was beautiful, man.

It was also proof that Coke and Pepsi could co-exist peacefully and profitably in one machine. And if they could, maybe there was hope for the rest of the world.

That's when it happened.

Our little testament to freedom and diversity was replaced. On the surface, not a bad thing. And not a complete surprise. The old machine was a little eccentric. It sometimes sucked in dollar bills and then refused to cough up a soda. And there were those times when it didn't agree with your choice of Diet Coke and gave you Dr Pepper instead.

We could hear the commotion down the hall as our old friend was scraped across the floor, lifted onto a dolly and unceremoniously rolled into the sunset.

When the noise died down, I made my way down the hall toward the small room where my cravings for "the real thing" had been satisfied for so many years.

My screams of horror could be heard throughout the building.

Standing before me was a modern gargantuan example of corporate greed. And staring back at me from behind its plexiglass lair were rows and rows of—Pepsi products.

"Noooooooooo!"

I thought perhaps I was mistaken. So after the initial shock, I scanned the machine's offerings again.

But it was true. There was bottled Pepsi in all its horrid and various forms. Wild Cherry Pepsi? I gagged.

There was also bottled water and juice. For the love of bourbon, we're not schoolteachers. We're journalists. There should be a row of Lynchburg Lemonade, not mango juice.

All this, but not one Coca-Cola product.

Avarice! Sheer avarice!

My shock turned to rebellion, and I went straight to The Trib's editor with the war cry of "Coke or death! Coke or death!" fresh upon my thirsty lips.

I laid out my cola complaint on behalf of myself and like-minded colleagues. My editor took immediate action. He called the soda people and told them we wouldn't put up with such a blatantly evil anti-Coke demonstration. He told them that Pepsi and Coke had been living in harmony lo these many years and The Tribune would not compromise its ideals to satisfy any attempt by Pepsi to monopolize our thirst for equality and diversity.

Or maybe he just asked if next time they could throw in a few more Cokes so we'd leave him alone. I'm not sure. But whatever was said, a row of Cokes and Diet Cokes was added. But over the past several weeks, slowly, insidiously, they have once again pushed Pepsi upon us. The balancing presence of "the real thing" has again been eliminated.

First the USA Patriot Act. Now this.

My friends, I fear for us all.

28. The Baseball—It's Something to Spit About

NOV. 5, 2004

Did you watch the World Series? Or as a friend of mine calls it, "the baseball"?

Very exciting for the Red Sox, I understand, who hadn't won a series since the Earth cooled. Now they've won and the world can breathe a great sigh of relief and continue spin-

ning happily on its axis. And I believe the players got a parade and a ring. Well worth years and years and years of taunting and sacrifice.

I tried to watch the baseball, but, well, there was something disturbing that distracted me completely from enjoying America's pastime.

I'm speaking, of course, of all the spitting. You know what I'm talking about.

There's always been spitting in the baseball, but over the last several years it has escalated to tsunami proportions. There's so much spitting on the field it gives "sliding home" a whole new, icky meaning.

Used to be you'd see some ballplayer with a wad of tobacco in his cheek the size of a golf ball. Very attractive. Chick magnet. But now, every man on the team looks as though he's got a giant softball-size meatball in his cheek. Some have tobacco, some have wads of gum. They look like a control group in some kind of grotesque medical study of cheeky tumors.

They spit on the field, they spit into their gloves, they spit on their hands, they spit on the bases, they spit on the baseball and they even spit in the dugout. I pity the poor janitor who gets the dugout gig. There are no words.

It made me think a lot about men and spitting in general. Hey, it's my job. I'm a columnist.

For the most part, men do not spit indoors. For that we are grateful. But as soon as they're outside, all bets are off.

Now, as a rule, women won't spit unless there's a bathroom sink available or a big, soft absorbent tissue suffused with aloe and vitamin E.

Apparently, a woman's salivary glands are not triggered by the outdoors. (There are those that believe the spitting is a sports thing. But I watched the Olympics and all the spitting and drooling happened off-camera from male correspondents during women's volleyball.)

I had a boyfriend once who never spit if we were on a long trek in which sidewalks were involved. But get him on some outdoor dirt trail and, "Hock-patooey!"

I asked him once why he spit. Did the outdoor air trigger some kind of uncontrollable testosterone spit font? Was it something macho he learned as a boy while playing sports? Were men born with a spit gene as part of their DNA construct? Was his swallower broken?

He blinked as if I was an alien from the planet Loogie, spit and said, "Beats me."

Today that man is clinically insane and wears a bib.

Now, I've interviewed tens of people about this. OK, five. Alright. Two. I've also perused football, basketball, tennis, golf and badminton and could only detect one or two incidents of spitting. And it was during a rather tense set of badminton.

It all leads me to this very important conclusion:

Men spit while playing the baseball because it's what ya do while playing the baseball. It's what Babe Ruth did. It's what Lou Gehrig did. It's what Sammy Sosa did. It's what Kevin Costner and Tim Robbins did in "Bull Durham." It's a tradition. I get it. But it's gotten out of hand.

(Now, this is all very different from that old guy you always see spitting up something heinous and possibly alive onto the sidewalk in public. He's an old guy and has had many years of life built up in his lungs and must get rid of it in order to stay alive. Give him a break.)

I guess in the baseball, if you're not salivating like a bull mastiff, then you're just not passionate enough to be playing the game. You need to go home. The baseball is not for you.

Look, I'm all for tradition and I love the baseball. All I'm asking is for a return to golf ball-size cheeks and intermittent, moderate spitting. And if you're a grown man and not even remotely involved in a sport, just cut it out.

If that happened, much like Gehrig, I'd consider myself "the luckiest (luckiest, luckiest, luckiest) gal (gal, gal, gal) on the face of the Earth (Earth, Earth, Earth)."

A conversation with
M.J. Wilde

An edited e-mail interview conducted by Poynter Institute Dean Keith Woods with M.J. Wilde, winner of the ASNE commentary/column writing award.

KEITH WOODS: If there were one or two primary sources of inspiration, which would you say provide most of your column ideas?

M.J. WILDE: Just plain old intense observation of this nutty world around us. No lack of material ripe to be ripped there. We have a common experience going on here, from the seemingly insignificant—like a trip to Wal-Mart or toasters with a mind of their own—to the frighteningly significant—like a trip to hell with George W. Bush. Everything is a potential column.

It would seem from these columns that you often mine your own life for stories. If that's true, how do you gather information about your life in order to turn it into a column?

I'll go again back to the common experience. My life is your life. Going to the doctor and slowly going mad in the waiting room. Outrage at discrimination. Fear of spiders. Procrastination. Feeling as though the world is conspiring to drive us all to our refrigerators. It's all right there if you're not afraid to look at it, poke fun at it, then turn tail and run away. Fast and far.

Tell me about your writing process. When you sit down at the keyboard, how do you decide on the column's focus?

Well, it's a funny thing. I never consciously map anything out. The closest thing I can compare it to is jazz improvisation. I've been a musician and singer all my life and that mind-set—knowing about melody, pace, tone, rhythm, improvisation without losing the focus of the melody—spills over creatively to my writing.

I sit down with the melody (topic) in my head and allow it to take me wherever it's going to take me, on whatever tangents it desires, never allowing it to get too far away from me. So the column eventually becomes a stream of tightly composed jazz solos with a strong melody at its core.

And sometimes, I just pull it out of my butt at the last minute to meet the deadline.

You seem to favor a conversational style in your writing. How did you arrive at that choice? Do you try others?

Well, it was never a choice. It's always been the way I write. I grew up in a family in which humor was in our everyday conversation. Some of the most profoundly funny experiences I've had in my life were and are conversations with family and friends. In a world in which conversation is a lost art, this style is intimate and personal, and I think it really puts the reader at ease. It's also a kind of verbal human contact. I've written in many styles, but this comes most naturally to me.

There's a touch of hyperbole in each of your columns. In the column about sodas, for example, you wrote, "My screams of horror could be heard throughout the building." What are you trying to accomplish by using exaggeration as a tool?

It gives readers a sense of place. It helps them picture the situation in a very realistic way, making the experience that much more enjoyable. It also enables you to say the things others want to express but can't because they fear the politically correct police.

You use deep sarcasm in writing the column about Rhea County, Tenn. To make the point that they've gone to extremes, you do, too. By identifying all the "gay" things that should be banned, you walk a thin line between sarcasm and stereotype. Did you worry about stepping over that line?

No, because I made sure it was clear that these "gay" things didn't come from my mind but from the simplistic and stereotypical ideas that roam the empty halls found so abundantly in the brains of the homophobic.

Humor is such a tough thing to pull off in print. How do you gauge from column to column whether you've achieved it?

I get a lot of feedback from readers, editors and colleagues, but, as a card-carrying member of the Me Me Me Foundation, I rely for the most part on—wait for it—me. I set the bar pretty high as far as humor goes, and if it's not funny, it doesn't get in the paper. Also, if I can go back in a week or a month or a year and a column still makes me laugh hard enough to choke, I know I'm on the right track.

How does your relationship with your editor work?

She's very tolerant, and when she thinks I may be getting too formulaic, she gently nudges me back toward the light. Most important, she "gets" the column, and she "gets" me and allows me the space to roll along. Bless her.

As you go through revisions in the column, do you read aloud?

No, but I sometimes write aloud. There are those times I have all the reporters sit in a semicircle on the floor while I read my columns aloud to them through a thinly disguised veil of condescension. Actually I am told folks enjoy reading the column to friends over the phone, so I guess I'm doing something right.

How many rewrites do you do on average with a column?

Zero to two. Mostly just a tweak here and there.

What other tactics do you use to be sure that your column is at its best before you hit the "send" key?

I read it through again and again until there's nothing more I can possibly do to screw it up.

I note your use of colloquialisms and other laid-back language such as "Win-win sitch" (in the bathing suit column) or "It was beautiful, man" (in the soda column) or "I don't think so, mister" (in the Rhea County column). How do you get so comfortable with your readers?

Well, for one thing, I like to write the way people in the real world actually talk. That in itself lets the reader know we're in this together. Sometimes I use it to conjure a certain universal character, like a surfer dude or a scolding mother, to illustrate a point quickly and directly. It can be a kind of shorthand. It all goes back to communicating our commonality.

How would you describe your writing voice?

Loud.

What's up with your e-mail name, "tvqueen"?

Well, 13 years ago I created a character named the "TV Queen," who became the *Tribune*'s TV critic. She is of royal television lineage and has a manservant named Xavier, who wears sparkly spandex and rubs her feet with warm oil as needed. The TV Queen loves TV, or as she calls it, "The Tube of Life." She also hates it and thinks we take it much too seriously. So basically she makes fun of TV while telling you to watch TV.

She is an enigma, dipped in chocolate, wrapped in a delusion, mailed overnight to a penthouse in Paris, unwrapped by George Clooney and now appearing in "Ocean's 12C: Do Not Disturb."

Hey, you asked.

Describe the typical reader for whom you're writing.

She's short, hairy, has no table manners and is slightly psychotic. That's why she lives in a cave. No. I'm not writing for a demographic or aiming for a "typical" reader. I'm writing for anyone who likes to laugh and think a little. It's all-inclusive, baby. The minute I start writing for some specialized group, shoot me.

Editor's Note: We also asked Wilde, "What lesson or lessons did you learn or re-learn during the writing of these columns that might be of help to others interested in the pursuit of excellence?" This is her response.

It always surprises me how connected we all are. How even the smallest aspect of an event can resonate outward to so many. Our collective unconscious works happily in my favor as a humor columnist. It's a simple thing, but well-remembered.

Thinking about it recently, I realized for me everything is a column. Everything. Waking and dreaming. Living and dying. A boulder in the road or a fart in the wind. Coke or Pepsi. Mammograms or the evils of bigotry. It's finding that precious bit of quirky language that makes it not only funny and original but bangs the reader right between the eyes with recognition—with a happy awareness that someone else out there gets it, whatever their "it" might be.

Because everything is a column, there's no down time for silly buggers like columnists. Even if I'm not officially working on a column, I know my brain is storing funny bits and odd angles. You never know what bit or angle is gonna be the spark for that perfect read.

It can be a headache. Your brain is always at full capacity and may crowd out useful things like social skills or grooming habits. It can be annoying to your friends and family, who on occasion give you that look that says, "Crap. This better not turn into a column."

That's the thing, you see. You wanna be a columnist, you have to be willing to pay all the storage costs.

To be honest—and I do hate to break it to you—as a humor columnist, my main objective is to make *myself* laugh. I've found that if it makes me laugh out loud or gets my hackles up or sets my subversive spine atingle, I'm on the right path. If I'm not having fun, no one else will either.

Again, it's a simple thing. Well-remembered.

Writers' Workshop

Talking Points

1. M.J. Wilde said that her ideas come from ordinary life—hers and everyone else's. Seen through the prism of her work, what column ideas does she inspire?

2. What do you think of Wilde's decision to employ stereotypes in order to lampoon the people in Rhea County, Tenn., who want to criminalize homosexual sex?

3. In the column "Life's Scary. Ask My Bosom Buddies," Wilde mixes contrasting emotions: mortal fear of breast cancer and lighthearted humor about a breast exam. What effect does she create by combining such opposites?

4. Each column ends with a punch line. How do those kickers influence the power of the column?

Assignment Desk

1. Comb through Wilde's columns and underscore those words or phrases in which her personality most shines through. Cut those words and phrases and see what effect it has on the strength of the column.

2. Write a column that combines contrasting emotions—love and hate, fear and humor, attraction and repulsion. Test the column on a friend or colleague and discuss the benefits and pitfalls of the form.

3. Interview a friend about his or her life and have the friend interview you. Write down the story ideas that come from the interviews. Write a column from one of those ideas.

4. Wilde's columns are written in a distinct, conversational tone. See if you can rewrite one of the columns without the first-person voice. What happens to the tone and message?

● SARASOTA

Herald-Tribune

Finalist

Rich Brooks

Commentary/Column Writing

29. Small Talk Becomes a Big Thing When You're No Longer Able to Do It

SEPT. 11, 2004

I'm no longer on speaking terms with my brother.

And things are pretty dicey with my wife, too.

It's no one's fault, either. Blame amyotrophic lateral sclerosis (ALS), also known as Lou Gehrig's disease.

Nine years ago this month I was diagnosed with ALS. And a year ago in July, I stopped breathing.

That's right. I haven't drawn a breath on my own since I was attached to a portable ventilator. I have room air pumped into my lungs through a plastic tube that connects the respirator to a stoma, which, in medical jargon, is called a HITT or hole in the throat.

The last nine years have seen lots of changes in my life, as well as the lives of my family.

I've been conscious of these changes, some of which have overtaken me incrementally. My speech is a good example of this.

A conversation last weekend with my older brother, who is half deaf, and a shopping excursion with my wife, who suffers from selective hearing loss, brought my communication problem into sharp focus.

Being unable to perform many of the tasks required of fatherhood, I sometimes ask others to act as my proxy. Noticing the dog in contented repose on the couch, I asked my brother to gently prod her from her satisfied slumber.

"Smack the dog," I implored.

He looked at me and smiled. He hadn't heard a word.

"Smack the dog," I said, raising the decibel level a notch.

This time he saw my lips move and walked to within shouting distance, which for him is about 2 feet.

"SMACK THE DOG," I yelled loud enough to be heard across the bay.

Desperate, he called for a translator—my wife.

"I think he said Magna Carta," he said to my wife.

"Smack the dog," I repeated.

"No. I think it was Madagascar," said she.

While the two of them discussed how history and geography often intersect, the dog, perhaps growing weary of the noise, sauntered out of the room.

The following day, I was in the back of our van with my wife driving. As we turned into a parking lot, I spied a man leaving a store with my alma mater's logo on his T-shirt.

"Look at that guy's shirt," I said.

I'm pretty sure I didn't say what she thought I said. And I'm fairly certain I don't want to know.

"Fine," she hissed. "I'll find a parking place. You know, sometimes you are a real pain in the !#@," she said.

I wanted to dispute her characterization, but let it slide. After all, it's better to have someone think you're a pain than to open your mouth and remove any doubt.

My gradual loss of diction has made me appreciate the gift of speech and how we take it for granted.

There are those who disdain small talk, but as one who can no longer engage in it I can testify to its importance.

"How are you?" "That was some storm last night, wasn't it?" and other Lilliputian phrases often open the door to more important topics. And the phrase carries different meanings to different people. For example, saying, "How're you doing?" to my son carries a different meaning than if spoken to a casual acquaintance.

It will probably be some time before I can no longer speak. When that happens, I plan to read Thomas Merton, who found sanctity in silence.

Until then, I plan to make myself understood, even to the point of being a pain in the !#@.

To read additional columns by Rich Brooks, go to
http://www.poynter.org/bnw2005.

Lessons Learned

BY RICH BROOKS

Forget nut graphs, summary paragraphs, inverted pyramids, anecdotal leads and anything else you think you might know about newswriting.

Those forms and formulas beaten into your head since Journalism 101 won't help you here. They don't apply.

Instead, I want to talk about a game I play with my readers every so often. The name of the game is "imagination," or "let's pretend."

Newspaper reporters, editors and their readers don't get to play this game much. That's too bad because, as a storytelling technique, this game can be a powerful tool that allows readers to identify with the characters or the author.

It's called empathy.

Typical news stories don't elicit much empathy from readers. That's because most news stories focus on events. These stories aren't really stories at all, at least not in the sense that people normally define a story. This definition of a story would include characters and a plot that has a beginning, middle and an end. Put another way, a story is what adults read to their children at bedtime. News stories are usually an organization and presentation of facts or events.

Empathy is why readers cheer Hansel and Gretel when the witch is pushed into the oven. It's why we're glad that Goldilocks escapes from the three bears.

The lack of empathy is why few read an account of the city planning and zoning board. The city planning board might put people to sleep, but that doesn't make it a good bedtime story.

Judging from the response I receive, newspaper readers are hungry for stories that evoke empathy. About six times a year I write about my disease process, and, in each case, responses from readers fill my e-mail box.

Sure, I get some letters from readers saying they feel sorry for me. But most of the letters are from readers who had a similar experience with a loved one, and they can relate to the experiences of my family and me.

Besides, playing to readers' sympathy can quickly turn stale.

To avoid what I call the sap trap, I try to focus on the incremental losses the disease—amyotrophic lateral sclerosis—has caused while using humor and dialogue to advance the story line. This holds readers' attention and keeps them from being overwhelmed by emotion.

By letting readers walk a mile in my shoes—playing "let's pretend"—I've been able to develop a relationship with them. This relationship has given readers a window into a place most of them have never been.

Rich Brooks is a senior editor at the Sarasota *(Fla.)* Herald-Tribune. *His career in journalism started at 17, when he wrote high school sports stories for a weekly newspaper. He currently writes a column that appears Saturdays in all* Herald-Tribune *editions.*

The Boston Globe

Finalist

Brian McGrory

Commentary/Column Writing

30. Back Bay's Dog Man

JAN. 9, 2004

When they found Richard Harmon that morning last week, it looked as if he had been praying. He was on his knees, his arms splayed forward, his head bowed so low that it rested against the ground in front of him.

He was in an alley behind Newbury Street, a homeless man living and dying in the midst of so much affluence. A contractor painting a women's boutique saw him around 9 a.m. and called 911. Police and medics declared him dead at the scene. They labeled him another John Doe and then carted him from the frigid streets to a refrigerated room at the state medical examiner's office. Sometimes it seems impossible to get warm.

There wasn't a reason in the world why anyone who handled Harmon's body would have known about the hundreds of creatures who would be heartbroken by his absence.

Harmon was a lot of things in life. He was as big and imposing as his native Maine, with a barrel chest and a scraggly gray beard. When he napped on a Commonwealth Avenue mall bench, you could hear him snoring a block away.

He was gruff. Words lurched from his mouth, especially when he told stories about an old manslaughter conviction, his time as a POW during the Korean War, or his former wives.

He was fiercely independent. He refused medical help in the days before he died, never stayed in a shelter, and "preferred to go through the Dumpsters than take the sandwiches from us on the van," said one homeless caregiver, Dr. James O'Connell.

But what he's best known for, what he'll always be missed for, is this: Harmon was the Dog Man of the Back Bay.

Some street people spend their days begging for money. Others struggle toward normalcy or drink themselves into oblivion or find a bench and stare at things no one else can see.

Harmon gave out dog biscuits. He gave them out to every dog who came his way, and come they did, urgently, their masters struggling to grip the leash. Some days it looked like he was leading a canine chorus, with bulldogs, retrievers, shepherds, terriers, all sitting rigid in front of him waiting for their treat. There's not a dog in the neighborhood who doesn't spend the better part of his or her walk thinking of Richard.

"That's my 72d customer today," he'd say to the owner as he handed a biscuit to his admirer. "They're out in force."

Put it in perspective: A 78-year-old man living on the absolute edge was spending money he barely had on the pampered dogs of wealthy people.

Didn't matter. Some days, he'd search for dogs as they searched for him. The reunion was always joyous. He often awoke from a nap on a bench to stare into the eyes of an entitled mutt who couldn't comprehend the delay.

When Harmon wasn't giving out biscuits, he slowly pushed his cart up and down the back alleys collecting bottles and cans so he could afford the treats. He refused most offers of money, unless it was all but forced on him. "I don't need it," he would say.

When dog owner Mary Kaitlin McSally gave him a Christmas gift, he quietly said, "I never get anything wrapped anymore."

He told people that he spent his nights in a rented room in the South End, but that appears to have been a lie born of pride. Yesterday, in the alley where he died, a homeless man named Paul said Harmon slept for years beneath the overhang of a sealed doorway behind the Jasmine Sola store. When it rained, he taped a plastic tarp across the brick. On cold days, he sat in the public library reading large-print editions of spy novels.

Other stories may or may not have been a stretch. There's no record of any manslaughter conviction in his past, and homeless advocates were having little luck confirming that he was a Korean War veteran, which would allow for a proper burial.

Meantime, hundreds of disappointed dogs continue to look in vain for their departed friend. And this city has lost another small piece of its fading soul.

To read additional columns by Brian McGrory, go to
http://www.poynter.org/bnw2005.

Lessons Learned

BY BRIAN McGRORY

I had initially approached Richard Harmon several years before his death, asking whether he would talk to me for a column that would portray him as the Dog Man of the Back Bay—the homeless guy who spent his money on biscuits for the pampered hounds of rich owners. He laughed his big garrulous laugh, and then he declined.

His reason: The streets were too dangerous; his fellow bench dwellers too fickle. He feared that if I gave him notoriety in the *Globe*, then he would be targeted by the sometimes-irrational men with whom he shared the Commonwealth Avenue Mall. He was adamant in his refusal to cooperate and could not be budged.

Still, I filed the idea away and continued to take mental notes on his comings and goings, always writing leads in my head about him—this man who lived in poverty among so much wealth, a gruff giant who gently devoted himself to animals that were not his. For many Back Bay residents, he was the only homeless person with whom they ever had contact. I always assumed he would give me an opportunity at some point to write about him.

That was lesson one that I learned from the experience: Don't abandon a good idea. When word trickled out that he was missing and might have died, I began to report the column. That led to two other key lessons I relearned in this exercise.

The first one is to always make the extra phone call and, even better than a phone call, to knock on one more door. In this case, I had heard that Harmon had died in an alley behind a fashionable women's clothing store. Early one freezing cold morning, I roamed up and down the alley and talked to the other homeless men who lived there, and they pointed out where Richard Harmon used to sleep. Afterward, I went into the store, wondering whether someone might have seen something on the day he died.

The woman at the register referred me to a contractor who was in the store doing repairs. He, in turn, told me that he was the one who found the body and described in detail the position and the scene that gave me my lead. Without that, the story would not have been the same.

This gets me to the second lesson: Things aren't always as they seem.

Harmon had always told me, and any of the hundreds of other people whom he talked to, that he was not, in fact, homeless, that he had a little basement apartment, that he was a combat veteran, that he had once been convicted of a manslaughter charge.

As I reported the column, I came to learn that none of this was true. He slept in an alley. By day, he sat in the Boston Public Library when the weather wasn't good enough for him to sit outside. He had no military record. He had no criminal record. He had no home.

In my mind, the fact that he was a serial fabricator at first weakened the story, but as I thought it through, I came to realize that it was all just part of the complicated life and death of this man who was seen and well-regarded by so many. I was glad I did the reporting. I was also confident that telling the truth in death would in no way diminish the life he led.

Brian McGrory is a metro columnist for The Boston Globe. *Previously, he worked as a suburban reporter, city reporter, national reporter, and as a White House correspondent covering the Clinton Administration from the newspaper's Washington bureau.*

St. Petersburg Times

■ Finalist

Howard Troxler
Commentary/Column Writing

31. Scapegoats Won't Make Bus Stops Any Safer

OCT. 14, 2004

Here is how it needs to work.

A parent calls the Pinellas County schools and says: "You're making my kid cross several lanes of traffic to get to and from the bus stop."

An alarm goes off or something. A big red light starts flashing in the school bus office. The school bus person says: "That is an emergency! It will be fixed RIGHT NOW."

And then they fix it. That hour. If all else fails, then the next day the incoming superintendent of schools, Clayton Wilcox, personally shows up to drive that kid to school.

Or if Wilcox's car is already full, then members of the School Board help out. Or several of the various administrators.

Yes, they all have important meetings to attend, and they all have important memos to write. But maybe the idea of not getting kids killed might be, you know, more important.

Maybe.

Unfortunately, that was not the case for Rebecca McKinney, a 16-year-old junior at Clearwater High School who was struck Friday as she and her sister scampered across McMullen-Booth Road. She died Sunday.

Rebecca McKinney's case is not unique. The anecdotal evidence now coming in from other parents is that they have tried, even begged, the school system not to make their kids cross busy highways.

I talked to the father of another Clearwater High student, Gary Williams. Last year his daughter Ashley, then a junior, had to cross busy, dangerous U.S. 19 to get to her bus stop.

"They put her in a position where she had to cross seven lanes," Williams told me. Even if she ran, the stoplight was too short.

He called the school system.

They said they would fix it.

She had to cross U.S. 19 the next day.

He called again. They said they would fix it.

She had to cross U.S. 19 the third day.

He called a third time. They told him: "Well, that's where the bus stop is." He did not allow her to ride the bus again.

It sounds very much like the response that the schools gave to McKinney's mother, according to a family friend: "It is where it is."

In 2002, our reporters wrote about six children assigned to Anona Elementary School on Indian Rocks Road. They included a 7-year-old first-grader who had to brave traffic without a stop light or stop sign. The school district refused to alter the bus route *by one block*. A mother said she was told she should "educate her child on how to cross the street."

Here is what the Pinellas school system's spokesman and career apologist, Ron Stone, said on Monday about the death: There had been no reports of any complaints from McKinney's mother this year.

No reports.

Let us parse that statement into its several levels.

First: It implies it's the mom's fault for not saying anything. (The family says she's been complaining for years.)

Second: What, they need a complaint first, before they can decide not to jettison kids from school buses into heavy traffic?

Third: What kind of report? Form 29-B, "Request Not To Endanger My Daughter," filled out in triplicate?

By Tuesday, school officials appeared to be trying out a new strategy: Offer Up the Bus Driver. The idea was that some poor, underpaid sucker suddenly could be responsible for setting and enforcing transportation policy for the School Board. Case solved!

Oh, and there also is the computer excuse. The School Board's computers can't tell four-lane roads from any others when they draw the bus routes. In this day and age of GPS and MapQuest and new technological miracles every day, the School Board can't tell McMullen-Booth Road from the alley behind my house. What, were the hamsters in the little wheels tired? Did the 386 computers break down? Maybe they should've stuck with the Macintoshes that they decided to get rid of.

Today, the Pinellas school district searches desperately for somebody else to blame, whether it be parent or bus driver or computer, while assuring the public that it is double-checking how many other students are so endangered. School Board member Mary Russell urged parents in this situation to "please call the district so it'll stop."

It doesn't work.

To read additional columns by Howard Troxler, go to http://www.poynter.org/bnw2005.

Lessons Learned

BY HOWARD TROXLER

Supposedly, if you put a frog in cold water and turn up the heat gradually, he doesn't notice. I do not know if this is true, but it is a useful image.

Sometimes a columnist's job is simply to poke that frog in the butt with a stick and yell, "Hey! It's HOT!" It's an obvious thing to say, but somebody needs to say it.

This column took a not-so-courageous stand against dumping students off school buses into heavy traffic and getting them killed. This does not strike me as an especially radical position. And yet, given the circumstance, it desperately needed to be said. Our local school board had allowed a bureaucratic culture to drift so far out of whack that not only were kids being dumped onto busy roads, but the busing office had developed an atmosphere of outright contempt for parents who objected.

After the death of 16-year-old Rebecca McKinney, the response of school officials was incredibly, stupidly out of touch. In best bureaucratic fashion, the first strategy was to try to shift the blame, impugn the mother, hint about the bus driver and, above all, admit nothing. Meanwhile our reporters were gathering anecdotal evidence from dozens of parents who had complained about the same problem and been given the brush-off. After initial denials, hems and haws, it turned out that hundreds of bus stops had been mapped in direct violation of the stated policy and that the mapping software's warning features had been disabled. People got fired or transferred.

But that all came later. At the outset, I was so mad about the initial bureaucratic response that I wanted to shove the issue all the way to the other end of the spectrum and make school officials acknowledge the responsibility *personally*. Hence the idea of red lights flashing and alarms going off in the bus office when a parent's complaint was received. Hence the sarcastic proposal that if the situation wasn't fixed within the hour, then the superintendent of schools or school board members should personally drive the kid to school the next morning. Hence, finally, the parsing of the spokesman's mealymouthed blame-shifting (making fun of mealymouthed spokesmen being one of the fringe benefits of the job).

This is my least favorite kind of column. It was my favorite kind when I switched to column writing 17 years ago, but over time I've grown tired of the obvious tack. An ongoing column ought to inform, provoke, challenge, amuse, surprise, move or be worth the reader's time somehow.

Yet, sometimes the job still boils down to poking the frog in the butt with a stick. *Somebody* needs to do it.

Howard Troxler is a metro columnist for the St. Petersburg *(Fla.)* Times. *He joined the* Times *as a columnist in 1991 and served as its political editor from July 1995 to November 1997. Troxler returned to writing in late 1997. His column currently appears Sundays, Tuesdays and Thursdays on the front of the newspaper's B section.*

PART 4

Obituary Writing

Alana Baranick

Obituary Writing

THE PLAIN DEALER

Each week in *The* (Cleveland) *Plain Dealer*, Alana Baranick shines a spotlight on someone in the community her readers may never have met.

She chooses with care the subjects of "A Life Story," her weekly obituary feature, searching for the remarkable within seemingly ordinary lives.

Readers have been introduced to Clementine Werfel, a longtime church housekeeper who was known for walking fast and for her occasional bad cooking, and George Kossoff, an orthopedic shoe salesman who chose fashion over function when it came to his own aching feet.

Baranick said she's interested in the accomplishments and honors her subjects have achieved, but she also wants to know about eccentricities, failed marriages and what made them laugh.

"Sure, rich white men—the movers and shakers of their generation—still dominate the obit page," Baranick said. " 'A Life Story' affords me the opportunity to write about the lesser-knowns. Men and women. Rich, poor and in between. Relatively young to very old. Various races and ethnicities, occupations and avocations, religions and socioeconomic backgrounds."

A reporter with *The Plain Dealer* since 1992, Baranick has become internationally recognized for her obituary writing. Her book, "Life on the Death Beat: A Handbook for Obituary Writers," draws on her nearly 20 years of experience in writing about the lives of northeast Ohioans.

Baranick has given presentations to obit professionals from Australia, Canada, England, and across the United States at Great Obituary Writers Conferences in 2001, 2002 and 2003. She has been quoted in obituary-related stories in *American Journalism Review*, the *Los Angeles Times* and *The Washington Times*. She has won several statewide awards for obituary writing.

A native of western Pennsylvania, Baranick wrote obits, reviewed rock concerts and edited the religion page for *The Chronicle-Telegram* in Elyria, Ohio, before taking a job as an obituary writer for *The Plain Dealer*.

—Sara Quinn

32. Selling Shoes Fit This Man Well

JULY 5, 2004

MAYFIELD HEIGHTS—Of the many jobs George Kossoff held in his life, none satisfied his soul more than selling orthopedic shoes.

In the 1950s, he fitted customers who hobbled into the Cleveland Orthopedic store with shoes that could help them walk straighter and with less pain. Kossoff, who died June 13 at 92, spent evenings at nursing homes, measuring the feet of clients who couldn't get to the store.

George Kossoff

- June 12, 1912–June 13, 2004
- Youngstown native, son of Russian immigrants.
- B'nai B'rith Youth Organization volunteer.
- Told his three daughters: *It's just as easy to marry a rich man as it is to marry a poor man.*

"He was just pleased to be able to be helpful," said Bob Levine, a family friend. "I don't know whether he made any money on it, but he got psychic income. He made people feel good about themselves."

Kossoff had genuine empathy for folks with foot problems. He walked in pain since the 1930s, when he was pinned against the metal gate of an elevator by a pallet of boxes while working as a stockboy.

"He injured his leg," said his wife, Millie. "The doctor said he'd never walk."

Although drab, clunky, specially-fitted shoes could ease his pain, Kossoff preferred to wear colorful Italian-made patent-leather dress shoes.

"At one time, he was a very spiffy dresser," said his daughter, Claire Nash. "He got a little less discriminating about mixing plaids and stripes toward the end, but he did like to look sharp."

Kossoff couldn't wear classy clothes while pumping gas, cleaning car windshields and changing tires at the Rockwell Service Station at East 12th Street and Rockwell Avenue, which he co-owned in the late 1930s.

"He hated that job," Millie said. "It was tough, dirty . . . When he came home, the kids were sleeping already. He didn't want to get near anyone until he took a shower."

Working conditions were better in the 1940s, when he owned Komar Sales and Service. He sold car accessories and such varying products as candy bars and new-fangled television sets with 10-inch screens.

At family gatherings, George Kossoff "invariably made some sort of speech about how lucky he was to have such a wonderful family," said his daughter Claire Nash. "We made family occasions 'occasions.' " In this photo, Kossoff gives a speech at his 75th birthday party during a family reunion in Hershey, Pa. (Photograph courtesy of the Kossoff family)

"We had a TV set because he sold them in his store," said his daughter, Linda Kemmerer. "People would come in our house and watch TV."

By the early 1950s, he was happily selling shoes. But his seemingly perfect career ended after four years due to a dispute over whether to keep the business open on Saturdays. Kossoff favored staying open, citing the potential for increased sales. His boss staunchly disagreed.

Kossoff went from selling shoes to peddling fish at the Woodland East 55th Street Market. "Only fresh fish," his wife said. "Some of the times, they would still be moving."

He and his wife also ran a concession at Catalano's Supermarket on Mayfield Road, where they sold fried fish on Fridays. When business dropped off in the late 1960s, Kossoff went to work for the Cleveland Vending Co. He serviced vending machines until he was 69. Then he returned to Catalano's to work part time until he was 80.

Kossoff struggled to support his family and "never thought he gave us enough," said daughter Claire. "But looking back at my childhood, I can't think of anything we wanted that we didn't get . . . Dancing lessons. Acting lessons. BBYO (B'nai B'rith Youth Organization). He always had money for us to do those things that were important to us."

The Kossoffs raised their kids in Cleveland Heights and South Euclid. After their youngest, Teri Alexander, graduated from high school, they lived in various apartments until moving into the Schnurmann House retirement center in Mayfield Heights.

In his latter years, Kossoff planned seniors' bus trips to such places as Amish country, Toronto and Washington, D.C. "We would rent a bus and fill it up with friends," Millie said.

One of those friends, Maury Feren, remembered Kossoff as a man who wanted seniors from his Jewish Community Center group "to spread their wings and do interesting things. George felt secure in himself and confident he could do anything with the group. He never worried about successes. He believed in the possibilities."

33. The Egg Lady of Avon Lake

JULY 26, 2004

AVON LAKE—Josephine Milbrandt kept three quarters, four dimes, two nickels and scads of trust in a Whitman Sampler candy box on her back porch.

Josephine Milbrandt

- June 8, 1911–June 27, 2004
- John Adams High School graduate.
- Her husband died in 1990.
- Philosophy about the past: *It's water over the duck's back.*

Alongside the box were dozens of fresh eggs.

Milbrandt, who died June 27 at age 93, sold eggs from the enclosed porch of her Avon Lake home for more than 40 years. She banked on people putting money in the box and taking only the change they were due—and, of course, their eggs.

"She had the honor system," said her neighbor and customer, Mary Mackin. "If you didn't have the money, you put an IOU in the box. Many times, she would be in the kitchen and come out and chat. She was very intelligent . . . very much aware of what was going on in Avon Lake and the world in general."

Milbrandt learned about entrepreneurship, customer relations and self-serve retail operations from her parents, the Blahas, in Cleveland in the 1920s and '30s.

Her father earned barely enough to support his wife and two kids at his stove factory job. Her mother, a native of Czechoslovakia, told him, "You're never going to get anywhere working for somebody else." So they opened a grocery store at East 131st Street.

To lighten their workload, they placed baskets at the door, so shoppers could take flour, canned vegetables and boxes of cereal from the shelves while the Blahas cut lunchmeat and ground coffee. Josephine was a youngster when she and her younger brother started working in the store.

After working for eight to 10 hours a day, Josephine liked to unwind by roller-skating at Euclid Beach Park. That's where she met her husband, George Milbrandt.

During the rationing days of World War II, "everybody on the street was raising rabbits or chickens for survival," said her daughter, Jo Grospitch. "After the war, stuff was plentiful. Neighbors complained

Josephine Milbrandt, known as the Egg Lady of Avon Lake, gets ready to go into the chicken coop to collect eggs to sell in 1948. (Photograph courtesy of the Milbrandt family)

about the chickens. We lived on a small, 40-foot lot. Mom wanted a better life for us. She said we should be on a farm."

In 1947, Milbrandt moved to Avon Lake with her husband, three kids and a dozen chickens. They ran a fruit farm and sold grapes to Welch's for jelly, but eggs became their bread and butter.

Each spring, egg seekers placed orders on a blackboard on the porch for dozens of eggs to be colored for Easter baskets.

"You'd say how many you need, and she'd hold them back," Mackin said. "The older the egg, the better the dye would take. She made sure she had them for you whenever you came."

Milbrandt also boarded horses in her barn. "My mother said she'd collect the eggs and feed the chickens, but wouldn't clean the horse barn," her daughter said. "That was man's work."

She donated eggs, time and money to Catholic churches in Avon Lake. She assisted with bake sales and raffles sponsored by the ladies guilds at St. Joseph and Holy Spirit parishes. She helped prepare chicken dinners—not using her own chickens—at St. Joe's summer festival.

Not long after St. Joseph School was started around 1949, Milbrandt came to the rescue of parochial school students, who were denied rides on a school bus because they didn't attend Avon Lake public schools.

"Anyone that was along that street and was kicked off, she picked them up in her station wagon and packed them in," said her son and former St. Joe pupil, George. "It was like one of these circus acts. She ran that wagon down the street to get those kids to school."

In recent years, the great-grandmother helped kids who visited the Bradley Bay nursing home with the Right-to-Read program improve their reading skills.

She also kept track of birds that stopped by for a snack at the bird feeders outside her window.

"She had bird feeders and a bird book," her daughter said. "If some new bird showed up, she'd look it up. She had a finch feeder. Mom fell in love with the yellow birds. People would show up at her room at 5 o'clock, when the birds came to eat."

34. A Spirit That Soared with the Stars

Willie Ray "Karimi" Mackey felt a kinship with the primitive Dogon people of West Africa, who have been mapping the stars for more than 800 years.

The 51-year-old NASA astrophysicist and African dance instructor was fascinated that the Dogon, who revere Sirius—known as the Dog Star—knew of its tiny companion star, Sirius B, centuries before modern astronomers identified it.

> **Willie Ray "Karimi" Mackey**
>
> ■ May 16, 1953–Aug. 6, 2004
>
> ■ Born in Memphis, Tenn.
>
> ■ African name: Osagyefo Karimi Salmone Faye.
>
> ■ To instruct someone to call him in his last months, liked to say: *Hit me up on my cell.*

Mackey was pronounced dead, apparently of a heart condition, Aug. 6—while Sirius was making its annual daytime appearance in the sky.

As a scientist, Mackey conducted far-ranging "fundamental research that doesn't reveal itself until years downstream but is critical to development," said Julian Earls, director of the NASA Glenn Research Center.

But he didn't look like a rocket scientist.

"He had his own style," said NASA colleague Eric Overton. "In appearance, he was so down to earth, you would be shocked to know he even had a job. Then you find out he worked at NASA, had a Ph.D."

Mackey grew up in St. Louis, the eldest of nine children in what was essentially a single-parent household. Ray, as he was known to his family, took care of his younger siblings while his mother worked the midnight shift at the post office. He got them ready for school in the morning and assigned them educational projects after school.

When his sisters saw a spider in the house, "not only did Ray kill it, he looked it up in the encyclopedia and gave a report," said his sister Karen. "He liked Radio Shack science kits. He outgrew those and started taking things apart in the house. Lamps, appliances. He always found a way to put it back together."

He watched public-television programs like "Nova" to learn about the stars. He tried to instill his passion for the heavens in his siblings and, later, his daughters.

Willie Ray "Karimi" Mackey, center, led this group at Lakeland Community College in an African circle dance at a Black History Month event in February 1996. (Photograph courtesy of C. H. Pete Copeland/*Plain Dealer* file photograph)

"He made us go in the back yard, and we'd have to look up in the sky," said his sister Yvonne. "He'd say, 'Analyze that.' "

In the early 1970s, Mackey enrolled at Oberlin College, where he and classmate Diaris Jackson were "roaring with ideology, pushing for change, angry that we'd missed the '60s, aware of the special gifts that made us leaders," Jackson said.

Mackey, whose African name, Karimi, means "one whose spirit travels with the stars," went to Boston to study astrophysics at the Massachusetts Institute of Technology. He also trained in African dance and drum under Raymond Sylla, an African cultural icon from Senegal.

After earning a doctorate from MIT in 1981, Mackey taught math at Wilberforce University in southern Ohio. Abasi Ojinjideka, with whom he collaborated on projects integrating cultural arts and science, met him at a Kwanzaa event 22 years ago.

"He was sitting on a drum, listening to music on headphones, reading a book and watching TV at the same time," Ojinjideka said.

Mackey started working for NASA in Brook Park in 1989 but later returned to Wilberforce through a space agency program that allows scientists to spend time at not-for-profit institutions. More recently, NASA lent him to Cheyney University in Pennsylvania.

"We worked together to provide NASA exposure and computer technology for students who lived in a homeless shelter in Philadelphia," said J. Otis Smith, a Cheyney professor. "He was fun to work with. He personally inspired some of our students to overcome their fear of science to explore those fields more closely."

He also did his best to get his twin daughters, Nyonu and Naima, excited about science.

"If you looked in the sky on a clear night, he could tell you the names of the stars," Naima said.

One weekend, while visiting his daughters at Hampton University in Virginia, Mackey woke them at 6:30 a.m., and said, "We're going to Norfolk State University. I want you to see the sunspots in the sky."

When they arrived, "he got out his little sunspot device with a mirror," Naima said. "We saw these little dots that would move across the paper. It was neat."

35. Housekeeper's Heavenly Touch

SEPT. 6, 2004

STRONGSVILLE—Clementine Werfel blessed priests at St. Joseph Catholic Church in Strongsville with heavenly desserts, memorable meals and seemingly miraculous coffee.

The retired parish housekeeper, who died Aug. 2 at age 96, routinely walked around the dining table in the rectory, offering coffee to each priest.

"Would Father like regular or decaf?" the 4-foot-something Werfel asked them one by one.

Clementine C. Werfel

- June 2, 1908–Aug. 2, 2004
- Her twin became a nun.
- Survived Palm Sunday tornado of 1965, which destroyed some parish buildings.
- Greeting to priests: *How's my little boy?*

Regardless of the priests' individual preferences, she filled all their cups with coffee from the same pot. The coffee drinkers silently accepted what they got, as though Werfel really could turn regular coffee into decaffeinated, much the way that the biblical Jesus turned water into wine.

"She was so comfortable with priests and anyone, she treated everybody the same," said the Rev. Mark Latcovich. "Clemmie made the rectory a home. She was like a mother and grandmother to you. She'd do anything for you."

But she didn't treat her charges with kid gloves. When a priest told her that he liked his beef "a little red," the diminutive Werfel handed him a bottle of ketchup and said, "Here. You can make it red."

She wasn't particularly fond of cooking, and sometimes it showed. She once boiled filet mignon, which is supposed to be broiled, until it looked like black tennis balls in a stew.

"She loved to clean the refrigerator out, put it in a pot and call it soup," Latcovich said.

Werfel did better with desserts. She made wicked fruitcake muffins, which she soaked in rum and brandy as they cooled. She drizzled hot pumpkin pie with honey to make it sweet. Whenever she baked pies, she made around 10 at a time, then froze them or gave them away.

"She enjoyed playing in flour," Latcovich said. "It was like dirt in the garden. She was really into gardening."

Clementine Werfel stands in front of St. Bernadette Catholic Church in Westlake and the statue of the Holy Family that she donated to the parish. She ordered an identical statue to stand in front of St. Joseph Catholic Church in Strongsville, where she was the housekeeper for 46 years. (Photograph courtesy of Hilda Monteleone)

Werfel got her first packet of flower seeds as a child growing up in Wilmore, Pa. She and her twin sister, Catherine, were the middle pair in a brood of 12 kids. Her parents, first generation German-Americans, ran a prosperous farm.

"We had heat in the house; we had a bathroom, and we had a car," said her only surviving sister, Mary Casey. "That was something for that day and age."

Werfel, who had polio as a baby, stayed on the farm, working as a cook for family and farm-hands until she was 31.

While visiting her sister Margaret in Cleveland in 1939, Werfel got a job as a housekeeper for the Hilkert family, who had eight kids. Two of them became priests. Werfel became house-keeper at St. Joe's when the parish was started in 1946.

When the Rev. Bob Sanson was appointed to St. Joe's in 1991, Werfel "was already 83, and she was still making delicious apple pies and scrubbing the garage carpet on her hands and knees," Sanson said.

As her ability to handle her duties diminished, "They let her stay there for a while and had someone else come in to cook," said retired parish bookkeeper, Hilda Monteleone. "This did not go well with her. She didn't want to give it up."

In 1994, Werfel reluctantly retired from the rectory and moved to the Harbor Court independent living community in Rocky River. The center provides one raised flowerbed for each of its gardening enthusiasts. Werfel had two.

Bill Parobechek, whose late father chauffeured Werfel around for decades, inherited the job of taking the ever-feisty housekeeper to church and gardening centers. He did his best to keep up with her as they walked to her room at the end of a long hallway at Harbor Court.

"She'd walk faster than I could, and I'm a mailman," Parobechek said. "She knew what she wanted, and she wanted it now. I would take her to lunch. We would be waiting to be served. She would ask the girl, 'Are you from out of state? It took you so long to serve us.' "

Werfel was accustomed to speaking her mind, even at the rectory. "She was a tough lady," Monteleone said. "If she didn't like something, she told the priests."

36. A Passion For Raising Rabbits

NOV. 22, 2004

SPENCER TOWNSHIP—Patty Crites' prize-winning rabbits were known for their long floppy ears, luxurious coats and unscheduled public demonstrations of bunny-birth.

The 63-year-old grandmother, who died of complications from congestive heart failure and other health problems Oct. 27, raised droopy-eared English lops and other breeds at Pat's Bunny Farm in Spencer Township for 30 years.

Patricia Ann Crites

■ Nov. 9, 1940–Oct. 27, 2004

■ Her mother, Helen Fetzer, lives in Spencer.

■ Former married name: Gerrick.

■ Enjoyed going with friends to movies, flea markets and country-music concerts.

She showed her best bunnies at rabbit-club events and county fairs throughout Ohio.

At a few Medina County Fair rabbit contests, Crites entered pregnant rabbits who ended up giving birth before the judging began.

"She didn't realize how far along they were," said her friend Renee Burns. "People loved it, to see these little tiny pink things coming out."

Crites had as many as 250 rabbits at one time, and every one of them had a name.

"She read a lot of novels," said her daughter Regina Manos. "Every time she saw a good name, she'd write it down."

She also raised ferrets and Peruvian guinea pigs. Over the years, she had a Vietnamese pot-bellied pig and a de-scented skunk as house pets. She kept a goat, ponies, horses, dogs and cats. She took care of two crows, Igor and J. J., a pig named Peggy and her nine piglets.

Crites also had an African parrot and cockatiels. Her part-time jobs at a veterinarian's office in Litchfield and at a pet shop in Ashland yielded opportunities to adopt even more exotic animals.

"We almost ended up with a tiger," said her husband of 32 years, Jim. "One time she tried to bring home an African anteater. She went to an auction in Wooster and brought an emu home. The only thing she never brought home was a monkey."

Crites, the daughter of a steel-hauling truck driver, was born Patricia Ann Fetzer at Berea Hospital. She started bringing stray animals home

Patty Crites, holding an angora rabbit, looks out from a barn window at Pat's Bunny Farm in Spencer Township in the late 1970s. (Photograph courtesy of Patricia Crites' family)

while growing up on Worthington Avenue near West 117th Street in Cleveland.

The location of her childhood home made Crites a city girl, but Crites really was a country girl at heart.

"We always used to go out to see my grandmother on the farm in Medina," said her younger sister, Beverly Magyar. "We weren't surprised when she started her bunny farm. She had trophies and all kinds of ribbons she'd won over the years. The hardest thing was for her to sell her rabbits when she was so sick."

Crites had three children— Brian Gerrick, Scott Gerrick and Regina—with her first husband, whom she married and divorced twice.

"They had some problems and were trying to patch things up," her sister said. "It didn't work. When I got married she said, 'Didn't you learn anything?'"

After her second divorce, she met Jim Crites, who also was divorced and had kids. They moved from Lakewood to a 17-acre farm in Spencer Township in the early 1970s.

Patty, her husband and her kids engaged in 18th-century re-enactments, where participants slept outdoors, wore pioneer garb, shot muzzle-loaders and paddled canoes.

"On all the campouts and everything, Patty always came out looking beautiful with perfect makeup on and never got dirty like the rest of us," said re-enactor Bob Wulff.

When she was younger, Crites hunted bear in Canada and deer in southern Ohio with her husband. She even went on rabbit hunts.

The only thing she ever shot was a fox.

But she was not averse to butchering the animals she raised—including bunnies that weren't suitable for show or too old or unattractive to be sold as pets—and cooking the meat for her family. The practice is common among rabbit breeders and farm folk.

"At rabbit shows, they'll have bunny-on-a-bun, creamed rabbit or barbecued rabbit," said Burns, a fellow bunny breeder. "How many animals can you raise and eat your mistakes?"

Crites grossed out her sister's kids one Easter when she tried serving them rabbit for dinner.

"They just thought that was amazing," her sister said. "You never knew what you were going to get on the holidays."

Housekeeper's Heavenly Touch

wonderful place name

STRONGSVILLE—Clementine Werfel blessed priests at St. Joseph Catholic Church in Strongsville with heavenly desserts, memorable meals and seemingly miraculous coffee.

writers love beautiful names

great reversal, she blessed priests

adjectives chosen with religious meaning

The retired parish housekeeper, who died Aug. 2 at age 96, routinely walked around the dining table in the rectory, offering coffee to each priest.

a gorgeous number

"Would Father like regular or decaf?" the 4-foot-something Werfel asked them one by one.

a rarity, dialogue in obit

soft humor, reveals character, not too deferential to priests

Regardless of the priests' individual preferences, she filled all their cups with coffee from the same pot. The coffee drinkers silently accepted what they got, as though Werfel really could turn regular coffee into decaffeinated, much the way that the biblical Jesus turned water into wine.

appropriate allusion to Christ's first public miracle

"She was so comfortable with priests and anyone, she treated everybody the same," said the Rev. Mark Latcovich. "Clemmie made the rectory a home. She was like a mother and grandmother to you. She'd do anything for you."

allows speaker to use affectionate nickname

But she didn't treat her charges with kid gloves. When a priest told her that he liked his beef "a little red," the diminutive Werfel handed him a bottle of ketchup and said, "Here. You can make it red."

She wasn't particularly fond of cooking, and sometimes it showed. She once boiled filet mignon, which is supposed to be broiled, until it looked like black tennis balls in a stew.

"She loved to clean the refrigerator out, put it in a pot and call it soup," Latcovich said.

Werfel did better with desserts. She made wicked fruitcake muffins, which she soaked in rum and brandy as they cooled. She drizzled hot pumpkin pie with honey to make it sweet. Whenever she baked pies, she made around 10 at a time, then froze them or gave them away.

"She enjoyed playing in flour," Latcovich said. "It was like dirt in the garden. She was really into gardening."

Werfel got her first packet of flower seeds as a child growing up in Wilmore, Pa. She and her twin sister, Catherine, were the middle pair in a brood of 12 kids. Her parents, first generation German-Americans, ran a prosperous farm.

"We had heat in the house; we had a bathroom, and we had

Margin annotations:

- telling
- polite word for "short"
- anecdote reveals character
- showing
- telling
- showing
- a bit of narrative
- nice balance to "miraculous"
- appeals to the senses
- easy transition of topics
- writer uses the speaker's analogy
- flashback
- good order: quote attribution quote
- unusual word, but fitting

a car," said her only surviving sister, Mary Casey. "That was something for that day and age."

Werfel, who had polio as a baby, stayed on the farm, working as a cook for family and farmhands until she was 31.

startling fact

While visiting her sister Margaret in Cleveland in 1939, Werfel got a job as a housekeeper for the Hilkert family, who had eight kids. Two of them became priests. Werfel became housekeeper at St. Joe's when the parish was started in 1946.

episode suggests a Catholic culture

When the Rev. Bob Sanson was appointed to St. Joe's in 1991, Werfel "was already 83, and she was still making delicious apple pies and scrubbing the garage carpet on her hands and knees," Sanson said.

reveals the strength of her body and character

As her ability to handle her duties diminished, "They let her stay there for a while and had someone else come in to cook," said retired parish bookkeeper, Hilda Monteleone. "This did not go well with her. She didn't want to give it up."

reinforces what has come before

In 1994, Werfel reluctantly retired from the rectory and moved to the Harbor Court independent living community in Rocky River. The center provides one raised flowerbed for each of its gardening enthusiasts. Werfel had two.

strong names

picks up the theme of her passionate interest

paragraph ends on good word

Bill Parobechek, whose late father chauffeured Werfel

around for decades, inherited the job of taking the ever-feisty housekeeper to church and gardening centers. **He did his best to keep up with her** as they walked to her room at the end of a long hallway at Harbor Court.

another nifty reversal

"She'd walk faster than I could, and I'm a mailman," Parobechek said. "She knew what she wanted, and she wanted it now. I would take her to lunch. We would be waiting to be served. She would ask the girl, 'Are you from out of state? It took you so long to serve us.' "

so she's not perfect: feisty, a bit provincial and impolite

Werfel was accustomed to speaking her mind, even at the rectory. "She was a tough lady," Monteleone said. "If she didn't like something, she told the priests."

Roy Peter Clark is senior scholar and vice president of The Poynter Institute.

A conversation with
Alana Baranick

An edited e-mail interview conducted by Poynter Institute faculty member Sara Quinn with Alana Baranick, winner of the ASNE obituary writing award.

SARA QUINN: How do you determine whom you will write about?

ALANA BARANICK: I write two kinds of obituaries for *The Plain Dealer*: standard daily obituaries and "A Life Story" features, which run every Sunday. My five ASNE award entries are for "A Life Story."

The movers and shakers of the community rank high in the selection process for standard daily obituaries, but they are for the most part ineligible for the "Life Story," which features northern Ohioans who are not widely known.

With both forms of obits, I strive for diversity. I consider the obit candidate's age, gender, race, ethnicity, religion, occupation, avocation and peculiarities. I also aim to represent communities throughout *The Plain Dealer*'s seven-county circulation area.

My goal is to represent every thread in the multicultural tapestry of Greater Cleveland.

I review obituary information submitted by families and friends of the deceased. I read paid death notices that run in *The Plain Dealer* and obituaries that are printed by our competitors. I never pass up an opportunity to chat with a caller (or e-chat with an e-mailer) about a suggested obituary. You never know when you're going to find a real gem.

How do you decide what the focus will be?

Serendipity. I get the information and see what rises to the top.

Are there surefire questions to get a source to tell you more than the subject's resume? What are they?

My favorite question is, "What set your loved one apart from the rest of the crowd?" It's not necessarily "surefire," but when it works, it's amazing.

I believe that interviews fall flat because the interviewee doesn't understand how to answer. With obit interviews, folks tend to say things they think you want to hear. They get into an "obitspeak" gutter.

I often say that the world would be a better place if the people I've written about had never died. Most of them were loving, caring, devoted to family, friends and God, hard-working, astute in business and generous to a fault. They never said an unkind word about anyone, and they never met a stranger. No wonder they will be (and I hate this phrase) sorely missed by all. (Obitspeak.)

Because the people whom I interview want me to succeed, I can take them by the hand and lead them to a better way. I tell them that they need to explain things to me in greater detail. "Assume I'm totally unfamiliar with this subject." (Sometimes I am.) "Help me paint a picture of Dad." "I want our readers to believe I knew your mom."

What do you do if the subject has something potentially embarrassing or unflattering about his or her biography that's crucial to the story?

If it's crucial to the story, I evaluate how to express it honestly. I don't want to diminish the severity of the transgression or flub or go overboard on it. The obit has to be done and the bad news included if the person was a public figure. For people who were not in the public eye, if the nasty stuff is too big to avoid, I might dump the story altogether.

How can you find the pattern in a person's life? Anecdotes, accomplishments, personality—how do you find the most important thread?

The most important thread usually emerges through interviews with family and friends, whether conducted individually or in a group setting. I ask questions, but I also let them ramble on. I latch onto similar anecdotes or facets of the person's life that are brought up by several interviewees. Sometimes I don't see it until I'm in the writing process.

How would you compare obituary writing with profile writing? Aren't they the same?

Obituaries are profiles, as long as the writer understands that they are news stories and not tributes to the dearly departed. The chief difference: The subject is not available to interview.

What do you think of the paid obits that many newspapers run, in which people can say whatever they want about a loved one?

I think they're great, as long as it's clear that they are family placed ads and not reporter-written stories. They tell you more about the person who composed the ad than they do about the deceased.

Where did the idea for the feature come from?

The idea for the "Life Story" feature came from Jim Sheeler's "A Colorado Life" in *The Denver Post*. I learned about the existence of that feature while attending the Third Great Obituary Writers Conference in Las Vegas, N.M.—not Nevada—in the summer of 2001. Garrett Ray, a retired journalism professor, shared copies of Sheeler's freelance features with us. Sheeler himself showed up at the 2002 conference and elaborated on how he did his fabulous stories. Sheeler now writes for the *Rocky Mountain News*, where he sometimes writes obits. "A Colorado Life" lives on in the hands of *Denver Post* staff reporters.

The annual obit writer's conference, which is the brainchild of Carolyn Gilbert, an obituary enthusiast who founded the International Association of Obituarists, has been a wonderful source of information and inspiration for me. I've learned from obituary writers from newspapers of all sizes from across the country, Australia, Canada and England.

Where and how do you collect information?

I find my subjects through information submitted by families hoping for an obit, from paid death notices, from obits in other newspapers and from tips from readers.

I contact relatives or friends of my subject. I visit with them in their homes or places of business. I look through their scrapbooks, at memorial picture boards from the funeral and photos displayed in the home. I borrow several photos. (Our photo editor makes the final decision on what to use.) I read through military discharge papers, old newspaper articles, awards programs and church bulletins.

I do a lot of phone interviews. I get phone numbers for all members of the immediate family and people who knew my subject from various points in his/her life.

I look up information on the person in our archives, old city directories, online public records and Google.

Sometimes I attend funeral or memorial services.

How do you organize your stories?

I compile a chronology of the person's life. I group related items together, then figure out where they fit in the chronology. I use a lively image of my subject in the lead. I usually make it clear in the second sentence that the person is dead. I select possible walk-offs (or closings, also known as kickers) and place them at the end of the chronology. I shuffle elements around to make the story flow. Sometimes I swap the lead and the walk-off. As I turn the elements into sentences, I determine what items could be eliminated. I put them aside for inclusion in the photo cutlines or the information box.

How many drafts do you do?

I keep tweaking a story until it's done. Then my editor suggests other tweaks.

What revisions did you make to these stories before publishing?

The revisions made in the "Life Story" features for Clementine Werfel, Willie Ray Mackey, Patty Crites, George Kossoff and Josephine Milbrandt were simple editing fixes.

I don't recall how I originally wrote the paragraph in Werfel's story that referred to the raised flowerbeds at the independent living community. I just recall that my editor revised it to make it easier to understand. The same type of fixes were made to explain Kossoff's job with the vending machine company, Mackey's cell phone and Crites' previous marriages. My editor also eliminated a portion of a quote in Crites' story.

What other role does your editor play?

This interview probably wouldn't be happening if it weren't for my editor, my champion, Chris Quinn. He was the first editor to support my vision for the "Life Story" feature. He sold the idea to his superiors. He lets me write the stories my way. When I miss the mark, he explains what's wrong with my story and tells me, "Give it another shot." He does not rewrite the story for me. He's awesome.

What's the best obituary you've written and why? What did you do right with it?

This is like asking me to tell you which of my two sons is my favorite. Should I say the best obituary I've ever written was the one for:

Fast Eddie Watkins, the colorful bank robber who made an estimated $1.5 million in unauthorized withdrawals from Cleveland to California?

Or Harriet Norris, a.k.a. the Banana Lady, who sardine-packed her ancient Bonneville sedan with produce, shoehorned herself behind the steering wheel and delivered the goods to local hunger centers so the homeless could have their daily requirements of fruits and veggies?

Perhaps the best was for Betty Ann Savage, the confidence-bolstering dress-boutique manager who, upon finding the perfect mother-of-the-bride dress for a client, would moisten her thumb with her tongue, touch her thumb to the woman's backside and make a hissing sound: "Ssss. Sssee? You sssizzle!"

On any given day, I might give you a different answer. Today I'll say the best obituary I've written was for Benedict Jablonski, mild-mannered clerk-typist for a metropolitan car dealership, who morphed into his alter ego, Ben Jason, BNF (Big Name Fan), whenever he entered the realm of SF (Science Fiction).

He was a big deal in old-time science fiction circles, but his only surviving brother didn't seem to appreciate how big. I persuaded the brother to give me phone numbers for Jablonski's SF friends from across the country. I got some wonderful insights on SF history and culture by interviewing his friends. I think I did a good job of conveying those insights. I wrote a comic-book superhero lead that set the tone for the rest of the story. I had fun with it.

Who would you like to write your obituary? What do you hope the person will include?

Realistically, the person who writes my obituary probably will be a reporter at *The Plain Dealer*. In that case, I'd prefer that it be written by either Richard Peery or Wally Guenther, who share obit duties with me, or my immediate editor, Chris Quinn. We have a talented staff of reporters at the paper, but the ones who regularly deal with obits would be best for this.

On a grander scale, if I could choose from all the writers in the world, I would want Jim Sheeler to pen my obit.

I'd want my obit to say: "She wrote about thousands of people she wished she had met."

Editor's Note: We also asked Baranick, "What lesson or lessons did you learn or re-learn during the writing of these stories that might be of help to others interested in the pursuit of excellence?" This is her response.

While doing research . . . I happened upon an awesome passage that has become the standard I follow in choosing "Life Story" subjects.

On Oct. 26, 1947, the bodies of 6,251 war dead—the first to be returned from military cemeteries in Europe, Iceland and Newfoundland after World War II—arrived in New York aboard the Liberty ship Joseph V. Connolly.

The bodies were en route to their final resting places in family plots or at Arlington National Cemetery. Only one unidentified body was taken off the ship and carried in a flag-draped coffin down Fifth Avenue to a dignitary-loaded memorial ceremony.

Bob Considine, who covered the event for the International News Service, brilliantly explained how this unknown soldier represented all those in caskets in the hold of the ship. They were commanders, sergeants, privates, commissioned officers, enlisted men, draftees. Men from every branch of the military. Only one woman, but even having one in that number was significant in those days. Jews, Catholics, Protestants.

"Men of every faith and of every known shade of skin and approach to life," Considine wrote.

This terrific definition of diversity has become my standard. (Of course, I changed it to "Men AND WOMEN of every . . . ") What better place than the obit page to celebrate diversity? After all, people from all walks of life die.

"A Life Story" affords me the opportunity to write about the lesser-knowns. Men and women. Rich, poor and in between. Relatively young to very old. Various races and ethnicities, occupations and avocations, religions and socioeconomic backgrounds.

I consider geography, too. I hope eventually to have written about at least one person from each city, town, village and township in *The Plain Dealer*'s seven-county circulation area.

I've learned to view obits as well-rounded profiles of real folks, not mournful one-dimensional tributes for the saintly. I want to share the deceased's accomplishments and good points, but I also want to know about his eccentric behavior, failed marriages and favorite jokes.

From summing up a life in 20 inches of copy, I've also learned to be selective with details and quotations, to make smooth transitions from one story element to another and to develop a structure that makes it all work.

Once I have completed the first round of interviews and research, I put together a chronology of my subject's life. Then I insert details, anecdotes and quotes, highlighting those I most want to include. If there are holes, I do more interviews and research.

I choose a lively image of the deceased for the beginning of the story. Most of the time, I casually mention the person's age and date of death near the top. I try to choose a knock-'em-dead or a full-circle ending, usually a setup with a quote. Then I string together details and quotes from start to finish, connecting the dots to make the story flow.

Writers' Workshop

Talking Points

1. How does writer Alana Baranick get someone to speak openly about the person she's writing about? What questions does she ask to help people say more than just what they think she wants to hear? Why are these techniques effective?

2. Baranick weaves subtle, humorous details about the person's life into her stories. Read through her story about Clementine Werfel. What details do we learn about Werfel that make us feel as though we have met her? What might draw readers to this story about a seemingly ordinary life?

3. How might it help Baranick's writing process to look through scrapbooks, old newspaper articles, photos on memorial picture boards and personal papers? How might this help the overall story presentation?

4. What criteria do Baranick and her editor use to determine whom to write about? How does this fit with the process at your publication? What sort of life stories are you drawn to as a reader? As a writer? Why?

Assignment Desk

1. Think about the last five people you interviewed for a story. List sources you might go to in order to collect anecdotes that would help you write this type of personal portrait for each of them.

2. Baranick's profiles sometimes include potentially embarrassing or unflattering details. How might you determine whether personal information is essential to a profile you might write? Who might be harmed? What steps might you take to minimize harm? Write or rewrite the obituary of a controversial public figure, modeling your story on Baranick's sensitive approach.

3. Write your own obit and have a colleague write your obit. Compare them. What did you put in yours that does not appear in your colleague's version? What did you leave out?

The Washington Post

Finalist

Adam Bernstein

Obituary Writing

37. Eleanor Whalen, 91; Effervescent Olympian

FEB. 3, 2004

Eleanor Whalen, 91, the saucy and irreverent Olympic swimmer who shot to fame in the water only to see her athletic ambitions felled by champagne, died Jan. 31 at her home in Miami. She had kidney failure.

Mrs. Whalen, known as Eleanor Holm or Eleanor Jarrett for much of her career, participated in the 1928 Games in Amsterdam and was a star of the 1932 Games in Los Angeles. In 1932, she won a gold medal in the 100-meter women's backstroke and later set unofficial records in the 200-meter and 220-yard backstroke in other competitions.

She resonated with the public not just as an athlete but as a glamorous society figure whose spicy quips and antics enlivened Depression Era America. A striking brunette, she had married popular crooner-bandleader Art Jarrett in 1933 and became a sensation as she stood before the band wearing a white hat, bathing suit and high heels singing "I'm an Old Cowhand."

This flashy behavior did not impress the formal American Olympic Committee president, Avery Brundage, a former Olympian. Still, Mrs. Whalen was chosen for the 1936 Olympic Games in Berlin—reportedly the only woman at the time to make three Olympic teams in succession.

Then came her downfall as an Olympian. Steaming over to Berlin on the SS Manhattan, she joined playwright Charles MacArthur in the first-class lounge and had several glasses of champagne.

A chaperone saw her and told her to go to bed. "Now, come on," she said years later to a New York Times reporter. "This was my third Olympics. I said to the chaperone, 'No one tells me how to train.' "

She added, "I was a plugger, plug, plug, plug, keep in shape, but I never over-trained like the girls now. Well, after 1932, I said to myself, 'Okay, kid, you're a girl, have some fun.' "

The next morning, she was dismissed from the team for breaking training rules. Livid, she said unprintable words about Brundage but largely tried to wait out the flap. She went on to Berlin writing about the Olympics for William Randolph Hearst's International News Service.

Soon she knew there was no further hope of making amends with Brundage.

"I've been a sap," she told the press in 1937. Her conclusion: "I decided to cash in."

She received a $30,000 contract to appear in the Great Lakes Exposition show in Cleveland in 1937. She was the ingenue opposite Glenn Morris, himself a former Olympian, in "Tarzan's Revenge" (1938). The film required working with alligators.

"Their jaws were wired," she told Sports Illustrated in 1992, "but they could still hit you with their tails, so that was pretty awful."

Afterward, she sang and swam with Johnny Weissmuller in Billy Rose's Aquacade for the 1939 World's Fair in New York.

She became a fashion icon, with her trademark white hair ribbon becoming a craze among young swimmers. She once challenged fan-dancer Sally Rand to a "curve-and-contour contest." She became a fixture at Cafe Society and a regular in gossip columns as she dated eligible millionaires. She told the columnist Dorothy Kilgallen she preferred small men "because they don't get into so much trouble."

She married Rose in 1939, after he divorced comedian Fanny Brice. Their stormy marriage, which ended in divorce in 1954, was described in the press as the War of the Roses. She then married Tommy Whalen, a St. Louis man reported to have underworld connections who then reinvented himself as a man of leisure.

According to Sports Illustrated, she and Whalen did not marry until 1974 because they lived well off Rose's alimony payments. They settled in Florida. Whalen died in the mid-1980s.

Eleanor Holm, the daughter of a Fire Department of New York official, was born in Brooklyn. She began swimming at age 12 after her parents bought a summer house on Long Island. "Two things appealed to me about this place—Long Island Sound and the handsome lifeguards who frequented the beach," she wrote in a serialized account of her life for The Washington Post.

She trained on water wings until she was unafraid of the water. Noticeably better than other children in swimming contests, she began receiving formal training.

After the 1928 Games, the fetching young swimmer was approached by Florenz Ziegfeld to appear in his Follies. She turned down the offer so she could train for the 1932 Games, but it marked only the first time she navigated the worlds of athletics and entertainment.

She spent her final years playing tennis and golf until she broke a shoulder bone while on the treadmill.

In 1999, she went to the White House for an event commemorating female athletes. The following exchange with President Bill Clinton was published around the world.

"You're a good-looking dude."

"I saw you sitting on that couch, and I'd love to have joined you there."

"Anytime, Mr. President, anytime."

To read additional obituaries written by Adam Bernstein, go to http://www.poynter.org/bnw2005.

Lessons Learned

BY ADAM BERNSTEIN

Good obituaries are intimate histories, not resumes with quotes.

They convey character, motivation and action, not merely names, dates and places.

Only to a degree do we select our subjects. As my former editor used to say, "God is our assignment editor."

Fortunately for my profession, the deceased are a vast and varied lot. On any given day, a reporter chooses among athletes, entertainers, politicians, scientists, community volunteers and criminals. There are the very young and the very old, the acknowledged and the anonymous, the famous and the infamous. This wide-ranging array of characters and situations makes obituary writing the gem job of the newsroom.

The responsibility of the writer is to find a subject who engages the imagination, just as the insolent Olympian Eleanor Whalen fascinated me. Once that happens, the writer's task is merely to stay out of the way. That is harder than it seems. Too many stories say someone was funny without giving an example. Too many use quotations from friends saying someone was kind and wonderful and generous without showing how. That is unfair to the subject and the newspaper subscriber, who hopes for insight, a dash of history and just a damn good read.

Whalen made my work easy. She was whimsical, slightly sarcastic, flirtatious and not for a moment regretful about how her enthusiasm for champagne undermined her athletic ambitions. When the Olympic authorities tried to saddle her with a chaperone, she was insulted. "I was a plugger, plug, plug, plug, keep in shape, but I never over-trained like the girls now," she said. "Well, after 1932, I said to myself, 'OK, kid, you're a girl, have some fun.'"

For research, one must find the best information and, in Whalen's case, the most difficult decisions involved what to omit. My sources were overwhelming—not a newspaper in the United States seemed to exclude her from its pages during the Depression—but I limited my sights to Whalen's serialized accounts of her life and a few key and, most important, reliable newspaper and magazine reports about her travails.

Sometimes, I have found, the best articles appear years after the initial limelight has faded, when a subject reflects on learned experience and puts his or her life in context. Later stories about Whalen were useful for fixing oft-repeated "facts" from earlier, more outlandish stories that appeared during the fever pitch of her celebrity when reporters struggled to out-do one another.

As I write, I generally imagine I am sitting in a bar exchanging stories over a beer. With Whalen, I made that a magnum of champagne at the "21" Club. A critical factor at this point is to hear the "tone" of Whalen's voice. The first paragraph must convey this clearly.

In persuading an editor why Whalen warranted some space, I offered, "She was great in the water, but champagne was the problem." I realized I had my lead, or some variation of an engaging opening.

Then it was only a matter of typing. I needed to present the reason for her initial fame—her athletic feats—and then leap into her saucy behavior and establish why she clashed with the Olympic overseers. I did this to support my opening paragraph and tell the reader, "This story will be a fun ride."

After some comparably quiet years away from public view, Whalen received a flurry of coverage when she was invited to the Clinton White House as a pioneering female athlete. I was lucky to find the ideal kicker among this batch of dispatches, which brought her story into a modern context.

Although I am relatively young, I have long been entranced by the fascinating figures of the Jazz Age, the Depression and the World War II era. I try to counter whenever possible the prejudice many my age have against historic personalities that they perceive only in black and white. To me, these figures are as colorful as they come, and the pleasure is in resuscitating a life, however fleetingly, on the printed page.

And then to see whom the Assignment Editor selects next.

Adam Bernstein is senior obituary writer at The Washington Post *and has been a staff writer at the* Post *since 1999. His one-act comedy "Period Piece" received a first-place award at the Rocky Mountain Playwriting Festival in 1992.*

The New York Times

▌ Finalist

Margalit Fox
Obituary Writing

38. R. W. Burchfield, Editor of Oxford Dictionary, Dies at 81

JULY 10, 2004

R. W. Burchfield, an internationally renowned lexicographer who wrestled the Victorian behemoth known as the Oxford English Dictionary into the era of "wimmin," "sexploitation" and "microwave oven," died on Monday at Abingdon Community Hospital in Abingdon, England. He was 81.

Mr. Burchfield, who lived in Sutton Courtenay, in Oxfordshire, had been ill with Parkinson's disease for some time, his wife, Elizabeth Burchfield, said.

Chief editor of the Oxford English Dictionaries from 1971 to 1984, Mr. Burchfield was best known for overseeing the dictionary's four-volume supplement, an undertaking of nearly 30 years.

He was also known for his unorthodox edition of the grammarian's bible, Fowler's Modern English Usage, which provoked heated, hyper-articulate debate when it appeared in 1996.

Published from 1972 to 1986, the supplement augmented the original O.E.D. by more than 60,000 words, including scientific terminology, trademarks and English vocabulary from around the globe.

It also added obscenities and racial epithets, a decision that would land Mr. Burchfield in court, provoke a threat on his life and illuminate the fundamental nature of the lexicographer's art.

A balding, scholarly man who captivated the public in television and radio appearances but could drive the dictionary's staff with relentless intensity, Mr. Burchfield never meant to be a lexicographer.

Robert William Burchfield was born Jan. 27, 1923, in Wanganui, New Zealand. In 1949, after earning an undergraduate degree at Victoria University College in Wellington, he accepted a Rhodes scholarship to Oxford.

There, he read Medieval English literature with C. S. Lewis and J. R. R. Tolkien. He also met C. T. Onions, who had supervised the O.E.D. after the death of its legendary editor, James Murray, in 1915.

Mr. Burchfield expected to lead a life of blissful scholarly obscurity. Mr. Onions had other plans. After a hiatus of nearly three decades, work on the O.E.D., published between 1884 and 1928, was gearing up again. In 1957, Mr. Burchfield was hired to edit the supplement. Nothing could prepare him for the heft of the job.

Oxford University Press, the dictionary's publisher, expected the supplement to comprise a single volume of 1,275 pages and take seven years to complete. Instead, it ran to four volumes, 6,000 pages and 29 years.

"I moved," Mr. Burchfield told The Chicago Tribune in 1986, "with the speed of an electric hare."

Nothing could prepare him, either, for the level of public passion his tweedy profession aroused.

When the O.E.D. established a telephone hot line for the lexically perplexed, calls flooded in. A sign painter left his post to ask whether "accommodation" had two m's. A frantic Scrabble player phoned from New Zealand to inquire into the legality of "vee." ("Vee," the 22nd letter of the alphabet, was in.)

Conceived in 1858, the original O.E.D. was every inch a Victorian enterprise. Though its editors had agonized over whether to include terms of scatology, sexual congress and racial opprobrium, delicacy won the day. With the exception of a very few entries late in the alphabet, when the restrictions had begun to ease (a breathtakingly vulgar synonym for "kestrel" can be found in the W's), offensive terms were excluded.

It fell to Mr. Burchfield to put them back. "As it happens, the two key taboo words both start with letters towards the beginning of the alphabet," John Simpson, the O.E.D.'s current chief editor, explained in a telephone interview. "It was a major point of interest to the first volume of the supplement that it did include a full historical coverage of the two words."

Even more troublesome were ethnic terms, like "street Arab" and "Jew down." In the early 1970s, a Jewish businessman sued Oxford University Press, seeking an injunction against publishing the derogatory definition. The suit raised fundamental questions about the lexicographer's job:

should the dictionary-maker be a warder, protecting the public from offensive words? Or should he be a watcher, recording language as it is really used?

Mr. Burchfield, despite having received a death threat during the trial, argued strenuously for the second position. The British High Court concurred.

The words stayed in, with Mr. Burchfield ensuring their pedigrees were carefully documented. "Jew" as a term of opprobrium, denoting "a grasping or extortionate person," is traced in meticulous detail to the early 17th century.

"If you look at the entry in the supplement, it's enormous, much larger than most entries," said Jesse Sheidlower, the O.E.D.'s North American editor. "And the reason was, he wanted to make absolutely clear that it was not something that was put in because they were anti-Semitic or because they thought it was funny, but that they had a lot of evidence for it."

After retiring from the dictionary, Mr. Burchfield turned his attention to grammar, heavily rewriting Henry Watson Fowler's 1926 classic. Some critics attacked his detached, lexicographer's stance: a grammarian, they argued, was supposed to tell people what to do. (The Guardian, however, wrote recently that Mr. Burchfield was "positively thrilling on the distinction between 'shall' and 'will.' ")

Mr. Burchfield, whose first marriage ended in divorce, is survived by his second wife, the former Elizabeth Knight; by two daughters and a son from his first marriage; and eight grandchildren. His other books include "The English Language" (1985) and "The Spoken Word" (1981).

A lexicographer to the core, Mr. Burchfield even marked the passage of time alphabetically. In 1986, his work on the supplement at an end, he told The New York Times: "I took particular delight when we arrived at such words as 'yo-yo' and 'yuck.' When we reached 'zilch' and 'zillionaire,' it was like having the finishing tape in sight in a marathon run and we were entering the stadium."

To read additional obituaries by Margalit Fox, go to
http://www.poynter.org/bnw2005.

Lessons Learned

BY MARGALIT FOX

The obituary of R. W. Burchfield, lexicographer of The Oxford English Dictionary, was atypical in three respects. First, it wasn't written on deadline. Second, I had a bulging, fiendishly accurate press kit about the O.E.D., rushed to me by the dictionary's publisher. Third, because of my training in linguistics, I knew something about lexicography.

With my three most customary problems—the ticking clock, the search for reliable sources and acute ignorance of the topic at hand—stripped away, this obit threw into relief the small, chronic craft decisions the obituary writer makes every day of her working life.

More than anything else in the paper, obits groan with boilerplate. Date of death, place of death, the subject's age and cause of death figure high in the story. Farther down are date and place of birth, education, marriages, divorces. Finally, there are the survivors: a paragraph-long list of spouse, siblings and children, and the space-consuming towns in which they live. This traditionally ends the piece, depriving writer and reader of a satisfying kicker.

Despite all this ballast, the obit must soar. The survivors are easy. Obit writers have lately been sneaking them in higher, freeing the last graph for a proper kicker. Because I'd found a lovely valedictory quote from Burchfield in the clips, I used it to end the story.

Far harder is the lead itself—or what's left of it after the writer's other obligations have been discharged. The obit writer doesn't get a full paragraph to grab the reader's attention. She doesn't even get a complete sentence. She gets a *clause*—a single, stingy dependent clause, the handful of words between "who" and "died."

The stricture chafes, but it has its benefits. It forces an economy of language often absent from the rest of the paper. At its best, the obituary lead is a kind of haiku, each spare, carefully chosen word pulling double its weight through added nuances of style and tone. To this end, there are four American writers whose crystalline prose should be read and reread like Scripture: Mark Twain, E. B. White, Red Smith, Murray Kempton.

An obituary lead should telegraph in elegant shorthand what is interesting or innovative about the subject's life. It justifies the existence of the story that follows. With Burchfield, I was able to do this by contrasting the stuffy Victorianism of the original O.E.D. with the outrageous late-20th century language Burchfield had to add.

Using a list helped enormously. My original lead was, "R.W. Burchfield ... who wrestled the Victorian behemoth known as the Oxford English Dictionary *into the modern age*, died . . ." Not awful, but a little flat. It struck me that in a story about new words colliding with old ones, the words themselves should figure prominently in the lead. I added the three most flamboyantly modern terms that came to mind—"wimmin," "sexploitation" and "microwave oven" (after double-checking that they actually appeared in Burchfield's dictionary)—and the lead crackled to life.

Obits aren't eulogies. Stanley Woodward, sports editor of the *New York Herald Tribune*, admonished his writers, "Stop Godding up those ballplayers." The same goes for obituary subjects. If they were less than angelic in life, find a way to say so. In reporting Burchfield, I learned that while he was respected professionally, he was disliked, even feared, personally. The reference to him as a man who "could drive the dictionary's staff with relentless intensity" gets at this.

An obit is more than the sum of its subject's doings. Ideally, it is a capsule work of history, in which the life lived is a window onto a larger social issue. With Burchfield, the issue was the continuing relevance of the seemingly dusty profession of dictionary-making, with its power to provoke debate, lawsuits, even death threats.

Finally, there is often room for humor in obits, though it should be used with care. In the Burchfield article, I managed to exploit to comic effect the *Times*'s longstanding reluctance to print obscenities. I needed to refer to an extremely naughty word that had somehow made it into the original O.E.D. I knew I'd never get it into the paper. So I described it obliquely: "a breathtakingly vulgar synonym for 'kestrel.'" The next morning, I had a gratifying barrage of e-mails from readers across the country, panting to learn what we would not print.

The word? You can look it up. In the O.E.D. it appears between *windflower* and *windgall*.

Margalit Fox is a staff reporter in the obituary news department of The New York Times. *She joined the* Times *in 1994 as an editor in the Sunday Book Review section after several years as a freelance cultural journalist. She has bachelor's and master's degrees in linguistics from the State University of New York at Stony Brook in addition to a master's from the Columbia University Graduate School of Journalism.*

PART 5

Editorial Writing

David Barham
Editorial Writing

David Barham understands Arkansas, perhaps better than Arkansas understands itself.

It's historically been a state of Democrats whose residents are really Republicans. They just don't know it yet.

"They're churchgoing folks. They're pro-capital punishment. They're anti-affirmative action. On most issues, they vote conservatively," Barham said.

Barham joined the *Arkansas Democrat-Gazette* in 2002, when the editorial page editor hired him to represent a conservative voice. The Louisiana native knows the territory. His father's family is from Arkansas, and Barham graduated from Southern Arkansas University.

He hunts and fishes. He has a dog named Three (One and Two have died). He calls his wife, Stephanie, his "bride." They have three boys—Hunter, Garrett and Jacob—and one daughter, Bailey Lynn, "who rules the roost." You can hear the voice of a father in many of his columns.

The family goes to a Methodist church, but Barham said, like most Arkansans, he keeps his faith in the background, a strong but unspoken influence.

Barham finds himself at odds with his neighbors and co-workers most often on two issues: the death penalty and football. As a parent and a Methodist, he's against executing convicts, particularly people convicted of committing crimes when they were minors. (His bosses are in favor of capital punishment, so he avoids the issue "like pink pork.") And because he was raised in Louisiana, a state that came to terms with its bipartisan orientation a long time ago, Barham often finds himself alone on fall Sundays, rooting for the New Orleans Saints instead of the Dallas Cowboys.

Barham's journalism career started in high school. After graduating from college, he joined the *Bastrop* (La.) *Daily Enterprise*. In 1992, he moved to *The News-Star* in Monroe, La. Ten years later, he joined the staff of the *Arkansas Democrat-Gazette*. He was one of two winners of the 2003 ASNE Distinguished Writing Award for Editorial Writing.

He takes a practical, constant view of journalism's trials and tribulations. Bias in newsrooms isn't really an issue, he said. It's the bosses, the guys who equate Democrats with John F. Kennedy and Republicans with Richard Nixon, who are out of touch. Once Barham's peers—the people who think Carter and Clinton when they think Democrat and Reagan and Bush when they think Republican—take over, this whole bias discussion will evaporate.

But don't expect Barham to be one of those bosses. He's pretty happy writing editorials at a place that encourages great writing and discourages meetings. "They'll have to burn me out of this office."

—Kelly McBride

39. Three Daughters: Crosses At the Intersection

MARCH 24, 2004

The strangest thought came to mind as we stood at the intersection of Arkansas Highways 5 and 89 early Monday afternoon:

What were their nicknames?

All daddies give their daughters nicknames, don't they? Maybe just the standard "Princess." Or, around these parts, "Darling Girl," or "Baby Doll," or "Sweet Girl." We liked what Paw called Laura in the *Little House* series: "Half-pint."

It was the strangest thought. Here we were looking at the memorials, and we were thinking about their *nicknames*. What goes on in the human mind. . .

If you haven't seen the papers lately—the news section and the obits—or watched the local news, or listened to any talk radio, or been to church, or shopped at any store, or got a haircut, or stepped outside your front door, or your back door, you may have missed it: Three young ladies—girls, really—were killed Thursday at the intersection of 5 and 89, right outside Cabot, at the Pulaski County/Lonoke County line.

Jae Lynn Russell. Alicia Rix. Taylor Hall.

Cheerleaders.

Going fishing.

Spring Break.

3:54 in the afternoon.

All wearing seatbelts.

Jae and Alicia were 16. Taylor was 15.

We stood on the west side of Highway 89, and looked to the left, north, up Highway 5. We were on the military crest of a hill. The cars simply disappeared as they drove north, and the south-bound vehicles coming at us had appeared out of nowhere. A driver going east on 89 has to stop at a stop sign before crossing. But if a truck or car is going south on Highway 5. . . You couldn't see it until it was right on top of you. You couldn't see it any more than Jae could on a Spring Break afternoon at 3:54.

We know a girl whose daddy calls her "Squirrel."

The intersection is so perfectly Arkansas. It's surrounded by pine thickets. There's a bit of litter in the ditch. Advertising signs are nailed to trees, complete with local phone numbers: "Cabot Truss, Inc." and "Clegg's Welding" and "Diamond Machine Shop." On one side of Highway 5 is a sign that says, "Lonoke County." On the other, "Pulaski County."

There's a man with a camera standing next to us this afternoon. He's a member of one of the extended families, which everybody seems to be in Arkansas.

Good gosh, look at the traffic, the inky wretch and the man with the camera say to each other. And at 1:30 in the afternoon, on a Monday no less! And look how fast they're going.

We wondered if one of the girls had ever been addressed as "Puddin-n-pie."

Somebody had put painting supplies under one of the crosses. One of the girls must have liked to paint.

There goes a full dump truck. Must be going 60 miles an hour, too. It's going south on Highway 5, just like the truck that plowed into the girls. It doesn't take long for an accident to be forgotten, and for truckers to floor it again. After all, the boss is waiting. Got to get the gravel to . . . wherever gravel goes.

One of the signs says only: "We love y'all."

Not "We love you." Whatever kid wrote that one knew the language Jae Lynn, Alicia and Taylor spoke.

Muffin? Short Stuff? Little Wiggle?

It must've been a devastating wreck. After all, the girls were wearing seatbelts. We could see the tire tracks where the poor truck driver—forever linked with these girls—did his best to stop.

We notice the glass on the side of the road, too. Is it from this wreck, or another? There have been several at the intersection of 5 and 89. Fatal ones. But the state hasn't got around to putting up a stop light. Just a yellow blinking light, which might as well be another pine tree for those who've gone through the intersection more than a few times. Just part of the scenery.

The Highway Department says it held some public meetings, got some federal money, and it expects it can hire a contractor to improve the intersection and make it safer by the end of the year.

By the end of the year.

"How many more?" reads another one of the signs by the side of the road.

By the end of the year. . .

Nicknames. When we got back to the office, we thought about calling one of the families, just out of curiosity. They had to have nicknames. It would add something to the editorial, give it a personal touch.

But we didn't call. Not now. Not ever. Some things can stay just between the daddies and their girls. Forever.

40. Letter to Europe: Special Delivery from Osama

APRIL 18, 2004

Dear European pig-dog radical Zionist crusader goat-faced sons of jackals:

In the name of Allah, the merciful, the beneficent, we send affectionate greetings, death and destruction, etc. Or, as they say in rotting American hovels like New York and Washington, Howdy. (Did I get that right?)

Forgive me if it's been a while since I've last communicated with you. I've been rather busy. I can't tell you how much time and planning it takes to avoid the commando raids, and dodge those pesky predator drones, and brush off the scorpions. Then there's the business of switching caves every night and always having to hire new food tasters. Good help is so hard to find nowadays. The best caves have a 30-day waiting list, the cost of bribes is skyrocketing, and don't get me started on the cooking around here.

But enough about me. On to business: Have I got a deal for you!

How's about a truce? Europe isn't the enemy of Allah. America is. And Israel. And Turkey. And Australia. And Britain. And, oh, yes, Poland. And Ukraine. And the Czech Republic. And Denmark. And Italy and. . . Well, the real Europe isn't our enemy. You know, the romantic, storied Europe of Vichy and Buchenwald, Malmedy and Auschwitz. Oh, those were the days, my friends, those were the days. European civilization was at its peak then, except of course when our hordes stood at the gates of Tours and Vienna ready to liberate you from your folly, property, and lives, O unbelieving ones.

What I mean to say is Europe no longer has to be the enemy of the true faith. Not if you buy my almost new truce offer. It's on sale. Today only. Worry beads thrown in free.

Al-Qaida will declare its war with European nations over—capital-O Over—if you Europeans will kindly agree to pull out of all Muslim countries immediately. As for the citizens of your countries who were lost on, after, or in connection with the glory of September 11th, we'll agree to let bygones be bygones if you will. If you'll stop defending yourselves, we'll stop killing you. Eventually.

How can you pass up a deal like that? Get out of Iraq, Afghanistan, Kuwait, the holy land of Saudi Arabia, and maybe Spain and the Balkans, **and every other true Realm of Islam or face the wrath of God just as the**

Spaniards did and we'll kill every last one of your sons in the Mother of All Wars and spread their rotting corpses over—

Ahem. Excuse me. I get carried away on occasion. Don't take it personally. I still dream of the gardens of Cordoba and yearn for the olives of Andalusia. I miss the golden days of the Inquisition and the auto-da-fe. Those people knew how to live, or rather kill. And then that heretic Ataturk comes along and abolishes the Caliphate without even thinking... But don't let my idle musings distract you, O, my brothers. Go about your business, enjoy your decadent pleasures, turn your back again, enroll my little friends in your flight schools...

And don't listen to those imperialist, colonialist, mass-marketing Americans. They just want to keep the good Muslims of the Middle East under their boots, so they can have all our oil, defile our religious sites, and stare luridly at our top-to-toe veiled women. They can't be trusted. Me you can trust.

The big problem is that the unilateralist Americans have too many allies in this war. So we are prepared to offer a separate peace until the Great Satan is destroyed. Then, of course, the whores of Paris and the charlatans of London **and the entire Western world will convert to Islam or feel the wrath of a thousand deaths as the blood of their children—**

(Cough.) Ahem. Sorry about that. Control. Must learn control.

If America's allies will pull out of the Middle East, America won't be far behind. That Bush! Do you really think he means business? Don't be fooled by his cowboy talk. He's weak! Weak, I tell you! You can take it direct from those of us cowering in my little cave. A few more months of this war, his poll numbers will drop, and he'll run from here like a scalded dog.

And once America is gone, proper order will be restored in the House of Islam, *i.e.,* the Middle East, and adjacent areas, *i.e.,* the world. We can overturn those liberal regimes in Turkey and Jordan, and the one to come in Iran, form approved Islamic governments, kill our heretics, keep our women home where they belong instead of in school, cut the throats of the infidels, drive our economy into the sand, and produce still more terrorists! Only then will we come after you in Europe. But that's *years* from now, decades maybe, so don't give it a second thought. In fact, I shouldn't have mentioned it. Forget it. That's an order.

And here's an Extra Added Bonus: By pulling out of this war, you get to embarrass the United States! Isn't that your real purpose in life, your *raison d'etre*—to escape America's clutching hegemony and let the United Nations handle all our little problems? Hey, I read the papers. This would

be an easy way to spit at the feet of your long-time ally and occasional lib-
erator. That'll show the Americans! Let no good deed go unpunished!

And if you don't, we will **fill your bowels with hell-fire lava and the
troops of al-Qaida will pull the flesh from your bones and give your meat
to our dogs for breakfast and use your innards for fish bait and, and, and—**

Anyway, sleep on it. You know you can trust an honest guy like me.
Have I ever lied to you? You can believe me when I promise you death,
destruction and general chaos—unless, of course, you're the American
FBI and CIA and have no eyes to see, ears to hear, phones to tap. . .

Your friend (and if you don't believe it I'll kill you dead),

OBL

41. 'You Guys' Moves South? Y'all Will Stand Like a Stone Wall

APRIL 29, 2004

Southerners! A call to arms!

A decaying, sinister, and determined force is marching down into these climes from Up Nawth. This force has all the manners of a Sherman. And all the romantic appeal of a Grant. Worse yet, it recruits our children—our very sons and daughters!—in its campaign to change Our Way of Life.

This force insults our women. It attempts to federalize the uniqueness of the South. It believes that overwhelming force—the mere presence of numbers!—will bowl over the states of the Old Confederacy. This force underestimates the fight of the Southern man, by Gawd, and the resolve of the Southern woman, by jingos. From Fayetteville, Arkansas, to Fayetteville, North Carolina, Southerners will fight this battle with all the rage and fury usually associated with something more serious, like football games. (Missouri may waver, but that state has always been on the fence.)

Of course we're enraged, as we know you are, about the dispatches from all fronts that the phrase "you guys" has infiltrated God's Country. And reports are that it's spreading, mostly advancing in house-to-house urban battles. And "you guys" is trying to gain footholds in those urban areas to launch attacks into rural communities.

Bring it on.

"You guys" . . . (Snort, indignantly.) The word around here for the plural You is Y'all, and it always will be. Because we were raised right. Y'all will never be taken prisoner by some green lieutenant of a Yankee phrase.

Another proper and wholly acceptable expression, You All, may be muttered on occasion, but only when addressing more than one person, and preferably by a Southern belle who's making a kind of art with her conversation, as Southern belles do: *Why don't You All go to the picture show without me tonight? I'm feeling poorly after visiting with Mama, bless her heart.*

But Y'all still dominates in these latitudes.

Of course, the left-leaning media help the enemy. Nothing new about that, right? But television is using more subtle techniques than it uses on *The West Wing* or *The CBS Evening News*. The tactic these days is to carpet-bomb programming with the Vile Phrase, and hope Southern chillen rally to its colors.

Which, by the way, is another reason to turn off the tube tonight and read to the kids. Preferably Mark Twain. Or Lewis Grizzard. Or, if they're a little older and in the mood for something serious, Robert Penn Warren.

We knew this war was coming years ago, in the 1970s. That's when a public television show for kids called *The Electric Company* began its propaganda each day with a shout to the easily persuaded: *Hey you guys!* We wish now that the South had taken a more proactive role in rolling back this menace before it posed such an imminent threat. What's next? "Youse guys"? "Lookit"? "Take off, eh"? "Go Yankees"?

We'd druther have snow in May.

* * *

We suspicion "you guys" will have a hard time establishing an area of operations in the South. Primarily because of the Southerner's love of history. Like Faulkner said, in the South, the past is never dead—it's not even past. And Southerners are good aims when it comes to using history as a weapon. Which reminds us:

Guess where the term "guy" came from? According to a dispatch from Newhouse News Service in Sunday's paper, the word "guy" is thought to come from Guy Fawkes, a conspirator in a failed 1605 plot to blow up the British Parliament. *Aha!*

Gradually, the word began to be used for any male. But Southerners will give up MoonPies and NASCAR before we'll let people use that word of questionable origins to be applied to our mothers, sisters and daughters! We'd just as soon address Mama with "What up, dog?"

Imagine a car salesman approaching a couple at Gwatney Chevrolet with, "What are you guys interested in today?" He may be asked why he can't help the lady, too.

Or imagine this verbal order as you leave a restaurant—preferably a restaurant that serves greens: "You guys come back now, heah?"

Ugh! On second thought, don't imagine any of that. This "you guys" invasion ain't nuthin but a thing. It will not take root. Not in this soil.

Not as long as Southerners paint words into their conversations just so, like artists adding a touch of blue where it's needed, and a slash of green where it's not expected. Not as long as those of us in God's Country recognize the difference between men and women, and the truly educated among us treat our ladies with a little more respect, and class, and never require them to open a door in our presence or see a baseball cap atop a gentlemen's head. Not as long as we all believe Suthun is a language all its own, and we use it not just to communicate an idea, but to communicate life itself.

"You guys" will last about as long as a hush puppy in an Arkadelphia buffet line.

Right, y'all?

42. Where Arkansas Leads: Schoolresults.org Is the Real Deal

MAY 1, 2004

Inside the meeting room were the usual suspects. By which we mean a handful of journalists, a handful of PR types, a handful of educators, and Stacy Pittman. (She always seems to be where education reform is being committed.) The projector was set up, the Internet was on the big screen, and people were passing out business cards all around. We could see it already: This is gonna call for some *serious* caffeine.

Not that we're against education reform, mind you. It's the endless talking about it, without ever doing anything, that unnerves. See the Arkansas Legislature, *circa* 2003–2004.

This was going to be just another meeting, to espouse just another idea, to blather on about another Technical Revolution in Education (how many have there been now?), and how Arkansas could benefit by it if the state would just get on board. The PR types and Education Experts would explain how bass-ackwards Arkansas is, what must be done to reverse that, how expensive it's going to be, how the future of our children is suffering because politicians and superintendents (but we repeat ourselves) stand in the way, how the lack of modern technology is hindering progress in the schools. And so depressingly on.

We dusted off Old Fogey Editorial No. 138, which starts like this:

(Clear throat.) In the Internet age, computers are becoming more and more important. On the one hand, children must learn basics like reading and math. On the other hand, try getting a job today without knowing how to Google somebody without getting fired for harassment. Arkansas must quit fighting technology, and, instead, get more of it into the classroom.

For too long now, Arkansas has fallen behind in several education categories. How long will Arkies allow their children to fall behind the nation? How long until they demand immediate accountability from their schools, and—

We had most of the editorial written when Jacqueline Lain, director of some outfit called Performance Evaluation Services, said the strangest thing:

"Arkansas is a leader."

Was that a jolt, or was the coffee kicking in?

Now, OFE No. 138 is a safe editorial, complete with the on-the-one-hand-but-on-the-other-hand prerequisite of any good, boring opinion piece. But the longer we listened to Ms. Lain describe, explain, and show off this new website called schoolresults.org, the more we began to realize No. 138 just isn't accurate anymore.

Arkansas is leading the nation.

* * *

Parents, educators, taxpayers or anybody else who's interested in education in Arkansas, do yourself a favor: Fire up the old computer, and surf on over to www.schoolresults.org. (Dot *org,* not dot *com!*) Notice that only a few states are blue, which indicates the state is online. Notice that Arkansas is one of 'em. A click on Arkansas (the state between Missouri and Louisiana), and a world opens up to the curious.

The website is full as a tick with stats, stats, and stats. And not just stats, stats, and stats, but numbers you—parents, teachers, etc.—can use. You can use them to improve your school, use them to find a home in a decent school district, or use them to bang over the heads of your local school board members.

We cracked our knuckles and began looking, er, typing around.

Lessee. . . We know a couple of kids at College Station Elementary in Little Rock. What's the level of reading proficiency there?

It took less than 20 seconds to find out. The number of kids making what educators call Adequate Yearly Progress is 85 percent. Not only that, but the number of kids who are, quote, Economically Disadvantaged, unquote, is 50 percent.

Which makes us wonder: What is College Station doing right with these poor kids that 85 percent can read on level? And how can other schools copy that?

Lessee, No. 2. . . We know some children at Nevada County High School. It's in poor and rural Nevada County. So we already know it's economically disadvantaged. But how does it compare to other schools in the same economic category?

A minute later. . . There are two other high schools, besides Nevada County, with an exact 59.2 percent of economically disadvantaged kids: Bruno-Pyatt High and Lakeside High. Nevada County is between the two in reading proficiency and well ahead in math. How can the math program there be improved and copied by others?

Hey, this is neat! Now *this* is transparency. Which leads to real accountability.

Lessee, No. 3. . . What about that massive Springdale High? How're they doin'? Go to the school's site, click on Quick Compare, and in a second, *voila!*

Yep, we guessed right. Its the biggest school in the state, with more than 2,500 kids. Its reading proficiency is on target at 61 percent, but—uh, oh—its math proficiency is right at 31 percent. Are the kids there having trouble grasping algebra? Or is it geometry? Is it just 10th-graders holding down the scores, or are most kids at the school having trouble? And, more importantly, who can fix this?

* * *

Okay, enough about numbers. What was that about Arkansas being a leader?

Well, not every state has its information up and running. It looks as though several others, in yellow, are in the process, but Arkansans can find out about the good, the bad, and the ugly test scores right now. And compare them to others across the state.

Arkansas is *one of the nation's leaders.* In a technical area of education, no less. (Mike Huckabee must be behind this.) And, more important, this website is something real, something tangible, something that parents and teachers and home buyers and anybody else can use.

Texas folks don't have this. California folks, either. Nor do those smarty-pants up in Vermont or New Hampshire or most of those other Canadian states.

"Arkansas is a leader," kept echoing around the room. It was a pleasant sound.

Of course, it's not a perfect world yet. You can't compare Arkansas schools and districts to those in other states, because Arkansas and those other states don't use the same tests. That should change. Why the feds don't strong-arm states into taking the same test—or why the feds don't strong-arm a little harder—we don't understand. We'd rather compare Arkansas kids to kids around the nation, and then the world, than compare Texarkana kids to those in Jonesboro.

But that's another editorial. (Old Fogey Editorial No. 141.)

Right now, we're just proud to point out this website to parents and taxpayers, and do a little bragging about our small, wonderfully technical state.

For now, No. 138 just has to go back into its file.

43. Taking a Stand

OCT. 13, 2004

Editorial writers must take a firm stand on the issues of the day. And after pondering this particular news story for most of a perfectly good morning, and after debating the pros and cons, the advantages and disadvantages amongst ourselves, and after doing our in-depth research and weighing the great effect that our opinion would surely have on all of society, we have to say we're foursquare against giant hornets.

YOW!

Did you see Chris Branam's story last Thursday? The European hornet—did we mention it's originally from Europe?—is also called the Giant Hornet because it's a big 'un. Its wingspan is 50 feet long, or at least 1¹/₂ inches. And people just began noticing them in this maybe too Natural State in 1999.

The article said this particular hornet is not threatening. But you know how the media lie.

This breed of hornet was first found in New York more than 150 years ago, and it's just now getting to God's Country. You want to talk about unwanted immigration this election season, let's talk about unwanted immigration. (Gee thanks, New York.)

"They are said to be mild-mannered, and not prone to attack, but they will defend their colony when their nest is threatened," according to the graphic that went with the story.

What does that mean, "but they will defend their colony when their nest is threatened"? What is threatening? Walking by? Trimming a tree? Throwing a football in the back yard and accidentally hitting the neighbor's hedge? Simply existing? How's a mere human to know?

Excuse, please, Monsieur Arkie. But I must say to you I consider such actions threatening to my nest. En garde!

Reports from the northern part of the state haven't been encouraging. These so-called mild-mannered suckers have been dive-bombing people in orchards and banging themselves against house windows at night. The "experts," a word that should always have quotation marks around it, say the dive-bombing thing is just a function of the bug's attraction to fruit, and the window-banging thing just its attraction to light.

Does it matter? They're still dive-bombing and window-banging.

Achtung! Vee vill attack, attack, attack und resistance es useless!

And this from a Mr. Jeffrey Barnes, curator of the Arthropod Museum at the University of Arkansas: "I don't know of any reports of it being detrimental ecologically, but that doesn't mean it's not."

Aha! That's all the proof we need. This critter is obviously a Menace to Civilization As We Know It. (And have you ever noticed that when scientists are quoted in the paper they always sound like white-coated actors in a B sci-fi movie *circa* 1955?)

"If this thing is taking up tree holes, it's certainly going to affect bird and squirrel populations," Mr. Barnes added.

Aha, again! This so-called mild-mannered hornet is picking off the bird and squirrel population! What next? Deer? Cows? Third graders? Attention must be paid!

And all this comes just in time for hunting season, when hundreds of thousands of Arkies are preparing to take to the woods. Our advice: Along with your mosquito spray, your tent pegs, and your doe scent, you'd better pack a can of Raid. Make that the over-sized, industrial-strength can. Take no chances. Say, we wonder if our taxidermist could mount one of them thangs. . .

Three Daughters: Crosses At the Intersection

the editorial "we"? writer on the scene, out of the office

word gets emphasis at end of paragraph

The strangest thought came to mind as we stood at the intersection of Arkansas Highways 5 and 89 early Monday afternoon:

What were their nicknames?

nicknames become a recurring theme

inventory of names forces readers to think of their own experiences

All daddies give their daughters nicknames, don't they? Maybe just the standard "Princess." Or, around these parts, "Darling Girl," or "Baby Doll," or "Sweet Girl." We liked what Paw called Laura in the *Little House* series: "Half-pint."

soft way of noting their deaths

It was the strangest thought. Here we were looking at the memorials, and we were thinking about their *nicknames*. What goes on in the human mind. . .

ellipses invite readers to complete the thought

parallel structures

If you haven't seen the papers lately—the news section and the obits—or watched the local news, or listened to any talk radio, or been to church, or shopped at any store, or got a haircut, or stepped outside your front door, or your back door, you may have missed it: Three young ladies—girls, really—were killed Thursday at the intersection of 5 and 89, right outside Cabot, at the Pulaski County/Lonoke County line.

inventory of ways news spreads in a community

pinpoints location

their real names

Jae Lynn Russell. Alicia Rix. Taylor Hall.

Cheerleaders.

Going fishing.

Spring Break.

3:54 in the afternoon.

litany of sentence fragments heightens emotional impact

raises question of how they died

All wearing seatbelts.

Jae and Alicia were 16. Taylor was 15.

writer puts self at scene

We stood on the west side of Highway 89, and looked to the left, north, up Highway 5. We were on the military crest of a hill. The cars simply disappeared as they drove north, and the south-bound vehicles coming at us had appeared out of nowhere.

explanation of problem

A driver going east on 89 has to stop at a stop sign before crossing. But if a truck or car is going south on Highway 5... You couldn't see it until it was right on top of you. You couldn't see it any more than Jae could on a Spring Break afternoon at 3:54.

again, readers must think the unspeakable

We know a girl whose daddy calls her "Squirrel."

odd intrusion of nickname motif

The intersection is so perfectly Arkansas. It's surrounded by pine thickets. There's a bit of litter in the ditch. Advertising signs are nailed to trees, complete with local phone numbers: "Cabot Truss, Inc." and "Clegg's Welding" and "Diamond Machine Shop." On one side of Highway 5 is a sign that says, "Lonoke County." On the other, "Pulaski County."

details create sense of place and regional culture

There's a man with a camera standing next to us this afternoon.

He's a member of one of the extended families, which everybody seems to be in Arkansas.

overstatement, but it fits, makes us feel like relatives of girls

folksy phrase — Good gosh, look at the traffic, the inky wretch and the man with the camera say to each other. And at 1:30 in the afternoon, on a Monday no less! And look how fast they're going.

even the editorial writer gets a nickname

We wondered if one of the girls had ever been addressed as "Puddin-n-pie."

power of eyewitness testimony

reiterates his theme — Somebody had put painting supplies under one of the crosses. One of the girls must have liked to paint.

There goes a full dump truck. Must be going 60 miles an hour, too. It's going south on Highway 5, just like the truck that plowed into the girls. It doesn't take long for an accident to be forgotten, and for truckers to floor it again. After all, the boss is waiting. Got to get the gravel to . . . wherever gravel goes.

longer paragraph develops a thought

return to the problem

shorter paragraph delivers a punch — One of the signs says only: "We love y'all."

Not "We love you." Whatever kid wrote that one knew the language Jae Lynn, Alicia and Taylor spoke.

three names

three nicknames — *Muffin? Short Stuff? Little Wiggle?*

It must've been a devastating wreck. After all, the girls were wearing seatbelts. We could see the tire tracks where the poor truck driver—forever linked with these girls—did his best to stop.

We notice the glass on the side of the road, too. Is it from this wreck, or another? There have been several at the intersection of 5 and 89. Fatal ones. But the state hasn't got around to putting up a stop light. Just a yellow blinking light, which might as well be another pine tree for those who've gone through the intersection more than a few times. Just part of the scenery.

state is complicit, makes point so readers share his outrage

The Highway Department says it held some public meetings, got some federal money, and it expects it can hire a contractor to improve the intersection and make it safer by the end of the year.

By the end of the year.

allows sign writer to editorialize

"How many more?" reads another one of the signs by the side of the road.

echo of three

By the end of the year. . .

ellipses return for dramatic effect

Nicknames. When we got back to the office, we thought about calling one of the families, just out of curiosity. They had to have nicknames. It would add something to the editorial, give it a personal touch.

completes the nicknames pattern

humanizes the writer

But we didn't call. Not now. Not ever. Some things can stay just between the daddies and their girls. Forever.

connotes love and eternity

Roy Peter Clark is senior scholar and vice president of The Poynter Institute.

A conversation with
David Barham

An edited e-mail interview conducted by Poynter Institute faculty member Kelly McBride with David Barham, winner of the ASNE editorial writing award.

KELLY McBRIDE: What's it like publishing without a byline?

DAVID BARHAM: Hey, it's great! You can say all the catty things you want, and nobody knows it's you!

If I were to shadow you from idea to editorial, what would I see?

You'd start off seeing somebody staring at a computer screen with a blank look on his face, breathing out of his mouth. Then I'd turn around to my office mate, assistant editorial page editor Kane Webb, and ask what he's doing for lunch. Then we'd go to lunch. Then I'd come back and stare at the computer screen again. Then Kane and I would go get a Pepsi. Then I'd come back and stare at the computer screen again. Then I'd get online or read the paper, then do some more staring at the computer screen and more mouth-breathing.

Then, out of nowhere, an idea will hit, and 15 minutes later the editorial will be done. Or as done as I can get it. The copy is then edited by Kane and Paul Greenberg, the editorial page editor here, and that's that. Writing editorials is like war or baseball. There's a lot of downtime, but every once in a while, when you're least expecting it, all hell breaks loose.

Give me an example of what you mean by all hell breaking loose.

All hell breaking loose? That's just a way of saying that once I've got the subject and an opinion on it, the writing just flows. And it flows fast. Sometimes I have to slow myself down or go take a walk around the block or something and come back and edit it with fresh eyes.

So you're a procrastinator. Why don't you do something about that like go to a time-management seminar or something?

Because it wouldn't help me to write better. Two things that have seriously harmed journalism: meetings and seminars. I say let's go to fewer meetings and think more about writing. And actually writing (when it happens). And editing others' writing.

What do you read?

Everything I can get my hands on. I've made a vow to myself to read the greatest books of all time by the time I'm 40. Remember when they were making all those lists after Y2K? The greatest 100 movies, the greatest 100 songs, the greatest 100 this or that? I printed out a copy of the greatest books. I was surprised how few I had read. I'm halfway through "Moby Dick" right now. I also read a lot of newspapers and online news.

What do you look for online and in the paper?

I look for something that interests me. That's the first step in almost all good editorial writing: finding something that interests the writer. After you've found that, the writing just comes naturally.

You use a couple of devices that many journalists have been taught to avoid. The editorial "we" is one of them. Why do you do that?

Because I've never been taught to avoid it. I didn't know that was a no-no. You're not going to take the award away from me, are you?

I don't think I'm allowed to, since you won the award. But who are you talking about when you say "we"?

I'm talking about the voice of The Newspaper (thunderclap). It's the publisher's paper. He's the ultimate voice. I write for Walter Hussman. He signs the checks. Mr. Hussman hired an editorial page editor who agrees with his points of view on public education, good government, et cetera, and Paul Greenberg hires writers who think that way. And when we write, we don't write for ourselves, as columnists do. We write for the newspaper. The editorial "we" you spoke of. It's an old and honorable tradition among newspapers.

You give yourself funny nicknames such as "the inky wretch" or "old fogey." That's strange since, as a reader, I don't know your name. (Well, I do, but your readers usually don't.) What purpose does that serve?

To make the writing interesting, or at least different. Too many editorials in this country sound like they could be printed in any newspaper. I'll bet if you switched the editorials in tomorrow's *USA Today*, *The New York Times* and *The Washington Post*, nobody would know the difference. They all sound exactly the same. We like our editorial page to have a personality.

You also use some creative spellings to convey the vernacular, stuff like "heah" and "ain't nuthin but a thing." Why?

Again, to make the editorial readable. To make it conversational. We strive for that every single day on this page. Even on serious subjects. Just because a subject is serious doesn't mean it has to be boring. I wish I could convince American editorial writers of that. (Sigh.)

How do you decide when to lapse into less than proper English?

I don't really "decide." It just happens. Whatever makes the editorial striking. Readable. Aggressive. Fun or emotional. But especially, above all else, readable. If an incomplete sentence is what it takes to make the point, use it. If it takes misspelling a word on purpose, use it. If it takes punctuation. To. Prove. The. Point. Use it. And when proper English is required, use that, too.

Occasionally you even use a passive sentence such as "Attention must be paid." Why do you do that?

"Attention must be paid" is actually a shot at boring editorials. We use it when we want to make fun of good, respectable, boring opinion writers. It's an inside joke.

I thought editorial pages were supposed to be measured and reasonable (boring). You seem to be pretty far out there in both your selection of topics and your style and tone. Where do you get your ideas?

Booze.

Just kidding.

One of the first editorials I wrote for this paper, I handed to Paul Greenberg. He read it over, called me back into his office and said it was a fine editorial. And it could run anywhere, for any newspaper. But it wasn't good enough for this newspaper. Working in these conditions is great. Fabulous. I love that we have high standards. We're always reaching for that second level. To say something that nobody else is saying and in a way nobody else says it.

As far as where I get my ideas, they can come from anywhere. The paper, online, the cable news holler shows, real life. Anywhere.

How do you manage to create in writing the illusion that you are speaking to me?

By speaking to you. I'll never write a headline like "Whither NATO?" And I'll never talk down to people in an editorial. Writing is so much easier to read when it's in a conversational tone.

Do you revise your work after the first draft?

You betcha. And not just me. Kane and Paul edit this stuff. And you should see some of their editing, especially Paul's.

In an interview when you won this award two years ago, you described a vigorous editing process that sounds a bit painful. Do you still go through that on every piece?

I hope what I said two years ago didn't come across as painful. It's a very healthy process. I write something. I ask Kane Webb to edit it. I then send the piece to the editorial page editor. If he agrees, it goes to the publisher. If either one of them disagrees, it goes into the wastebasket. But if it clears, it goes into the paper. And I don't mind at all if something gets thrown out. At least I'm not writing for a board of people and trying to please—or worse, trying not to displease—a committee of 12 to 15 people.

What percentage of your stuff ends up in the garbage?

Oh, about 10 percent, and that's a high-end estimate. I'm not going to write an editorial saying, "Let's get rid of public schools in Arkansas and put all the kids to work at the chicken processing plant" because I know that's probably not going to go down well with the bosses. But every now and then I'll write something and Paul will send a two-word message at the top of it: "Let's not." Which is his polite way of asking, "Are you crazy, smoking something, or what?"

Give me an example of something that didn't get published.

I can't seem to think of one specifically right now. But I do know that my views on capital punishment (agin it) don't fit with the newspaper's editorial point of view, so when I write, I avoid that topic. Unless I want to write an individual column about it.

Does it hurt your feelings? (Or if you want the manly version of this question: Is it hard on your ego?)

Having an editorial spiked never hurts my feelings. It may, if I didn't have the utmost respect for those above my pay grade. Besides, if I ever want to say something and the bosses don't agree, they always leave open the possibility of my running the piece as an individual column.

Talk a bit about the "You Guys" editorial. Where did that idea come from?

From a news story on the subject. I picked up the paper one day, and there it was: a story about how many kids in the South were picking up "you guys." I about had a heart attack. That one was easy to write.

How did you collect information for that topic?

I didn't. I just started writing.

Define these terms for me: Arkadelphia, MoonPies, full as a tick.

Arkadelphia is a state of mind. When you're sitting on the couch watching the Weather Channel, trying to decide whether to water the bell peppers or let the rain do it tomorrow, so full of fried catfish that a tick couldn't stick to your belly, with your spouse gossiping on the phone with her sister in the background about what the preacher's wife was wearing Sunday, you're in Arkadelphia. (It's also a pretty little town between Little Rock and Texarkana. If you pass through Arkansas, you really must stop in Arkadelphia and get a plate lunch.) "Full as a tick" means you couldn't eat another bite . . . except for one more little slice of pecan pie. MoonPies, though, are like jazz. If I have to explain it, you'll never get it.

OK, we have to talk about "Letter to Europe." Satire can be pretty dangerous business. How did you decide to take this approach?

I couldn't believe the gall of Osama bin Hiden. Didn't some of the Nazis try to negotiate a separate peace with the West in 1944 or '45, so they could turn on Russia again? No, sir. You started this war, jerk, now the allies are going to kick your backside for you.

What did you hope to accomplish?

I hoped to accomplish writing something somebody would find interesting. Something that would be well read. And talked about over breakfast.

How did the readers respond?

I don't remember.

Did people think you were making fun of Arab people?

I don't think so. But I can only be responsible for what I write. I can't be responsible for what others read.

Finally, how has your writing changed since you won this same award two years ago? In other words, how do you sustain growth and development?

If I ever sustain growth and development, I'm going to quit writing. Sounds too boring.

Editor's Note: We also asked Barham, "What lesson or lessons did you learn or re-learn during the writing of these editorials that might be of help to others interested in the pursuit of excellence?" This is his edited response:

Death to editorial boards!

Editorial boards are no good. Editorial writing would be so much better nowadays if all the editorial boards at all the newspapers in this country were disbanded.

Editorial boards kill good writing. I know. I worked for one for five years. I'm telling you, editorial boards aren't interested in good writing or even in saying anything. Well, those may be secondary concerns, but taking a stand isn't the top priority. The No. 1 priority for an editorial board is *consensus*.

It works like this: You have a group of people in a room, maybe up to a dozen, maybe more. You might have a publisher, an editor, a managing editor or three (depending on the size of the paper), the editorial page editor and a couple of editorial writers. And you have to "reflect the community," so you get a few people from out in the real world to sit on the board. And don't forget diversity. Must have it. So everybody is of different tribes, different ages, different religions, different economic backgrounds. And, of course, different political opinions. Now try to get this group of people to come up with an aggressive position on . . . *anything*. It won't happen. Not on abortion. Not on gun control. Not on gay marriage. Not on the important issues of our day. The members of this board argue and argue, they all have different points of view, and the editorial page editor (after 30 minutes of sometimes-heated discussion) bangs the table with his palm and asks, "What's the consensus of the board?"

The consensus is . . . sometimes a real nose picker. Like, "Abortion should be rare." Hell, who doesn't believe that? The preacher down the street and those protesting at the NOW march believe abortion should be rare. *Abortion doctors* believe abortion should be rare.

Or, "We can all agree that murder with guns is wrong." Yeah, we can. So why are you saying it? Readers should be falling over themselves to get to the curb at 5 in the morning to be told murder with guns is wrong?

But that's what you get when you ask for a consensus of the board of very different people. You also get milksop.

So these poor editorial writers, who aren't allowed to write an editorial opinion that would offend any member of the board, are sent out to fill the editorial column. But they must do so without having a strong opinion. (Poor guys.) They now downshift into "news analysis." Which is fine, I guess. There's a place for news analysis. But if you're going to write news analysis, mark it "news analysis," give it to the news side, and let them run it on their pages. But don't write news analysis, lie to your readers and mark it an "editorial" and put it on the opinion page.

I believe that the reason so few people read newspaper editorials is because editorials are so incredibly boring. Reading some of those yawners is like watching a moth climb a drape.

How is it done here at the *Arkansas Democrat-Gazette*?

I write. Then re-write. Then edit. Then re-edit. Then give it to the editorial page editor. Then it goes to the publisher. If one of them disagrees, the thing goes into the trash. After all, I know who signs the checks. I really don't mind one of my editorials getting killed (that much). It's not my paper, and I'm writing editorials for the paper; I'm not writing an individual column. But at least—thank God almighty—I'm not sleepwalking through this life writing committee reports.

If I wanted to do that, I'd go to work for Exxon or State Farm and write committee reports all day and make a million dollars doing it. I got into this business to write well, be read and make a difference.

All too often, editorial boards across the country keep that from happening.

Damn shame, too.

Writers' Workshop

Talking Points

1. David Barham said, "I'll never talk down to people in an editorial. Writing is so much easier to read when it's in a conversational tone." Does he achieve his goal of being conversational? How would you describe his "voice"?

2. Barham occasionally refers to himself by a funny name. In the "Three Daughters" editorial he calls himself "the inky wretch." Did you "get it" the first time you saw the reference? What effect does the personal reference have on the reader?

3. In several of the editorials in this collection, Barham switches voices. He takes on the personalities of a hornet, a Southern belle and a terrorist losing his composure. He uses type differently in "Three Daughters." What effect does the switch to italics achieve in this editorial? Does it work?

4. After reading these editorials, can you decipher the writer's political ideology? The *Democrat-Gazette* deliberately hired Barham because he is conservative. Do you think his appeal is greater among like-minded readers? Why or why not?

Assignment Desk

1. Read Barham's editorial about the phrase "you guys." Now scan the features section, the entertainment news, the sports section or other places where you might find lighthearted news stories. See if you can write a 400-word editorial on an interesting but less serious issue, yet do so in a very serious tone.

2. Barham avoids writing editorials that take a stance that would contradict the beliefs of his publisher. He also doesn't write editorials that contradict his own beliefs. Search today's news for a controversial topic on which you have a personal opinion. Write an editorial in support of your opinion. Now write an editorial in support of an opposing opinion. Is it possible to write a convincing persuasive piece when you don't agree with the stance you are taking?

3. Barham said that readers wouldn't know whether editorials in *USA Today*, *The New York Times* and *The Washington Post* were switched because "they all sound exactly the same." Compare the editorials from those three newspapers. Do the editorial voices sound similar? How do they compare with the editorial voice of the *Arkansas Democrat-Gazette*? How do they compare with your local newspaper?

THE
POST★STAR

▮ Finalist

Mark Mahoney
Editorial Writing

44. Baby Steps Needed to Fight Teen Drinking

MAY 23, 2004

If you ever get a chance, take a moment to watch a child sleep.

It could be your own child, but it doesn't have to be. It could be the neighbor's toddler. A nephew or a young cousin. Your baby brother.

A child's sleep is not always the most peaceful event. Kids toss and turn and flop and grunt and scratch their noses hard. They contort their arms and legs into positions that defy the rules of anatomy and geometry. They mumble incomprehensibly in cryptic messages only their dreams understand.

And sometimes, too, they are frighteningly still, so absolutely motionless that it takes all your concentration just to catch them taking a breath.

It's beautiful and perplexing at the same time. It's as if they disappear into an ocean of slumber to deal with the harsh realities of the wakened world, to rejuvenate and to guild themselves for what's to come with the dawn.

When they're asleep, they're taking care of themselves. When they're awake, that duty falls to us.

We can't always protect our children—from the world or from their own actions. A teenager's life, especially, is a difficult one, their own complex inner workings attacked by intangible pressures and unfamiliar situations. And whether they admit it or not, they need us to help them through it, especially avoiding the dangers they can't see.

One of those dangers is alcohol.

One reason it's dangerous is because we treat it so lightly.

Positive images of alcohol are everywhere—in magazines, on TV. Our children's sports heroes promote it. Race cars have beer logos pasted all over them. Some of our most beloved movie characters were happy drunks.

We also promote the positive image of alcohol at home. We enjoy a cold beer or a glass of wine after work. We have a keg in the bucket at the family picnics, and everyone's having a great time. Mom or Dad plays softball with the gang after work, then heads over to the local pub for a pitcher.

But alcohol is dangerous to teenagers. As adults, we have a responsibility to stop teen alcohol abuse. But it's not something that can be accomplished with one single action or turned on a single event.

If we as a society are going to do something about the problem of teen alcohol abuse, we're going to have to do it in baby steps, over time.

First, we have to change our basic personal behaviors. How much do we talk about alcohol in a positive way? How available do we make it? How much appeal do we pass on to our children? Children, it's been shown, are guided not by words, but by example. What kind of example are we setting by our own actions in our own homes? An act as simple as having iced tea instead of a beer at dinner sends a message.

OUR VIEW

Kids are unpredictable creatures, but it's up to adults to protect them.

Then we have to act as a community.

Tougher laws do help control behavior. Make kids more responsible by punishing those who abuse alcohol. Make parental notification a requirement for courts when children are arrested on alcohol offenses. Make parents responsible for the actions of their children by forcing them to pay their children's fines and requiring them to attend counseling. Make it a felony to provide alcohol to minors.

Schools, where our children spend a significant portion of their days, should be allowed to freely address the problems, punish offenders unencumbered by the fear of litigation or retribution. Attach conditions to participating in sports teams and extracurricular activities, and be consistent in enforcing them.

Community leaders, businessmen, government officials, individuals and parents have to come together and examine whether their community is doing enough to steer its children away from alcohol use, and whether it's giving kids enough reasonable alternatives to drinking.

Most of all, we have to be willing to talk to our children about the dangers. Start as early as you can, when they're most impressionable and open to your input. But no matter how old your kids are, you have to talk to them. Be open and compassionate and non-judgmental. Reach out to them, even when they don't want to be reached.

We can stop alcohol abuse among our teenagers. We have the ability. And we have the support. All we need is the will. Start making the effort, a little bit at a time.

Once we start addressing this enormous problem, we'll all be able to sleep a little easier at night.

To read additional editorials by Mark Mahoney, go to
http://www.poynter.org/bnw2005.

Lessons Learned

BY MARK MAHONEY

This editorial was the last of four editorials on the issue of teen drinking that accompanied a monthlong series on the subject. Since this was the last word, I needed to hit all the elements of the past editorials and of the entire series. I couldn't approach this editorial like an ordinary opinion on a tax hike or legislative blunder. This one in particular had to resonate with people and really get them to think.

Amazingly, there's not universal support for fighting teen drinking. The pervasive attitude is that it's OK as long as the kids don't drive. I wanted to send a message to the entire community—parents, businesses, police, government and school officials—that it's not OK and that there are reasonable steps they can take to fight the problem.

Here's what I learned from writing this piece.

Don't be afraid to get personal. The most important element of an editorial, even more than a solid argument, is its ability to strike a chord with people. A lot of editorial writers take too distant an approach to their writing, thinking their editorials can't be personal because they're supposed to be an opinion written by a detached "editorial board." You can have the best justification for your position in the world, but if it doesn't resonate with readers, they're just going to ignore it. Then what have you accomplished?

Editorial writers shouldn't be afraid to use their personal experiences to send home a message. I've always used my kids, my parents, my life experiences, stories and even jokes—any tool in the bag—to make a connection with readers.

Don't be afraid to write colorfully—paint a picture for readers. Along the same lines as not being afraid to get personal, you also can't be afraid to use your writing, reporting and observation skills to make your point clear. In describing what children look like when they're sleeping, I closed my eyes and pictured everything I could remember about my own experiences. Then I wrote them down.

Don't go for the cliche or generic descriptions. Offer detailed color so readers can actually conjure in their minds the image that you're describing. Editorial writing can be so formulaic and dull. Break the mold. Surprise people, and use your writing to draw them into your piece.

If you want people to act, you have to give them specific suggestions. Nothing annoys me more than an editorial that gets people all worked up but then leaves them hanging without anything to do. If you want people to take action, you have to spell out what you expect of them. At the very least, it will serve as a starting point for discussion, perhaps inspiring them to come up with ideas of their own.

Every time we write an editorial about our dysfunctional state Legislature, for example, we provide the phone numbers or e-mail addresses of the legislators, governor and other top officials. The next day, I get calls from the officials telling me how bombarded they were with calls. That's an effective editorial.

If the suggestions aren't there, the readers will just read the piece, nod thoughtfully and move on. People want to act, but they need constructive prodding.

This particular editorial on teen drinking told readers why the problem of teen drinking needed to be addressed. It then listed specific, detailed steps they could take to combat the problem. Without that, it wouldn't have been received as much more than a temperance lecture.

Show readers that you understand the depth of the problem. Readers won't take you seriously if they think you don't *get* the problem you're describing. You have to convey, "I understand why you feel that way." Stating facts isn't enough. You have to demonstrate that you know what they're thinking and that you empathize with them. That establishes credibility in your argument and, therefore, in your proposed solutions.

Keep beating the drum. A single editorial usually isn't going to make much of a difference, no matter how brilliant your prose. If you really want to effect change, use a variety of approaches and angles to drive home your message over an extended period of time.

Mark Mahoney started at The Post-Star *(Glens Falls, N.Y.) in 1988 as a night general assignment reporter. For the past 13 years, he has served at various times as regional editor and city editor. Mahoney is currently the paper's editorial page editor and the 2004 winner of the ASNE award for editorial writing. He was a finalist for the same award in 2003.*

Community Service
Photojournalism

Carol Guzy
Community Service Photojournalism

Carol Guzy has been a staff photographer at *The Washington Post* since 1988. Her assignments include domestic and international stories and documentary reporting. While at the *Post*, she has won two Pulitzer Prizes for spot news photography and one for feature photography.

The Pennsylvania native received an associate degree in registered nursing in 1978. A change of heart led her to the Art Institute of Fort Lauderdale in Florida to study photography. She received an associate degree in applied science in photography and subsequently spent eight years at *The Miami Herald* before moving to the *Post*.

In addition to the Pulitzers, she has been named Photographer of the Year three times by the National Press Photographers Association and eight times by the White House News Photographers' Association. Her other honors include the Robert F. Kennedy award for international photojournalism, an Overseas Press Club award and a National Headliner Award.

In her ASNE award-winning project, "A Year At Ballou," Guzy chronicles the story of a young man at a crossroads. She documents how John Thomas made a conscious decision to avoid the violence and turmoil of his neighborhood and high school, focusing instead on academic achievement and sports.

—Kenny Irby

The Washington Post

"When I first met John Thomas, I kinda took a liking to him 'cause he had talent and I made him like a project and I was like—if I could turn this kid around and make him see differently, then maybe, just maybe, he may turn a corner." —Renaldo Gillis

In a time when male role models are scarce, coach Renaldo Gillis became a surrogate father to John Thomas (pictured second from left). Gillis grew up on the same block, graduated from Ballou and now owns a real estate appraisal company. He lives in what might be considered a mansion by public housing residents.

45. About "A Year At Ballou"

John Thomas' journey began on a familiar but dangerous road. Like many of his peers, he stole cars, was arrested and faced a future of little promise. His father went to prison when Thomas was 5 years old. His mother overcame her struggle with drugs. An older brother spent time in jail awaiting trial, and his sister survived a shooting while she was pregnant.

In a Washington, D.C., neighborhood that makes it easy to be bad but hard to be good, Thomas grabbed a foothold somewhere in the middle. With street smarts and good grades, he was neither a nerd nor a troublemaker. Instead, he was a star basketball player who graduated with honors from Ballou Senior High School.

He became a role model in a world fraught with the temptation to fail. His was the voice of reason for friends heading toward peril.

"That's what it's all about—making choices," said Thomas.

In telling Thomas' story, staff photographer Carol Guzy creates a visual narrative of dignity and concern, one that has inspired a community thirsty for hope.

—Adapted from *The Washington Post* ASNE contest entry

A conversation with
Carol Guzy

An edited e-mail interview conducted by Poynter Institute faculty member Kenny Irby with Carol Guzy, winner of the ASNE community service photo-journalism award. Captions for the images include material written by Manny Fernandez.

KENNY IRBY: Where did the project idea come from?

CAROL GUZY: The project began as a daily assignment. Reporter Manny Fernandez decided to write about the students who were excelling at Ballou Senior High School in spite of the turmoil of a chaotic year that included a mercury spill, frequent brawls and a rising number of students slain. Our photo assignments editor planned to cover the story with different staff as events warranted. I suggested having the continuity of one photographer so the faculty would recognize a familiar face and the images would potentially have more depth.

The school was somewhat distrustful of the media and felt that negative press had burned them so often. The door was probably opened to this story as an attempt to balance the dire news reports with the silent population of students who do their work and avoid trouble, or even blossom, but are often invisible in the shadows of dramatic events.

Where and how did you research your information?

I spent time with Manny as he interviewed students who were making honor roll in an attempt to find a person who would be representative for the story. After a lengthy conversation with John Thomas, we both knew he was the subject we hoped to pursue.

How did you decide that the focus would be John Thomas?

His life mirrored that of many youth in the community who are faced with daily challenges and the dangerous lure of the streets. His father has been in jail since he was 5, his mother is a recovered drug addict and, sadly, he couldn't count how many people he knew who were killed or wounded by gun violence.

He was candid and open about his earlier mistakes and judgment, with a past checkered by run-ins with law enforcement, like many of his peers. He appeared levelheaded, quiet and wise beyond his years, with the haunting eyes of someone who knew tragedy on an intimate basis. He was a popular student and a star basketball player who made a conscious decision to change the direction his life appeared headed.

A young man who exuded a certain poise and dignity, he also had the elusive quality of remaining himself under the scrutiny of a camera lens. He didn't ham it up or play it down.

How much time did you put into the coverage?

During the previous year's final semester, both Manny and I agreed we would follow John through graduation. The paper wanted a general story sooner so we initially spent time with the principal, who was beloved by students but later fired amid controversy, adding to the upheaval of the tumultuous year.

In early 2004 we started slowly getting to know John, as well as struggling with the difficulties of obtaining access to the school. At first we were required to make formal requests in advance for any time we spent there and were questioned each time upon entering. By the end of the school year I had a virtual open pass to the grounds, and most security and faculty expected that where John went, I usually followed. (Although if I asked for John Thomas, I got only puzzled expressions, as most referred to him by his nickname, "Flood.")

It was a remarkable amount of trust given by a school with reason to be wary of uncensored coverage, especially after the homicide in February of John's childhood friend, James "J-Rock" Richardson. A student allegedly involved in a rival feud managed to slip a gun through security and shoot him outside the crowded cafeteria. It caused an uproar among families who worried about the safety of their own children.

Except for a month documenting the rebellion in Haiti, I spent an increasing amount of time with John until his graduation in June, probably to his eternal chagrin. However, he remained polite and accommodating the entire time, even when faced with initial teasing by his peers.

He was a typical teenager in many ways and not the best at returning calls. So if I didn't catch him early, it was easy to lose him to an erratic schedule with school and sports. Also, while hanging out with him I would hear about things that might be interesting to photograph that may not have seemed important to mention when I inquired about future events.

Though not ideal, writers can still write about events they don't witness. Our eyes need to see it.

What revisions did you make to the story before publishing?

We were mindful to balance the edit and display of pictures with the variety of positive and negative influences in his life. We weighed whether to publish a photo of the hallway fight and determined it was critical to the story to highlight John's ability to walk away from mayhem as other classmates rushed up to witness it. The student in the photo was not identifiable and it spoke to the general atmosphere of unpredictability. Parental permission slips were sometimes difficult to obtain and some photos were not considered if we did not have one.

What role did your picture editor play?

Assignments editor Ray Saunders was open to the idea of following John through graduation, and he kept me posted about events pertinent to the story and needs of the word side.

Ultimately, Michel duCille was instrumental in the success of the visual reportage by supporting my initial instincts and allowing the freedom and luxury of time to delve deeper into the life of this young man. Too often, it seems, photo editors applaud great work and expect it from staff but don't allocate the time required to give stories intimacy. Michel understood the potential of this piece and also the importance it held for a struggling community many times forgotten until calamity occurs.

The criticism the media receive about focusing too often on the negative aspects of life may warrant careful self-evaluation by news organizations regarding balance in coverage.

Tell me about your reporting partnership with Manny Fernandez.

Manny was phenomenal to work with. He is a pure professional with sensitivity to the nuances of the story. He was intuitive about John's feelings and treated all those involved in the story with fairness and decorum. He was also respectful of the visual aspects necessary to provide a complete package, and our working relationship was flawless and rewarding.

What were some of the challenges you faced? How did you overcome them?

There existed an initial wariness on the part of the faculty and students, as well as the expected frenzy of attention that a camera provokes. Age and other differences with the young, spirited students were also apparent, and for a while it was difficult to be inconspicuous and document John's experiences without affecting the scene.

He was teased mercilessly about the media attention, at first, but took it in stride. Eventually the novelty of my presence wore off, and there was a certain acceptance that evolved.

Many obstacles to coverage can be overcome by simply being flexible, patient and earnest. I never could master the handshake though. John finally gave up on it and just nodded in greeting.

How did you organize your final photographic narrative?

The edit was different for the paper than the Web due to space limitations. It was gratifying to work with the layout person on the newspaper pages and also with the editor at Washingtonpost.com to package the Web site piece. In my opinion, it is imperative for the photographer to be a vital part of the final product, yet so often that is not the case.

Later, an expanded edit of the story was published on The Photography Channel Web site (www.everypicture.tv) with audio by John and his coach, which enhanced the package.

The visual narrative was not composed of a string of dramatic images but, rather, the subtle pieces of a puzzle. When placed together, they revealed various aspects of a young man's trials and triumphs and a view of his world. Some photos might be deemed cliched, but it seems an unfair word to use since moments in our own lives seldom feel cliched but are, in fact, deeply personal.

What were the more memorable lessons you learned during this assignment?

Attitude is everything.

Were there any major surprises for you while reporting this story?

We began the story before J-Rock was killed. The fact that it happened *inside* the school was particularly disturbing. However, it did not reflect the everyday reality. Some folks reacted with a shudder when I said I was spending time at Ballou. One person asked if I could possibly be safe there. It seemed a poignant statement of the disparity of our coverage that this school could be deemed a virtual no man's zone. There were indeed serious problems that faced the beleaguered school, but most of the time it was similar to any other high school, filled with laughter and lessons and raucous teenage hormones.

Why do you do what you do as a photojournalist?

To tell stories.

What outcome had you hoped for when covering this story?

John became a role model for other students precariously balanced on a hazardous precipice, influenced by tragic circumstance and faced with decisions at a vulnerable age that could affect the course of their lives. He embodied a strong statement about the necessity to accept responsibility for the choices one makes and proof that destiny need not be dictated by environment but rather by attitude.

It was important to highlight the influence of a mentor like John's coach, Renaldo Gillis, who believed in him, didn't cut him any slack, pushed him to shine and celebrated his success like a proud father.

How different was this story from the kinds of stories that you have covered on foreign soil: war, famine and destruction?

Many staff and students at the school felt as if they lived in a community under siege and at war with itself. Teen homicides have risen dramatically in the area. The cycle of poverty and despair embraces many young people, as it does in countries across the globe. I have tried to cover foreign stories in the same manner as local ones, believing there are universal emotions—fears, desires and dreams—that run through us all. The challenge is to offer the link between people of different cultures and backgrounds to evoke empathy for their common humanity.

What advice can you offer younger photographers when it comes to being a visual reporter?

Tread lightly. Trust your instincts—they are seldom erroneous; we just fail to listen closely. Try to take yourself out of the equation. It's about their story, not your pictures. Open your eyes to the unexpected and don't let preconceived ideas cloud reality. Embrace concern, fairness and dignity. Be patient and persistent. If you care enough about a story, you will tell it well. Don't let others break your spirit by insisting you "can't." Take a lesson from John Thomas. You can indeed.

The Story Behind the Photographs

KENNY IRBY: What picture represents a valuable lesson learned during the course of the coverage?

CAROL GUZY: Actually it seems the contrast between two photographs is most compelling: John's farewell to his childhood friend in the coffin dressed in a Ballou football jersey (below) and the photo of John carrying the girl down the hallway at school (next page). They represent the dramatic extremes of his life—a battle between the treacherous enticement

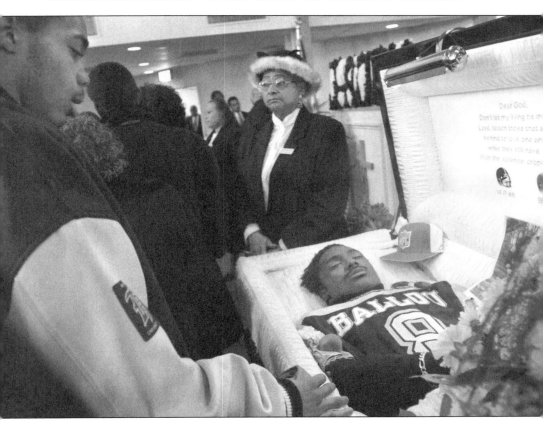

"I seen a lot of my friends get killed and a lot of friends been locked up. And I said I didn't want to go that way, but I felt like ain't no other choice." —John Thomas
   John attends the funeral of his childhood friend, James "J-Rock" Richardson, who was shot and killed inside the school by another student in an ongoing dispute between two rival gangs. The emotional service was held at Paramount Baptist Church, where he was baptized. As gospel music filled the air and mourners wailed, a steady stream of students filed by the coffin to pay their respects to a life cut short by the violence that plagues their city.

"I started feeling proud of him. I said, 'I told ya you can do it.'" —Renaldo Gillis, coach and mentor

John gallantly carries classmate Sade Dunn, who hurt her leg dancing for Ballou in a competition. He has become a role model for other students and the voice of reason at times when his friends appeared headed for trouble. John was selected "Most Improved" of the senior class.

of the streets and the carefree and exhilarating moments of youth. This story was an attempt to provide balance.

The hallway picture is significant in order to dispel misconceptions that Ballou is a virtual no man's land, a war zone. The school was indeed troubled, but much of the time it was like other high schools, filled with spirit, hopes and dreams.

Prom Night

It was very endearing to see the enthusiasm of his family. John was followed by an increasingly large crowd of relatives on his prom night, all of them eager to take his picture and celebrate the moment (facing page). He visited both grandmothers (one lives in the same complex as J-Rock) before heading to his date's home. Both families gathered excitedly as he waited for her. He appeared a bit embarrassed by all the attention. After he greeted Janae with a hug, everyone proceeded to take pictures but had to turn off the TV when John was distracted watching the basketball game, his obsession. He and Janae spent most of the time at school teasing each other but after prom night he bought her a ring.

"They act like we're getting married or something." —*John Thomas*
John was bewildered and slightly embarrassed as a roomful of excited family members gathered at the home of his prom date, Janae West. With cameras ready, they watched the stairs for her to descend in a delicate yellow dress. The couple received a joyful sendoff with applause and pictures on their big night.

"Just Keep Walking"

I had been shadowing John at Ballou for a while. There were frequent fights at the school but the few times when they involved more than a scuffle, I was not there. The hallways were heavily monitored by security guards and D.C. police after the shooting of J-Rock.

As we were walking from his last class, the scene erupted with a bloody young man walking down the hall and arguing with the guards, who quickly rushed to grab him (next page). The agitation level rose with students gathering to watch, but John kept going to the library, looking around inquisitively but not stopping.

I took two frames before his classmates began yelling, and the level of hostility directed at me was a bit unnerving. I put the camera down and continued to follow John as a girl kicked something on the floor at me.

I'm not sure if I handled it properly and have second-guessed myself about the decision to stop photographing the dramatic scene, but it seemed more important to respect the reaction of the students. In the library I explained to John that I understood the sensitivity among his

"Just keep walking." —John Thomas
    When other students rushed up to see the melee as security guards and D.C. police subdued a blood-ied, angry classmate involved in a fight at Ballou, John Thomas kept going to the library down the hall to finish an English project, quietly ignoring the commotion. D.C. police and security guards were positioned throughout the troubled public school, breaking up frequent brawls. Students passed through metal detec-tors and were searched upon entering the building, but a gun slipped by on the day J-Rock was shot out-side the crowded cafeteria.

friends about portraying negative aspects of his school and community. However, even though their point was valid, I stressed to him that I couldn't sugarcoat reality either.

    Some of what he faced every day was challenging, and it was crucial to document how he reacted and rose above it. I recognized the girl who was so angry and kicked the object, having photographed her at other school activities. I asked John to give her my number so I could explain that I respected her feelings but felt the action was inappropriate. It was unclear if the students understood my role in documenting John's story. We played phone tag for a few days and didn't ultimately discuss it, but she later greeted me cordially and it seemed the situation was diffused. Of the two frames I made, only one was reasonably sharp and didn't reveal the identity of the student.

Graduation

John was positively giddy on his graduation night (facing page). He was usu-ally very stoic and not visibly emotional, so it was touching to see him that

"I told him, 'The only thing you owe me is, when you graduate from college, you come back to the 'hood and you grab somebody and bring them up, same as I grabbed you. . . . Then your debt would be repaid.'"
—Renaldo Gillis
   John Thomas says it is a promise he will keep.

happy. He had a calm demeanor, cool and quiet in many ways. However, this was his day to celebrate a major milestone in his life. He started school with low to failing grades but graduated on the honor roll. Some people joked that I deserved a diploma as well, considering the amount of time I spent in class.

All the ASNE award-winning work by Carol Guzy, as well as work by ASNE finalists Manny Crisostomo and Robert Gauthier, is displayed at News University (http://www.newsu.org/bnw2005) in a course called "Community Service Photojournalism: Lessons from a Contest." The course examines three approaches to community service photojournalism and offers judges' comments about the honored work. News University is a journalism-training project of The Poynter Institute funded by the John S. and James L. Knight Foundation.

The Sacramento Bee

Finalist

Manny Crisostomo
Community Service Photojournalism

46. About "The Leftover People"

In "The Leftover People," photographer Manny Crisostomo and reporter Stephen Magagnini introduce Sacramento to its future neighbors—one of the last waves of Hmong refugees long stuck in Thailand. The photographs, published as a special section, brought an outpouring of offers of assistance and donations of clothing and food for the newcomers.

It's no wonder. Crisostomo, a Pulitzer Prize–winning photographer, spent five months documenting a complete portrait of who would be coming, and who would not, plus what the future might hold for them and for Sacramento.

He began with a visit to the squatter's camp in Thailand where many of the refugees had lived for years. He had to talk his way into the camp, past Thai guards who previously had prevented access beyond staged events and public areas. Then, Crisostomo traveled to the Thai villages where former camp residents had moved in search of better lives, only to discover that by doing so they may have missed the chance to come to America. On his return, he delved into the Hmong communities locally and in the Midwest to get a sense of where these newcomers might fit in.

Crisostomo's evocative images capture the hopes and emotions of the Hmong as they journey to America to find a new home. His photographs bring to life a struggle to overcome history without losing it and tell the story of our neighbors, whether next door or across the ocean, and the basic human essence we all share: the desire for our families to have a home.

—Adapted from *The Sacramento Bee* ASNE contest entry

The first taste of freedom terrified Tia Vang, 9, who arrived at Sacramento International Airport in July carrying her little brother Ger on her back. They are the advance guard for the 16,000 Hmong refugees headed for America, the families of Vietnam War era veterans who have been scraping by in an illegal squatters camp north of Bangkok, Thailand. Soon, 2,000 will be neighbors in Sacramento.

Manny Crisostomo joined The Sacramento Bee *in August 2002 as senior photographer. He began his career at Guam's* Pacific Daily News, *graduated with a degree in photojournalism from the University of Missouri and joined the* Detroit Free Press *in 1982. While at the* Free Press, *Crisostomo's work garnered him many awards, including the 1989 Pulitzer Prize for feature photography for his series depicting life at a Detroit high school.*

A conversation with

Manny Crisostomo

Manny Crisostomo came away from his work on "The Leftover People" with a better appreciation of some traditional journalistic values, especially collaboration and respect, and just a little paranoia.

Shortly after joining reporter Stephen Magagnini and others on the project, Crisostomo began by reading some of what Magagnini had written earlier about the Hmong. He also worked closely with the Bee's *assistant director of photography, Tim Reese, who pushed Crisostomo to "get up early and stay late."*

Crisostomo puts respect at the core of his professional values. "Respect yourself and your subject . . . and honor the profession," he said.

He also finds that "a little paranoia" can be the right mind-set for addressing the bane of journalists everywhere—the danger of assuming everything will go as planned.

In an edited e-mail interview conducted by Poynter Institute faculty member Kenny Irby, Crisostomo shares other lessons learned.

KENNY IRBY: Where did "The Leftover People" project idea come from?

MANNY CRISOSTOMO: The origin of the project came from Amy Pyle, our projects editor, and then was expanded by our executive editor, Rick Rodriguez, with further input from senior writer Stephen Magagnini. I joined the process just after that, with assistant director of photography Tim Reese, to discuss what the visual components of the project would be.

Where and how did you research your information?

I read some of Magagnini's earlier work on the Hmong. I also looked at coverage of the Hmong by the newspapers in St. Paul and Minneapolis, which had sent a reporter and photographer team to the Wat Tham Krabok refugee camp in Thailand a month before our planned trip to the same camp.

How much time did you put into the coverage?

It took about five months for the research, prep, shooting, editing, layout and design. However, during that time I also worked on another project and a personal photo series on the California state fair. The *Bee* photo department is committed to special projects and advocates giving staffers the time to do the work.

What role did your picture editor play?

I worked closely with Tim Reese from the beginning to the end. We bounced around ideas, discussed logistics and coverage in Thailand and Minnesota. He pushed me to get up early and stay late, to hang out and document the Hmong families during their first days in America.

There was a lot of give and take during the editing process. It wasn't quite painless, but it wasn't like pulling teeth either.

We got early drafts of the stories and tried to synergize the pictures with the text. We also shared the photographs with the writer, who used them to help guide portions of his storytelling.

What were some of the challenges that you faced? How did you overcome them?

I think the biggest challenge was getting in the Wat Tham Krabok, the Hmong refugee camp north of Bangkok. The Thai government runs the camp, and access is controlled and monitored by the Thai military. We had to check in with the guards every morning and had a "minder" following us the whole time.

Nothing is ever guaranteed when dealing with foreign military personnel. Cultural and language differences make things tenuous at best. Just when we thought things were going smoothly, we arrived one morning to discover we were banned from entering the camp. It took a day of phone calls to the State Department, Thai government officials and U.S. resettlement folks to get back in.

On our last day there, we planned to ask hard questions of the Thai military officials. As a precaution the night before, I culled my edited selects (about 600 images from a week of shooting) burned them on several CDs and mailed the CDs to *The Sacramento Bee*. I wanted to be prepared for a worst-case scenario should they confiscate my cameras and my laptop with my whole take in the hard drive. Luckily nothing of that sort happened. I feel a little paranoia in foreign countries is a good thing.

How did you organize your final photographic narrative?

Director of photography Mark Morris stresses the importance of our (the photo department's) role in special projects and preaches a more even partnership with the word side. I bought into Mark's vision and decided to be proactive and push the envelope.

When it came time to present photo's contribution to "The Leftover People" project, we set up a premiere atmosphere.

We gathered the executive editor, managing editor, assistant managing editor for graphics, the projects editor and the senior reporter, served them soda and popcorn and presented a multimedia presentation on DVD.

While the presentation was "photo's vision" of the project, we were cognizant of the premise that the images we edited and presented matched the text.

In the end we got the space we had hoped for—a 20-page special section.

Were there any major surprises for you while reporting this story?

No major surprises, but it is really cool to see the Hmong refugees enjoy a different standard of living—from their dirt-floor shacks without running water to a home with a washing machine, refrigerator and air conditioning. But what was even cooler was to see the children relishing going to school and their insatiable appetite to learn. One of the teachers told me, "They are sponges—they just soak everything in."

Why do you do what you do as a photojournalist?

I feel being a photojournalist at a newspaper that is committed to photography is one of the greatest jobs there is. Every day is an adventure and an opportunity to engage people and learn more about ourselves. As much as I enjoy the daily assignments (at least 99 percent of them) it's the long-term documentary projects that really shape my heart and soul.

Spending time with the Hmong on "The Leftover People" project left me humbled and inspired and, to a larger degree, more appreciative of what I have and who I am.

What advice can you offer younger photographers when it comes to being a visual reporter?

I would stress respect—respect yourself and your subject. In the course of our business we will run into mass murderers and Mother Teresas. There will be people we admire and people we despise, but it is important we remain fair and show respect. The other component is to respect yourself and honor the profession.

With respect at the core, one can then build on technical expertise, talent development and stuff of the heart—passion, desire, dedication and commitment.

The complete ASNE entry by Manny Crisostomo, as well as entries by Carol Guzy and Robert Gauthier, is displayed at News University (http://www.newsu.org/bnw2005) in a course called "Community Service Photojournalism: Lessons from a Contest." The course exam- ines three approaches to community service photojournalism and offers judges' comments about the honored work. News University is a journalism-training project of The Poynter Institute funded by the John S. and James L. Knight Foundation.

Los Angeles Times

Finalist

Robert Gauthier

Community Service Photojournalism

47. About "The Troubles at King/Drew"

How do you illustrate the politics of race?

How do you show the ways fear and timidity crippled a hospital named for the Rev. Martin Luther King Jr., a hospital that frequently harmed, rather than healed, the African-American and Latino communities it was built to serve?

When the *Los Angeles Times* began a yearlong look at Martin Luther King Jr./Drew Medical Center, photographer Rob Gauthier was given the toughest of assignments: to help tell a story that combined medicine and race, that was imbued with all the nuance and tangled tensions of South Los Angeles.

Gauthier's photos became a key element of the *Times'* investigation, vividly documenting the troubles of King/Drew over the course of a five-day series published in December 2004. His portrait of Sulma Tasejo, her eyes staring in despair, is a body blow, an immediate moment of recognition for anyone who has entrusted the care of a loved one, especially a child, to a hospital. Tasejo's 9-year-old daughter, who arrived with two broken teeth, died after a series of errors by King/Drew doctors and nurses.

Gauthier worked with great sensitivity. He is white; the hospital's ardent defenders and most of its employees are black. He was accused, sometimes publicly, of being a racist for pursuing the story. Nonetheless, Gauthier persisted with tremendous grace and courage, ever respectful of those who would defend the hospital, but never letting his focus stray far from the victims of its failings, themselves almost exclusively black and Latino.

—Adapted from the *Los Angeles Times* ASNE contest entry

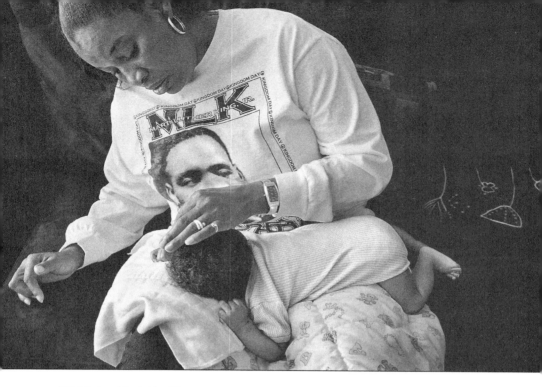

Still Grieving: Johnnie Mae Williams, here with her great-niece, had a hysterectomy after Dr. Dennis G. Hopper said she had cancer. He was wrong, according to her medical records.

Robert Gauthier has been a staff photographer at the Los Angeles Times *since 1994. Before joining the* Times, *he was a photographer at* The San Diego Union-Tribune, *the* Escondido *(Calif.)* Times-Advocate *and* The Bernardo News *in San Diego. Gauthier's photographs for "The Troubles at King/Drew" were part of the* Los Angeles Times *series that won the 2005 Pulitzer Prize for public service.*

A conversation with
Robert Gauthier

For Robert Gauthier, a white photographer pursuing a tough story in a community of color, it was a moment he says he will always remember. Working on his paper's coverage of the Martin Luther King Jr./Drew Medical Center, Gauthier was photographing a community meeting when a member of the Congressional Black Caucus stopped him in his tracks.

Rep. Maxine Waters, D-Calif., called him a racist and told him he could not take her picture during the meeting. Later, in a one-on-one conversation, she told Gauthier about the racist hate mail she receives whenever she appears angry in a news photograph. Waters' reaction also reflected a common perception among people in under-covered communities: Journalists show up mostly when there is trouble.

Gauthier didn't back off his reporting, but he pursued a relationship of trust with Waters that developed over the course of the Los Angeles Times' *yearlong investigation.*

In an edited e-mail interview conducted by Poynter Institute faculty member Kenny Irby, Gauthier shares other lessons learned.

KENNY IRBY: Where did the King/Drew Medical Center project idea come from?

ROBERT GAUTHIER: *Times* reporters Charles Ornstein and Tracy Weber began looking at the Los Angeles County public hospital system in the spring of 2003 after a lawsuit raised allegations of substandard care at the largest public hospital, County-USC Medical Center. Their research indicated that the most severe problems plagued Martin Luther King Jr./Drew Medical Center, formed after the 1965 Watts riots to serve the poor of South Los Angeles.

Where and how did you research your information?

I did minimal research at the outset of the project. As issues arose and principal characters developed within the story, I spent as much time as possible becoming familiar with both. Most of my time was spent talking with and getting to know victims and their families.

How did you decide that the focus would be on a series of individuals?

Illustrating an investigative report offers a myriad of challenges. I tried to keep it simple and work very closely with the reporters. As we went along, it became clear that the stories of both victims and bad guys would be key to the visual presentation.

How much time did you put into the coverage?

Twelve months.

What role did your picture editor play?

Senior photo editor Gail Fisher worked closely with me from the beginning, providing numerous edits and direction throughout the year. At publication, Fisher worked with deputy managing editor Joe Hutchinson to shape the photoplay to match the narrative of the stories. She fought many battles and was open to many of my ideas.

Tell me about your reporting partnerships with your writing colleagues.

Less than halfway through the project, I was working with four reporters, each covering different aspects of the story. I depended on them to keep me constantly updated, and they trusted me to be an extra set of eyes and ears.

What were some of the challenges that you faced? How did you overcome them?

As it became apparent that racial politics was to be a key component of the story, I found myself torn between the facts and my feelings. It was hard for me to agree with the concept that community activists who defend the hospital were also responsible for many of its problems. I tried to avoid stereotypical images of angry black men and women.

Ultimately, there was still a published image of an angry doctor dressing down a county worker at a community meeting, but it ran only after a lot of discussion among editors, reporters and myself.

While shooting in and around the hospital, I faced many people who distrusted and downright hated the *Los Angeles Times*. They usually felt like all we were interested in was closing the hospital. I tried to blend in with the background and found it hard to gain their trust or disinterest.

The victims and their families also posed many challenges. Many felt unsure about the attention and a little reluctant to criticize a place that was once considered the jewel of the community. Dozens of phone calls, house visits and e-mails would result in only minimal access. In a few cases, family members cut off all access after only one visit.

How did you organize your final photographic narrative?

I'm fairly satisfied with the photographic narrative. I think some important faces were lost in the interest of space and that left a few holes. Gail

Fisher and I worked closely with the reporters during the final stages of writing and tried to closely illustrate the written narrative.

What were the more memorable lessons you learned during this assignment?

I'll always remember Congresswoman Maxine Waters calling me out specifically during a community meeting, calling me racist and announcing that I would not be allowed to take her picture during the meeting. We talked one-on-one at a later news conference, and I learned that she considers it a disservice to the African-American community every time we publish a picture showing someone like her as angry. She talked about all the racist hate mail she gets when something like that is published. I told her that I thought it was good to show there are people who care enough to act when an issue like this exists. It was an eye-opening experience for me and shaped the way I covered rallies from that point forward.

I will also always remember the strength and resilience shown ... by the victims and their families. Dealing with emotional, physical and financial hardships with strength and grace while hearing the community loudly defend an institution that betrayed their trust showed me a level of courage I would have a hard time mustering.

Were there any major surprises for you while reporting this story?

I was surprised to realize how little we cover the African-American community and how distrusted we (the *Times*) are in South Los Angeles.

Why do you do what you do as a photojournalist?

After more than 20 years in journalism, I'm still an idealist. I believe we can make a difference with our work. This series is an extreme example of what can be done.

The complete ASNE entry submitted by Robert Gauthier, as well as entries by Carol Guzy and Manny Crisostomo, is displayed at News University (http://www.newsu.org/bnw2005) in a course called "Community Service Photojournalism: Lessons from a Contest." The course examines three approaches to community service photojournalism and offers judges' comments about the honored work. News University is a journalism-training project of The Poynter Institute funded by the John S. and James L. Knight Foundation.

Suggested Readings

RECENT RESOURCES

Brady, John Joseph. "The Interviewer's Handbook." Waukesha, Wis.: Writer Books, 2004. Review of interviewing techniques used by professional journalists and writers.

Brooks, Brian S., James Pinson and Jean Gaddy Wilson. "Working with Words." 5th edition. New York: Bedford/St. Martin's, 2003. Handbook for media writers and editors.

Cappon, Rene J. "The Associated Press Guide to News Writing." Forest City, Calif.: IDG Books Worldwide, 2000. Practical guide dealing with the essentials of good writing.

Clark, Roy Peter, and Don Fry. "Coaching Writers." 2nd edition. New York: Bedford/St. Martin's, 2003. Guidelines on how to improve communication between editors and reporters.

Dunsky, Marda. "Watch Your Words." Lanham, Md.: Rowman & Littlefield, 2003. Language-skills handbook for journalists.

Garrison, Bruce. "Professional Feature Writing." 4th edition. Mahwah, N.J.: Lawrence Erlbaum, 2004. Introduction to feature writing.

Goldstein, Norm, ed. "The Associated Press Stylebook and Briefing on Media Law." Scranton, Pa.: Perseus Books Group, 2002. AP rules on grammar, spelling, punctuation, capitalization, word usage and more.

Harrigan, Jane, and Karen F. Dunlap. "The Editorial Eye." 2nd edition. New York: Bedford/St. Martin's, 2003. Discussion of the technical and management elements of professional editing.

Houston, Brant, Len Bruzzese and Steve Weinberg. "The Investigative Reporter's Handbook." Boston: Bedford/St. Martin's, 2002. Valuable advice and tools for investigative reporters.

Jackson, Dennis, and John Sweeney, eds. "The Journalist's Craft." New York: Allworth Press, 2002. Guide to writing well and reporting accurately.

LaRocque, Paula. "The Book on Writing: The Ultimate Guide to Writing Well." Oak Park, Ill.: Marion Street Press, 2003. Useful tips about many aspects of writing.

Mencher, Melvin. "News Reporting and Writing." 9th edition. Boston: McGraw-Hill, 2003. Journalism textbook.

Murray, Donald M. "Writing to Deadline: The Journalist at Work." Portsmouth, N.H.: Heinemann, 2000. Insights for journalists on the writing process.

Poynter's Reporting, Writing and Editing Bibliography, http://poynter.org/writingbib.

Pumario, Jim. "Bad News and Good Judgment." Oak Park, Ill.: Marion Street Press, 2005. Guide to reporting on sensitive issues in a small-town newspaper.

Rich, Carole. "Writing and Reporting News: A Coaching Method." 4th edition. Belmont, Calif.: Wadsworth, 2003. Introduction for students to the basic skills required of a news reporter.

Roush, Chris. "Show Me the Money: Writing Business and Economic Stories for Mass Communication." Mahwah, N.J.: Lawrence Erlbaum, 2004. Advice for reporting on business.

Ryan, Buck, Michael O'Connell and Leland B. Ryan. "The Editor's Toolbox." Ames: Iowa State University Press, 2001. Reference for beginning and professional journalists.

Scanlan, Christopher. "Reporting and Writing: Basics for the 21st Century." New York: Oxford University Press, 2000. Practical guide to professional journalism skills.

Smith, Sarah Harrison. "The Fact Checker's Bible." New York: Anchor Books, 2004. Manual on how to get the facts right.

WRITING AND REPORTING ANTHOLOGIES

Clark, Roy Peter, and Christopher Scanlan, eds. "America's Best Newspaper Writing." New York: Bedford/St. Martin's, 2000. Thirty-six ASNE Distinguished Writing Award–winning stories and eight classic news reports.

Cramer, Richard Ben, ed. "The Best American Sports Writing 2004." Boston: Houghton Mifflin, 2004. Annual series presenting excellent sports writing.

Garlock, David, ed. "Pulitzer Prize Feature Stories." Ames: Iowa State University Press, 2003. Twenty-five Pulitzer Prize–winning feature stories published from 1979 to 2003.

Leckey, Andy, ed. "The Best Business Stories of the Year 2004." New York: Vintage Books, 2004. Anthology of well-written and interesting business stories.

Menand, Louis, ed. "The Best American Essays 2004." Boston: Houghton Mifflin, 2004. Annual showcase for the country's finest writing.

Penzler, Otto. "Best American Crime Writing: 2004 Edition." New York: Pantheon, 2004. Annual anthology of 20 nonfiction crime stories originally published in magazines.

Pinker, Steven, ed. "The Best American Science and Nature Writing 2004." Boston: Houghton Mifflin, 2004. Some of the year's finest writing on a wide range of scientific topics.

Remnick, David, ed. "Life Stories: Profiles from *The New Yorker*." New York: Random House, 2001. Compilation of some of the best profiles to appear in *The New Yorker*.

Staff of *The New York Times*. "Tales from the Times." New York: St. Martin's Griffin, 2004. Compilation (by Lisa Belkin) of human-interest stories from *The New York Times*.

Thomas Jr., Robert McG., Thomas Mallon and Chris Calhoun, eds. "52 McGs." New York: Scribner, 2003. Best obituaries from *New York Times* writer Robert McG. Thomas Jr.

Wells, Ken, ed. "Floating Off the Page." New York: Simon & Schuster, 2002. Collection of stories from *The Wall Street Journal*'s "Middle Column."

CLASSICS

Blundell, William E. "The Art and Craft of Feature Writing." New York: Plume, 1988. Step-by-step guide to reporting and editing.

Brande, Dorothea. "Becoming a Writer." Los Angeles: J. P. Tarcher; Boston: distributed by Putnam Publishing, 1981. Timeless writing advice.

Franklin, Jon. "Writing for Story." New York: Plume, 1994. Lessons on how to write dramatic nonfiction.

Harrington, Walt. "Intimate Journalism: The Art and Craft of Reporting Everyday Life." Thousand Oaks, Calif.: Sage, 1997. Award-winning articles describing the process of combining traditional feature writing with in-depth reporting.

Snyder, Louis L., and Richard B. Morris, eds. "A Treasury of Great Reporting." New York: Simon & Schuster, 1962. Historical examples of great reporting and writing.

Stewart, James B. "Follow the Story: How to Write Successful Nonfiction." New York: Simon & Schuster, 1988. Guide to the techniques of compelling narrative writing.

Strunk, William, Jr., and E. B. White. "The Elements of Style." 4th edition. New York: Macmillan, 1999. Reference on the rules of usage and the principles of composition.

Zinsser, William. "On Writing Well." New York: Harper Resource, 2001. Twenty-fifth-anniversary edition of a respected writing guide.

David Shedden, director of the Eugene Patterson Library at The Poynter Institute for Media Studies, compiled this listing.